P9-CAD-793

healthy cooking

Taste of Home

cooking

annual recipes

RDA ENTHUSIAST BRANDS, LLC • MILWAUKEE, WI

healthy cooking
Taste of Home
annual recipes

72

29

84

EDITORIAL
EDITOR-IN-CHIEF Catherine Cassidy
CREATIVE DIRECTOR Howard Greenberg
EDITORIAL OPERATIONS DIRECTOR
Kerri Balliet

MANAGING EDITOR/PRINT & DIGITAL
BOOKS Mark Hagen
ASSOCIATE CREATIVE DIRECTOR
Edwin Robles Jr.

EDITORS Christine Rukavena,
Michelle Rozumalski
ASSOCIATE EDITOR Molly Jasinski
ART DIRECTOR Jessie Sharon
LAYOUT DESIGNER Catherine Fletcher
EDITORIAL PRODUCTION MANAGER
Dena Ahlers
COPY CHIEF Deb Warlaumont Mulvey
COPY EDITORS Mary-Liz Shaw, Dulcie Shoener,
Kaitlin Stainbrook, Joanne Weintraub
CONTRIBUTING COPY EDITORS
Valerie Phillips, Lisa Michel

CHIEF FOOD EDITOR Karen Berner
FOOD EDITORS James Schend,
Peggy Woodward, RD
RECIPE EDITORS Mary King, Jenni Sharp, RD,
Irene Yeh
CONTENT OPERATIONS MANAGER
Colleen King
CONTENT OPERATIONS ASSISTANT
Shannon Stroud
EXECUTIVE ASSISTANT Marie Brannon

TEST KITCHEN & FOOD STYLING MANAGER
Sarah Thompson
TEST COOKS Nicholas Iverson (lead),
Matthew Hass, Lauren Knoelke
FOOD STYLISTS Kathryn Conrad (senior),
Shannon Roum, Leah Rekau
PREP COOKS Megumi Garcia, Melissa Hansen,
Bethany Van Jacobson, Sara Wirtz

PHOTOGRAPHY DIRECTOR Stephanie Marchese
PHOTOGRAPHERS Dan Roberts, Jim Wieland
PHOTOGRAPHER/SET STYLIST
Grace Natoli Sheldon
SET STYLISTS Stacey Genaw, Melissa Haberman,
Dee Dee Jacq

PHOTO STUDIO ASSISTANT Ester Robards
CONTRIBUTORS Mark Derse (photography),
Laurel Zimienski (food stylist), Pam Stasney
(set stylist)

EDITORIAL BUSINESS MANAGER
Kristy Martin
EDITORIAL BUSINESS ASSOCIATE
Samantha Lea Stoeger

EDITOR, *TASTE OF HOME* Jeanne Ambrose
ASSOCIATE CREATIVE DIRECTOR,
TASTE OF HOME Erin Burns
ART DIRECTOR, *TASTE OF HOME*
Kristin Bowker

BUSINESS
VICE PRESIDENT, CHIEF SALES OFFICER
Mark S. Josephson
GENERAL MANAGER, TASTE OF HOME
COOKING SCHOOL Erin Puariea

THE READER'S DIGEST ASSOCIATION, INC.
PRESIDENT AND CHIEF EXECUTIVE OFFICER
Bonnie Kintzer
CHIEF FINANCIAL OFFICER Colette Chestnut
VICE PRESIDENT, CHIEF OPERATING
OFFICER, NORTH AMERICA Howard Halligan
VICE PRESIDENT, ENTHUSIAST BRANDS,
BOOKS & RETAIL Harold Clarke
VICE PRESIDENT, NORTH AMERICAN
OPERATIONS Philippe Cloutier
CHIEF MARKETING OFFICER Leslie Dukker Doty
VICE PRESIDENT, NORTH AMERICAN
HUMAN RESOURCES Phyllis E. Gebhardt, SPHR
VICE PRESIDENT, BRAND MARKETING
Beth Gorry
VICE PRESIDENT, GLOBAL
COMMUNICATIONS Susan Russ
VICE PRESIDENT, NORTH AMERICAN
TECHNOLOGY Aneel Tejwaney
VICE PRESIDENT, CONSUMER MARKETING
PLANNING Jim Woods

COVER PHOTOGRAPHY
PHOTOGRAPHER Mark Derse
FOOD STYLIST Kathryn Conrad
SET STYLIST Stacey Genaw

© 2015 RDA ENTHUSIAST BRANDS, LLC
1610 N. 2ND ST., SUITE 102, MILWAUKEE WI 53212-3906

INTERNATIONAL STANDARD BOOK NUMBER: 978-1-61765-350-6
INTERNATIONAL STANDARD SERIAL NUMBER: 1944-7736
COMPONENT NUMBER: 117900035H00
ALL RIGHTS RESERVED.
TASTE OF HOME IS A REGISTERED TRADEMARK OF THE READER'S DIGEST ASSOCIATION, INC.
PRINTED IN CHINA
13 5 7 9 10 8 6 4 2

PICTURED ON THE FRONT COVER: Mama Rachel's Tomato & Kalamata Pizzas (p. 181).
PICTURED ON THE BACK COVER: Strawberry Cream Cheese Pie (p. 224), Makeover Creamy Mac & Cheese (p. 184), Cherry-Chicken Lettuce Wraps (p. 124) and Veggie Chowder (p. 40).

Contents

Get inspired to try something new, fresh and healthy. With hundreds of satisfying recipes to choose from, you'll find everything you need for casual weeknight dinners, holiday entertaining, vegetarian cooking and more.

243

Starters & Snacks 6

Salads 20

Soups.. 36

Side Dishes..52

Good Mornings..................................... 66

Ready in 30 80

Slow Cooker... 94

Beef Entrees 106

Chicken Favorites 118

Turkey Specialties 134

Pork Entrees 146

Fish & Seafood 160

Meatless Mains 176

The Bread Basket 188

Table for Two 202

Cakes & Pies 216

Treat Yourself 230

Indexes 246

Healthy Home-Cooked Meals on Your Timetable

With *Healthy Cooking Annual Recipes*, it's never been easier!

There's nothing better than coming home to a healthy home-cooked meal. The trouble is, somebody has to make it! I love to cook, and I enjoy baking even more. It's hard to find the time to get it all done, however, especially on busy weeknights.

That's why we've added more than 30 slow-cooked dishes to this year's edition of *Healthy Cooking Annual Recipes*. You'll find slow-simmered dinners guaranteed to make your mouth water when you walk in the door. Three cheers for an evening meal that's more relaxed, less rushed and reliably delicious! After all, these easy, delicious recipes come from home cooks just like you.

Every recipe features healthy ingredients and from-scratch taste, which is great news for this registered dietitian and mother of two. These wholesome slow-cooked dinners include old-fashioned favorites such as Meat Loaf with Chili Sauce (p. 99) and Chicken Cacciatore (p. 104), plus contemporary twists like Fiesta Beef Bowls (p. 105) and Tropical Pulled Pork Sliders (p. 102).

Make-ahead meals are just the start of how *Healthy Cooking* will help set nutritious meals on the table, fast. You'll also find Overnight Maple Oatmeal (p. 74) and freezer-friendly Veggie Egg Casserole (p. 69) for no-fuss breakfasts with a hearty dose of protein and fiber to keep you energized until lunchtime.

Next up, your options are virtually endless to mix and match your lunch from dozens of tasty soups, salads and sandwiches. Whether you are lunching at home or brown-bagging at work, you're sure to find nutritious and tasty dishes perfect for at home or on the go!

There's even time to savor homemade dessert. From five-ingredient meringue cookies (p. 235) to a frosty orange pie that's freezer-ready in just 20 minutes (p. 220), you'll be able to whip up special sweets for your family—treats that you can feel good about—at any time you like.

So, close the book on frantic weeknights. Start a new chapter with the hundreds of easy-to-fix recipes in this year's edition of *Healthy Cooking Annual Recipes*.

Happy Cooking,

Peggy Woodward, RD

Peggy Woodward, RD
Food Editor

About Our Nutrition Facts

NUTRITIONAL GUIDELINES
All the recipes in *Healthy Cooking Annual Recipes* cookbook fit the lifestyle of health-conscious cooks and families. The recipes represent a variety of foods that fit into any meal plan within the standards of the USDA's "MyPlate" recommendations for moderately active adults (see the Daily Nutrition Guide on p. 5).

FACTS
- Nutrition Facts are based on one serving. For appetizers, cookies, rolls and other per-piece foods, serving information is based on one piece.
- Whenever a choice of ingredients is given in a recipe (such as ⅓ cup of sour cream or plain yogurt), the first ingredient listed is always the one calculated in the Nutrition Facts.
- When a range is given for an ingredient (such as 2 to 3 teaspoons), we calculate using the first amount.
- Only the amount of a marinade absorbed during preparation is calculated.
- Optional ingredients are not included in our calculations.

DIABETIC EXCHANGES
All recipes in *Healthy Cooking Annual Recipes* have been reviewed by a registered dietitian. Diabetic Exchanges are assigned to recipes in accordance with guidelines from the American Diabetes Association and the Academy of Nutrition and Dietetics.

The majority of recipes in this cookbook are suitable for people with diabetes, but please check the Diabetic Exchanges to make sure the recipe is in accordance with your doctor's instructions and fits your particular dietary guidelines.

SPECIAL DIET INDICATORS
To help those on restricted diets easily find dishes to suit their needs, we clearly mark recipes that are especially low in fat, sodium or carbohydrates, as well as those that contain no meat. You will find these colored diet indicators directly after the recipe title, where appropriate:

F One serving contains 3 fat grams or less

S One serving contains 140 milligrams sodium or less

C One serving contains 15 grams carbohydrates or less

M Recipe contains no meat, gelatin, Worcestershire or other animal products

FOR OTHER TASTE OF HOME BOOKS
AND PRODUCTS, VISIT
ShopTasteofHome.com

201

241

173

115

The Year's Best Tips

People often ask us for advice on cooking delicious meals that are healthy. Check out some of our favorite ideas from this edition, along with recipes:

Everybody knows that whole wheat bread is a smarter choice than white bread or a whole wheat blend. But achieving a light and tender whole wheat loaf isn't always easy. Add vital wheat gluten (found in the baking section) to the recipe to pump up the dough's structure, making it lighter and softer.
SEEDED WHOLE GRAIN LOAF, P. 201

Let the fruit's natural sweetness work for you. Tart fruits in desserts generally reign supreme, but using a sweeter fruit such as Bing cherries or Golden Delicious apples (instead of tart Montmorency cherries or Granny Smith apples) means you can use less sugar in the recipe.
ALMOND CHERRY COBBLER, P. 241

The hearty texture and slightly nutty taste of whole wheat pasta make it ideal for Asian recipes, including those that call for soba noodles or buckwheat. Even if you don't enjoy the taste of whole wheat pasta in your favorite Italian dishes, don't be afraid to try it in Asian specialties.
SESAME NOODLES WITH SHRIMP & SNAP PEAS, P. 173

An unexpected spice blend turns lean ground beef into a tempting version of Middle Eastern kofta. A sweet and savory blend of seasonings also pairs perfectly with sliced tomatoes, cucumbers, watermelon salad and other garden-fresh foods.
JUICY & DELICIOUS MIXED SPICE BURGERS, P. 115

DAILY NUTRITION GUIDE

	Women 25-50	Women over 50	Men 50-65
CALORIES	2,000	1,800	2,400
FAT	67 g or less	60 g or less	80 g or less
SATURATED FAT	22 g or less	20 g or less	27 g or less
CHOLESTEROL	300 mg or less	300 mg or less	300 mg or less
SODIUM	2,300 mg or less	1,500 mg or less	1,500 mg or less
CARBOHYDRATES	300 g	270 g	360 g
FIBER	20-30 g	20-30 g	30-40 g
PROTEIN	50 g	45 g	60 g

This chart is only a guide. Requirements vary, depending on age, weight, height and amount of activity.
Children's dietary needs vary as they grow.

16

18

19

Starters & Snacks

“I threw this together after an overzealous trip to the farmers market. My family loved it from the first bite. You can serve it right away, but I think it tastes best after it has rested in the refrigerator a few hours.”

—ANDREA HEYART AUBREY, TX
about her recipe, Watermelon Salsa, on page 11

CHUNKY MANGO GUACAMOLE

Chunky Mango Guacamole C M

To prep ahead, chop the veggies and mango in advance. Then simply stir in the avocados right before serving.
—DIANA NIENBERG MCCOMB, OH

START TO FINISH: 15 MIN.
MAKES: 16 SERVINGS (¼ CUP EACH)

- 3 medium ripe avocados, peeled and chopped
- 1 large mango, peeled and chopped
- 1 large tomato, chopped
- 1 small red onion, chopped
- ¼ cup chopped fresh cilantro
- 3 tablespoons lime juice
- 1 teaspoon salt
  Assorted fresh vegetables and tortilla chips

In a large bowl, combine the first five ingredients; stir in lime juice and salt. Serve with vegetables and chips.
PER SERVING *67 cal., 5 g fat (1 g sat. fat), 0 chol., 151 mg sodium, 6 g carb., 3 g fiber, 1 g pro.* **Diabetic Exchanges:** *1 fat, ½ starch.*

Thai Veggie Dip F S C M

This delicious dip is full of flavor, color and crunch, but not full of calories. There's mild sweetness from the honey with a bit of heat at the end from the pepper flakes.
—JEANNE HOLT MENDOTA HEIGHTS, MN

PREP: 15 MIN. + CHILLING
MAKES: 12 SERVINGS (¼ CUP EACH)

- 3 tablespoons reduced-fat creamy peanut butter
- 1 tablespoon reduced-sodium soy sauce
- 1 tablespoon honey
- 1 cup (8 ounces) reduced-fat sour cream
- 1 cup fat-free plain Greek yogurt
- 1 cup fresh baby spinach, chopped
- ½ cup sliced water chestnuts, chopped
- 1 small sweet red pepper, finely chopped
- 3 tablespoons finely chopped green onions
- 3 tablespoons minced fresh cilantro
- 1 tablespoon minced fresh mint
- 1 teaspoon crushed red pepper flakes
  Assorted fresh vegetables

In a large bowl, combine peanut butter, soy sauce and honey. Stir in sour cream, yogurt, spinach, water chestnuts, pepper, onions, herbs and pepper flakes. Chill 1-2 hours. Serve with vegetables.
PER SERVING *73 cal., 3 g fat (1 g sat. fat), 7 mg chol., 99 mg sodium, 7 g carb., 1 g fiber, 5 g pro.* **Diabetic Exchanges:** *½ starch, ½ fat.*

THAI VEGGIE DIP

Chipotle Avocado Dip C M

Thanks to the avocado base, this dip provides a bonus of healthy fats and fiber. Try spooning it on tacos, too.

—**BARBARA OLIPHANT** VALLEY CENTER, KS

START TO FINISH: 15 MIN.
MAKES: 24 SERVINGS (2 TBSP. EACH)

- 3 medium ripe avocados, peeled
- 1 cup reduced-fat mayonnaise
- ¼ cup finely chopped onion
- 1 tablespoon finely chopped banana pepper
- 1 tablespoon minced pickled hot cherry peppers
- 1½ teaspoons garlic powder
- 1 to 1½ teaspoons ground chipotle pepper
- 1 teaspoon onion powder
- 1 teaspoon seasoned salt
  Assorted fresh vegetables

In a small bowl, mash avocados. Stir in the mayonnaise, onion, peppers and seasonings. Chill until serving. Serve with vegetables.

NOTE *Wear disposable gloves when cutting hot peppers; the oils can burn skin. Avoid touching your face.*

PER SERVING *72 cal., 7 g fat (1 g sat. fat), 4 mg chol., 153 mg sodium, 3 g carb., 2 g fiber, 1 g pro.* **Diabetic Exchange:** *1½ fat.*

Tri-Color Miniature Peppers F S C

My mom used to make a stuffed-pepper entree using ground beef and white rice. I switched up her recipe to make it healthier with ground turkey and brown rice, and then I decided to use cute little tri-color peppers to create an irresistible appetizer.

—**ROSE MUCCIO** METHUEN, MA

PREP: 55 MIN. • **BAKE:** 20 MIN.
MAKES: 2 DOZEN

- 8 each miniature sweet red, orange and yellow peppers
- 4 ounces ground turkey
- ½ cup finely chopped fresh mushrooms
- ¼ cup chopped sweet onion
- 1 garlic clove, minced
- 1 can (15 ounces) tomato sauce, divided
- ¼ cup cooked brown rice
- 1 tablespoon grated Parmesan cheese
- 1 tablespoon shredded part-skim mozzarella cheese
- ½ teaspoon dried basil
- ¼ teaspoon salt
- ¼ teaspoon cayenne pepper
- ¼ teaspoon pepper

1. Cut tops off peppers and reserve; remove seeds. Cut thin slices from bottoms of peppers; set peppers aside.
2. In a large skillet, cook the turkey, mushrooms, onion and garlic over medium heat until meat is no longer pink. Remove from the heat; let stand for 5 minutes.
3. Stir in ¼ cup tomato sauce, rice, cheeses and seasonings; spoon mixture into peppers. Place upright in a greased 11x7-in. baking dish. Spoon remaining tomato sauce over peppers; replace pepper tops. Cover and bake at 400° for 18-22 minutes or until heated through and peppers are crisp-tender.
PER SERVING *23 cal., 1 g fat (trace sat. fat), 4 mg chol., 116 mg sodium, 3 g carb., 1 g fiber, 1 g pro.*

TRI-COLOR MINIATURE PEPPERS

ZESTY MARINATED SHRIMP

Zesty Marinated Shrimp F S C

These easy shrimp look impressive on a buffet table and taste even better! I love this recipe because I can make it ahead.
—MARY JANE GUEST ALAMOSA, CO

PREP: 5 MIN. + CHILLING
MAKES: ABOUT 2 DOZEN

- ½ cup canola oil
- ½ cup lime juice
- ½ cup thinly sliced red onion
- 12 lemon slices
- 1 tablespoon minced fresh parsley
- ½ teaspoon salt
- ½ teaspoon dill weed
- ⅛ teaspoon hot pepper sauce
- 2 pounds medium shrimp, cooked, peeled and deveined

In a large bowl, combine the first eight ingredients. Stir in shrimp. Cover and refrigerate 4 hours, stirring shrimp occasionally. Drain before serving.
PER SERVING *1 shrimp equals 43 cal., 2 g fat (trace sat. fat), 38 mg chol., 54 mg sodium, 1 g carb., trace fiber, 5 g pro.*

Rosemary Beet Phyllo Bites F S C M

Sweet-and-sour pickled beets paired with rich and tangy goat cheese is a match made in heaven. These pretty tartlets will make a splash on the buffet table.
—*TASTE OF HOME* TEST KITCHEN

START TO FINISH: 25 MIN.
MAKES: 6 DOZEN

- 1 jar (16 ounces) pickled whole beets, drained and chopped
- 1 tablespoon olive oil
- 2 teaspoons minced fresh rosemary
- 1 teaspoon grated orange peel
- 2 cups fresh arugula, torn
- 72 frozen miniature phyllo tart shells
- ¾ cup crumbled feta cheese

1. Pat beets dry with paper towels; place in a bowl. Add the olive oil, rosemary and orange peel; toss to combine.
2. Divide arugula among tart shells; top with beet mixture. Sprinkle with feta cheese.
PER SERVING *31 cal., 1 g fat (trace sat. fat), 1 mg chol., 33 mg sodium, 3 g carb., trace fiber, 1 g pro.*

Watermelon Salsa F S C M

I threw this together after an overzealous trip to the farmers market. My family loved it from the first bite. You can serve it right away, but I think it tastes best after it has rested in the refrigerator a few hours.
—ANDREA HEYART AUBREY, TX

START TO FINISH: 25 MIN.
MAKES: 15 SERVINGS (⅓ CUP EACH)

- ¼ cup lime juice
- 3 tablespoons brown sugar
- 2 tablespoons cider vinegar
- 1 tablespoon honey
- ¼ teaspoon salt
- 3 cups seeded chopped watermelon
- 1 medium cucumber, seeded and chopped
- 1 small red onion, finely chopped
- 2 jalapeno peppers, seeded and finely chopped
- ¼ cup finely chopped sweet yellow pepper
- ¼ cup minced fresh cilantro
- 2 tablespoons minced fresh basil

In a large bowl, combine the first five ingredients. Add remaining ingredients; toss to combine. Refrigerate, covered, until serving. If necessary, drain before serving.
PER SERVING *32 cal., trace fat (trace sat. fat), 0 chol., 42 mg sodium, 8 g carb., 1 g fiber, 1 g pro.* **Diabetic Exchange:** *½ starch.*

ZUCCHINI CRAB CAKES

Zucchini Crab Cakes C

Here's a great way to use up garden zucchini. These tender crab cakes are easy to double for a crowd: Just use 1 whole egg instead of having to measure.
—JACQUELINE CORREA LANDING, NJ

PREP: 15 MIN. + CHILLING • **COOK:** 10 MIN.
MAKES: 4 SERVINGS

- ½ cup shredded zucchini
- 1 green onion, thinly sliced
- 3 teaspoons olive oil, divided
- 2 tablespoons beaten egg
- ¼ cup seasoned bread crumbs
- 1½ teaspoons Dijon mustard
- ¼ teaspoon minced fresh thyme
  Dash cayenne pepper
- ¾ cup lump crabmeat, drained

1. In a large skillet, saute zucchini and onion in 1 teaspoon oil until tender. In a small bowl, combine the egg, bread crumbs, mustard, thyme, cayenne and zucchini mixture. Fold in crabmeat. Refrigerate for at least 30 minutes.
2. With floured hands, shape mixture into four ¾-in.-thick patties. In the same skillet, cook crab cakes in remaining oil over medium heat for 3-4 minutes on each side or until golden brown.
PER SERVING *86 cal., 5 g fat (1 g sat. fat), 51 mg chol., 325 mg sodium, 7 g carb., 1 g fiber, 5 g pro.*

WATERMELON SALSA

? Did you know?

The shrink-wrapped long, thin English cucumbers at the store don't have a protective wax coating like most other cukes. That means you can eat the peel and all. Ditto for cucumbers from the farmers market.

Tangy Pickled Mushrooms F S C M

Home-canned pickled mushrooms are a great addition to your pantry. Not only are they light, but they're an ideal addition to appetizers, salads and relish trays.

—**JILL HIHN** WEST GROVE, PA

PREP: 50 MIN. • **PROCESS:** 20 MIN./BATCH • **MAKES:** 8 PINTS

- 5 pounds small fresh mushrooms
- 2 large onions, halved and sliced
- 2 cups white vinegar
- 1½ cups canola oil
- ¼ cup sugar
- 2 tablespoons canning salt
- 3 garlic cloves, minced
- 1½ teaspoons pepper
- ¼ teaspoon dried tarragon

1. Place all ingredients in a stockpot. Bring to a boil. Reduce heat; simmer, uncovered, 10 minutes. Carefully ladle hot mixture into eight hot 1-pint jars, leaving ½-in. headspace.
2. Remove air bubbles and adjust headspace, if necessary, by adding hot mixture. Wipe rims. Center lids on jars; screw on bands until fingertip tight. Place jars into canner, ensuring that they are completely covered with water. Bring to a boil. Process for 20 minutes. Remove jars and cool.

TANGY PICKLED MUSHROOMS

GRILLED NECTARINE & CHEESE CROSTINI

NOTE *The processing time listed is for altitudes of 1,000 feet or less. For altitudes up to 3,000 feet, add 5 minutes; 6,000 feet, add 10 minutes; 8,000 feet, add 15 minutes; 10,000 feet, add 20 minutes.*
PER SERVING *¼ cup equals 18 cal., 1 g fat (trace sat. fat), 0 chol., 35 mg sodium, 2 g carb., 1 g fiber, 1 g pro.* **Diabetic Exchange:** *Free food.*

Grilled Nectarine & Cheese Crostini F S C M

At our house, we love the refreshing flavors of garden basil and sweet grilled nectarines over goat cheese. I can usually find all the ingredients at the farmers market.

—**BRANDY HOLLINGSHEAD** GRASS VALLEY, CA

START TO FINISH: 25 MIN. • **MAKES:** 12 SERVINGS

- ½ cup balsamic vinegar
- 1 tablespoon olive oil
- 12 slices French bread baguette (¼ inch thick)
- 2 medium nectarines, halved
- ¼ cup fresh goat cheese, softened
- ¼ cup loosely packed basil leaves, thinly sliced

1. In a small saucepan, bring vinegar to a boil; cook 10-15 minutes or until liquid is reduced to 3 tablespoons. Remove from heat.
2. Brush oil over both sides of baguette slices. Grill, uncovered, over medium heat until golden brown on both sides. Grill nectarines 45-60 seconds on each side or until tender and lightly browned. Cool slightly.
3. Spread goat cheese over toasts. Cut nectarines into thick slices; arrange over cheese. Drizzle with balsamic syrup; sprinkle with basil. Serve immediately.
PER SERVING *48 cal., 2 g fat (1 g sat. fat), 5 mg chol., 55 mg sodium, 6 g carb., trace fiber, 1 g pro.* **Diabetic Exchange:** *½ starch.*

Strawberry Salsa S C M

START TO FINISH: 25 MIN. • **MAKES:** 24 SERVINGS (¼ CUP EACH)

- 2 pints cherry tomatoes, quartered
- 1 pint fresh strawberries, chopped
- 8 green onions, chopped
- ½ cup minced fresh cilantro
- 6 tablespoons olive oil
- 2 tablespoons balsamic vinegar
- ½ teaspoon salt

In a large bowl, combine tomatoes, strawberries, green onions and cilantro. In a small bowl, whisk oil, vinegar and salt; gently stir into tomato mixture. Refrigerate until serving.

PER SERVING *41 cal., 4 g fat (trace sat. fat), 0 chol., 53 mg sodium, 3 g carb., 1 g fiber, trace pro.*

Here's a sweet and tangy salsa that's miles away from the spicy version people expect. Serve it as an appetizer with tortilla chips for scooping, or make it part of the main event and spoon it over poultry.
—**AMY HINKLE** TOPEKA, KS

STRAWBERRY SALSA

CAJUN CRAWFISH SLIDERS

Cajun Crawfish Sliders F S C

Add a touch of Southern hospitality to your festivities with our corn bread-based version of a slider. Crawfish gets a touch of spicy goodness from the chipotle mayonnaise and jalapeno.
—*TASTE OF HOME* TEST KITCHEN

PREP: 25 MIN. • **BAKE:** 10 MIN. + COOLING • **MAKES:** 4 DOZEN

- 1 package (8½ ounces) corn bread/muffin mix
- 1 egg
- ⅓ cup 2% milk
- 3 cups fresh baby spinach, thinly sliced
- 12 ounces frozen cooked crawfish tail meat, thawed and shredded
- 1 cup reduced-fat chipotle mayonnaise
- 48 pickled jalapeno slices

1. In a large bowl, combine the corn bread mix, egg and milk. Spread into a greased 13x9-in. baking pan. Bake at 400° for 9-11 minutes or until a toothpick inserted near the center comes out clean. Cool on a wire rack.

2. Cut corn bread into 1½-in. squares. Top each with spinach, crawfish, mayonnaise and a jalapeno slice.

EDITOR'S NOTE *1 cup reduced-fat mayonnaise and 1 tablespoon minced chipotle pepper in adobo sauce may be substituted for 1 cup reduced-fat chipotle mayonnaise.*

PER SERVING *1 square equals 43 cal., 2 g fat (trace sat. fat), 17 mg chol., 92 mg sodium, 4 g carb., trace fiber, 2 g pro.*
Diabetic Exchange: *½ starch.*

I love Mediterranean food, and the flavors in this dip are so vibrant. We make our own mini sandwiches with flatbreads, olives, veggies and this sensational dip. —**STACY MULLENS** GRESHAM, OR

MEDITERRANEAN EGGPLANT DIP

Mediterranean Eggplant Dip S C M

PREP: 20 MIN. • **BAKE:** 40 MIN.
MAKES: 16 SERVINGS (¼ CUP EACH)

- 1 large eggplant (about 1½ pounds), peeled
- 1 small onion, coarsely chopped
- 6 garlic cloves, peeled
- 3 tablespoons olive oil
- 2 cups (16 ounces) reduced-fat sour cream
- 4 teaspoons lemon juice
- ¾ teaspoon salt
- ½ teaspoon pepper
- 10 drops liquid smoke, optional
   Minced fresh parsley
   Optional ingredients: naan flatbread wedges or miniature pitas, cherry tomatoes, celery sticks, julienned red pepper, baby carrots and Greek olives

1. Preheat oven to 400°. Cut eggplant crosswise into 1-in. slices; place on a greased 15x10x1-in. baking pan. Top with onion and garlic cloves. Drizzle with oil.

2. Roast 40-45 minutes or until eggplant is very soft, turning and stirring vegetables once. Cool slightly.

3. Place eggplant mixture in a food processor; process until blended. Transfer to a large bowl; stir in sour cream, lemon juice, salt, pepper and, if desired, liquid smoke.

4. Sprinkle with parsley. Serve with flatbread and vegetables as desired.

PER SERVING *77 cal., 5 g fat (2 g sat. fat), 10 mg chol., 132 mg sodium, 5 g carb., 2 g fiber, 3 g pro.*

From the Web

I made this for a large crowd, so I doubled the amount of eggplant and other ingredients, but used only 8 ounces of sour cream for the whole dip so the flavor of the roasted eggplant was not lost. It was delicious and made a huge quantity.
—DOLLARGIRL TASTEOFHOME.COM

Roast Beef Aioli Bundles S C

Everyone will want to try these delicious, dainty bundles. And while they look impressive, they're actually quite easy!
—*TASTE OF HOME* TEST KITCHEN

START TO FINISH: 30 MIN.
MAKES: 16 APPETIZERS

- 16 fresh asparagus spears, trimmed
- ⅓ cup mayonnaise
- 1 garlic clove, minced
- 1 teaspoon Dijon mustard
- 1 teaspoon lemon juice
- ⅛ teaspoon ground cumin
- 8 thin slices deli roast beef, cut in half lengthwise
- 1 medium sweet yellow pepper, thinly sliced
- 1 medium sweet orange pepper, thinly sliced
- 1 medium sweet red pepper, thinly sliced
- 16 whole chives

1. In a large skillet, bring 1 in. of water to a boil. Add asparagus; cover and cook for 3 minutes. Drain asparagus and immediately place in ice water. Drain and pat dry.

2. In a small bowl, combine the mayonnaise, garlic, mustard, lemon juice and cumin. Place roast beef slices on a work surface; spread each slice with 1 teaspoon aioli. Top each with an asparagus spear and pepper strips. Roll up tightly; tie bundles with chives. Serve immediately.

PER SERVING *52 cal., 4 g fat (1 g sat. fat), 6 mg chol., 74 mg sodium, 2 g carb., 1 g fiber, 2 g pro.* **Diabetic Exchange:** *1 fat.*

ROAST BEEF AIOLI BUNDLES

Yogurt & Honey Fruit Cups F S M

This tasty combo of fresh fruit and creamy orange-kissed yogurt will disappear fast.

—*TASTE OF HOME* TEST KITCHEN

START TO FINISH: 10 MIN.
MAKES: 6 SERVINGS

4½ cups cut-up fresh fruit (pears, apples, bananas, grapes, etc.)
¾ cup (6 ounces) orange yogurt
1 tablespoon honey
½ teaspoon grated orange peel
¼ teaspoon almond extract

Divide fruit among six individual serving bowls. Combine the yogurt, honey, orange peel and extract; spoon over the fruit.

PER SERVING *97 cal., trace fat (trace sat. fat), 2 mg chol., 22 mg sodium, 23 g carb., 2 g fiber, 2 g pro.* **Diabetic Exchanges:** *1 fruit, ½ starch.*

Shrimp Salad Appetizers F S C

This refreshing hors d'oeuvre has gained a big following since a friend shared her family recipe with me. The celery and shrimp are so good together.

—**SOLIE KIMBLE** KANATA, ON

START TO FINISH: 15 MIN.
MAKES: 2 DOZEN

1 pound peeled and deveined cooked shrimp, chopped
1 can (6 ounces) lump crabmeat, drained
2 celery ribs, finely chopped
¼ cup Dijon-mayonnaise blend
24 Belgian endive leaves (3-4 heads) or small butterhead lettuce leaves

In a large bowl, combine the shrimp, crabmeat and celery. Add mayonnaise blend; toss to coat. To serve, top each leaf with about 2 tablespoons shrimp mixture.

PER SERVING *31 cal., trace fat (trace sat. fat), 35 mg chol., 115 mg sodium, 1 g carb., trace fiber, 5 g pro.*

SHRIMP SALAD APPETIZERS

ASIAN CHICKEN DUMPLINGS

Asian Chicken Dumplings F S C

To celebrate my two daughters' Chinese heritage, we occasionally make special meals for holidays like Chinese New Year. I took a traditional pork dumpling recipe and modified it to use ground chicken.
—JOY OLCOTT MILLERSVILLE, PA

PREP: 40 MIN. • **COOK:** 10 MIN./BATCH
MAKES: 2½ DOZEN

- 1 pound ground chicken
- 4 green onions, chopped
- ½ cup chopped cabbage
- ¼ cup minced fresh cilantro
- 2 teaspoons minced fresh gingerroot
- 1 teaspoon salt
- ¼ teaspoon Chinese five-spice powder
- 2 tablespoons water
- 1 package (10 ounces) pot sticker or gyoza wrappers
  Cabbage leaves
  Reduced-sodium soy sauce

1. Place the first seven ingredients in a food processor; cover and process until finely chopped. Add water; cover and process until blended.

2. Place 1 tablespoon chicken mixture in the center of one wrapper. (Keep remaining wrappers covered with a damp paper towel to prevent them from drying out.) Moisten edges with water. Fold wrapper over filling to form a semicircle; press edges firmly to seal, pleating the front side to form three to five folds.

3. Holding sealed edges, stand each dumpling on an even surface; press to flatten bottom. Repeat with remaining wrappers and filling; cover dumplings with plastic wrap.

4. Line a steamer basket with four cabbage leaves. Arrange dumplings in batches 1 in. apart over cabbage; place in a large saucepan over 1 in. of water. Bring to a boil; cover and steam for 10-12 minutes or until a thermometer reads 165°. Discard cabbage. Repeat. Serve with soy sauce.

PER SERVING *1 dumpling equals 45 cal., 1 g fat (trace sat. fat), 10 mg chol., 109 mg sodium, 6 g carb., trace fiber, 3 g pro.*

Moo Shu Chicken Cones F C

My Asian-inspired cones make a unique dish for holiday open houses and game-day parties.
—SUSAN ROTH NAZARETH, PA

PREP: 20 MIN. • **COOK:** 15 MIN.
MAKES: 32 APPETIZERS

- ¾ cup sliced fresh shiitake mushrooms
- 1 tablespoon canola oil
- 1½ teaspoons minced fresh gingerroot
- 1½ teaspoons minced garlic
- 3 cups coleslaw mix
- 2 cups shredded rotisserie chicken
- 3 green onions, sliced
- ½ cup hoisin sauce
- 1 tablespoon honey
- 1½ teaspoons sesame oil
- 16 flour tortillas (6 inches), warmed

1. In a large skillet, saute the mushrooms in oil over medium heat until tender. Add ginger and garlic; cook 1 minute longer.

2. Stir in the coleslaw mix, chicken, green onions, hoisin sauce, honey and sesame oil; heat through.

3. To serve, cut tortillas in half. Roll up each into a cone shape. Spoon 2 tablespoons filling into each cone. Arrange cones, seam side down, on a serving platter.

PER SERVING *92 cal., 3 g fat (1 g sat. fat), 8 mg chol., 174 mg sodium, 11 g carb., 1 g fiber, 4 g pro.* **Diabetic Exchange:** *1 starch.*

MOO SHU CHICKEN CONES

TOMATO & ARTICHOKE BRUSCHETTA

Tomato & Artichoke Bruschetta F S C M

I enjoy serving healthy and delicious bruschetta any time of the year. It's great for entertaining, too. Just mix up the topping and chill until party time.

—**GINA BERGAMINO** CHANHASSEN, MN

START TO FINISH: 30 MIN.
MAKES: ABOUT 6½ DOZEN

- 4 cups grape tomatoes, chopped
- 1 cup (4 ounces) shredded part-skim mozzarella cheese
- ¾ cup water-packed artichoke hearts, rinsed, drained and chopped
- 3 green onions, chopped
- 3 tablespoons pine nuts, toasted
- ¼ cup olive oil
- 3 tablespoons red wine vinegar
- 3 garlic cloves, minced
- ¾ teaspoon pepper
- ¼ teaspoon salt
- 1 French bread baguette (10½ ounces), cut into ¼-inch slices

1. Preheat oven to 425°. In a large bowl, combine tomatoes, cheese, artichokes, green onions and pine nuts. Whisk the oil, vinegar, garlic, pepper and salt; pour over tomato mixture and toss to coat.
2. Place bread on ungreased baking sheets. Bake 4-5 minutes on each side or until golden brown. Top with tomato mixture.
PER SERVING *1 slice equals 24 cal., 1 g fat (trace sat. fat), 1 mg chol., 37 mg sodium, 3 g carb., trace fiber, 1 g pro.*

 Bruschetta Know-How

Try rubbing the bread for this classic Italian appetizer with a half-clove of garlic or lightly brushing it with a garlic-olive oil blend before toasting. Add finely shredded Parmesan or chopped olives for a more salty flavor. During the summer, be sure to use plenty of garden basil.

Pomegranate Orange Salsa F S C M

Pomegranates give this salsa a wonderful sweet-tart flavor. About 4 to 5 medium fruits will yield enough for this recipe.
—NANCEE MAYNARD BOX ELDER, SD

PREP: 10 MIN. + CHILLING
MAKES: 16 SERVINGS (¼ CUP EACH)

- 1 can (15 ounces) mandarin oranges
- 3⅓ cups pomegranate seeds
- ¼ cup minced fresh cilantro
- 2 jalapeno peppers, seeded and finely chopped
- Tortilla chips

Drain the mandarin oranges, reserving 2 tablespoons juice. Cut orange segments in half; transfer to a large bowl. Add the pomegranate seeds, cilantro, jalapenos and reserved juice. Chill 2 hours. Serve with chips.
NOTE *Wear disposable gloves when cutting hot peppers; the oils can burn skin. Avoid touching your face.*
PER SERVING *37 cal., trace fat (trace sat. fat), 0 chol., 3 mg sodium, 9 g carb., trace fiber, trace pro.* **Diabetic Exchange:** *½ fruit.*

Grilled Shrimp Appetizer Kabobs S C

PREP: 15 MIN. + MARINATING • **GRILL:** 5 MIN.
MAKES: 10 SERVINGS

- ⅓ cup tomato sauce
- ⅓ cup olive oil
- 3 tablespoons minced fresh basil
- 3 tablespoons red wine vinegar
- 5 garlic cloves, minced
- ¾ teaspoon salt
- ½ teaspoon cayenne pepper
- 10 uncooked jumbo shrimp, peeled and deveined (8-10 ounces)
- 10 fresh pineapple chunks
- 1 small onion, cut into 1-inch chunks

1. In a large bowl, whisk the first seven ingredients until blended. Reserve ¼ cup marinade for basting. Add shrimp to remaining marinade; toss to coat. Refrigerate, covered, for 30 minutes.
2. On each of 10 metal or soaked wooden appetizer skewers, alternately thread one shrimp, one pineapple chunk and onion. Grill, covered, over medium heat or broil 4 in. from heat 4-6 minutes or until shrimp turn pink, turning occasionally and basting with reserved marinade during the last 2 minutes.

PER SERVING *68 cal., 4 g fat (1 g sat. fat), 31 mg chol., 138 mg sodium, 4 g carb., trace fiber, 4 g pro.* **Diabetic Exchanges:** *1 lean meat, ½ fat.*

The simple combination of pineapple, onion and marinated shrimp has turned me into a big fan of seafood appetizers.
—MICHELE TUNGETT ROCHESTER, IL

GRILLED SHRIMP APPETIZER KABOBS

24

27

32

Salads

"This fast, fresh salad is a winner at every get-together. It's an easygoing side dish for kabobs, chicken or anything hot off the grill."

—**BLAIR LONERGAN** ROCHELLE, VA
about her recipe, Balsamic Cucumber Salad, on page 32

GINGER-SESAME STEAMED VEGETABLE SALAD

Ginger-Sesame Steamed Vegetable Salad C

A homage to my father's Laotian roots, this warm salad is traditionally prepared with baby bok choy, snow peas, peapod shoots and baby mustard greens. Use any seasonal green vegetables you like.

—**MONNIE NORASING** MANSFIELD, TX

PREP: 25 MIN. • **COOK:** 10 MIN.
MAKES: 6 SERVINGS

- 2 **tablespoons grated fresh gingerroot**
- 2 **tablespoons sesame oil**
- 1 **tablespoon fish sauce or reduced-sodium soy sauce**
- 1 **teaspoon sugar**
- ½ **teaspoon reduced-sodium soy sauce**
- ¼ **teaspoon salt**
- 1 **cup cut fresh green beans (2-inch pieces)**
- 4 **cups fresh broccoli florets**
- 2 **large carrots, julienned**
- 1 **package (9 ounces) fresh spinach**
- ½ **cup finely chopped unsalted dry roasted peanuts**
  Coarsely chopped fresh cilantro and julienned fresh gingerroot

1. In a small bowl, mix the first six ingredients.
2. In a stockpot, place steamer insert or basket over 2 in. of water. Place green beans, broccoli and carrots in insert. Bring water to a boil. Reduce heat to maintain a simmer; steam vegetables, covered, 5-7 minutes or just until crisp-tender. Add spinach; cook, covered, 1-2 minutes longer or until spinach is wilted.

3. Transfer vegetables to a large bowl. Add ginger mixture; toss to combine. Just before serving, sprinkle with peanuts, cilantro and julienned ginger.
PER SERVING *156 cal., 11 g fat (2 g sat. fat), 0 chol., 407 mg sodium, 11 g carb., 5 g fiber, 6 g pro.* **Diabetic Exchanges:** *2 vegetable, 2 fat.*

Red & Green Salad with Toasted Almonds S C M

During long winters in the Midwest, I crave greens and tomatoes from the garden. This salad has a fantastic out-of-the-garden taste.

—**JASMINE ROSE** CRYSTAL LAKE, IL

START TO FINISH: 25 MIN.
MAKES: 12 SERVINGS (1⅓ CUPS EACH)

- ¼ **cup red wine vinegar**
- 1 **tablespoon reduced-sodium soy sauce**
- 2 **garlic cloves, minced**
- 2 **teaspoons sesame oil**
- 2 **teaspoons honey**
- 1 **teaspoon minced fresh gingerroot or ½ teaspoon ground ginger**
- ⅛ **teaspoon Louisiana-style hot sauce**
- ½ **cup grapeseed or canola oil**

SALAD
- 2 **heads Boston or Bibb lettuce, torn**
- 1 **head red leaf lettuce**
- 1 **medium sweet red pepper, julienned**
- 2 **celery ribs, sliced**
- 1 **cup sliced English cucumber**
- 1 **cup frozen peas, thawed**
- 1 **cup grape tomatoes, halved**
- 1 **cup sliced almonds, toasted**

1. In a small bowl, whisk the first seven ingredients. Gradually whisk in grapeseed oil until blended.
2. In a large bowl, combine lettuces, red pepper, celery, cucumber, peas and tomatoes. Just before serving, pour dressing over salad and toss to coat. Sprinkle with almonds.
NOTE *To toast nuts, spread in a 15x10x1-in. baking pan. Bake at 350° for 5-10 minutes or until lightly browned, stirring occasionally. Or, cook in a dry skillet over low heat until lightly browned, stirring occasionally.*
PER SERVING *168 cal., 14 g fat (1 g sat. fat), 0 chol., 90 mg sodium, 8 g carb., 3 g fiber, 4 g pro.* **Diabetic Exchanges:** *3 fat, 1 vegetable.*

RED & GREEN SALAD WITH TOASTED ALMONDS

MANDARIN ORANGE & ROMAINE SALAD

Mandarin Orange & Romaine Salad S C M

A salad of romaine, celery and oranges, dressed with tarragon vinaigrette, makes a delightful accompaniment to savory turkey or chicken dishes.

—CATHY PAWLOWSKI NAPERVILLE, IL

START TO FINISH: 20 MIN.
MAKES: 10 SERVINGS (1 CUP EACH)

- ¼ cup canola oil
- 2 tablespoons sugar
- 2 tablespoons tarragon vinegar
- ½ teaspoon salt
- ¼ teaspoon hot pepper sauce
- ⅛ teaspoon pepper
- 10 cups torn romaine
- 1 cup (15 ounces) mandarin oranges, drained
- 2 celery ribs, chopped
- 2 green onions, sliced
- 2 tablespoons minced fresh parsley

In a small bowl, whisk the first six ingredients until blended. In a large bowl, combine remaining ingredients. Drizzle with dressing; toss to coat.
PER SERVING 84 cal., 6 g fat (trace sat. fat), 0 chol., 132 mg sodium, 8 g carb., 2 g fiber, 1 g pro. **Diabetic Exchanges:** 1 vegetable, 1 fat, ½ starch.

top tip

From the Web

This is a simple salad with a refreshing dressing. I used white wine vinegar and added 1 tsp. dried tarragon instead of tarragon vinegar. I'll try it with toasted almond slices and a sprinkling of feta or blue cheese next time.

—CATMURPHY TASTEOFHOME.COM

Tomatoes with Buttermilk Vinaigrette S C M

START TO FINISH: 20 MIN.
MAKES: 12 SERVINGS (¾ CUP EACH)

- ¾ cup buttermilk
- ¼ cup minced fresh tarragon
- ¼ cup white wine vinegar
- 3 tablespoons canola oil
- 1½ teaspoons sugar
- ½ teaspoon ground mustard
- ¼ teaspoon celery salt
- ¼ teaspoon pepper
- 4 pounds cherry tomatoes, halved
- ⅓ cup minced fresh chives

1. In a small bowl, whisk the first eight ingredients until blended. Refrigerate, covered, until serving.
2. Just before serving, arrange tomatoes on a platter; drizzle with vinaigrette. Sprinkle with chives.
PER SERVING 79 cal., 4 g fat (trace sat. fat), 1 mg chol., 63 mg sodium, 10 g carb., 2 g fiber, 2 g pro. **Diabetic Exchanges:** 1 vegetable, ½ starch, ½ fat.

> I like to make the most of tomatoes when they are in season and plentiful, and I love an old-fashioned homemade dressing with a summery taste.
>
> —JUDITH FOREMAN ALEXANDRIA, VA

TOMATOES WITH BUTTERMILK VINAIGRETTE

Salmon Salad with Glazed Walnuts C

This main-dish salad was inspired by something I ate while on a trip. The glazed walnuts give it a little something special. I've also topped it with grilled chicken or portobello mushrooms when they're on hand.

—**JOANNA KOBERNIK** BERKLEY, MI

START TO FINISH: 15 MIN.
MAKES: 2 SERVINGS

- 2 **salmon fillets (4 ounces each)**
- 6 **tablespoons reduced-fat balsamic vinaigrette, divided**
- ⅛ **teaspoon pepper**
- 4 **cups spring mix salad greens**
- ¼ **cup glazed walnuts**
- 2 **tablespoons crumbled blue cheese**

1. Brush salmon with 2 tablespoons vinaigrette; sprinkle with pepper. Moisten a paper towel with cooking oil; using long-handled tongs, lightly coat the grill rack. Grill salmon, covered, over medium heat or broil 4 in. from heat 3-4 minutes on each side or just until fish begins to flake easily with a fork.

2. In a bowl, toss salad greens with remaining vinaigrette. Divide between two plates; sprinkle with walnuts and cheese. Top with salmon.

PER SERVING *374 cal., 25 g fat (5 g sat. fat), 64 mg chol., 607 mg sodium, 13 g carb., 4 g fiber, 24 g pro.* **Diabetic Exchanges:** *3 lean meat, 3 fat, ½ starch.*

Roasted Butternut Tossed Salad M

Here's an easy side dish that's special enough for Thanksgiving dinner. It's packed with nutritious veggies, almonds, berries and squash.

—**KATIE WOLLGAST** FLORISSANT, MO

PREP: 20 MIN. • **BAKE:** 20 MIN.
MAKES: 8 SERVINGS

- 4 **cups cubed peeled butternut squash (about 1 pound)**
- 1 **large onion, chopped**
- 1 **tablespoon honey**
- ½ **teaspoon salt**
- ½ **teaspoon garlic powder**
- ¼ **teaspoon pepper**
- 1 **package (6 ounces) fresh baby spinach**
- 2 **cups coarsely chopped iceberg lettuce**
- ½ **cup shredded fat-free cheddar cheese**
- 6 **tablespoons reduced-fat poppy seed salad dressing, divided**
- ½ **cup seasoned stuffing cubes**
- ½ **cup dried cranberries**
- ¼ **cup slivered almonds, toasted**
- 4 **bacon strips, cooked and crumbled**

1. Preheat oven to 400°. In a large bowl, toss squash and onion with honey, salt, garlic powder and pepper. Transfer to a 15x10x1-in. baking pan coated with cooking spray. Bake 20-25 minutes or until vegetables are tender, stirring once. Cool slightly.

2. In another bowl, combine spinach, lettuce, cheese and squash mixture. Just before serving, drizzle with 4 tablespoons dressing and toss to coat. Divide salad among eight plates; top with stuffing cubes, cranberries, almonds and bacon. Drizzle with remaining dressing.

NOTE *To toast nuts, spread in a 15x10x1-in. baking pan. Bake at 350° for 5-10 minutes or until lightly browned, stirring occasionally. Or, spread in a dry nonstick skillet and heat over low heat until lightly browned, stirring occasionally.*

PER SERVING *165 cal., 4 g fat (1 g sat. fat), 5 mg chol., 453 mg sodium, 28 g carb., 4 g fiber, 7 g pro.* **Diabetic Exchanges:** *2 starch, ½ fat.*

ROASTED BUTTERNUT TOSSED SALAD

SALMON SALAD WITH GLAZED WALNUTS

Sweet Potato Salad with Orange Dressing M

For a unique side dish that pairs well with almost any entree, try my delightful salad. The sweet potatoes, crunchy apples and nuts tossed in a citrusy dressing make it a favorite in my home.

—MARIE RIZZIO INTERLOCHEN, MI

PREP: 25 MIN. • **COOK:** 15 MIN.
MAKES: 10 SERVINGS

- 2 pounds medium sweet potatoes, peeled and cubed (about 6 cups)
- 1 cup fat-free mayonnaise
- 2 tablespoons orange juice
- 1 tablespoon honey
- 1½ teaspoons grated orange peel
- 1½ teaspoons minced fresh gingerroot
- ¼ teaspoon salt
- ¼ teaspoon pepper
- 1 medium Granny Smith apple, peeled and chopped
- 1 cup finely chopped fennel bulb
- ½ cup dried cranberries
- ½ cup chopped pecans, toasted
- ¼ cup chopped walnuts, toasted

1. Place sweet potatoes in a Dutch oven; cover with water. Bring to a boil. Reduce heat; cook, covered, 8-10 minutes or just until tender. Drain.

2. Meanwhile, in a large bowl, mix mayonnaise, orange juice, honey, orange peel, ginger, salt and pepper. Stir in apple, fennel, cranberries, pecans and walnuts. Add sweet potatoes; toss gently to coat. Serve warm or refrigerate, covered, and serve cold.

PER SERVING *183 cal., 7 g fat (1 g sat. fat), 3 mg chol., 300 mg sodium, 30 g carb., 5 g fiber, 2 g pro.* **Diabetic Exchanges:** *2 starch, 1 fat.*

 ## Did you know?

Wild salmon is 20% leaner than farm-raised fish, while being higher in heart-healthy omega-3 fatty acids. Some people prefer its flavor over farm-raised fish, too. Fresh wild salmon is available from May through October, as the different species travel upstream to spawn.

SWEET POTATO SALAD
WITH ORANGE DRESSING

Italian Fresh Vegetable Salad C M

Garden-fresh veggies are a hit at community potlucks. I like to carry the dressing along in a jar to add just before serving.
—**JEANETTE HILDEBRAND** STAFFORD, KS

START TO FINISH: 25 MIN. • **MAKES:** 20 SERVINGS (1 CUP EACH)

SALAD
- 1 bunch romaine, torn
- 4 cups fresh baby spinach
- 2 cups grape tomatoes
- 1 can (14 ounces) water-packed artichoke hearts, rinsed, drained and quartered
- 1 medium zucchini, thinly sliced
- 1 small green pepper, sliced
- 1 small sweet red pepper, sliced
- 1 cup thinly sliced fresh mushrooms
- 1 cup thinly sliced red onion
- 1 cup (4 ounces) shredded part-skim mozzarella cheese
- ½ cup sliced pepperoncini
- 1 can (2¼ ounces) sliced ripe olives, drained

VINAIGRETTE
- ⅔ cup canola oil
- ½ cup red wine vinegar
- ¼ cup minced fresh basil
- 1½ teaspoons garlic powder
- 1½ teaspoons ground mustard
- 1 teaspoon honey
- ½ teaspoon salt

1. In a large bowl, combine the salad ingredients. In a small bowl, whisk the vinaigrette ingredients.
2. Just before serving, pour ¾ cup vinaigrette over salad; toss to coat. Refrigerate remaining vinaigrette for another use.
PER SERVING 84 cal., 6 g fat (1 g sat. fat), 3 mg chol., 149 mg sodium, 5 g carb., 1 g fiber, 3 g pro. *Diabetic Exchanges: 1 vegetable, 1 fat.*

Grilled Vegetable Orzo Salad M

Vegetables that are in season make great additions to this incredibly versatile orzo salad. It's the perfect side dish for a picnic, it can easily be doubled for a crowd, or you can add grilled chicken to make it a filling entree.
—**DANIELLE MILLER** WESTFIELD, IN

PREP: 35 MIN. • **GRILL:** 10 MIN. • **MAKES:** 8 SERVINGS

- 1¼ cups uncooked orzo pasta
- ½ pound fresh asparagus, trimmed
- 1 medium zucchini, cut lengthwise into ½-inch slices
- 1 medium sweet yellow or red pepper, halved
- 1 large portobello mushroom, stem removed
- ½ medium red onion, halved

DRESSING
- ⅓ cup olive oil
- ¼ cup balsamic vinegar
- 3 tablespoons lemon juice
- 4 garlic cloves, minced
- 1 teaspoon lemon-pepper seasoning

SALAD
- 1 cup grape tomatoes, halved
- 1 tablespoon minced fresh parsley
- 1 tablespoon minced fresh basil
- ½ teaspoon salt
- ¼ teaspoon pepper
- 1 cup (4 ounces) crumbled feta cheese

1. Cook orzo according to package directions. Place vegetables in a large bowl. In a small bowl, whisk dressing ingredients. Add to vegetables and toss to coat.
2. Remove vegetables, reserving dressing. Grill mushroom, pepper and onion, covered, over medium heat 5-10 minutes or until tender, turning occasionally. Place asparagus and zucchini in a closed grill basket; grill 3-4 minutes or until desired doneness, turning occasionally.
3. When cool enough to handle, cut vegetables into bite-size pieces. In a large bowl, combine cooked orzo, grilled vegetables, tomatoes, parsley, basil, salt, pepper and reserved dressing; toss to combine. Serve at room temperature or refrigerate until cold. Just before serving, stir in cheese.
PER SERVING 260 cal., 12 g fat (3 g sat. fat), 8 mg chol., 352 mg sodium, 30 g carb., 2 g fiber, 8 g pro. *Diabetic Exchanges: 2 fat, 1½ starch, 1 vegetable.*

ITALIAN FRESH VEGETABLE SALAD

Red Potato Salad Dijon Ⓜ

PREP: 25 MIN. • **COOK:** 15 MIN. • **MAKES:** 12 SERVINGS (¾ CUP EACH)

- 3½ pounds red potatoes (about 12 medium), cubed
- ¼ cup Dijon-mayonnaise blend
- 3 tablespoons seasoned rice vinegar
- 3 tablespoons olive oil
- 4 teaspoons minced fresh tarragon
- 1½ teaspoons salt
- ¾ teaspoon pepper
- 6 green onions, thinly sliced

1. Place potatoes in a Dutch oven; add water to cover. Bring to a boil. Reduce heat; cook, uncovered, 10-15 minutes or until tender. Drain; transfer to a large bowl.
2. In a small bowl, mix mayonnaise blend, vinegar, oil, tarragon, salt and pepper. Drizzle over potatoes; toss to coat. Gently stir in green onions. Serve warm. Refrigerate leftovers.

PER SERVING *139 cal., 4 g fat (1 g sat. fat), 0 chol., 557 mg sodium, 24 g carb., 2 g fiber, 3 g pro.* **Diabetic Exchanges:** *1½ starch, 1 fat.*

My mother made the best warm potato salad, and now it's a tradition at all of our tables. Sometimes I use Yukon Gold potatoes to make it even prettier.
—**PATRICIA SWART** GALLOWAY, NJ

RED POTATO SALAD DIJON

TURKEY TACO SALAD

Turkey Taco Salad

I discovered this taco salad while I was on a health kick. My husband and I love it now. When I served it at a family birthday party, everyone eagerly asked for the recipe.
—**ANGELA MATSON** AMBOY, WA

START TO FINISH: 30 MIN. • **MAKES:** 4 SERVINGS

- 12 ounces ground turkey
- 1 medium sweet red pepper, chopped
- 1 small sweet yellow pepper, chopped
- ⅓ cup chopped onion
- 3 garlic cloves, minced
- 1½ cups salsa
- ½ cup canned kidney beans, rinsed and drained
- 2 teaspoons chili powder
- 1 teaspoon ground cumin
- 8 cups torn romaine
- 2 tablespoons fresh cilantro leaves
  Optional toppings: chopped tomatoes, shredded cheddar cheese and crushed tortilla chips

1. In a large skillet, cook turkey, peppers, onion and garlic over medium heat 6-8 minutes or until turkey is no longer pink and vegetables are tender, breaking up turkey into crumbles; drain.
2. Stir in salsa, beans, chili powder and cumin; heat through. Divide romaine among four plates. Top with turkey mixture; sprinkle with cilantro and toppings of your choice. Serve immediately.

PER SERVING *275 cal., 13 g fat (4 g sat. fat), 58 mg chol., 525 mg sodium, 21 g carb., 6 g fiber, 18 g pro.* **Diabetic Exchanges:** *2 medium-fat meat, 1½ starch.*

Crunchy apples and ripe, juicy pears are fantastic when tossed with crisp, cool cukes and a spicy dressing. This fun combination of ingredients comes together beautifully in one flavorful dish.

—**JEAN ECOS** HARTLAND, WI

FRESH APPLE & PEAR SALAD

Fresh Apple & Pear Salad F M

START TO FINISH: 20 MIN.
MAKES: 8 SERVINGS

- 4 medium apples, thinly sliced
- 2 medium pears, thinly sliced
- 1 medium cucumber, seeded and chopped
- 1 medium red onion, halved and thinly sliced
- ¼ cup apple cider or juice
- 1 tablespoon snipped fresh dill or minced fresh tarragon
- 1 tablespoon olive oil
- 1 tablespoon spicy brown mustard
- 2 teaspoons brown sugar
- ½ teaspoon salt
- ¼ teaspoon pepper

In a large bowl, combine apples, pears, cucumber and onion. In a small bowl, whisk remaining ingredients until blended. Pour over apple mixture and toss to coat. Refrigerate until serving.
PER SERVING *96 cal., 2 g fat (trace sat. fat), 0 chol., 175 mg sodium, 20 g carb., 4 g fiber, 1 g pro.* **Diabetic Exchanges:** *1 fruit, ½ fat.*

Mandarin Watermelon Salad F S C M

Fruit tossed with feta? You bet! There's nothing better. Fresh mint, cilantro and parsley add the perfect pop. I'm always looking for something different to serve my vegetarian mom, and she loved this!
—**JADE BAUSELL** MIAMI, FL

START TO FINISH: 20 MIN.
MAKES: 8 SERVINGS

- 4½ cups cubed seedless watermelon
- 1 can (11 ounces) mandarin oranges, drained
- ½ small red onion, sliced
- ¼ cup crumbled feta cheese
- 2 tablespoons minced fresh mint
- 2 tablespoons minced fresh cilantro
- 2 tablespoons lime juice
- 1 tablespoon minced fresh parsley

Place all ingredients in a bowl; gently toss to combine. Serve immediately.
PER SERVING *48 cal., 1 g fat (trace sat. fat), 2 mg chol., 39 mg sodium, 12 g carb., 1 g fiber, 1 g pro.* **Diabetic Exchange:** *1 fruit.*

RUBY RED SPINACH SALADS

Ruby Red Spinach Salads M

These fabulous salads blend contrasting flavors deliciously. Pomegranate seeds add vibrant color, a pleasant crunch and a healthy dose of vitamin C.
—**VERONICA CALLAGHAN** GLASTONBURY, CT

START TO FINISH: 20 MIN.
MAKES: 4 SERVINGS

- 3 tablespoons red grapefruit juice
- 1 tablespoon olive oil
- ½ teaspoon honey
- ¼ teaspoon kosher salt
- ⅛ teaspoon pepper
- 1 large fennel bulb
- 2 large red grapefruit, sectioned
- 1 cup fresh baby spinach
- ¼ cup shaved Romano cheese
- ½ cup pomegranate seeds

1. In a bowl, whisk the first five ingredients. Remove fronds from fennel; set aside for garnish. Cut bulb into thin slices and coarsely chop the slices. In a bowl, combine the chopped fennel, grapefruit and spinach. Drizzle dressing over salad; toss to coat.
2. Divide salad among four plates; sprinkle cheese and pomegranate seeds over salads. Garnish with fennel fronds.
PER SERVING *132 cal., 4 g fat (1 g sat. fat), 3 mg chol., 190 mg sodium, 23 g carb., 4 g fiber, 3 g pro.* **Diabetic Exchanges:** *1 vegetable, 1 fruit, 1 fat.*

Shrimp Salad with Cilantro Vinaigrette

This pretty dish has such authentic flavor, you'll think you're sitting at a beachside cantina in Acapulco.

—**HEIDI HALL** NORTH ST. PAUL, MN

START TO FINISH: 25 MIN.
MAKES: 4 SERVINGS

- 3 **tablespoons olive oil**
- 2 **tablespoons lime juice**
- 1 **to 2 teaspoons dried cilantro flakes**
- 1 **small garlic clove, minced**
- ¾ **teaspoon sugar**
- ¼ **teaspoon salt**
- ⅛ **teaspoon pepper**

SALAD

- 1 **teaspoon olive oil**
- ½ **pound uncooked large shrimp, peeled and deveined**
- ¼ **teaspoon chili powder**
- ⅛ **teaspoon salt**
- ⅛ **teaspoon ground cumin**
- 1 **small garlic clove, minced**
- 5 **cups chopped hearts of romaine**
- 1 **cup fresh or frozen corn, thawed**
- 1 **cup frozen peas, thawed**
- ½ **cup chopped sweet red pepper**
- 1 **medium ripe avocado, peeled and thinly sliced**

1. In a bowl, whisk the first seven ingredients until blended. In a skillet, heat oil over medium-high heat. Add shrimp, chili powder, salt and cumin; cook and stir 2-3 minutes or until shrimp turn pink. Add garlic; cook 1 minute longer. Remove from heat.

2. In a bowl, combine romaine, corn, peas and red pepper; drizzle with dressing and toss to coat. Top with avocado and shrimp.

PER SERVING *305 cal., 20 g fat (3 g sat. fat), 69 mg chol., 359 mg sodium, 22 g carb., 8 g fiber, 15 g pro.*

Texas Tabbouleh ᴹ

I used to live in Texas and since moving away, I missed those classic Tex-Mex flavors that were always a big part of my meals. I decided to create a fresh and healthy salad that reminds me of traditional pico de gallo.

—**TAMMY DAVIS** ARLINGTON, VA

PREP: 40 MIN. + CHILLING
MAKES: 10 SERVINGS

- 1 **cup bulgur**
- 2 **cups boiling water**
- 3 **medium tomatoes**
- 1 **cup finely chopped red onion**

TEXAS TABBOULEH

- 2 **green onions, thinly sliced**
- ½ **cup chopped sweet red pepper**
- ½ **cup chopped green pepper**
- 2 **jalapeno peppers, seeded and chopped**
- ½ **cup fresh cilantro leaves, chopped**
- ¼ **cup lime juice**
- 3 **tablespoons canola oil**
- 2 **garlic cloves, minced**
- ¼ **teaspoon salt**
- ¼ **teaspoon coarsely ground pepper**
- 1 **can (15 ounces) black beans, rinsed and drained**
- 1 **cup (4 ounces) crumbled queso fresco or feta cheese**

1. Place bulgur in a large bowl; stir in boiling water. Let stand, covered, 30 minutes or until bulgur is tender and most of the liquid is absorbed. Drain well, pressing out excess water. Cool completely.

2. Stir in tomatoes, onions, peppers, cilantro, lime juice, oil and seasonings. Add beans; toss to combine. Refrigerate, covered, at least 30 minutes. Serve with cheese.

NOTE *Wear disposable gloves when cutting hot peppers; the oils can burn skin. Avoid touching your face.*

PER SERVING *139 cal., 4 g fat (1 g sat. fat), 4 mg chol., 161 mg sodium, 21 g carb., 5 g fiber, 6 g pro.* **Diabetic Exchanges:** *1 starch, ½ fat.*

SHRIMP SALAD WITH CILANTRO VINAIGRETTE

Minted Sugar Snap Pea Salad M

You'll catch spring fever with just one bite of this lovely salad. Shallot, honey and mustard add piquant and savory elements to crisp spring peas.

—DARLENE MORRIS FRANKLINTON, LA

START TO FINISH: 25 MIN.
MAKES: 4 SERVINGS

- 1½ **pounds fresh sugar snap peas, trimmed and strings removed**
- ¼ **cup crumbled goat cheese**
- **DRESSING**
- 3 **tablespoons minced fresh mint**
- 3 **tablespoons olive oil**
- 1 **small shallot, finely chopped**
- 1 **tablespoon lemon juice**
- 1 **teaspoon grated lemon peel**
- 1 **teaspoon Dijon mustard**
- 1 **teaspoon honey**
- ½ **teaspoon salt**
- ¼ **teaspoon pepper**

1. In a large saucepan, bring 2 quarts water to a boil. Add peas; cook, uncovered, 2-3 minutes or just until crisp-tender. Drain and immediately place in ice water. Drain and pat dry. Cut in half crosswise; place in a large bowl. Sprinkle with goat cheese.

2. In a small bowl, whisk dressing ingredients. Pour over pea mixture; toss to coat.
PER SERVING *197 cal., 12 g fat (3 g sat. fat), 9 mg chol., 368 mg sodium, 16 g carb., 5 g fiber, 7 g pro.* **Diabetic Exchanges:** *2½ fat, 2 vegetable.*

Honey-Lime Berry Salad F S M

I picked up this dish a couple of years ago, and really like the mint and fruit combo. Cilantro is one of my favorite herbs, so sometimes I use it instead.

—KAYLA SPENCE WILBER, NE

START TO FINISH: 15 MIN.
MAKES: 10 SERVINGS

- 4 **cups fresh strawberries, halved**
- 3 **cups fresh blueberries**
- 3 **medium Granny Smith apples, cubed**
- ⅓ **cup lime juice**
- ¼ **to ⅓ cup honey**
- 2 **tablespoons minced fresh mint**

In a large bowl, combine the strawberries, blueberries and apples. In a small bowl, whisk lime juice, honey and mint. Pour over fruit and toss to coat.

HONEY-LIME BERRY SALAD

PER SERVING *93 cal., trace fat (trace sat. fat), 0 chol., 2 mg sodium, 24 g carb., 3 g fiber, 1 g pro.* **Diabetic Exchanges:** *1 fruit, ½ starch.*

Fiesta Rice and Bean Salad F M

My entire family, including the grandkids, loves this salad, so it's a good one for me to serve during the summer months when we have everyone over for dinner. This is a fresh and healthy side dish that goes well with your favorite barbecue meal. I like to prepare it with fresh sweet corn bought from our local farmer.

—DIANE LYNCH SUGAR GROVE, IL

PREP: 40 MIN. + CHILLING
MAKES: 10 SERVINGS

- 1 **package (6.2 ounces) fast-cooking long grain and wild rice mix**
- 2 **cups fresh or frozen corn**
- 1 **can (15 ounces) black beans, rinsed and drained**
- 1 **bunch green onions, chopped**
- 1 **small sweet red pepper, chopped**
- 1 **small sweet orange pepper, chopped**
- ½ **cup minced fresh cilantro**
- 1 **can (2¼ ounces) sliced ripe olives, drained**
- ½ **cup reduced-fat Italian salad dressing**
- 1 **tablespoon lime juice**
- ¼ **teaspoon pepper**

1. Prepare rice mix according to package directions; cool. Meanwhile, in a large saucepan, bring 4 cups water to a boil. Add corn; cover and cook for 5-6 minutes or until tender. Drain corn and rinse in cold water.

2. In a large bowl, combine the rice, corn, black beans, green onions, red and orange peppers, cilantro and olives. Combine the salad dressing, lime juice and pepper; drizzle over salad and toss to coat. Cover and refrigerate salad for at least 2 hours before serving.
PER SERVING *155 cal., 3 g fat (trace sat. fat), trace chol., 470 mg sodium, 28 g carb., 4 g fiber, 5 g pro.* **Diabetic Exchanges:** *2 starch, ½ fat.*

Broccoli Slaw with Lemon Dressing C M

Our family absolutely loves broccoli, so I'm so happy there's finally a slaw mix in stores that features it. I like this slaw best after it's chilled 20 minutes or so for the flavors to meld.
—**DONNA MARIE RYAN** TOPSFIELD, MA

START TO FINISH: 15 MIN. • **MAKES:** 10 SERVINGS

- ½ cup sour cream
- 3 tablespoons lemon juice
- 2 tablespoons mayonnaise
- 1 tablespoon white wine vinegar
- 2 teaspoons grated lemon peel
- 1 teaspoon Dijon mustard
- ½ teaspoon salt
- ¼ teaspoon freshly ground pepper
- 1 package (12 ounces) broccoli coleslaw mix
- 2 large red apples, juliennned

In a large bowl, mix the first eight ingredients. Add coleslaw mix and apples; toss to coat. Refrigerate salad, covered, until serving.
PER SERVING *79 cal., 4 g fat (2 g sat. fat), 9 mg chol., 152 mg sodium, 9 g carb., 2 g fiber, 1 g pro.* **Diabetic Exchanges:** *1 fat, ½ starch.*

Balsamic Cucumber Salad C M

This fast, fresh salad is a winner at every get-together. It's an easygoing side dish for kabobs, chicken or anything hot off the grill.
—**BLAIR LONERGAN** ROCHELLE, VA

START TO FINISH: 15 MIN. • **MAKES:** 6 SERVINGS

- 1 large English cucumber, halved and sliced
- 2 cups grape tomatoes, halved
- 1 medium red onion, halved and thinly sliced
- ½ cup balsamic vinaigrette
- ¾ cup crumbled reduced-fat feta cheese

In a large bowl, combine cucumber, tomatoes and onion. Add vinaigrette; toss to coat. Refrigerate, covered, until serving. Just before serving, stir in cheese. Serve with a slotted spoon.
PER SERVING *90 cal., 5 g fat (1 g sat. fat), 5 mg chol., 356 mg sodium, 9 g carb., 1 g fiber, 4 g pro.* **Diabetic Exchanges:** *1 vegetable, 1 fat.*

Chicken Salad with Dijon Vinaigrette C

I find myself turning to this quick and easy chicken salad for many weeknight dinners. It's the perfect combination of crunchy, savory and salty.
—**LYNNE KEAST** MONTE SERENO, CA

START TO FINISH: 15 MIN. • **MAKES:** 8 SERVINGS

- 2 **tablespoons champagne vinegar or rice vinegar**
- 4 **teaspoons Dijon mustard**
- ¼ **teaspoon salt**
- ¼ **teaspoon pepper**
- ¼ **cup olive oil**
- 10 **cups torn Bibb or Boston lettuce**
- 1 **rotisserie chicken, skin removed, shredded**
- ⅓ **cup crumbled blue cheese**
- ½ **cup sliced almonds, optional**

1. In a small bowl, whisk vinegar, mustard, salt and pepper. Gradually whisk in oil until blended.
2. In a large bowl, combine lettuce, chicken, cheese and, if desired, almonds. Drizzle with vinaigrette; toss to coat.
PER SERVING *275 cal., 17 g fat (4 g sat. fat), 74 mg chol., 275 mg sodium, 4 g carb., 1 g fiber, 26 g pro.* **Diabetic Exchanges:** *3 lean meat, 2½ fat.*

Kale Salad C M

I love to make meals that wow everyone at the table. The flavor and nutrition in kale set it apart from many other salads.
—**GINA MYERS** SPOKANE, WA

START TO FINISH: 15 MIN. • **MAKES:** 8 SERVINGS

- 10 **cups sliced kale (about 1 bunch)**
- 1 **medium apple, thinly sliced**
- 3 **tablespoons olive oil**
- 2 **tablespoons lemon juice**
- 1 **teaspoon salt**
- ½ **teaspoon pepper**
- ¼ **cup crumbled feta cheese**
- ¼ **cup salted pumpkin seeds or pepitas**

1. Place kale in a large bowl. With clean hands, massage kale until leaves become soft and darkened, about 2-3 minutes; stir in apple.
2. In a small bowl, whisk oil, lemon juice, salt and pepper until blended. Drizzle over salad; toss to coat. Sprinkle with cheese and pumpkin seeds.
PER SERVING *113 cal., 9 g fat (2 g sat. fat), 2 mg chol., 381 mg sodium, 6 g carb., 1 g fiber, 4 g pro.* **Diabetic Exchanges:** *2 fat, ½ starch.*

GARDEN-FRESH CHEF SALAD

Bow Tie Pasta Salad F C M

This was originally a vegetable dish, but I added pasta to stretch it for family gatherings and church potlucks. You can also add sliced mushrooms and diced tomatoes before serving.

—BARBARA BURKS HUNTSVILLE, AL

PREP: 30 MIN. + CHILLING • **COOK:** 10 MIN.
MAKES: 24 SERVINGS (¾ CUP EACH)

- 1 medium cucumber
- 1 medium yellow summer squash
- 1 medium zucchini
- 1 medium sweet red pepper
- 1 medium green pepper
- 4 cups fresh broccoli florets
- 3 cups fresh cauliflowerets
- 1 small red onion, finely chopped
- 2 packages Italian salad dressing mix
- 4½ cups uncooked bow tie pasta
- ¼ cup olive oil
- ¼ cup red wine vinegar
- ¾ teaspoon salt
- ½ teaspoon pepper

1. Wash the first five ingredients, but do not dry; chop and transfer to a large bowl. Add remaining vegetables. Sprinkle with dry dressing mix; toss to coat. Refrigerate, covered, 4-6 hours or overnight.

2. Cook pasta according to package directions. Drain; rinse with cold water. Add to vegetable mixture. In a small bowl, whisk the remaining ingredients. Add to salad; toss to coat.

PER SERVING *89 cal., 3 g fat (trace sat. fat), 0 chol., 296 mg sodium, 14 g carb., 2 g fiber, 3 g pro.* **Diabetic Exchanges:** *1 vegetable, ½ starch, ½ fat.*

BOW TIE PASTA SALAD

Garden-Fresh Chef Salad C

For much of the year, I use my garden's produce when I make this cool salad. In spring, it's salad mix and radishes, and in summer, we have tomatoes, cabbage and carrots. What a good feeling!

—EVELYN GUBERNATH BUCYRUS, OH

START TO FINISH: 25 MIN.
MAKES: 6 SERVINGS

- 6 cups spring mix salad greens
- 2 medium tomatoes, coarsely chopped
- 6 hard-cooked eggs, coarsely chopped
- 3 slices deli turkey, cut into thin strips
- 3 slices deli ham, cut into thin strips
- ½ cup shredded cabbage
- 4 green onions, sliced
- 4 fresh baby carrots, sliced
- 4 radishes, thinly sliced
- ¼ teaspoon garlic powder
- ¼ teaspoon pepper
- ½ cup reduced-fat Thousand Island salad dressing or dressing of your choice

In a large bowl, combine the first nine ingredients. Sprinkle with garlic powder and pepper; toss to coat. Serve with salad dressing.

PER SERVING *171 cal., 9 g fat (2 g sat. fat), 227 mg chol., 508 mg sodium, 11 g carb., 2 g fiber, 12 g pro.* **Diabetic Exchanges:** *2 lean meat, 2 vegetable, 1 fat.*

CASHEW-CURRY
CHICKEN SALAD

Cashew-Curry Chicken Salad

My husband and I fell hard for the curried chicken salad from our grocery store deli, and I knew I could find a way to make something similar. This version has become one of our favorites to take on trips to the beach.

—JANINE COOPER-MOREN PORTLAND, OR

START TO FINISH: 20 MIN.
MAKES: 6 SERVINGS

- 3 cups cubed cooked chicken breast
- 4 celery ribs, chopped
- 2 medium carrots, chopped
- ⅔ cup golden raisins
- ½ cup chopped cashews

DRESSING

- ⅔ cup honey Greek yogurt
- 4 teaspoons lemon juice
- 4 teaspoons honey
- 1 teaspoon curry powder
- ¼ teaspoon salt
- ¼ teaspoon garlic powder
- ¼ teaspoon pepper
- ⅛ teaspoon ground ginger

1. In a large bowl, combine chicken, celery, carrots, raisins and cashews.
2. In a small bowl, mix yogurt, lemon juice, honey and spices. Pour over chicken mixture; toss to coat.
PER SERVING *287 cal., 10 g fat (3 g sat. fat), 60 mg chol., 267 mg sodium, 27 g carb., 2 g fiber, 24 g pro.* **Diabetic Exchanges:** *3 lean meat, 1½ starch, 1 vegetable, ½ fruit.*

My Underground Vegetable Salad Ⓜ

PREP: 20 MIN. • **BAKE:** 40 MIN.
MAKES: 8 SERVINGS

- 1 pound medium fresh mushrooms, halved
- 8 small carrots, peeled and halved lengthwise
- 2 cups cubed peeled celery root (about ½ pound)
- 2 cups cubed peeled rutabaga (about 1 medium)
- 2 cups cubed peeled sweet potatoes (about 1 medium)
- 2 tablespoons olive oil
- ¼ teaspoon salt
- 2 cups cherry tomatoes, halved
- 8 cups torn curly endive

VINAIGRETTE

- 3 tablespoons apple cider or juice
- 2 tablespoons lemon juice
- 2 tablespoons cider vinegar
- 1 teaspoon stone-ground mustard
- 1 teaspoon grated lemon peel
- ½ teaspoon fennel seed, crushed
- ¼ teaspoon salt
- ¼ teaspoon pepper
- ½ cup olive oil

1. Preheat oven to 400°. In a large bowl, combine the first five ingredients. Add oil and salt; toss to coat. Transfer to a greased shallow roasting pan. Roast 30-35 minutes or until vegetables are tender, stirring occasionally. Add tomatoes; bake 10 minutes longer.
2. Place endive in a large bowl. In a small bowl, whisk the first eight vinaigrette ingredients. Gradually whisk in oil until blended. Pour over endive; toss to coat. Divide endive among eight plates; top with roasted vegetables.
PER SERVING *261 cal., 18 g fat (2 g sat. fat), 0 chol., 261 mg sodium, 24 g carb., 7 g fiber, 4 g pro.*

I've found that roasting is a delicious and easy way to bring out the subtle sweetness of rich, earthy root vegetables. Serving them over endive with a homemade vinaigrette is just a bonus!
—PETER HALFERTY CORPUS CHRISTI, TX

MY UNDERGROUND VEGETABLE SALAD

40

42

50

Soups

❝This heartwarming soup has become a favorite because it uses kitchen staples, is packed with healthy ingredients and is a cinch to prepare. If I can't find escarole, I just use fresh spinach instead!❞

—GINA SAMOKAR NORTH HAVEN, CT
about her recipe, White Bean Soup with Escarole, on page 51

BEAN SOUP WITH SAUSAGE

Bean Soup with Sausage ◧

This soup is so simple to put together, and it calls for ingredients that are easy to keep on hand. The tomato-based broth is loaded with meat, potatoes and veggies.

—**GAIL WILKERSON** HOUSE SPRINGS, MO

PREP: 10 MIN. • **COOK:** 25 MIN.
MAKES: 10 SERVINGS (2½ QUARTS)

8	ounces bulk lean turkey breakfast sausage
1	medium onion, chopped
1	medium green pepper, chopped
2	cans (16 ounces each) kidney beans, rinsed and drained
1	medium potato, peeled and cubed
4	cups water
1	bay leaf
½	teaspoon each garlic salt, seasoned salt and pepper
½	teaspoon dried thyme
1	can (28 ounces) diced tomatoes, undrained

1. In a large saucepan, cook sausage, onion and green pepper over medium heat 4-6 minutes or until vegetables are tender and sausage is no longer pink, breaking up the sausage into crumbles; drain.

2. Stir in beans, potato, water and seasonings; bring to a boil. Reduce heat; simmer, uncovered, 10-15 minutes or until potato is tender. Stir in tomatoes and heat through. Remove bay leaf.

PER SERVING *1 cup equals 160 cal., 2 g fat (1 g sat. fat), 24 mg chol., 645 mg sodium, 23 g carb., 6 g fiber, 13 g pro.* ***Diabetic Exchanges:*** *1 starch, 1 lean meat, 1 vegetable.*

❓ Did you know?

A medium green pepper, chopped, will yield about 1 cup. A large green pepper, chopped, results in about 1⅓ to 1½ cups. A medium onion, chopped, offers about ½ cup; a large onion will yield about 1 cup.

ROASTED SWEET POTATO SOUP

Roasted Sweet Potato Soup F

I like to serve this golden soup from my great-grandmother at holiday dinners. Not only is it a great first course, it also makes a satisfying meal for my health-minded friends.

—TRISHA KRUSE EAGLE, ID

PREP: 40 MIN. • **COOK:** 10 MIN.
MAKES: 12 SERVINGS (ABOUT 2 QUARTS)

- 3 pounds sweet potatoes, peeled and cut into 1-inch cubes
- 2 large sweet onions, coarsely chopped
- 1 can (49½ ounces) chicken broth, divided
- 2 tablespoons reduced-sodium soy sauce
- 2 tablespoons maple syrup
- 1 garlic clove, minced
- ¼ teaspoon pepper
  Salted pumpkin seeds or pepitas, optional

1. Place sweet potatoes and onions in separate greased 15x10x1-in. baking pans. Bake, uncovered, at 425° for 15 minutes, stirring once.

2. Meanwhile, combine ½ cup broth, soy sauce, maple syrup and garlic; drizzle over onions and toss to coat. Bake potatoes and onions 15-20 minutes longer or until tender.

3. In a blender, cover and process potatoes and remaining broth in batches until smooth. Transfer the mixture to a Dutch oven; add the onion mixture and pepper. Heat through. Garnish with pumpkin seeds if desired.

PER SERVING ¾ *cup equals 107 cal., trace fat (trace sat. fat), 3 mg chol., 618 mg sodium, 24 g carb., 3 g fiber, 2 g pro.* **Diabetic Exchange:** *1½ starch.*

Tuscan Turkey Soup C

START TO FINISH: 30 MIN.
MAKES: 8 SERVINGS (2 QUARTS)

- 2 tablespoons olive oil
- 1 cup chopped onion
- 1 cup chopped celery
- 2 garlic cloves, minced
- 2 cans (14½ ounces each) reduced-sodium chicken broth
- 1 can (15 ounces) solid-pack pumpkin
- 1 can (15 ounces) white kidney or cannellini beans, rinsed and drained
- 2 cups cubed cooked turkey
- ½ teaspoon salt
- ½ teaspoon dried basil
- ¼ teaspoon pepper
  Grated Parmesan cheese, optional

1. In a large saucepan, heat oil over medium-high heat. Add onion and celery; cook and stir until tender. Add garlic; cook 1 minute longer.

2. Stir in broth, pumpkin, beans, turkey, salt, basil and pepper. Bring to a boil. Reduce heat; simmer, uncovered, 10-15 minutes or until heated through, stirring occasionally. If desired, serve with cheese.

PER SERVING *167 cal., 6 g fat (1 g sat. fat), 27 mg chol., 549 mg sodium, 14 g carb., 5 g fiber, 15 g pro.* **Diabetic Exchanges:** *2 lean meat, 1 starch, 1 fat.*

Transform leftover turkey into a change-of-pace pumpkin soup that's sure to satisfy hungry family and friends. It's so easy, even a beginner in the kitchen can pull this one off!

—MARIE MCCONNELL SHELBYVILLE, IL

TUSCAN TURKEY SOUP

Cool as a Cucumber Soup F C M

This chilled soup makes a wonderful appetizer or side dish on a hot summer day. Bright bursts of dill provide a pleasant contrast to the mild cucumber flavor.

—DEIRDRE COX KANSAS CITY, MO

PREP: 15 MIN. + STANDING • **MAKES:** 5 SERVINGS

- 1 pound cucumbers, peeled, seeded and sliced
- ½ teaspoon salt
- 1½ cups fat-free plain yogurt
- 1 green onion, coarsely chopped
- 1 garlic clove, minced
- 4½ teaspoons snipped fresh dill
  Additional chopped green onion and snipped fresh dill

1. In a colander set over a bowl, toss cucumbers with salt. Let stand for 30 minutes. Squeeze and pat dry.
2. Place the cucumbers, yogurt, onion and garlic in a food processor; cover and process until smooth. Stir in dill. Serve immediately in chilled bowls. Garnish soup with additional onion and dill.
PER SERVING *40 cal., trace fat (trace sat. fat), 2 mg chol., 279 mg sodium, 8 g carb., 1 g fiber, 3 g pro.* **Diabetic Exchange:** *½ fat-free milk.*

Veggie Chowder

This lightened-up version of chowder is so easy to put together for dinner. And since it's not too heavy, it also pairs wonderfully with sandwiches.

—VICKI KERR PORTLAND, ME

START TO FINISH: 30 MIN. • **MAKES:** 6 SERVINGS (1¾ QUARTS)

- 2 cups cubed peeled potatoes
- 2 cups reduced-sodium chicken broth
- 1 cup chopped carrots
- ½ cup chopped onion
- 1 can (14¾ ounces) cream-style corn
- 1 can (12 ounces) fat-free evaporated milk
- ¾ cup shredded reduced-fat cheddar cheese
- ½ cup sliced fresh mushrooms
- ¼ teaspoon pepper
- 2 tablespoons bacon bits

1. In a large saucepan, combine potatoes, broth, carrots and onion; bring to a boil. Reduce heat; simmer, uncovered, 10-15 minutes or until vegetables are tender.
2. Add corn, milk, cheese, mushrooms and pepper; cook and stir 4-6 minutes longer or until heated through. Sprinkle with bacon bits.
PER SERVING *208 cal., 4 g fat (2 g sat. fat), 14 mg chol., 637 mg sodium, 34 g carb., 3 g fiber, 12 g pro.* **Diabetic Exchanges:** *2 starch, ½ fat.*

Hearty Vegetable Split Pea Soup F M

This slow-cooker soup is my secret weapon on busy days. It's delicious served with oyster crackers that are tossed in a bit of melted butter and herbs, and then lightly toasted in the oven.

—**WHITNEY JENSEN** SPRING LAKE, MI

PREP: 10 MIN. • **COOK:** 7 HOURS • **MAKES:** 8 SERVINGS (2 QUARTS)

- 1 **package (16 ounces) dried green split peas, rinsed**
- 1 **large carrot, chopped**
- 1 **celery rib, chopped**
- 1 **small onion, chopped**
- 1 **bay leaf**
- 1½ **teaspoons salt**
- ½ **teaspoon dried thyme**
- ½ **teaspoon pepper**
- 6 **cups water**

In a 3- or 4-qt. slow cooker, combine all ingredients. Cook, covered, on low 7-9 hours or until peas are tender. Stir before serving. Discard bay leaf.

PER SERVING *202 cal., 1 g fat (trace sat. fat), 0 chol., 462 mg sodium, 36 g carb., 15 g fiber, 14 g pro.* **Diabetic Exchanges:** *2 starch, 1 lean meat.*

Summer's Bounty Soup F S C M

This soup, chunky with garden-fresh veggies, is so versatile. You can add or omit just about any vegetable to make the most of what you have. Best of all, a slow cooker does the work!

—**VICTORIA HAHN** NORTHAMPTON, PA

PREP: 5 MIN. • **COOK:** 7 HOURS
MAKES: 14 SERVINGS (ABOUT 3½ QUARTS)

- 4 **medium tomatoes, chopped**
- 2 **medium potatoes, peeled and cubed**
- 2 **cups halved fresh green beans**
- 2 **small zucchini, cubed**
- 1 **medium yellow summer squash, cubed**
- 4 **small carrots, thinly sliced**
- 2 **celery ribs, thinly sliced**
- 1 **cup cubed peeled eggplant**
- 1 **cup sliced fresh mushrooms**
- 1 **small onion, chopped**
- 1 **tablespoon minced fresh parsley**
- 1 **tablespoon salt-free garlic and herb seasoning**
- 4 **cups reduced-sodium V8 juice**

Combine all ingredients in a 5-qt. slow cooker. Cook, covered, on low 7-8 hours or until vegetables are tender.

PER SERVING *67 cal., trace fat (trace sat. fat), 0 chol., 62 mg sodium, 15 g carb., 3 g fiber, 2 g pro.* **Diabetic Exchange:** *2 vegetable.*

Cider Turkey Soup 🅕

Save the turkey carcass from special dinners to make this savory soup the next day! Apple cider gives the broth a hint of sweetness you'll adore.
—*TASTE OF HOME* TEST KITCHEN

PREP: 15 MIN. • **COOK:** 2½ HOURS
MAKES: 15 SERVINGS (3¾ QUARTS)

- 1 leftover turkey carcass (from a 12-pound turkey)
- 3½ quarts water
- 4 cups apple cider or juice
- 2 celery ribs, cut into 2-inch pieces
- 1 large onion, cut into wedges
- 1 large apple, cut into wedges
- 1 large carrot, cut into 2-inch pieces
- 8 sprigs fresh thyme
- 2 sprigs fresh sage

SOUP

- 3 cups shredded cooked turkey breast
- 2 cups cooked long grain and wild rice
- 2 large carrots, shredded
- 1 large onion, chopped
- 1 cup chopped celery
- 1 teaspoon salt
- ½ teaspoon dried thyme
- ¼ teaspoon pepper

1. Place the first nine ingredients in a stockpot. Slowly bring to a boil over low heat; cover and simmer for 1½ hours.

2. Discard the carcass. Strain broth through a cheesecloth-lined colander; discard vegetables and herbs. If using immediately, skim fat. Or cool, then refrigerate for 8 hours or overnight.

3. Remove fat from surface before using. Broth may be refrigerated for up to 3 days or frozen for 4-6 months.

4. Place the soup ingredients in a stockpot; add broth. Bring to a boil. Reduce heat; cover and simmer for 30 minutes or until the vegetables are tender.

PER SERVING *1 cup equals 24 cal., 1 g fat (trace sat. fat), 25 mg chol., 342 mg sodium, 16 g carb., 1 g fiber, 10 g pro.* **Diabetic Exchanges:** *1 starch, 1 lean meat.*

Cincinnati-Style Chili

My husband had this type of chili when visiting a friend in Ohio and was thrilled when I made it at home. You can enjoy it with just chili and spaghetti, but our favorite version has all three toppings.
—*TARI AMBLER* SHOREWOOD, IL

PREP: 35 MIN. • **COOK:** 6 HOURS
MAKES: 10 SERVINGS

- 2 pounds extra-lean ground turkey
- 2 medium onions, finely chopped
- 4 garlic cloves, minced
- 2 cans (8 ounces each) no-salt-added tomato sauce
- 1 can (14½ ounces) reduced-sodium beef broth
- 2 tablespoons cider vinegar
- ½ ounce unsweetened chocolate, chopped
- 3 tablespoons chili powder
- 1 bay leaf
- 2 teaspoons Worcestershire sauce
- 1 teaspoon ground cumin
- ¾ teaspoon salt
- ¾ teaspoon ground cinnamon
- ¼ teaspoon ground allspice
- ⅛ teaspoon ground cloves
- ⅛ teaspoon cayenne pepper
- 1 package (16 ounces) whole wheat spaghetti

TOPPINGS

- 1 can (16 ounces) kidney beans, rinsed and drained
- 1¼ cups (5 ounces) shredded reduced-fat cheddar cheese
- 1 medium onion, chopped

1. In a nonstick Dutch oven coated with cooking spray, cook turkey, onions and garlic until turkey is no longer pink. Transfer to a 3-qt. slow cooker.

2. In a large bowl, combine tomato sauce, broth, vinegar, chocolate and seasonings; pour over turkey mixture. Cook, covered, on low 6-8 hours.

3. Cook spaghetti according to package directions; drain. Remove bay leaf from chili. For each serving, place ¾ cup spaghetti in a bowl. Top with about ⅔ cup chili, 3 tablespoons kidney beans, 2 tablespoons cheese and 1 tablespoon chopped onion.

PER SERVING *388 cal., 6 g fat (3 g sat. fat), 47 mg chol., 523 mg sodium, 52 g carb., 10 g fiber, 37 g pro.*

CINCINNATI-STYLE CHILI

KALE & BEAN SOUP

Kale & Bean Soup 🄵 🄼

Loaded with veggies, this soup soothes both the body and the spirit. The kale is packed with nutrients, including omega-3s, and the beans add a natural heartiness that can't be beat!

—BETH SOLLARS DELRAY BEACH, FL

PREP: 20 MIN. • **COOK:** 70 MIN.
MAKES: 8 SERVINGS (2½ QUARTS)

- 2 medium onions, chopped
- 2 cups cubed peeled potatoes
- 1 tablespoon olive oil
- 4 garlic cloves, minced
- 1 bunch kale, trimmed and coarsely chopped
- 3½ cups vegetable broth
- 1 can (28 ounces) diced tomatoes, undrained
- 1½ cups water
- 1 teaspoon Italian seasoning
- 1 teaspoon paprika
- ½ teaspoon pepper
- 1 bay leaf
- 1 can (15 ounces) white kidney or cannellini beans, rinsed and drained

1. In a Dutch oven, saute onions and potatoes in oil until tender. Add garlic; cook 1 minute longer. Stir in the kale, broth, tomatoes, water, Italian seasoning, paprika, pepper and bay leaf. Bring to a boil. Reduce heat; cover and simmer for 50-60 minutes or until kale is tender.
2. Cool slightly. Discard bay leaf. In a blender, process 3 cups soup until smooth. Return to pan; add beans and heat through.

PER SERVING *152 cal., 2 g fat (trace sat. fat), 0 chol., 622 mg sodium, 29 g carb., 6 g fiber, 5 g pro.* **Diabetic Exchanges:** *2 vegetable, 1 starch, 1 lean meat.*

Turkey Gnocchi Soup

PREP: 15 MIN. • **COOK:** 25 MIN.
MAKES: 6 SERVINGS (2 QUARTS)

- 1 tablespoon butter
- 3 medium carrots, chopped
- 4 garlic cloves, minced
- 6 cups water
- 3 teaspoons reduced-sodium chicken base
- ¾ teaspoon Italian seasoning
- 1 package (16 ounces) potato gnocchi
- 2 cups cubed cooked turkey breast
- 1 cup frozen peas
- ½ teaspoon pepper
- ½ cup shredded Parmesan cheese

1. In a Dutch oven, heat butter over medium heat. Add carrots; cook and stir 8-10 minutes or until crisp-tender. Add garlic; cook 1 minute longer.
2. Stir in water, chicken base and Italian seasoning; bring to a boil. Add gnocchi. Reduce heat; simmer, uncovered, 3-4 minutes or until gnocchi float. Stir in turkey, peas and pepper; heat through. Top servings with cheese.

PER SERVING *307 cal., 6 g fat (3 g sat. fat), 55 mg chol., 782 mg sodium, 39 g carb., 4 g fiber, 24 g pro.* **Diabetic Exchanges:** *3 lean meat, 2 starch, ½ fat.*

TURKEY GNOCCHI SOUP

While trying to find a creative use for leftover turkey, we decided to add gnocchi instead of noodles. If you don't have leftover turkey, a rotisserie chicken works just as well. —AMY BABINES VIRGINIA BEACH, VA

Turkey Sausage Soup with Fresh Vegetables

PREP: 30 MIN. • **COOK:** 6 HOURS
MAKES: 10 SERVINGS (3½ QUARTS)

- 1 package (19½ ounces) Italian turkey sausage links, casings removed
- 3 large tomatoes, chopped
- 1 can (15 ounces) garbanzo beans or chickpeas, rinsed and drained
- 3 medium carrots, thinly sliced
- 1½ cups cut fresh green beans (1-inch pieces)
- 1 medium zucchini, quartered lengthwise and sliced
- 1 large sweet red or green pepper, chopped
- 8 green onions, chopped
- 4 cups chicken stock
- 1 can (12 ounces) tomato paste
- ½ teaspoon seasoned salt
- ⅓ cup minced fresh basil

1. In a large skillet, cook sausage over medium heat 8-10 minutes or until no longer pink, breaking into crumbles; drain and transfer to a 6-qt. slow cooker.
2. Add tomatoes, beans, carrots, green beans, zucchini, pepper and green onions. In a large bowl, whisk stock, tomato paste and seasoned salt; pour over vegetables.
3. Cook, covered, on low 6-8 hours or until vegetables are tender. Just before serving, stir in basil.

PER SERVING *167 cal., 5 g fat (1 g sat. fat), 20 mg chol., 604 mg sodium, 21 g carb., 5 g fiber, 13 g pro.* **Diabetic Exchanges:** *2 lean meat, 2 vegetable, ½ starch.*

Our family is big on soup. This favorite is quick to make, very tasty and gives me plenty of time to have fun with the family while it simmers in the slow cooker.
—**NANCY HEISHMAN** LAS VEGAS, NV

TURKEY SAUSAGE SOUP WITH FRESH VEGETABLES

Lemon Chicken & Rice Soup

Lemon, Swiss chard and cooked brown rice create a tasty spin on classic chicken soup...without much extra effort on your part. Consider this new favorite tonight.
—**KRISTIN CHERRY** BOTHELL, WA

PREP: 35 MIN. • **COOK:** 4¼ HOURS
MAKES: 12 SERVINGS (4 QUARTS)

- 2 tablespoons olive oil
- 2 pounds boneless skinless chicken breasts, cut into ½-inch pieces
- 5 cans (14½ ounces each) reduced-sodium chicken broth
- 8 cups coarsely chopped Swiss chard, kale or spinach
- 2 large carrots, finely chopped
- 1 small onion, chopped
- 1 medium lemon, halved and thinly sliced
- ¼ cup lemon juice
- 4 teaspoons grated lemon peel
- ½ teaspoon pepper
- 4 cups cooked brown rice

1. In a large skillet, heat 1 tablespoon oil over medium-high heat. Add half of the chicken; cook and stir until browned. Transfer to a 6-qt. slow cooker. Repeat with remaining oil and chicken.
2. Stir broth, vegetables, lemon slices, lemon juice, peel and pepper into chicken. Cook, covered, on low 4-5 hours or until chicken is tender. Stir in rice; heat through.

PER SERVING *1⅓ cup equals 203 cal., 5 g fat (1 g sat. fat), 42 mg chol., 612 mg sodium, 20 g carb., 2 g fiber, 20 g pro.* **Diabetic Exchanges:** *2 lean meat, 1 starch, 1 vegetable, ½ fat.*

? Did you know?

When you purchase chicken at the butcher's counter you can ask to have it cubed. Most will do it for free! Not only does this save you time during dinner preparation, but it cuts down on cleanup as well.

LEMON CHICKEN & RICE SOUP

GUILT-FREE CHICKEN CHILI

Guilt-Free Chicken Chili

This chili is a keeper. Make it for Sunday dinner, and you'll have lunch for the rest of the week, too.

—AMY CHALMERS POUGHKEEPSIE, NY

PREP: 20 MIN. • **COOK:** 25 MIN.
MAKES: 8 SERVINGS

- 1 pound lean ground chicken
- 1 medium onion, chopped
- 1 medium sweet red pepper, chopped
- 4 garlic cloves, minced
- 2 cans (15 ounces each) pinto beans, rinsed and drained
- 1 can (28 ounces) diced tomatoes, undrained
- 1 cup water
- 1 tablespoon tomato paste
- 2 tablespoons baking cocoa
- 2 tablespoons chili powder
- 1 tablespoon ground cumin
- ½ teaspoon coarsely ground pepper
- ¼ teaspoon salt
- 4 cups hot cooked brown rice
  Optional toppings: Greek yogurt, reduced-fat shredded cheddar cheese and/or sliced jalapeno peppers

1. In a Dutch oven, cook chicken, onion, red pepper and garlic over medium heat 6-8 minutes or until chicken is no longer pink and vegetables are tender, breaking up chicken into crumbles; drain.

2. Add beans, tomatoes, water, tomato paste, cocoa and seasonings. Bring to a boil. Reduce heat; simmer, uncovered, 15-20 minutes or until flavors are blended.

3. Serve with rice and, if desired, toppings of your choice.

PER SERVING *326 cal., 5 g fat (1 g sat. fat), 41 mg chol., 411 mg sodium, 50 g carb., 10 g fiber, 21 g pro.*

Golden Clam Chowder

My recipe makes it easy to enjoy delicious homemade clam chowder any night. Bits of crispy bacon are not only traditional; they make the chowder rich, savory and a bit indulgent.

—**AMANDA BOWYER** CALDWELL, ID

PREP: 20 MIN. • **COOK:** 20 MIN.
MAKES: 7 SERVINGS

- 2 **celery ribs**
- 2 **medium carrots**
- 1 **medium onion**
- 2 **teaspoons olive oil**
- 4 **garlic cloves, minced**
- 4 **medium potatoes, peeled and diced**
- 2 **cans (6½ ounces each) minced clams, undrained**
- 1 **bottle (8 ounces) clam juice**
- 1 **cup plus 1 tablespoon water, divided**
- 1 **teaspoon dried thyme**
- ½ **teaspoon salt**
- ½ **teaspoon pepper**
- 1 **can (12 ounces) evaporated milk**
- 2 **teaspoons cornstarch**
- 2 **bacon strips, cooked and crumbled**

1. Finely chop the celery, carrots and onion. In a Dutch oven, saute vegetables in oil until tender. Add garlic; cook 1 minute longer. Stir in the potatoes, clams, clam juice, 1 cup water, thyme, salt and pepper. Bring to a boil. Reduce heat; cover and simmer for 12-15 minutes or until potatoes are tender.

2. Gradually stir in milk; heat through. Combine cornstarch and remaining water until smooth; stir into chowder. Bring to a boil; cook and stir for 2 minutes or until thickened. Stir in bacon.

PER SERVING *195 cal., 5 g fat (3 g sat. fat), 27 mg chol., 574 mg sodium, 28 g carb., 2 g fiber, 10 g pro.* **Diabetic Exchanges:** *1 starch, 1 lean meat, 1 vegetable, 1 fat.*

GOLDEN CLAM CHOWDER

Roasted Tomato Soup with Fresh Basil C M

Roasting brings out a rich, sweet tomato flavor in this soup. Fresh summertime basil is the classic companion.

—MARIE FORTE RARITAN, NJ

PREP: 40 MIN. • **COOK:** 5 MIN. • **MAKES:** 6 SERVINGS

- 3½ pounds tomatoes (about 11 medium), halved
- 1 small onion, quartered
- 2 garlic cloves, peeled and halved
- 2 tablespoons olive oil
- 2 tablespoons fresh thyme leaves
- 1 teaspoon salt
- ¼ teaspoon pepper
- 12 fresh basil leaves
    Salad croutons and thinly sliced fresh basil leaves

1. Preheat oven to 400°. Place tomatoes, onion and garlic in a greased 15x10x1-in. baking pan; drizzle with oil. Sprinkle with thyme, salt and pepper; toss to coat. Roast 25-30 minutes or until tender, stirring once. Cool slightly.
2. Process tomato mixture and basil leaves in batches in a blender until smooth. Transfer to a large saucepan; heat through. If desired, top with croutons and sliced basil.
PER SERVING *107 cal., 5 g fat (1 g sat. fat), 0 chol., 411 mg sodium, 15 g carb., 4 g fiber, 3 g pro.* **Diabetic Exchanges:** *1 starch, 1 fat.*

BLACK BEAN 'N' PUMPKIN CHILI

ROASTED TOMATO SOUP WITH FRESH BASIL

Black Bean 'n' Pumpkin Chili

My family is crazy about this slow cooker dish because it uses ingredients you don't usually find in chili. Believe it or not, I discovered that pumpkin is what makes this dish so special. Cook up a big batch and freeze some for later; it tastes even better after the flavors have blended.

—DEBORAH VLIET HOLLAND, MI

PREP: 20 MIN. • **COOK:** 4 HOURS • **MAKES:** 10 SERVINGS (2½ QUARTS)

- 2 tablespoons olive oil
- 1 medium onion, chopped
- 1 medium sweet yellow pepper, chopped
- 3 garlic cloves, minced
- 2 cans (15 ounces each) black beans, rinsed and drained
- 1 can (15 ounces) solid-pack pumpkin
- 1 can (14½ ounces) diced tomatoes, undrained
- 3 cups chicken broth
- 2½ cups cubed cooked turkey
- 2 teaspoons dried parsley flakes
- 2 teaspoons chili powder
- 1½ teaspoons ground cumin
- 1½ teaspoons dried oregano
- ½ teaspoon salt
    Cubed avocado and thinly sliced green onions, optional

1. In a large skillet, heat oil over medium-high heat. Add onion and pepper; cook and stir until tender. Add garlic; cook 1 minute longer.
2. Transfer to a 5-qt. slow cooker; stir in the remaining ingredients. Cook, covered, on low 4-5 hours. If desired, top with avocado and green onions.
PER SERVING *192 cal., 5 g fat (1 g sat. fat), 28 mg chol., 658 mg sodium, 21 g carb., 7 g fiber, 16 g pro.* **Diabetic Exchanges:** *2 lean meat, 1½ starch, ½ fat.*

Creamless Creamy Squash Soup M

Here's my go-to recipe for get-togethers with family and friends. Everyone asks for seconds, and they can't believe they are eating something so healthy! It's also a hearty dish for vegetarians and those with food allergies.

—**SHARON VEREA** THOMASVILLE, GA

PREP: 20 MIN. • **COOK:** 35 MIN. • **MAKES:** 8 SERVINGS (2 QUARTS)

- 2 **tablespoons olive oil**
- 2 **small onions, chopped**
- 2 **celery ribs, chopped**
- 2 **medium carrots, chopped**
- 1 **medium butternut squash (3 pounds), peeled, seeded and cut into 1-inch cubes**
- 1 **medium sweet potato (about 8 ounces), peeled and cut into 1-inch cubes**
- 1 **yellow summer squash, halved lengthwise and sliced**
- 4 **garlic cloves, minced**
- 4 **cups vegetable broth**
- 2 **teaspoons dried savory or herbes de Provence**
- ¼ **teaspoon pepper**
  Grated Parmesan cheese, optional

1. In a Dutch oven, heat oil over medium heat. Add onions, celery and carrots; cook and stir 6-8 minutes or until onion is tender. Stir in butternut squash, sweet potato and summer squash. Cook and stir 5-7 minutes or until squash and potato are lightly browned. Add garlic; cook 1 minute longer.
2. Add broth, savory and pepper; bring to a boil. Reduce heat; simmer, uncovered, 20-25 minutes or until vegetables are tender.
3. Puree soup using an immersion blender, or cool slightly and, in batches, puree in a blender and return to pan; heat through. If desired, serve with cheese.
PER SERVING *138 cal., 4 g fat (1 g sat. fat), 0 chol., 497 mg sodium, 27 g carb., 7 g fiber, 2 g pro.* **Diabetic Exchanges:** *1½ starch, 1 vegetable, ½ fat.*

FRESH CORN AND TOMATO SOUP

Fresh Corn and Tomato Soup

Pressing the vegetables through a sieve creates a lovely base for this light soup. The flavor of the sweet corn shines through in every spoonful.

—**CLYDA CONRAD** YUMA, AZ

PREP: 30 MIN. • **COOK:** 30 MIN. • **MAKES:** 6 SERVINGS

- 1 **celery rib, chopped**
- 1 **small onion, chopped**
- ¼ **cup chopped green pepper**
- 2 **tablespoons butter**
- 4 **cups chopped seeded peeled tomatoes**
- 2 **cups chicken broth**
- 1 **teaspoon sugar**
- ½ **teaspoon salt**
- ⅛ **teaspoon white pepper**
- 2 **cups fresh sweet corn**
- 1 **tablespoon minced fresh basil**
- 2 **tablespoons minced fresh parsley**
- 1 **green onion, finely chopped**

1. In a large saucepan, saute the celery, onion and green pepper in butter until tender. Stir in tomatoes and broth. Bring to a boil. Reduce heat; cover and simmer for 20 minutes.
2. Press through a sieve or food mill; return to the pan. Add the sugar, salt and white pepper. Bring to a boil. Stir in corn and basil. Reduce heat; simmer, uncovered, for 3-5 minutes or until corn is tender. Garnish with parsley and green onion.
PER SERVING *115 cal., 5 g fat (3 g sat. fat), 12 mg chol., 571 mg sodium, 17 g carb., 3 g fiber, 3 g pro.* **Diabetic Exchanges:** *1 vegetable, 1 fat, ½ starch.*

CREAMLESS CREAMY SQUASH SOUP

Nothing cures the winter blahs like tasty comfort food, including this beefy soup I first cooked on a snowy winter day. Serve it alongside crusty bread or rolls.

—BILLY HENSLEY MOUNT CARMEL, TN

Chunky Beef & Vegetable Soup

PREP: 25 MIN. • **COOK:** 2¾ HOURS
MAKES: 8 SERVINGS (3 QUARTS)

- 1½ pounds beef stew meat, cut into ½-inch pieces
- 1 teaspoon salt, divided
- 1 teaspoon salt-free seasoning blend, divided
- ¾ teaspoon pepper, divided
- 2 tablespoons olive oil, divided
- 4 large carrots, sliced
- 1 large onion, chopped
- 1 medium sweet red pepper, chopped
- 1 medium green pepper, chopped
- 2 garlic cloves, minced
- 1 cup Burgundy wine or additional reduced-sodium beef broth
- 4 cups reduced-sodium beef broth
- 1 can (14½ ounces) diced tomatoes, undrained
- 2 tablespoons tomato paste
- 2 tablespoons Worcestershire sauce
- 1 bay leaf
- 4 medium potatoes (about 2 pounds), cut into ½-inch cubes

1. Sprinkle beef with ½ teaspoon each salt, seasoning blend and pepper. In a Dutch oven, heat 1 tablespoon oil over medium heat. Brown beef in batches. Remove from pan.

2. In same pan, heat remaining oil over medium heat. Add carrots, onion and peppers; cook and stir until carrots are crisp-tender. Add garlic; cook 1 minute longer.

3. Add wine, stirring to loosen browned bits from pan. Stir in broth, tomatoes, tomato paste, Worcestershire sauce, bay leaf and remaining seasonings. Return beef to pan; bring to a boil. Reduce heat; simmer, covered, 2 hours.

4. Add potatoes; cook 30-40 minutes longer or until beef and potatoes are tender. Skim fat and discard bay leaf.

PER SERVING *312 cal., 10 g fat (3 g sat. fat), 55 mg chol., 695 mg sodium, 31 g carb., 5 g fiber, 21 g pro.* **Diabetic Exchanges:** *2 starch, 2 lean meat, ½ fat.*

CHUNKY BEEF & VEGETABLE SOUP

White Bean Soup with Escarole F

This heartwarming soup has become a favorite because it uses kitchen staples, is packed with healthy ingredients and is a cinch to prepare. If I can't find escarole, I just use fresh spinach instead!
—**GINA SAMOKAR** NORTH HAVEN, CT

PREP: 15 MIN. • **COOK:** 35 MIN.
MAKES: 8 SERVINGS (2 QUARTS)

- 1 tablespoon olive oil
- 1 small onion, chopped
- 5 garlic cloves, minced
- 3 cans (14½ ounces each) reduced-sodium chicken broth
- 1 can (14½ ounces) diced tomatoes, undrained
- ½ teaspoon Italian seasoning
- ¼ teaspoon crushed red pepper flakes
- 1 cup uncooked whole wheat orzo pasta
- 1 bunch escarole or spinach, coarsely chopped (about 8 cups)
- 1 can (15 ounces) white kidney or cannellini beans, rinsed and drained
- ¼ cup grated Parmesan cheese

1. In a Dutch oven, heat oil over medium heat. Add onion and garlic; cook and stir until tender. Add broth, tomatoes, Italian seasoning and pepper flakes; bring to a boil. Reduce heat; simmer, uncovered, 15 minutes.

2. Stir in orzo and escarole. Return to a boil; cook 12-14 minutes or until orzo is tender. Add beans; heat through, stirring occasionally. Sprinkle servings with cheese.

PER SERVING *174 cal., 3 g fat (1 g sat. fat), 2 mg chol., 572 mg sodium, 28 g carb., 8 g fiber, 9 g pro.* **Diabetic Exchanges:** *1 starch, 1 lean meat, 1 vegetable, ½ fat.*

WHITE BEAN SOUP WITH ESCAROLE

54

59

61

Side Dishes

❝Simple and flavorful, this recipe is a tasty, healthful way to use up all those zucchini taking over the garden. And it's ready in no time!❞

—**BOBBY TAYLOR** ULSTER PARK, NY
about his recipe, Thymed Zucchini Saute, on page 56

FRESH GREEN BEANS & GARLIC

Fresh Green Beans & Garlic C

I am a firm believer that fresh is best. I developed this recipe to take advantage of our garden veggies. It really shows off the full flavor of the green beans.
—**CAROL MAYER** SPARTA, IL

START TO FINISH: 25 MIN.
MAKES: 8 SERVINGS

- 2 tablespoons canola oil
- 2 tablespoons butter
- 4 garlic cloves, sliced
- 2 pounds fresh green beans
- 1 cup reduced-sodium chicken broth
- ½ teaspoon salt
- ¼ teaspoon pepper

1. In a Dutch oven, heat oil and butter over medium-high heat. Add garlic; cook and stir 45-60 seconds or until golden. Using a slotted spoon, remove garlic from pan; reserve. Add green beans to pan; cook and stir 4-5 minutes or until crisp-tender.
2. Stir in broth, salt and pepper. Bring to a boil. Reduce heat; simmer, uncovered, 8-10 minutes or just until beans are tender and broth is almost evaporated, stirring occasionally. Stir in reserved garlic.
PER SERVING *91 cal., 6 g fat (2 g sat. fat), 8 mg chol., 245 mg sodium, 8 g carb., 3 g fiber, 2 g pro.* **Diabetic Exchanges:** *1½ fat, 1 vegetable.*

Spring Green Risotto F M

Once a week, I create a new recipe for my blog, An Officer and a Vegan. I first made this risotto when I needed something cheerful and satisfying. It would also be good with asparagus or zucchini, but use whatever veggies are in season.
—**DEANNA MCDONALD** KALAMAZOO, MI

PREP: 15 MIN. • **COOK:** 30 MIN.
MAKES: 8 SERVINGS

- 1 carton (32 ounces) vegetable stock
- 1 to 1½ cups water
- 1 tablespoon olive oil
- 2 cups sliced fresh mushrooms
- 1 medium onion, chopped
- 1½ cups uncooked arborio rice
- 2 garlic cloves, minced
- ½ cup white wine or additional vegetable stock
- 1 teaspoon dried thyme
- 3 cups fresh baby spinach
- 1 cup frozen peas
- 3 tablespoons grated Parmesan cheese
- 1 tablespoon red wine vinegar
- ½ teaspoon salt
- ¼ teaspoon pepper

1. In a large saucepan, bring stock and water to a simmer; keep hot. In a Dutch oven, heat oil over medium-high heat. Add mushrooms and onion; cook and stir 5-7 minutes or until tender. Add rice and garlic; cook and stir 1-2 minutes or until rice is coated.
2. Stir in wine and thyme. Reduce heat to maintain a simmer; cook and stir until wine is absorbed. Add hot stock mixture, ½ cup at a time, cooking and stirring until stock has been absorbed after each addition, until rice is tender but firm to the bite and risotto is creamy. Stir in spinach, peas, cheese, vinegar, salt and pepper; heat through. Serve immediately.
PER SERVING *198 cal., 3 g fat (1 g sat. fat), 2 mg chol., 477 mg sodium, 37 g carb., 2 g fiber, 5 g pro.*

SPRING GREEN RISOTTO

BUTTERNUT SQUASH & POTATO MASH

Tuscan-Style Roasted Asparagus C M

PREP: 20 MIN. • **BAKE:** 15 MIN.
MAKES: 8 SERVINGS

- 1½ **pounds fresh asparagus, trimmed**
- 1½ **cups grape tomatoes, halved**
- 3 **tablespoons pine nuts**
- 3 **tablespoons olive oil, divided**
- 2 **garlic cloves, minced**
- 1 **teaspoon kosher salt**
- ½ **teaspoon pepper**
- 1 **tablespoon lemon juice**
- ⅓ **cup grated Parmesan cheese**
- 1 **teaspoon grated lemon peel**

1. Preheat oven to 400°. Place the asparagus, tomatoes and pine nuts on a foil-lined 15x10x1-in. baking pan. Mix 2 tablespoons oil, garlic, salt and pepper; add to asparagus and toss to coat.

2. Bake 15-20 minutes or just until asparagus is tender. Drizzle with remaining oil and the lemon juice; sprinkle with cheese and lemon peel. Toss to combine.

PER SERVING *95 cal., 8 g fat (2 g sat. fat), 3 mg chol., 294 mg sodium, 4 g carb., 1 g fiber, 3 g pro.* **Diabetic Exchanges:** *1½ fat, 1 vegetable.*

Butternut Squash & Potato Mash M

Some people like squash, some people like potatoes. Mash the two together and you've got true love. This is a great way to get kids to eat their veggies.

—**JASMINE ROSE** CRYSTAL LAKE, IL

PREP: 25 MIN. • **COOK:** 20 MIN.
MAKES: 10 SERVINGS (¾ CUP EACH)

- 8 **cups cubed peeled butternut squash (about 4 pounds)**
- 4 **cups cubed peeled potatoes (about 4 medium)**
- 16 **garlic cloves, peeled**
- 2 **tablespoons sesame seeds**
- 1 **teaspoon ground cumin**
- 1 **cup (4 ounces) shredded Colby-Monterey Jack cheese**
- 2 **tablespoons butter**
- 1½ **teaspoons salt**
- ½ **teaspoon pepper**

1. Place squash, potatoes and garlic in a Dutch oven; add water to cover. Bring to a boil. Reduce heat; cook, uncovered, 10-15 minutes or until tender.

2. Meanwhile, in a dry small skillet, toast sesame seeds and cumin over medium-low heat 3-4 minutes or until aromatic, stirring frequently. Remove from heat.

3. Drain squash mixture. Mash vegetables, adding cheese, butter, salt and pepper. Sprinkle with sesame seed mixture.

PER SERVING *190 cal., 7 g fat (4 g sat. fat), 16 mg chol., 448 mg sodium, 31 g carb., 4 g fiber, 6 g pro.* **Diabetic Exchanges:** *2 starch, 1½ fat.*

> This is especially wonderful when locally grown asparagus is in season. It's easy for celebrations because it can be served hot or cold.
>
> —**JANNINE FISK** MALDEN, MA

TUSCAN-STYLE ROASTED ASPARAGUS

Roasted Carrot Fries F C M

Turn carrot sticks into crispy baked fries with a happier health profile than the old familiar ones. These are delicious with sweet and spicy ketchup.

—*TASTE OF HOME* TEST KITCHEN

START TO FINISH: 20 MIN. • **MAKES:** 5 SERVINGS

- 1 **pound fresh carrots, cut into ½-inch sticks**
- 2 **teaspoons olive oil**
- ½ **teaspoon salt**

Place carrots in a greased 15-in. x 10-in. x 1-in. baking pan. Drizzle with oil and sprinkle with salt; toss to coat. Bake, uncovered, at 450° for 10-12 minutes or until crisp-tender.
PER SERVING *53 cal., 2 g fat (trace sat. fat), 0 chol., 299 mg sodium, 9 g carb., 3 g fiber, 1 g pro. **Diabetic Exchange:** 2 vegetable.*

Thymed Zucchini Saute S C M

Simple and flavorful, this recipe is a tasty, healthful way to use up all those zucchini taking over the garden. And it's ready in no time!
—**BOBBY TAYLOR** ULSTER PARK, NY

START TO FINISH: 15 MIN. • **MAKES:** 4 SERVINGS

- 1 **tablespoon olive oil**
- 1 **pound medium zucchini, quartered lengthwise and halved**
- ¼ **cup finely chopped onion**
- ½ **vegetable bouillon cube, crushed**
- 2 **tablespoons minced fresh parsley**
- 1 **teaspoon minced fresh thyme or ¼ teaspoon dried thyme**

In a large skillet, heat oil over medium-high heat. Add zucchini, onion and bouillon; cook and stir 4-5 minutes or until zucchini is crisp-tender. Sprinkle with herbs.
PER SERVING *53 cal., 4 g fat (1 g sat. fat), 0 chol., 135 mg sodium, 5 g carb., 2 g fiber, 2 g pro. **Diabetic Exchanges:** 1 vegetable, ½ fat.*

Lemon Parmesan Orzo M

Fresh lemon peel and minced parsley make this orzo one of my family's most-requested springtime sides. It's fantastic with chicken, pork and fish.
—**LESLIE PALMER** SWAMPSCOTT, MA

START TO FINISH: 20 MIN. • **MAKES:** 4 SERVINGS

- 1 **cup uncooked whole wheat orzo pasta**
- 1 **tablespoon olive oil**
- ¼ **cup grated Parmesan cheese**
- 2 **tablespoons minced fresh parsley**
- ½ **teaspoon grated lemon peel**
- ¼ **teaspoon salt**
- ¼ **teaspoon pepper**

Cook orzo according to package directions; drain. Transfer to a small bowl; drizzle with oil. Stir in remaining ingredients.
PER SERVING *191 cal., 6 g fat (1 g sat. fat), 4 mg chol., 225 mg sodium, 28 g carb., 7 g fiber, 7 g pro.* ***Diabetic Exchanges:*** *2 starch, ½ fat.*

Dilled New Potatoes M

With six kids at home, I try to grow as much of our own food as possible, and our big potato patch means easy and affordable meals for much of the year. For this fresh and tasty side dish, I season red potatoes with homegrown dill.
—**JENNIFER FERRIS** BRONSON, MI

START TO FINISH: 25 MIN. • **MAKES:** 8 SERVINGS

- 2 **pounds baby red potatoes (1¾ inches wide, about 24)**
- ¼ **cup butter, melted**
- 2 **tablespoons snipped fresh dill**
- 1 **tablespoon lemon juice**
- 1 **teaspoon salt**
- ½ **teaspoon pepper**

1. Place potatoes in a Dutch oven; add water to cover. Bring to a boil. Reduce heat; cook, uncovered, 15-20 minutes or until tender.
2. Drain; return to pan. Mix remaining ingredients; drizzle over potatoes and toss to coat.
PER SERVING *180 cal., 8 g fat (5 g sat. fat), 20 mg chol., 447 mg sodium, 27 g carb., 2 g fiber, 3 g pro.* ***Diabetic Exchanges:*** *2 starch, 1½ fat.*

My husband, Matt, grills this recipe for both breakfast and dinner gatherings. Besides our company, his potatoes are one of the best parts of the meal!
—**SUSAN NORDIN** WARREN, PA

GRILLED POTATOES & PEPPERS

Grilled Potatoes & Peppers F S M

PREP: 20 MIN. • **GRILL:** 40 MIN.
MAKES: 10 SERVINGS

- 8 **medium red potatoes, cut into wedges**
- 2 **medium green peppers, sliced**
- 1 **medium onion, cut into thin wedges**
- 2 **tablespoons olive oil**
- 5 **garlic cloves, thinly sliced**
- 1 **teaspoon paprika**
- 1 **teaspoon steak seasoning**
- 1 **teaspoon Italian seasoning**
- ¼ **teaspoon salt**
- ¼ **teaspoon pepper**

1. In a large bowl, combine all ingredients. Divide between two pieces of heavy-duty foil (about 18 in. square). Fold foil around potato mixture and crimp edges to seal.
2. Grill, covered, over medium heat 40-45 minutes or until potatoes are tender. Open foil carefully to allow steam to escape.
PER SERVING *103 cal., 3 g fat (trace sat. fat), 0 chol., 134 mg sodium, 18 g carb., 2 g fiber, 2 g pro.* **Diabetic Exchanges:** *1 starch, ½ fat.*

Walnut Zucchini Saute C M

I know I can get my family to eat their veggies when I serve this recipe.
—**ANGELA STEWART** WEST SENECA, NY

START TO FINISH: 15 MIN.
MAKES: 4 SERVINGS

- 2 **medium zucchini, cut into ¼-inch slices**
- ⅓ **cup chopped walnuts**
- 2 **teaspoons olive oil**
- 1 **teaspoon butter**
- 3 **garlic cloves, minced**
- ¼ **teaspoon salt**
- ¼ **teaspoon pepper**

Saute zucchini and walnuts in oil and butter in a large skillet until zucchini is tender. Add the garlic, salt and pepper; cook and stir for 1 minute.
PER SERVING *111 cal., 10 g fat (2 g sat. fat), 3 mg chol., 165 mg sodium, 5 g carb., 2 g fiber, 3 g pro.* **Diabetic Exchanges:** *2 fat, 1 vegetable.*

Slow Cooker Mushroom Rice Pilaf

A few modifications to dear Great Aunt Bernice's recipe made it convenient for potlucks, barbecues and get-togethers. It'll be a favorite in your household, too!
—**AMY WILLIAMS** RIALTO, CA

PREP: 20 MIN. • **COOK:** 3 HOURS
MAKES: 6 SERVINGS

- 1 **cup medium grain rice**
- ¼ **cup butter**
- 6 **green onions, chopped**
- 2 **garlic cloves, minced**
- ½ **pound sliced baby portobello mushrooms**
- 2 **cups warm water**
- 4 **teaspoons beef base**

1. In a large skillet, saute rice in butter until lightly browned. Add green onions and garlic; cook and stir until tender. Stir in mushrooms.
2. Transfer to a 1½-qt. slow cooker. In a small bowl, whisk water and beef base; pour over rice mixture. Cover and cook on low for 3 to 3½ hours or until rice is tender and liquid is absorbed. Fluff with a fork.
NOTE *Look for beef base near the broth and bouillon.*
PER SERVING *210 cal., 8 g fat (5 g sat. fat), 20 mg chol., 512 mg sodium, 30 g carb., 1 g fiber, 4 g pro.* **Diabetic Exchanges:** *2 starch, 2 fat.*

SLOW COOKER MUSHROOM RICE PILAF

Rainbow Vegetable Skillet M

Even my kids love this nicely spiced skillet. It's pretty and absolutely scrumptious. Sometimes, I turn it into a main dish by stirring in pieces of cooked chicken.

—JENNIFER SCHMIDT DICKENS, TX

START TO FINISH: 30 MIN.
MAKES: 9 SERVINGS

- 1 **medium butternut squash (about 2 pounds)**
- ¼ **cup reduced-fat butter, melted**
- 2 **tablespoons brown sugar**
- 1 **tablespoon chili powder**
- 1 **tablespoon minced fresh cilantro**
- 1 **teaspoon salt**
- ½ **teaspoon pepper**
- ¼ **teaspoon ground cinnamon**
- 1 **medium green pepper, cut into 1-inch pieces**
- 1 **medium sweet yellow pepper, cut into 1-inch pieces**
- 1 **medium red onion, cut into wedges**
- 1 **tablespoon olive oil**
- 2 **cups grape tomatoes**

ROASTED FALL VEGETABLES

1. Cut squash in half; discard seeds. Place cut side down in a microwave-safe dish; add ½ in. water. Microwave, uncovered, on high for 10-12 minutes or until almost tender.
2. Meanwhile, in a bowl, combine the butter, brown sugar, chili powder, cilantro, salt, pepper and cinnamon; set aside. When squash is cool enough

RAINBOW VEGETABLE SKILLET

to handle, peel and discard rind. Cut squash into ½-in. pieces.
3. In a large skillet, saute peppers and onion in oil until tender. Add tomatoes and squash; heat through. Transfer to a large bowl; add butter mixture and toss to coat.
NOTE *This recipe was tested with Land O'Lakes light stick butter in a 1,100-watt microwave.*
PER SERVING *106 cal., 5 g fat (2 g sat. fat), 7 mg chol., 322 mg sodium, 18 g carb., 4 g fiber, 2 g pro.* **Diabetic Exchanges:** *1 starch, 1 vegetable, ½ fat.*

Roasted Fall Vegetables M

I love serving these tender roasted veggies on a chilly fall night. The cayenne pepper lends zippy flavor that's not overpowering.

—JULI MEYERS HINESVILLE, GA

PREP: 30 MIN. • **BAKE:** 40 MIN.
MAKES: 14 SERVINGS

- 1 **large acorn squash, peeled and cut into 1½-inch cubes**
- 1 **large rutabaga, peeled and cut into 1-inch cubes**
- 1 **medium pie pumpkin or butternut squash, peeled and cut into 1-inch cubes**
- 3 **large carrots, peeled and cut into 1½-inch pieces**
- 1 **medium parsnip, peeled and cut into 1-inch pieces**
- ¼ **cup grated Parmesan cheese**
- ¼ **cup canola oil**
- 3 **tablespoons minced fresh parsley**
- 2 **tablespoons paprika**
- 2 **teaspoons salt**
- 1 **teaspoon garlic powder**
- ½ **teaspoon cayenne pepper**

1. In a large bowl, combine the first five ingredients. In a small bowl, combine the remaining ingredients. Pour over vegetables; toss to coat.
2. Transfer to two greased 15-in. x 10-in. x 1-in. baking pans. Bake, uncovered, at 425° for 40-50 minutes or until tender, stirring occasionally.
PER SERVING *110 cal., 5 g fat (1 g sat. fat), 1 mg chol., 384 mg sodium, 17 g carb., 3 g fiber, 3 g pro.* **Diabetic Exchanges:** *1 vegetable, 1 fat, ½ starch.*

Sweet Onion & Carrot Medley F C M

Carrots, onion and peas, oh my! Tender veggies are tossed in a tasty honey-garlic mixture. Keep in mind that olive oil pours quickly, so it's a good idea to measure it—even an extra teaspoon adds 40 calories.

—FRAN SCOTT BIRMINGHAM, MI

START TO FINISH: 30 MIN.
MAKES: 6 SERVINGS

- 2 **cups fresh baby carrots**
- ½ **pound fresh sugar snap peas, trimmed**
- 1 **large sweet onion, halved and thinly sliced**
- 4 **teaspoons olive oil**
- 2 **garlic cloves, minced**
- 1 **tablespoon minced chives**
- 2 **teaspoons honey**
- ½ **teaspoon salt**
- ¼ **teaspoon pepper**

1. Place 1 in. of water in a large skillet; add carrots. Bring to a boil. Reduce heat; cover and simmer for 5 minutes. Stir in peas; cover and cook 3 minutes longer. Drain; remove from pan and set aside.

2. In the same skillet, saute onion in oil until tender. Add garlic; cook 1 minute longer. Stir in the chives, honey, salt, pepper and vegetables; heat through.
PER SERVING 86 cal., 3 g fat (trace sat. fat), 0 chol., 240 mg sodium, 13 g carb., 2 g fiber, 2 g pro. **Diabetic Exchanges:** 1 vegetable, ½ fat.

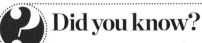

Did you know?

Sweet onions are typically available in just the spring and summer months. But some South American varieties, such as the Oso Sweet, are imported to large North American markets in winter. If you can't find sweet onions such as Vidalia (from Georgia), Walla Walla (from Washington) or Hawaii's Maui onion, red onion is always a good substitute.

Basil Corn & Tomato Bake

When sweet Jersey corn is in season, I turn to this recipe. Studded with summer tomatoes, zucchini and basil, the luscious corn casserole is great for brunch, lunch or dinner.

—ERIN CHILCOAT CENTRAL ISLIP, NY

PREP: 30 MIN. • **BAKE:** 45 MIN. + STANDING
MAKES: 10 SERVINGS

- 2 **teaspoons olive oil**
- 1 **medium onion, chopped**
- 2 **eggs**
- 1 **can (10¾ ounces) reduced-fat reduced-sodium condensed cream of celery soup, undiluted**
- 4 **cups fresh or frozen corn**
- 1 **small zucchini, chopped**
- 1 **medium tomato, seeded and chopped**
- ¾ **cup soft whole wheat bread crumbs**
- ⅓ **cup minced fresh basil**
- ½ **teaspoon salt**
- ½ **cup shredded part-skim mozzarella cheese**
  Additional minced fresh basil, optional

1. Preheat oven to 350°. In a small skillet, heat oil over medium heat. Add onion; cook and stir until tender. In a large bowl, whisk eggs and condensed soup until blended. Stir in vegetables, bread crumbs, basil, salt and onion. Transfer mixture to an 11x7-in. baking dish coated with cooking spray.

2. Bake, uncovered, 40-45 minutes or until bubbly. Sprinkle with cheese. Bake 5-10 minutes longer or until cheese is melted. Let stand 10 minutes before serving. If desired, sprinkle with additional basil.

NOTE *To make soft bread crumbs, tear bread into pieces and place in a food processor or blender. Cover and pulse until crumbs form. One slice of bread yields ½ to ¾ cup crumbs.*

PER SERVING *131 cal., 4 g fat (1 g sat. fat), 47 mg chol., 299 mg sodium, 20 g carb., 3 g fiber, 6 g pro.* **Diabetic Exchanges:** *1 starch, ½ fat.*

BASIL CORN & TOMATO BAKE

Mediterranean Mashed Potatoes M

It's hard for our family to imagine eating mashed potatoes any other way than this. The dish tastes great on its own or drizzled with tahini sauce.

—NIKKI HADDAD GERMANTOWN, MD

PREP: 25 MIN. • **COOK:** 15 MIN.
MAKES: 16 SERVINGS (¾ CUP EACH)

- 8 **large potatoes (about 6½ pounds), peeled and cubed**
- 3 **garlic cloves**
- 1 **teaspoon plus ¾ teaspoon salt, divided**
- ½ **cup olive oil**
- ¼ **cup lemon juice**
- ½ **cup pine nuts, toasted**

1. Place potatoes in a stockpot; add water to cover. Bring to a boil. Reduce heat; cook, uncovered, for 10-15 minutes or until tender.

2. Meanwhile, mince garlic; sprinkle with 1 teaspoon salt. Mash garlic with flat side of the knife blade, forming a smooth paste. In a small bowl, whisk oil, lemon juice, garlic mixture and remaining salt until blended.

3. Drain potatoes; return to pan. Mash potatoes, gradually adding oil mixture. Transfer to a serving dish; sprinkle with pine nuts.

NOTE *To toast nuts, spread in a 15x10x1-in. baking pan. Bake at 350° for 5-10 minutes or until lightly browned, stirring occasionally. Or, spread in a dry nonstick skillet and heat over low heat until lightly browned, stirring occasionally.*

PER SERVING *192 cal., 9 g fat (1 g sat. fat), 0 chol., 262 mg sodium, 26 g carb., 2 g fiber, 3 g pro.* ***Diabetic Exchanges:*** *1½ starch, 1½ fat.*

ROASTED GARLIC GREEN BEANS WITH CASHEWS

Roasted Garlic Green Beans with Cashews C M

My mom got a garlic roaster and soon my kitchen was overflowing with heads of sweet, gooey roasted garlic. This recipe, one of my many experiments, was a favorite of my family. The garlic is mild and adds a rich, buttery taste to the beans.

—VIRGINIA STURM SAN FRANCISCO, CA

PREP: 40 MIN. • **COOK:** 15 MIN. • **MAKES:** 8 SERVINGS

- 10 **garlic cloves, unpeeled**
- 2 **teaspoons plus ¼ cup olive oil, divided**
- 2 **pounds fresh green beans, trimmed**
- 1 **cup water**
- 1 **cup lightly salted cashews, coarsely chopped**
- ½ **teaspoon salt**
- ¼ **teaspoon pepper**

1. Preheat oven to 375°. Cut stem ends off unpeeled garlic cloves. Place cloves on a piece of foil. Drizzle with 2 teaspoons oil; wrap in foil. Bake 25-30 minutes or until cloves are soft. Unwrap and cool slightly. Squeeze garlic from skins; mash with a fork to form a paste.

2. In a Dutch oven, heat remaining oil over medium-high heat. Add green beans and garlic; cook and stir 2-3 minutes. Add water; bring to a boil. Reduce heat; simmer, uncovered, 7-10 minutes or until beans are crisp-tender and water is almost evaporated, stirring occasionally. Add cashews, salt and pepper; toss to combine.

PER SERVING *208 cal., 16 g fat (3 g sat. fat), 0 chol., 187 mg sodium, 13 g carb., 4 g fiber, 6 g pro.*

MEDITERRANEAN
MASHED POTATOES

Thyme-Roasted Vegetables M

PREP: 25 MIN. • **BAKE:** 45 MIN. • **MAKES:** 10 SERVINGS

- 2 pounds red potatoes, cubed (about 9 cups)
- 3 cups sliced sweet onions (about 1½ large)
- 3 medium carrots, sliced
- ½ pound medium fresh mushrooms, halved
- 1 large sweet red pepper, cut into 1½-inch pieces
- 1 large sweet yellow pepper, cut into 1½-inch pieces
- 2 tablespoons butter, melted
- 2 tablespoons olive oil
- 1 tablespoon minced fresh thyme or 1 teaspoon dried thyme
- 1 teaspoon salt
- ¼ teaspoon pepper

1. Preheat oven to 400°. In a large bowl, combine vegetables. Add remaining ingredients; toss to coat.
2. Transfer to a 15x10x1-in. baking pan. Roast 45-50 minutes or until tender, stirring occasionally.

PER SERVING *151 cal., 5 g fat (2 g sat. fat), 6 mg chol., 274 mg sodium, 24 g carb., 4 g fiber, 3 g pro.* **Diabetic Exchanges:** *1 starch, 1 vegetable, 1 fat.*

The aroma as this is baking calls everyone to dinner. Normally, it serves 10, but my husband's been known to have more than just one serving at a time. It's that good.
—JASMINE ROSE CRYSTAL LAKE, IL

THYME-ROASTED VEGETABLES

BLACK-EYED PEAS & HAM

Black-Eyed Peas & Ham F

We have these black-eyed peas regularly at our house. They're reputed to bring good luck!
—DAWN FRIHAUF FORT MORGAN, CO

PREP: 20 MIN. • **COOK:** 6 HOURS
MAKES: 12 SERVINGS (¾ CUP EACH)

- 1 package (16 ounces) dried black-eyed peas, rinsed and sorted
- ½ pound fully cooked boneless ham, finely chopped
- 1 medium onion, finely chopped
- 1 medium sweet red pepper, finely chopped
- 5 bacon strips, cooked and crumbled
- 1 large jalapeno pepper, seeded and finely chopped
- 2 garlic cloves, minced
- 1½ teaspoons ground cumin
- 1 teaspoon reduced-sodium chicken bouillon granules
- ½ teaspoon salt
- ½ teaspoon cayenne pepper
- ¼ teaspoon pepper
- 6 cups water
  Minced fresh cilantro, optional
  Hot cooked rice

In a 6-qt. slow cooker, combine the first 13 ingredients. Cover and cook on low for 6-8 hours or until peas are tender. Sprinkle with cilantro if desired. Serve with rice.

NOTE *Wear disposable gloves when cutting hot peppers; the oils can burn skin. Avoid touching your face.*

PER SERVING *170 cal., 3 g fat (1 g sat. fat), 13 mg chol., 386 mg sodium, 24 g carb., 7 g fiber, 13 g pro.* **Diabetic Exchanges:** *1½ starch, 1 lean meat.*

BAKED PARMESAN BREADED SQUASH

Grilled Tomato with Fresh Corn C M

Grilling the tomatoes and corn makes this side dish special and it's so simple to do. I like to serve it with French bread.

—ROXANNE CHAN ALBANY, CA

START TO FINISH: 30 MIN.
MAKES: 6 SERVINGS

- 6 tomato slices (½ inch thick)
- ½ teaspoon salt
- ½ teaspoon pepper

GRILLED CORN TOPPING

- 2 large ears sweet corn, husked
- 3 tablespoons olive oil, divided
- 1 green onion, finely chopped
- 2 tablespoons minced fresh parsley
- 2 tablespoons sliced ripe olives
- 1 tablespoon capers, drained
- 1 garlic clove, minced
- 1 teaspoon lemon juice
- ½ teaspoon grated lemon peel
- ¼ cup crumbled queso fresco or feta cheese
  Toasted baguette slices, optional

1. Sprinkle tomatoes with salt and pepper. Brush corn with 1 tablespoon oil. Grill, covered, over medium heat 10-12 minutes or until lightly browned, turning occasionally. Grill tomato slices 1-2 minutes on each side or until lightly browned.
2. Cool corn slightly. Cut corn from cobs; transfer to a small bowl. Stir in onion, parsley, olives, capers, garlic, lemon juice, peel and remaining oil.
3. Serve corn mixture over tomatoes; sprinkle with cheese. If desired, serve with baguette slices.
PER SERVING *123 cal., 8 g fat (2 g sat. fat), 3 mg chol., 263 mg sodium, 11 g carb., 2 g fiber, 3 g pro.* **Diabetic Exchanges:** *1½ fat, 1 starch.*

Baked Parmesan Breaded Squash C M

Summer squash crisps up beautifully when it's baked. You don't have to turn the pieces, but do keep an eye on them.

—DEBI MITCHELL FLOWER MOUND, TX

PREP: 20 MIN. • **BAKE:** 20 MIN.
MAKES: 6 SERVINGS

- 4 cups thinly sliced yellow summer squash (3 medium)
- 3 tablespoons olive oil
- ½ teaspoon salt
- ½ teaspoon pepper
- ⅛ teaspoon cayenne pepper
- ¾ cup panko (Japanese) bread crumbs
- ¾ cup grated Parmesan cheese

1. Preheat oven to 450°. Place squash in a large bowl. Add oil and seasonings; toss to coat.
2. In a shallow bowl, mix bread crumbs and cheese. Dip squash in crumb mixture to coat both sides, patting to help coating adhere. Place on parchment paper-lined baking sheets. Bake 20-25 minutes or until golden brown, rotating pans halfway through baking.
PER SERVING *137 cal., 10 g fat (2 g sat. fat), 7 mg chol., 346 mg sodium, 8 g carb., 2 g fiber, 5 g pro.* **Diabetic Exchanges:** *2 fat, 1 vegetable.*

? Did you know?

Capers are the flower buds of a small bush from the Mediterranean and Middle East. The smallest capers, French nonpareils, are considered the finest. Caper berries, from Spain, are the olive-size fruit of the caper shrub. Rinse capers well before using to remove excess salt and brine.

HERB-ROASTED MUSHROOMS

Herb-Roasted Mushrooms C M

My husband grows herbs, and we use whatever's abundant. Our favorite blend is oregano, rosemary and basil, but we suggest trying parsley, dill and mint, too.
—**JENNIFER NIEMI** TUCSON, AZ

START TO FINISH: 30 MIN.
MAKES: 4 SERVINGS

- ½ **pound medium fresh mushrooms**
- ½ **pound baby portobello mushrooms**
- 5 **ounces fresh shiitake mushrooms, stems removed**
- 2 **tablespoons olive oil**
- 2 **tablespoons minced fresh basil**
- 1 **tablespoon minced fresh oregano**
- 1 **tablespoon minced fresh rosemary**
- ¼ **teaspoon salt**
- ¼ **teaspoon pepper**
- 2 **tablespoons balsamic vinegar**

1. Cut mushrooms into quarters; place in a large bowl. Add oil, herbs, salt and pepper; toss to combine. Place on two 15-in. x 10-in. x 1-in. baking pans coated with cooking spray.
2. Bake, uncovered, at 425° for 9-11 minutes or until tender. Transfer to a bowl. Drizzle with vinegar; toss to coat.
PER SERVING *104 cal., 7 g fat (1 g sat. fat), 0 chol., 154 mg sodium, 8 g carb., 2 g fiber, 4 g pro.* **Diabetic Exchanges:** *1½ fat, 1 vegetable.*

Roasted Brussels Sprouts with Cranberries C M

PREP: 15 MIN. • **BAKE:** 20 MIN.
MAKES: 12 SERVINGS (½ CUP EACH)

- 3 **pounds fresh Brussels sprouts, trimmed and halved**
- 3 **tablespoons olive oil**
- 1 **teaspoon kosher salt**
- ½ **teaspoon pepper**
- ½ **cup dried cranberries**

Preheat oven to 425°. Divide Brussels sprouts between two greased 15x10x 1-in. baking pans. Drizzle with oil; sprinkle with salt and pepper. Toss to coat. Roast 20-25 minutes or until tender, stirring occasionally. Transfer to a large bowl; stir in cranberries.
PER SERVING *94 cal., 4 g fat (1 g sat. fat), 0 chol., 185 mg sodium, 14 g carb., 5 g fiber, 4 g pro.* **Diabetic Exchanges:** *1 vegetable, 1 fat.*

The preparation and cooking are so quick, there's practically nothing to this recipe. I throw in dried cranberries, but you can let your imagination take over. Add a handful of raisins or walnuts at the end...even sliced oranges. If your Brussels sprouts are large, cut them in half. —**ELLEN RUZINSKYS** YORKTOWN HEIGHTS, NY

ROASTED BRUSSELS SPROUTS WITH CRANBERRIES

72

74

79

Good Mornings

❝If you're looking for a grab-and-go breakfast for busy mornings, this sandwich is high in protein, low in fat and keeps you full all morning. Plus, it's only about 200 calories!❞

—**BRENDA OTTO** REEDSBURG, WI
about her recipe, Microwave Egg Sandwich, on page 70

FRUIT-FILLED PUFF PANCAKE

Fruit-Filled Puff Pancake M

My husband and I will often make a meal of this fruity puff pancake. The cinnamon, blueberries and bananas are a wonderful combination.
—**LEANNE SENGER** OREGON CITY, OR

START TO FINISH: 25 MIN.
MAKES: 4 SERVINGS

- 3 **eggs**
- ½ **cup 2% milk**
- ⅓ **cup all-purpose flour**
- ¼ **teaspoon salt**
- 3 **tablespoons sugar, divided**
- 1 **tablespoon butter**
- 1½ **cups fresh or frozen blueberries, thawed**
- 1 **medium ripe banana, sliced**
- ¼ **teaspoon ground cinnamon**

1. Preheat oven to 400°. In a large bowl, whisk eggs, milk, flour, salt and 1 tablespoon sugar until smooth. Place butter in a 9-in. pie plate. Place in oven 2-3 minutes or until melted.
2. Tilt pie plate to coat evenly with butter. Pour batter into hot plate. Bake 10-12 minutes or until sides are puffed and golden brown.
3. Meanwhile, in a bowl, combine blueberries and banana. Remove pancake from oven. Top with fruit. Mix cinnamon and remaining sugar; sprinkle over top. Cut into wedges; serve immediately.
PER SERVING *232 cal., 8 g fat (4 g sat. fat), 171 mg chol., 240 mg sodium, 34 g carb., 2 g fiber, 8 g pro.* **Diabetic Exchanges:** *1 starch, 1 medium-fat meat, 1 fruit, ½ fat.*

Slow Cooker Honey Granola M

PREP: 10 MIN. • **COOK:** 2 HOURS + COOLING
MAKES: ABOUT 8 CUPS

- 4 **cups old-fashioned oats**
- 1 **cup sunflower kernels**
- 1 **cup flaked coconut**
- ½ **teaspoon salt**
- ½ **cup canola oil**
- ½ **cup honey**
- 1 **cup chopped dried pineapple**
- 1 **cup chopped dried mangoes**

1. In a 3-qt. slow cooker, combine oats, sunflower kernels, coconut and salt. In a small bowl, whisk oil and honey until blended. Stir into oats mixture. Cook, covered, on high 2 hours, stirring well every 20 minutes.
2. Remove granola to baking sheets, spreading evenly; cool completely. Stir in pineapple and mangoes. Store in airtight containers.
PER SERVING *½ cup equals 295 cal., 15 g fat (3 g sat. fat), 0 chol., 167 mg sodium, 38 g carb., 4 g fiber, 5 g pro.*

> It's simple to put this granola together, and it really helps with breakfast on busy mornings. Change the fruits to fit your preference or the seasons.
> —**ARISA CUPP** WARREN, OR

SLOW COOKER HONEY GRANOLA

VEGGIE EGG CASSEROLE

Veggie Egg Casserole M

A few years ago, I worked in the kitchen at Delaware's first oncology camp for kids. I ended up making a variety of breakfast casseroles that week, and this is the one the campers loved most. We even used the leftovers to supplement our dinner one evening.

—KIMBERLEY PITMAN SMYRNA, DE

PREP: 1 HOUR • **BAKE:** 25 MIN.
MAKES: 8 SERVINGS

- 6 **medium potatoes**
- 1 **cup chopped fresh mushrooms**
- 1 **medium onion, chopped**
- ½ **cup chopped green pepper**
- 2 **tablespoons butter**
- 1 **teaspoon seasoned salt**
- 1 **package (10 ounces) frozen chopped broccoli, thawed**
- 4 **eggs**
- 2 **cups egg substitute**
- ½ **teaspoon salt**
- ¼ **teaspoon pepper**
- 1 **cup (4 ounces) shredded cheddar cheese**

1. Scrub and pierce potatoes. Bake at 400° for 45-50 minutes or until tender. When cool enough to handle, peel and cube potatoes. Reduce heat to 350°.

2. In a large skillet, saute the mushrooms, onion and green pepper in butter until crisp-tender. Add potatoes and seasoned salt; cook until lightly browned. Stir in broccoli.

3. Transfer to a 13-in. x 9-in. baking dish coated with cooking spray. In a large bowl, whisk the eggs, egg substitute, salt and pepper. Add cheese; pour over potato mixture. Bake, uncovered, for 25-30 minutes or until a knife inserted near the center comes out clean. Or, before baking, cover and freeze for up to 3 months.

TO USE FROZEN CASSEROLE *Thaw in the refrigerator overnight. Remove from the refrigerator 30 minutes before baking. Bake as directed.*

PER SERVING *288 cal., 10 g fat (6 g sat. fat), 128 mg chol., 622 mg sodium, 35 g carb., 4 g fiber, 17 g pro.*

Asparagus Omelet Tortilla Wrap M

Since whole grains, veggies and protein are included in this omelet, all I have to do is add a side of fresh fruit for a healthy breakfast before work. Sometimes I make this omelet with fresh spinach in place of the asparagus.

—BONITA SUTER LAWRENCE, MI

START TO FINISH: 20 MIN.
MAKES: 1 SERVING

- 1 **egg**
- 2 **egg whites**
- 1 **tablespoon fat-free milk**
- 2 **teaspoons grated Parmesan cheese**
- ⅛ **teaspoon pepper**
- 4 **fresh asparagus spears, trimmed and sliced**
- 1 **teaspoon butter**
- 1 **green onion, chopped**
- 1 **whole wheat tortilla (8 inches), warmed**

1. In a small bowl, whisk the first five ingredients until blended. Place a small nonstick skillet coated with cooking spray over medium heat; add asparagus. Cook and stir 3-4 minutes or until crisp-tender. Remove from the pan.

2. In same skillet, heat butter over medium-high heat. Pour in egg mixture. Mixture should set immediately at edges. As eggs set, push cooked portions toward the center, letting the uncooked eggs flow underneath. When eggs are thickened and no liquid egg remains, spoon green onion and asparagus on one side. Fold omelet in half; serve in tortilla.

PER SERVING *319 cal., 13 g fat (5 g sat. fat), 225 mg chol., 444 mg sodium, 28 g carb., 3 g fiber, 21 g pro.* **Diabetic Exchanges:** *2 lean meat, 2 fat, 1½ starch.*

ASPARAGUS OMELET TORTILLA WRAP

Microwave Egg Sandwich

If you're looking for a grab-and-go breakfast for busy mornings, this sandwich is high in protein, low in fat and keeps you full all morning. Plus, it's only about 200 calories!

—**BRENDA OTTO** REEDSBURG, WI

START TO FINISH: 15 MIN.
MAKES: 1 SERVING.

- 1 **piece Canadian bacon**
- ¼ **cup egg substitute**
- 1 **tablespoon salsa**
- 1 **tablespoon shredded reduced-fat cheddar cheese**
- 1 **whole wheat English muffin, split, toasted**
- 3 **spinach leaves**

1. Place Canadian bacon on bottom of a 6-oz. ramekin or custard cup coated with cooking spray. Pour egg substitute over top. Microwave, uncovered, on high for 30 seconds; stir. Microwave 15-30 seconds or until egg is almost set. Top with salsa; sprinkle with cheese. Microwave just until cheese is melted, about 10 seconds.
2. Line bottom of English muffin with spinach. Place egg and Canadian bacon over spinach; replace English muffin top.
NOTE *This recipe was tested in a 1,100-watt microwave.*
PER SERVING *218 cal., 4 g fat (2 g sat. fat), 12 mg chol., 751 mg sodium, 30 g carb., 5 g fiber, 17 g pro.* **Diabetic Exchanges:** *2 starch, 2 lean meat.*

Egg Substitute vs. Whole Eggs

If you prefer, use 1 beaten egg in the recipe instead of ¼ cup egg substitute. A real egg will add 45 calories, 5 grams of fat and 210 milligrams cholesterol. The extra calories in eggs all come from fat: Whole eggs and egg substitute contain the same amount of protein and carbohydrates.

MICROWAVE EGG SANDWICH

Blueberry-Stuffed French Toast 🅂 🅼

I came across this recipe in a local newspaper several years ago. It's perfect for company because you can bake all eight servings at once.

—**MYRNA KOLDENHOVEN** SANBORN, IA

PREP: 35 MIN. • **BAKE:** 15 MIN.
MAKES: 8 SERVINGS

- 1½ cups fresh or frozen blueberries
- 3 tablespoons sugar, divided
- 8 slices Italian bread (1¼ inches thick)
- 4 eggs
- 1 teaspoon grated orange peel
- ½ cup orange juice
  Dash salt

SAUCE

- ¼ cup orange juice
- ¼ cup cold water
- 3 tablespoons sugar
- 1 tablespoon cornstarch
- ⅛ teaspoon salt
- 1½ cups orange sections
- 1 cup fresh or frozen blueberries
- ⅓ cup sliced almonds, toasted

1. Preheat oven to 400°. In a small bowl, toss the blueberries with 2 tablespoons sugar. Cut a pocket horizontally in each slice of bread. Fill with blueberries.

2. In a shallow bowl, whisk eggs, orange peel, orange juice, salt and remaining sugar. Dip both sides of bread in egg mixture, being careful to not squeeze out berries. Place in a greased 15x10x1-in. baking pan. Bake 14-17 minutes or until golden brown, carefully turning once.

3. Meanwhile, in a small saucepan, whisk the first five sauce ingredients until smooth. Bring to a boil, stirring constantly; cook and stir 1-2 minutes or until thickened. Reduce heat; stir in fruit and heat through. Serve with French toast; sprinkle with almonds.

NOTE *To toast nuts, spread in a 15x10x1-in. baking pan. Bake at 350° for 5-10 minutes or until lightly browned, stirring occasionally. Or, spread in a dry nonstick skillet and heat over low heat until lightly browned, stirring occasionally.*

AUTUMN POWER PORRIDGE

PER SERVING *167 cal., 5 g fat (1 g sat. fat), 106 mg chol., 118 mg sodium, 27 g carb., 3 g fiber, 5 g pro.* **Diabetic Exchanges:** *1½ starch, 1 fat, ½ fruit.*

Autumn Power Porridge 🅼

This rib-sticking porridge is made with oats and protein-rich quinoa. Pumpkin, maple syrup, walnuts and dried cranberries make it a delicious and kid-friendly breakfast.

—**JENNIFER WICKES** PINE BEACH, NJ

PREP: 15 MIN. • **COOK:** 30 MIN.
MAKES: 4 SERVINGS

- 3 cups water
- ¾ cup steel-cut oats
- ½ cup quinoa, rinsed
- ¼ teaspoon salt
- ¾ cup canned pumpkin
- 1 teaspoon pumpkin pie spice
- 3 tablespoons agave nectar or maple syrup
- ½ cup dried cranberries
- ⅓ cup coarsely chopped walnuts, toasted
  Milk

1. In a large saucepan, combine the water, oats, quinoa and salt. Bring to a boil. Reduce heat; cover and simmer for 20 minutes.

2. Stir in the pumpkin, pie spice and agave nectar. Remove from the heat; cover and let stand for 5 minutes or until water is absorbed and grains are tender. Stir in cranberries and walnuts. Serve with milk if desired.

NOTE *Steel-cut oats are also known as Scottish oats or Irish oatmeal.*
PER SERVING *361 cal., 10 g fat (1 g sat. fat), 0 chol., 155 mg sodium, 65 g carb., 7 g fiber, 9 g pro.*

BLUEBERRY-STUFFED FRENCH TOAST

Cranberry-Walnut Oatmeal 🅼

My family loves cranberries, but we can only get them fresh during the holiday season. Using cranberry sauce in this recipe, however, lets us enjoy the flavors we crave—along with the comfort of oatmeal—no matter what time of year.

—TEENA PETRUS JOHNSTOWN, PA

START TO FINISH: 15 MIN. • **MAKES:** 4 SERVINGS

- 3½ cups water
- ¼ teaspoon salt
- 2 cups quick-cooking oats
- 3 tablespoons sugar
- 1 teaspoon vanilla extract
- 2 teaspoons cinnamon-sugar
- ½ cup whole-berry cranberry sauce
- ¼ cup chopped walnuts, toasted

1. In a large saucepan, bring water and salt to a boil. Stir in oats. Cook for 1 minute over medium heat, stirring occasionally.

2. Remove from heat; stir in sugar and vanilla. Top servings with cinnamon-sugar, cranberry sauce and walnuts.

NOTE *To toast nuts, spread in a 15x10x1-in. baking pan. Bake at 350° for 5-10 minutes or until lightly browned, stirring occasionally. Or, spread in a dry nonstick skillet and heat over low heat until lightly browned, stirring occasionally.*

PER SERVING *293 cal., 8 g fat (1 g sat. fat), 0 chol., 156 mg sodium, 53 g carb., 5 g fiber, 7 g pro.*

CRANBERRY-WALNUT OATMEAL

WHOLE-GRAIN WAFFLE MIX

Whole-Grain Waffle Mix 🅼

My mother-in-law shared the recipe for these golden waffles with me, and my daughter Kayla just loves them. Simply add a few ingredients to the mix and you'll be enjoying their homemade taste in minutes.

—MICHELLE SHELDON EDMOND, OK

START TO FINISH: 20 MIN. • **MAKES:** 5 SERVINGS PER BATCH

- 4 cups whole wheat flour
- 2 cups all-purpose flour
- 1 cup toasted wheat germ
- 1 cup toasted oat bran
- 1 cup buttermilk blend powder
- 3 tablespoons baking powder
- 2 teaspoons baking soda
- 1 teaspoon salt

ADDITIONAL INGREDIENTS

- 2 eggs
- 1 cup water
- 2 tablespoons canola oil
- 2 tablespoons honey

In a large bowl, combine the first eight ingredients. Store in an airtight container in the refrigerator for up to 6 months.

YIELD *8½ cups mix (about 4 batches).*

TO PREPARE WAFFLES *Place 2 cups waffle mix in a bowl. Combine the eggs, water, oil and honey; stir into waffle mix just until moistened. Bake in a preheated waffle iron according to manufacturer's directions until golden brown.*

NOTE *Look for buttermilk blend powder next to the powdered milk in your grocery store.*

PER SERVING *284 cal., 9 g fat (2 g sat. fat), 89 mg chol., 482 mg sodium, 43 g carb., 5 g fiber, 12 g pro.* **Diabetic Exchanges:** *3 starch, 1½ fat.*

Rhubarb Compote with Yogurt & Almonds 🅂Ⓜ

PREP: 10 MIN. • COOK: 15 MIN. + CHILLING • MAKES: 6 SERVINGS

- 2   cups finely chopped fresh rhubarb
- ¼   cup sugar
- 2   tablespoons water
- 3   cups reduced-fat plain Greek yogurt
- 2   tablespoons honey
- ¾   cup sliced almonds, toasted

1. In a small saucepan, combine rhubarb, sugar and water. Bring to a boil. Reduce heat; simmer, uncovered, 10-15 minutes or until rhubarb is tender, stirring occasionally. Transfer to a bowl; cool slightly. Refrigerate until cold.
2. In a small bowl, whisk yogurt and honey until blended. Spoon into serving dishes. Top with compote and almonds.
PER SERVING *218 cal., 8 g fat (2 g sat. fat), 7 mg chol., 49 mg sodium, 23 g carb., 2 g fiber, 14 g pro.* **Diabetic Exchanges:** *1 starch, 1 reduced-fat milk, 1 fat.*

My grandma Dot used to make rhubarb compote and always had some in the freezer when I came to visit. This breakfast is a tribute to her. No two stalks of rhubarb are exactly alike, so make sure to taste your compote before you chill it. It should be tart, but sometimes needs a little extra sugar.
—MICHAEL HOFFMAN BROOKLYN, NY

RHUBARB COMPOTE WITH YOGURT & ALMONDS

FETA SCRAMBLED EGG WRAPS

Feta Scrambled Egg Wraps Ⓜ

My daughter jokes that I am too predictable when it comes to dining out; I always order chicken souvlaki. So I thought, why not incorporate my favorite Greek dish into a breakfast wrap? It's healthy, tasty and easy to make.
—MARY JO KEMPF WEST SENECA, NY

START TO FINISH: 15 MIN. • MAKES: 4 SERVINGS

- 1½   cups Southwestern-style egg substitute
- ¾   cup crumbled feta cheese
- 2   tablespoons sliced pepperoncini, chopped
- 4   whole wheat tortillas (8 inches), warmed

Place a large nonstick skillet coated with cooking spray over medium heat. Pour in egg substitute; cook and stir until thickened and no liquid egg remains. Gently stir in cheese and pepperoncini; heat through. Serve in tortillas.
PER SERVING *239 cal., 6 g fat (2 g sat. fat), 11 mg chol., 560 mg sodium, 24 g carb., 3 g fiber, 17 g pro.* **Diabetic Exchanges:** *2 lean meat, 1½ starch.*

Overnight Maple Oatmeal S M

I tried muesli on a trip to Switzerland, and when I came home, I made it my way. Keep things interesting (and avoid the mid-morning munchies) by adding different fruits and nuts every day.
—MADDIE KIRK SPRINGFIELD, PA

PREP: 10 MIN. + CHILLING
MAKES: 6 SERVINGS

- 2 cups old-fashioned oats
- 1 cup fat-free milk
- ¼ cup maple syrup
- 2 teaspoons vanilla extract
- 1 cup vanilla yogurt
- ½ cup chopped walnuts, toasted
  Assorted fresh fruit

1. In a large bowl, combine oats, milk, syrup and vanilla. Refrigerate, covered, overnight.
2. Just before serving, stir in yogurt. Top with walnuts and fruit.
NOTE *To toast nuts, spread in a 15x10x1-in. baking pan. Bake at 350° for 5-10 minutes or until lightly browned, stirring occasionally. Or, spread in a dry nonstick skillet and heat over low heat until lightly browned, stirring occasionally.*
PER SERVING *249 cal., 9 g fat (1 g sat. fat), 3 mg chol., 46 mg sodium, 36 g carb., 3 g fiber, 9 g pro.* **Diabetic Exchanges:** *2½ starch, 1 fat.*

Black Bean & White Cheddar Frittata C M

This is one of my favorite comfort foods for breakfast or even a quick dinner. I like to make it with a cool lime salsa, but if you're looking for something with more kick, use hot salsa or add some minced chipotle pepper.
—AYSHA SCHURMAN AMMON, ID

PREP: 20 MIN. • **COOK:** 15 MIN.
MAKES: 6 SERVINGS

- 6 eggs
- 3 egg whites
- ¼ cup salsa
- 1 tablespoon minced fresh parsley
- ¼ teaspoon salt
- ¼ teaspoon pepper
- 1 tablespoon olive oil
- ⅓ cup finely chopped green pepper
- ⅓ cup finely chopped sweet red pepper
- 3 green onions, finely chopped
- 2 garlic cloves, minced
- 1 cup canned black beans, rinsed and drained
- ½ cup shredded white cheddar cheese
  Optional toppings: minced fresh cilantro, sliced ripe olives and additional salsa

1. Preheat broiler. In a large bowl, whisk the first six ingredients until blended.
2. In a 10-in. ovenproof skillet, heat oil over medium-high heat. Add peppers and green onions; cook and stir 3-4 minutes or until peppers are tender. Add garlic; cook 1 minute longer. Stir in beans. Reduce heat to medium; stir in egg mixture. Cook, uncovered, 4-6 minutes or until nearly set. Sprinkle with cheese.
3. Broil 3-4 in. from heat 3-4 minutes or until light golden brown and eggs are completely set. Let stand for 5 minutes. Cut into wedges. If desired, serve with toppings.
PER SERVING *183 cal., 10 g fat (4 g sat. fat), 196 mg chol., 378 mg sodium, 9 g carb., 2 g fiber, 13 g pro.* **Diabetic Exchanges:** *2 medium-fat meat, ½ starch, ½ fat.*

OVERNIGHT MAPLE OATMEAL

BLACK BEAN & WHITE
CHEDDAR FRITTATA

Ginger Cardamom Tea F S C M

I like to add a little spice to my tea, which is why I mix in the ginger and cardamom. Kick up your feet and relax with a steaming mugful of this warming drink.

—TRISHA KRUSE EAGLE, ID

START TO FINISH: 25 MIN. • **MAKES:** 4 SERVINGS

- 2 **cups water**
- 4 **teaspoons honey**
- 1 **tablespoon minced fresh gingerroot**
- ½ **teaspoon ground cardamom**
- 6 **individual tea bags**
- 1½ **cups fat-free milk**

1. In a small saucepan, combine water, honey, ginger and cardamom; bring to a boil. Reduce heat; simmer 10 minutes.
2. Pour over tea bags in a 2-cup glass measuring cup. Steep 3-5 minutes according to taste. Strain tea back into saucepan, discarding ginger and tea bags. Stir in milk; heat through.
PER SERVING *55 cal., trace fat (trace sat. fat), 2 mg chol., 39 mg sodium, 11 g carb., trace fiber, 3 g pro.* **Diabetic Exchange:** *½ starch.*

Carrot Cake Oatmeal F S M

This hot cereal can be made in the slow cooker overnight so you can wake up to a healthy breakfast. For extra crunch, I garnish individual servings with ground walnuts or pecans.

—DEBBIE KAIN COLORADO SPRINGS, CO

PREP: 10 MIN. • **COOK:** 6 HOURS • **MAKES:** 8 SERVINGS

- 4½ **cups water**
- 1 **can (20 ounces) crushed pineapple, undrained**
- 2 **cups shredded carrots**
- 1 **cup steel-cut oats**
- 1 **cup raisins**
- 2 **teaspoons ground cinnamon**
- 1 **teaspoon pumpkin pie spice**
  Brown sugar, optional

In a 4-qt. slow cooker coated with cooking spray, combine the first seven ingredients. Cover and cook on low for 6-8 hours or until oats are tender and liquid is absorbed. Sprinkle with brown sugar if desired.
PER SERVING *197 cal., 2 g fat (trace sat. fat), 0 chol., 23 mg sodium, 46 g carb., 4 g fiber, 4 g pro.*

Fruity Frappe F S M

Making a taste-alike of a restaurant drink is fun, but better yet, I know exactly what's in this one. My frappe gets all of its sweetness from berries, juice and honey.
—**PATRICIA CROUSE** WARREN, PA

START TO FINISH: 10 MIN. • **MAKES:** 4 SERVINGS

- 1 **cup water**
- 1 **cup fat-free milk**
- ⅔ **cup thawed orange juice concentrate**
- 3 **tablespoons honey**
- ½ **teaspoon vanilla extract**
- 1 **cup ice cubes**
- 1 **cup frozen unsweetened mixed berries**

Place all ingredients in a blender; cover and process until blended. Serve immediately.
PER SERVING *166 cal., trace fat (trace sat. fat), 1 mg chol., 28 mg sodium, 39 g carb., 1 g fiber, 3 g pro.*

Michigan Fruit Baked Oatmeal S M

Whole-grain oatmeal is a delicious way to start every day, and this is perfect if you're making breakfast for two. It also works great with fresh chopped apples instead of dried fruit.
—**JEANETTE KASS** RAVENNA, MI

PREP: 15 MIN. • **BAKE:** 45 MIN. • **MAKES:** 3 SERVINGS

- 1 **cup old-fashioned oats**
- ¼ **cup dried cranberries or cherries**
- 1 **tablespoon brown sugar**
- 2 **cups fat-free milk**
- ½ **cup chunky applesauce**
- ¼ **teaspoon almond extract**
- 2 **tablespoons sliced almonds**
  Optional toppings: vanilla yogurt and additional dried cranberries and sliced almonds

1. In a large bowl, combine the first six ingredients. Transfer to a 3-cup baking dish coated with cooking spray; sprinkle with almonds.
2. Bake, uncovered, at 350° for 45-50 minutes or until set. Serve with toppings if desired.
PER SERVING *259 cal., 4 g fat (1 g sat. fat), 3 mg chol., 73 mg sodium, 48 g carb., 4 g fiber, 10 g pro.*

TURKEY SAUSAGE PATTIES

Berry Granola Pancakes M

Nuts are a nice addition to pancakes because they add a toasty crunch. Even better is adding a cup of crunchy granola.

—ELIZABETH STEWART CRAB ORCHARD, WV

PREP: 15 MIN. • **COOK:** 5 MIN./BATCH
MAKES: 1½ DOZEN

- 2 **cups whole wheat flour**
- 3 **tablespoons sugar**
- 4 **teaspoons baking powder**
- ½ **teaspoon salt**
- 2 **eggs, lightly beaten**
- 2 **cups fat-free milk**
- ⅓ **cup unsweetened applesauce**
- 1 **tablespoon canola oil**
- ½ **teaspoon vanilla extract**
- 1 **cup granola with fruit and nuts**
- 1 **cup fresh or frozen blueberries**
- ½ **cup fresh or frozen blackberries or raspberries**

1. In a large bowl, whisk flour, sugar, baking powder and salt. In another bowl, whisk eggs, milk, applesauce, oil and vanilla until blended. Add to dry ingredients, stirring just until moistened. Fold in granola and berries.
2. Heat a griddle coated with cooking spray on medium heat. Pour batter by ¼ cupfuls onto griddle. Cook until bubbles on top begin to pop and bottoms are golden brown. Turn; cook until second side is golden brown.
NOTE *If using frozen blueberries, use without thawing to avoid discoloring the batter.*
PER SERVING *3 pancakes equals 321 cal., 8 g fat (1 g sat. fat), 72 mg chol., 543 mg sodium, 54 g carb., 7 g fiber, 12 g pro.*

BERRY GRANOLA PANCAKES

Turkey Sausage Patties S C

People are always surprised that my breakfast sausage is made from turkey. But what's even more surprising is how easy it is to make your own sausage using everyday seasonings.

—SALLY BRASSFIELD CALIFORNIA, MD

START TO FINISH: 30 MIN.
MAKES: 6 SERVINGS

- 2 **to 3 teaspoons rubbed sage**
- 1 **teaspoon brown sugar**
- ¼ **teaspoon crushed red pepper flakes**
- ¼ **teaspoon ground nutmeg**
- ¼ **teaspoon pepper**
   Pinch allspice
- 1 **pound lean ground turkey**

1. In a bowl, combine the first six ingredients. Add turkey; mix lightly but thoroughly. Shape into six patties.
2. Lightly coat a skillet with cooking spray. Cook patties over medium heat until browned on both sides and the meat is no longer pink, about 15-20 minutes.
PER SERVING *117 cal., 6 g fat (2 g sat. fat), 60 mg chol., 71 mg sodium, 1 g carb., trace fiber, 13 g pro.* **Diabetic Exchange:** *2 lean meat.*

CHERRY COBBLER SMOOTHIES

1 medium sweet red pepper, chopped
1 tablespoon canola oil
1 teaspoon garlic powder
1 teaspoon smoked paprika
¾ teaspoon ground chipotle pepper
½ teaspoon salt
¼ teaspoon pepper
⅔ cup canned black beans, rinsed and drained
4 eggs
½ cup reduced-fat sour cream
2 tablespoons lime juice
2 teaspoons adobo sauce
½ medium ripe avocado, peeled and sliced, optional
2 tablespoons minced fresh cilantro

1. Preheat oven to 400°. Place sweet potatoes, onion and red pepper in a 15x10x1-in. baking pan coated with cooking spray. Drizzle with oil; sprinkle with seasonings. Toss to coat. Roast 25-30 minutes or until potatoes are tender, adding beans during the last 10 minutes of cooking time.

2. Place 2-3 in. of water in a large saucepan or skillet with high sides. Bring to a boil; adjust heat to maintain a gentle simmer. Break cold eggs, one at a time, into a small bowl; holding bowl close to surface of water, slip egg into water.

3. Cook, uncovered, 3-5 minutes or until whites are completely set and yolks begin to thicken but are not hard. Using a slotted spoon, lift eggs out of the water.

4. In a small bowl, mix sour cream, lime juice and adobo sauce. Serve sweet potato mixture with egg, sour cream mixture and, if desired, avocado. Sprinkle with cilantro.

PER SERVING *304 cal., 12 g fat (3 g sat. fat), 222 mg chol., 520 mg sodium, 37 g carb., 6 g fiber, 13 g pro.* **Diabetic Exchanges:** *2 starch, 1½ fat, 1 medium-fat meat.*

Cherry Cobbler Smoothies F S M

It's been said that breakfast is the most important meal of the day. I want to make it count, so I created this fruity and refreshing smoothie packed with good-for-you cherries and vanilla yogurt.
—**SHERRY MOTE** MARIETTA, GA

START TO FINISH: 10 MIN.
MAKES: 5 SERVINGS

2 cups vanilla yogurt
½ cup orange juice
¼ cup honey
1 teaspoon vanilla extract
1 teaspoon almond extract
2 cups ice cubes
2 cups frozen pitted dark sweet cherries
2 teaspoons ground cinnamon

In a blender, combine all ingredients; cover and process for 30 seconds or until smooth. Pour into chilled glasses; serve immediately.
PER SERVING *197 cal., 2 g fat (1 g sat. fat), 5 mg chol., 66 mg sodium, 40 g carb., 2 g fiber, 6 g pro.*

Southwest Hash with Adobo-Lime Crema M

PREP: 20 MIN. • **BAKE:** 25 MIN.
MAKES: 4 SERVINGS

3 medium sweet potatoes (about 1½ pounds), cubed
1 medium onion, chopped

Add a splash of white vinegar to the poaching water right before you drop in the eggs. It helps keep them from separating. If you have leftover pulled pork, it's delicious tossed into this satisfying hash. —**BROOKE KELLER** LEXINGTON, KY

SOUTHWEST HASH WITH ADOBE-LIME CREMA

85

91

93

Ready in 30

"I work for a priest who loves to cook, and he shared a terrific stir-fry recipe with me. Perfect for the day after Thanksgiving, this quick-and-easy dish is a delicious way to use up holiday leftovers."

—**STEFEN LOVELACE** MARRIOTTSVILLE, MD
about his recipe, Day-After-Thanksgiving Turkey Stir-Fry, on page 84

Wasabi Beef Fajitas

Beef fajitas take on Asian flavor when you add soy sauce, coleslaw mix, fresh ginger and Japanese horseradish, also known as wasabi. Look for it in the Asian food section of your supermarket.

—**TASTE OF HOME** TEST KITCHEN

START TO FINISH: 20 MIN.
MAKES: 8 SERVINGS

- 2 **teaspoons cornstarch**
- 3 **tablespoons reduced-sodium soy sauce**
- 2 **teaspoons prepared wasabi**
- 2 **teaspoons minced fresh gingerroot**
- 1 **garlic clove, minced**
- 2 **tablespoons sesame oil, divided**
- 1 **pound uncooked beef stir-fry strips**
- 12 **green onions with tops, cut in half lengthwise**
- 1 **large sweet red pepper, julienned**
- 8 **flour tortillas (8 inches), warmed**
- 1 **cup coleslaw mix**

1. In a small bowl, mix the cornstarch, soy sauce, wasabi, ginger and garlic until blended. In a large skillet, heat 1 tablespoon oil over medium-high heat. Add beef; stir-fry 4-6 minutes or until no longer pink. Remove from pan.
2. Stir-fry the onions and pepper in the remaining oil 2-3 minutes or until vegetables are crisp-tender.
3. Stir the cornstarch mixture and add to the pan. Bring to a boil; cook and stir 1-2 minutes or until sauce is thickened. Return the beef to pan; heat through. Serve with tortillas and coleslaw mix.
PER SERVING *273 cal., 9 g fat (2 g sat. fat), 23 mg chol., 533 mg sodium, 30 g carb., 1 g fiber, 18 g pro.* **Diabetic Exchanges:** *2 starch, 2 lean meat.*

WASABI BEEF FAJITAS

A friend of mine wanted a filling dish she and her husband could enjoy hot or cold. I started with a hearty quinoa base and went from there. It turned out great!
—**LINDSAY MCSWEENEY** WINCHESTER, MA

BLACK BEAN & CORN QUINOA

Black Bean & Corn Quinoa Ⓜ

START TO FINISH: 30 MIN.
MAKES: 4 SERVINGS

- 2 **tablespoons canola oil**
- 1 **medium onion, finely chopped**
- 1 **medium sweet red pepper, finely chopped**
- 1 **celery rib, finely chopped**
- 2 **teaspoons chili powder**
- ¼ **teaspoon salt**
- ¼ **teaspoon pepper**
- 2 **cups vegetable stock**
- 1 **cup frozen corn**
- 1 **cup quinoa, rinsed**
- 1 **can (15 ounces) black beans, rinsed and drained**
- ⅓ **cup plus 2 tablespoons minced fresh cilantro, divided**

1. In a large skillet, heat the oil over medium-high heat. Add onion, red pepper, celery and seasonings; cook and stir 5-7 minutes or until vegetables are tender.
2. Stir in vegetable stock and corn; bring to a boil. Stir in quinoa. Reduce heat; simmer, covered, 12-15 minutes or until liquid is absorbed.
3. Add the beans and ⅓ cup cilantro; heat through, stirring occasionally. Sprinkle with remaining cilantro.
NOTE *Look for quinoa in the cereal, rice or organic food aisle.*
PER SERVING *375 cal., 10 g fat (1 g sat. fat), 0 chol., 668 mg sodium, 60 g carb., 10 g fiber, 13 g pro.*

Apricot-Lemon Chicken c

I discovered this simple, fuss-free recipe in college and have used it to treat my friends and family ever since. The tender chicken spread with an apricot and lemon sauce is not only elegant enough for company, but also healthy enough to include in my regular menu rotation.

—KENDRA DOSS COLORADO SPRINGS, CO

START TO FINISH: 30 MIN.
MAKES: 4 SERVINGS

- 4 boneless skinless chicken breast halves (6 ounces each)
- 1 teaspoon curry powder
- ½ teaspoon salt
- ¼ teaspoon coarsely ground pepper
- 2 teaspoons canola oil
- ⅓ cup apricot spreadable fruit
- 2 tablespoons water
- 2 tablespoons lemon juice
- 2 teaspoons grated lemon peel

1. Flatten chicken to ½-in. thickness. Combine the curry powder, salt and pepper; sprinkle over chicken.
2. In a large skillet, cook chicken in oil over medium heat for 5-6 minutes on each side or until a thermometer reads 170°. Remove to a serving plate; keep warm.
3. Add the apricot spreadable fruit, water and lemon juice to the pan; cook and stir for 1-2 minutes or until syrupy. Serve over the chicken; sprinkle with lemon peel.
PER SERVING *261 cal., 6 g fat (1 g sat. fat), 94 mg chol., 377 mg sodium, 15 g carb., trace fiber, 34 g pro.* **Diabetic Exchanges:** *5 lean meat, 1 starch, ½ fat.*

Did you know?

Also known as rabe and rapini, broccoli rabe is green and has small bud clusters. Resembling broccoli and available year-round, it has a bitter taste that mellows during cooking. Smaller leaves are more tender and have a milder flavor.

Linguine with Broccoli Rabe & Peppers M

Broccoli rabe is one of my favorite green vegetables. Because it cooks right with the linguine, you can multitask. And before you know it, dinner is served!

—GILDA LESTER MILLSBORO, DE

START TO FINISH: 25 MIN.
MAKES: 6 SERVINGS

- 1 pound broccoli rabe
- 1 package (16 ounces) linguine
- 3 tablespoons olive oil
- 2 anchovy fillets, finely chopped, optional
- 3 garlic cloves, minced
- ½ cup sliced roasted sweet red peppers
- ½ cup pitted Greek olives, halved
- ½ teaspoon crushed red pepper flakes
- ¼ teaspoon pepper
- ⅛ teaspoon salt
- ½ cup grated Romano cheese

1. Cut ½ in. off the ends of broccoli rabe; trim woody stems. Cut stems and leaves into 2-in. pieces. Cook linguine according to the package directions, adding broccoli rabe during the last 5 minutes of cooking. Drain, reserving ½ cup pasta water.
2. Meanwhile, in a large skillet, heat the oil over medium-high heat. Add the anchovies and garlic; cook and stir 1 minute. Stir in red peppers, olives, pepper flakes, pepper and salt.
3. Add the linguine and broccoli rabe to the skillet; toss to combine, adding the reserved pasta water as desired to moisten. Serve with cheese.
PER SERVING *426 cal., 15 g fat (4 g sat. fat), 10 mg chol., 495 mg sodium, 60 g carb., 5 g fiber, 17 g pro.*

LINGUINE WITH BROCCOLI RABE & PEPPERS

DAY-AFTER-THANKSGIVING
TURKEY STIR-FRY

Day-After-Thanksgiving Turkey Stir-Fry

I work for a priest who loves to cook, and he shared a terrific stir-fry recipe with me. Perfect for the day after Thanksgiving, this quick-and-easy dish is a delicious way to use up holiday leftovers.

—STEFEN LOVELACE MARRIOTTSVILLE, MD

START TO FINISH: 30 MIN.
MAKES: 2 SERVINGS

- 1 **cup cut fresh green beans**
- 1 **small red onion, chopped**
- 1 **tablespoon peanut or canola oil**
- 1 **garlic clove, minced**
- 2 **tablespoons whole-berry cranberry sauce**
- 1 **tablespoon soy sauce**
- 1 **teaspoon white vinegar**
- ⅛ **teaspoon salt**
- ⅛ **teaspoon pepper**
- 1½ **cups cubed cooked turkey breast**
- 2 **tablespoons chopped cashews**
  Minced fresh cilantro, optional
  Hot cooked rice

1. In a large skillet, saute beans and onion in oil until tender. Add garlic; cook 1 minute longer.
2. Meanwhile, in a small bowl, combine the cranberry sauce, soy sauce, vinegar, salt and pepper; pour over the bean mixture. Add turkey; simmer, uncovered, for 4-6 minutes or until heated through. Sprinkle with cashews and, if desired, cilantro. Serve with rice.
PER SERVING *320 cal., 12 g fat (2 g sat. fat), 90 mg chol., 730 mg sodium, 17 g carb., 3 g fiber, 36 g pro.*

Sweet-and-Sour Beef with Broccoli

We combined a variety of colorful veggies and inexpensive ground beef to put a new spin on classic Chinese beef and broccoli. For a change of pace, serve it over rice noodles—available in the Asian section of grocery stores—instead of rice.
—TASTE OF HOME TEST KITCHEN

START TO FINISH: 30 MIN.
MAKES: 6 SERVINGS

- 1 **can (20 ounces) unsweetened pineapple tidbits**
- 2 **tablespoons cornstarch**
- 1 **cup reduced-sodium beef broth**
- ¼ **cup reduced-sodium soy sauce**
- 2 **teaspoons minced fresh gingerroot**
- 1 **teaspoon minced garlic**
- 2½ **cups uncooked instant rice**
- 2 **cups fresh broccoli florets**
- ½ **pound sliced fresh mushrooms**
- 1 **medium sweet red pepper, julienned**
- 1 **can (8 ounces) sliced water chestnuts, drained**
- 1 **tablespoon sesame oil**
- 1 **pound lean ground beef (90% lean)**

1. Drain pineapple, reserving juice; set pineapple aside. In a small bowl, combine the cornstarch, broth, soy sauce, ginger, garlic and reserved juice until blended; set aside.
2. Cook the rice according to the package directions. Meanwhile, in a large skillet, stir-fry the broccoli, mushrooms, red pepper and water chestnuts in oil for 3-5 minutes or until crisp-tender; remove and set aside. In the same pan, cook the beef over medium heat until no longer pink; drain.
3. Stir the cornstarch mixture and add to the skillet. Bring to a boil; cook and stir for 1-2 minutes or until thickened. Stir in the reserved vegetable mixture and pineapple; heat through. Serve with rice.
PER SERVING *385 cal., 8 g fat (3 g sat. fat), 38 mg chol., 548 mg sodium, 58 g carb., 4 g fiber, 21 g pro.*

SPICY SHRIMP 'N' SCALLOP SKEWERS

Spicy Shrimp 'n' Scallop Skewers C

I absolutely adore shrimp. Throw in some scallops, and I'm in heaven! We usually pair these spicy skewers with grilled steaks and add a garden salad on the side.
—TRACI WYNNE DENVER, PA

START TO FINISH: 30 MIN.
MAKES: 6 SERVINGS

- 2 **tablespoons butter**
- ½ **teaspoon chili powder**
- ¼ **teaspoon dried oregano**
- ¼ **teaspoon ground cumin**
- ⅛ **teaspoon dried thyme**
- ⅛ **teaspoon each white pepper, cayenne pepper and black pepper**
- 18 **uncooked large shrimp (about ¾ pound)**
- 12 **sea scallops (1½ pounds)**

1. In a small saucepan, melt butter. Stir in the seasonings; set aside and keep warm. Peel and devein shrimp, leaving tails on. On six metal or soaked wooden skewers, alternately thread shrimp and scallops.
2. Moisten a paper towel with cooking oil; using long-handled tongs, lightly coat the grill rack. Grill seafood, covered, over medium heat or broil 4 in. from heat for 3-5 minutes on each side or until shrimp turn pink and scallops are firm and opaque, basting occasionally with butter mixture.

PER SERVING *176 cal., 5 g fat (3 g sat. fat), 128 mg chol., 316 mg sodium, 3 g carb., trace fiber, 28 g pro.* **Diabetic Exchanges:** *4 lean meat, 1 fat.*

Lemony Parsley Baked Cod S C

When you have a good piece of fish to fix for dinner, the last thing you want to do is overcook it. The key is cooking the fillets for a short time at a high temperature.
—SHERRY DAY PINCKNEY, MI

START TO FINISH: 25 MIN.
MAKES: 4 SERVINGS

- 3 **tablespoons minced fresh parsley**
- 2 **tablespoons lemon juice**
- 1 **tablespoon grated lemon peel**
- 1 **tablespoon olive oil**
- 2 **garlic cloves, minced**
- ¼ **teaspoon salt**
- ⅛ **teaspoon pepper**
- 4 **cod fillets (6 ounces each)**
- 2 **green onions, chopped**

Preheat oven to 400°. In a small bowl, mix the first seven ingredients. Place cod in an ungreased 11x7-in. baking dish; top with the parsley mixture. Sprinkle with green onions. Bake, covered, 10-15 minutes or until fish flakes easily with a fork.
PER SERVING *161 cal., 4 g fat (1 g sat. fat), 65 mg chol., 95 mg sodium, 2 g carb., 1 g fiber, 27 g pro.* **Diabetic Exchanges:** *4 lean meat, ½ fat.*

LEMONY PARSLEY BAKED COD

Chinese Takeout-on-a-Stick 🄒

Try serving rice and a side of pineapple or other fresh fruit with this tasty entree. Leftovers (if there are any) are great the next day in a salad, or wrapped in a flour tortilla with a little mayo.

—BETHANY SEELEY WARWICK, RI

START TO FINISH: 30 MIN. • **MAKES:** 4 SERVINGS

- 3 **tablespoons reduced-sodium soy sauce**
- 3 **tablespoons sesame oil**
- 4 **teaspoons brown sugar**
- 4 **teaspoons minced fresh gingerroot**
- 2 **garlic cloves, minced**
- ½ **teaspoon crushed red pepper flakes**
- 1 **pound boneless skinless chicken breasts, cut into 1-inch cubes**
- 3 **cups fresh broccoli florets**

1. In a large bowl, combine the first six ingredients; remove 3 tablespoons soy sauce mixture for basting. Add chicken to the remaining soy sauce mixture; toss to coat. On four metal or soaked wooden skewers, alternately thread the chicken and broccoli.

2. Moisten a paper towel with cooking oil; using long-handled tongs, lightly coat the grill rack. Grill skewers, covered, over medium heat or broil 4 in. from the heat for 10-15 minutes or until chicken is no longer pink, turning occasionally; baste with reserved soy sauce mixture during the last 4 minutes of cooking.

PER SERVING *261 cal., 13 g fat (2 g sat. fat), 63 mg chol., 534 mg sodium, 10 g carb., 2 g fiber, 25 g pro.* **Diabetic Exchanges:** *3 lean meat, 2 fat, ½ starch.*

CHINESE TAKEOUT-ON-A-STICK

CHILI STEAK & PEPPERS

Chili Steak & Peppers 🄒

In the mood for a steak dinner? Enjoy one guilt-free! A blend of chili sauce, lime juice, brown sugar and seasonings will kick up the flavor while keeping the calorie count under 275.

—TASTE OF HOME TEST KITCHEN

START TO FINISH: 30 MIN. • **MAKES:** 4 SERVINGS

- 2 **tablespoons chili sauce**
- 1 **tablespoon lime juice**
- 1 **teaspoon brown sugar**
- ½ **teaspoon crushed red pepper flakes**
- ½ **teaspoon salt, divided**
- 1 **beef top sirloin steak (1¼ pounds), cut into four steaks**
- 1 **medium onion, halved and sliced**
- 1 **medium green pepper, cut into strips**
- 1 **medium sweet yellow pepper, cut into strips**
- 2 **teaspoons olive oil**
- 1 **small garlic clove, minced**
- ⅛ **teaspoon pepper**
- ¼ **cup reduced-fat sour cream**
- 1 **teaspoon prepared horseradish**

1. Combine the chili sauce, lime juice, brown sugar, red pepper flakes and ¼ teaspoon salt; brush over the steaks. Broil steaks 4-6 in. from the heat for 5-7 minutes on each side or until the meat reaches the desired doneness (for medium-rare, a thermometer should read 145°; medium, 160°; well-done, 170°).

2. Meanwhile, in a large skillet, saute onion and green and yellow peppers in oil until tender. Add the garlic, pepper and remaining salt; cook 1 minute longer. In a small bowl, combine sour cream and horseradish. Serve steaks with pepper mixture and sauce.

PER SERVING *265 cal., 9 g fat (3 g sat. fat), 62 mg chol., 491 mg sodium, 12 g carb., 2 g fiber, 32 g pro.* **Diabetic Exchanges:** *4 lean meat, 1 vegetable, 1 fat.*

Simple Sesame Chicken with Couscous

START TO FINISH: 25 MIN. • **MAKES:** 4 SERVINGS

1½ cups water
1 cup uncooked whole wheat couscous
1 tablespoon olive oil
2 cups coleslaw mix
4 green onions, sliced
2 tablespoons plus ½ cup reduced-fat Asian toasted sesame salad dressing, divided
2 cups shredded cooked chicken breast
2 tablespoons minced fresh cilantro
Chopped peanuts, optional

1. In a small saucepan, bring the water to a boil. Stir in the couscous. Remove from the heat; let stand, covered, 5-10 minutes or until water is absorbed. Fluff with a fork.
2. In a nonstick skillet, heat the oil over medium heat. Add coleslaw mix; cook and stir 3-4 minutes or just until tender. Add green onions, 2 tablespoons dressing and couscous; heat through. Remove couscous from pan; keep warm.
3. In the same skillet, add chicken and remaining dressing; cook and stir over medium heat until heated through. Serve over couscous; top with cilantro and, if desired, peanuts.
PER SERVING *320 cal., 9 g fat (1 g sat. fat), 54 mg chol., 442 mg sodium, 35 g carb., 5 g fiber, 26 g pro.* **Diabetic Exchanges:** *3 lean meat, 2 starch, 1 fat.*

After my kids sampled Chinese takeout and requested more, I came up with this recipe. Use a rotisserie chicken from the deli for a super-fast, super-easy meal.
—**NAYLET LAROCHELLE** MIAMI, FL

SIMPLE SESAME CHICKEN WITH COUSCOUS

FIG-GLAZED PORK TENDERLOIN

Fig-Glazed Pork Tenderloin

I like to experiment with unusual ingredients and make food look photo-worthy, too. But as far as my husband is concerned, it just has to taste good! Here's a dish that pleases us both.
—**JEAN GOTTFRIED** UPPER SANDUSKY, OH

START TO FINISH: 30 MIN. • **MAKES:** 4 SERVINGS

1 pork tenderloin (1 pound), cut into 8 slices
½ teaspoon salt
½ teaspoon pepper
1 tablespoon olive oil
⅓ cup fig preserves
3 tablespoons apple juice
2 tablespoons cider vinegar
1½ teaspoons Worcestershire sauce
1 garlic clove, minced
¾ teaspoon curry powder

1. Sprinkle the pork with salt and pepper. In a large skillet, heat oil over medium-high heat. Brown pork on both sides; remove from pan.
2. Add the preserves, juice, vinegar, Worcestershire sauce, garlic and curry powder to same pan; bring to a boil. Return pork to pan. Reduce heat; simmer, covered, 5-7 minutes or until a thermometer inserted into pork reads 145°. Let stand 5 minutes before serving.
PER SERVING *239 cal., 7 g fat (2 g sat. fat), 63 mg chol., 509 mg sodium, 20 g carb., trace fiber, 23 g pro.*

APPLE-BALSAMIC
PORK CHOPS

Shrimp with Tomatoes & Feta c

Any dish that's special enough for guests but quick enough for a weeknight is a star in my book. Here's a real standout! Serve crusty French bread for sopping up the delicious tomato broth.

—**SUSAN SEYMOUR** VALATIE, NY

START TO FINISH: 30 MIN.
MAKES: 6 SERVINGS

- 3 tablespoons olive oil
- 2 shallots, finely chopped
- 2 garlic cloves, minced
- 6 plum tomatoes, chopped
- ½ cup white wine or chicken broth
- 1 tablespoon dried oregano
- ½ teaspoon salt
- ½ teaspoon crushed red pepper flakes
- ¼ teaspoon sweet paprika
- 2 pounds uncooked large shrimp, peeled and deveined
- ⅔ cup crumbled feta cheese
- 2 teaspoons minced fresh mint
  Hot cooked rice

1. In a large skillet, heat the oil over medium-high heat. Add the shallots and garlic; cook and stir until tender. Add the plum tomatoes, white wine, oregano, salt, red pepper flakes and paprika; bring to a boil. Reduce heat; simmer, uncovered, 5 minutes.

2. Stir in the shrimp and cheese; cook 5-6 minutes or until shrimp turn pink. Stir in mint. Serve with rice.

PER SERVING *261 cal., 11 g fat (3 g sat. fat), 191 mg chol., 502 mg sodium, 8 g carb., 2 g fiber, 28 g pro.* **Diabetic Exchanges:** *4 lean meat, 1 vegetable, 1 fat.*

Apple-Balsamic Pork Chops

My favorite main courses are easy, fast and frugal. These sweet, delicious pork chops score on all three counts.

—**JAMI WELLS** BOISE, ID

START TO FINISH: 20 MIN.
MAKES: 4 SERVINGS

- 4 boneless pork loin chops (5 ounces each)
- ½ teaspoon salt
- ½ teaspoon pepper
- 2 teaspoons olive oil
- ¼ cup apple cider or juice
- 1 cup reduced-sodium chicken broth
- ¼ cup apple jelly
- 2 teaspoons balsamic vinegar
- 1 tablespoon butter

1. Sprinkle pork chops with salt and pepper. In a large skillet, brown pork chops in oil. Remove and keep warm.

2. Add the apple cider to the skillet, stirring to loosen the browned bits from the pan. Stir in the chicken broth, apple jelly and balsamic vinegar. Bring to a boil; cook until liquid is reduced to ⅓ cup.

3. Return the pork chops to the skillet. Cover and simmer for 8-10 minutes or until the meat is tender, turning once. Add butter and stir until melted.

PER SERVING *298 cal., 13 g fat (5 g sat. fat), 76 mg chol., 499 mg sodium, 16 g carb., trace fiber, 28 g pro.* **Diabetic Exchanges:** *4 lean meat, 1 starch, 1 fat.*

SHRIMP WITH TOMATOES & FETA

Strawberry-Teriyaki Glazed Salmon

I'm always up for a good salmon dinner, and this one is the best I've ever tasted. Strawberry jam might seem surprising in an Asian-inspired recipe, but it makes a sweet-savory glaze that goes over well with everyone—even people who say they normally don't care for fish.
—**KRYSTINA CAHALAN** WINTER PARK, FL

START TO FINISH: 25 MIN.
MAKES: 4 SERVINGS

- ¼ cup seedless strawberry jam
- 2 tablespoons reduced-sodium soy sauce
- 1 garlic clove, minced
- ½ teaspoon ground ginger
- 4 salmon fillets (4 ounces each)
- ¼ teaspoon salt
- ¼ teaspoon pepper

1. Preheat broiler. In a small saucepan, combine the jam, soy sauce, garlic and ginger; cook and stir until the mixture comes to a boil. Reduce heat; simmer, uncovered, 6-8 minutes or until the mixture is reduced by half.
2. Sprinkle the salmon fillets with salt and pepper. Place in an ungreased 15x10x1-in. baking pan. Broil 4-6 in. from heat 8-10 minutes or until the fish just begins to flake easily with a fork, brushing with 2 tablespoons jam mixture during the last 2 minutes of cooking. Just before serving, brush with remaining jam mixture.
PER SERVING *234 cal., 10 g fat (2 g sat. fat), 57 mg chol., 507 mg sodium, 14 g carb., trace fiber, 20 g pro.* **Diabetic Exchanges:** *3 lean meat, 1 starch.*

top tip › Fillets in Your Freezer

Salmon and other oily types of fish such as whitefish, mackerel and lake trout may be frozen for up to 3 months. Lean types of fish like cod, tilapia, catfish and haddock may be frozen for up to 6 months. Wrap fish in freezer paper, heavy-duty plastic bags or heavy-duty foil before freezing.

STRAWBERRY-TERIYAKI GLAZED SALMON

CREOLE BLACKENED CHICKEN

Creole Blackened Chicken C

I love blackened chicken and was thrilled to discover I can easily prepare it at home. I adjusted the original recipe, making it spicier to suit my taste. If your family prefers food that's milder, just omit or reduce the amount of cayenne pepper.
—LAUREN HARDY JACKSONVILLE, FL

START TO FINISH: 30 MIN.
MAKES: 8 SERVINGS

- 2 tablespoons ground cumin
- 2 tablespoons Creole seasoning
- 2 tablespoons salt-free Southwest chipotle seasoning blend
- 4 teaspoons lemon-pepper seasoning
- 1 teaspoon cayenne pepper
- 8 boneless skinless chicken breast halves (6 ounces each)
- 2 tablespoons canola oil

1. Preheat oven to 350°. Mix the first five ingredients; sprinkle over chicken. In a large skillet, heat oil over medium-high heat. Brown chicken in batches on both sides; transfer to a greased 15x10x1-in. baking pan.
2. Bake, uncovered, 12-15 minutes or until a thermometer reads 165°.
PER SERVING *222 cal., 8 g fat (1 g sat. fat), 94 mg chol., 813 mg sodium, 1 g carb., 1 g fiber, 35 g pro.* **Diabetic Exchanges:** *5 lean meat, 1 fat.*

Margherita Pita Pizzas M

My husband plants our vegetable garden. When harvesttime arrives, I happily pick and cook the fruits of his labor. We make good use of our plum tomatoes by putting them on top of these individual pita-bread pizzas. They're so good!
—ROSEMARIE WELESKI NATRONA HEIGHTS, PA

START TO FINISH: 20 MIN.
MAKES: 4 SERVINGS

- 4 pita breads (6 inches)
- 2 teaspoons olive oil
- 2 garlic cloves, minced
- 2 cups (8 ounces) shredded part-skim mozzarella cheese
- 3 plum tomatoes, thinly sliced
- ¼ teaspoon garlic powder
- 1 teaspoon Italian seasoning
  Thinly sliced fresh basil, optional

1. Place pita breads on an ungreased baking sheet; brush with oil. Top with minced garlic, 1 cup cheese, tomatoes, garlic powder and remaining cheese; sprinkle with Italian seasoning.
2. Bake at 425° for 10-12 minutes or until cheese is melted. Top with basil if desired.
PER SERVING *340 cal., 12 g fat (6 g sat. fat), 33 mg chol., 588 mg sodium, 38 g carb., 2 g fiber, 20 g pro.* **Diabetic Exchanges:** *2 starch, 2 medium-fat meat, ½ fat.*

Zippy Zucchini Pasta M

Here's a wonderful meal for two, with leftovers for one the next day. We like the zip from the crushed red pepper flakes.
—KATHLEEN TIMBERLAKE DEARBORN HEIGHTS, MI

START TO FINISH: 15 MIN.
MAKES: 3 SERVINGS

- 1 package (7 ounces) angel hair pasta or thin spaghetti
- 2 small zucchini, cut into ¼-inch pieces
- 2 garlic cloves, minced
- 3 tablespoons olive oil
- 1 can (14½ ounces) Mexican diced tomatoes, undrained
- ¼ cup minced fresh parsley
- 1 teaspoon dried oregano
- ⅛ to ½ teaspoon crushed red pepper flakes

1. Cook pasta according to package directions. Meanwhile, in a large skillet, saute zucchini and garlic in oil until zucchini is crisp-tender.
2. Add the tomatoes, parsley, oregano and pepper flakes; heat through. Drain pasta; serve with zucchini mixture.
PER SERVING *412 cal., 15 g fat (2 g sat. fat), 0 chol., 299 mg sodium, 59 g carb., 5 g fiber, 11 g pro.*

ZIPPY ZUCCHINI PASTA

Sweet-Chili Salmon with Blackberries C

START TO FINISH: 25 MIN.
MAKES: 4 SERVINGS

- 1 **cup fresh or frozen blackberries, thawed**
- 1 **cup finely chopped English cucumber**
- 1 **green onion, finely chopped**
- 2 **tablespoons sweet chili sauce, divided**
- 4 **salmon fillets (6 ounces each)**
- ½ **teaspoon salt**
- ½ **teaspoon pepper**

1. In a small bowl, combine the blackberries, cucumber, green onion and 1 tablespoon sweet chili sauce; toss to coat. Moisten a paper towel with cooking oil; using long-handled tongs, rub on grill rack to coat lightly. Sprinkle the salmon fillets with salt and pepper.

2. Place the salmon fillets on grill rack, skin side down. Grill, covered, over medium-high heat or broil 4 in. from heat 10-12 minutes or until the fish flakes easily with a fork, brushing with remaining chili sauce during the last 2-3 minutes of cooking. Serve with blackberry mixture.

PER SERVING *303 cal., 16 g fat (3 g sat. fat), 85 mg chol., 510 mg sodium, 9 g carb., 2 g fiber, 30 g pro.* **Diabetic Exchanges:** *5 lean meat, ½ starch.*

LIME-GINGER CHICKEN TENDERS

> My garden is frequently my cooking inspiration. I have a large patch of berries, and I especially enjoy using those little gems in savory dishes to add a little bit of natural sweetness or tartness.
> —**ROXANNE CHAN** ALBANY, CA

SWEET-CHILI SALMON WITH BLACKBERRIES

Lime-Ginger Chicken Tenders C

I prepare chicken breasts often because they're low in fat, high in protein and almost always reasonably priced at the grocery store. To keep things exciting, I add a few of our favorite ingredients like jalapenos, lime and fresh ginger.
—**SAMANTHA ANDERSON** FORT WORTH, TX

START TO FINISH: 30 MIN.
MAKES: 4 SERVINGS

- ⅓ **cup minced fresh cilantro**
- 1 **jalapeno pepper, seeded and minced**
- 2 **tablespoons lime juice**
- 2 **tablespoons olive oil**
- 3 **garlic cloves, minced**
- 1½ **teaspoons minced fresh gingerroot**
- 1½ **teaspoons grated lime peel**
- ½ **teaspoon salt**
- ½ **teaspoon ground cumin**
- 1½ **pounds chicken tenderloins**

Preheat oven to 375°. In a large bowl, mix the first nine ingredients. Add the chicken; toss to coat. Transfer to a greased 15x10x1-in. baking pan. Bake, uncovered, 20-25 minutes or until the chicken is no longer pink.

NOTE *Wear disposable gloves when cutting hot peppers; the oils can burn skin. Avoid touching your face.*

PER SERVING *226 cal., 8 g fat (1 g sat. fat), 100 mg chol., 368 mg sodium, 2 g carb., trace fiber, 39 g pro.* **Diabetic Exchanges:** *5 lean meat, 1 fat.*

Grilled Turkey Burgers

On whole wheat buns, these juicy patties make wholesome, satisfying sandwiches.

—SHERRY HULSMAN ELKTON, FL

START TO FINISH: 30 MIN.
MAKES: 6 SERVINGS

- 1 egg, lightly beaten
- ⅔ cup soft whole wheat bread crumbs
- ½ cup finely chopped celery
- ¼ cup finely chopped onion
- 1 tablespoon minced fresh parsley
- 1 teaspoon Worcestershire sauce
- 1 teaspoon dried oregano
- ½ teaspoon salt
- ¼ teaspoon pepper
- 1¼ pounds lean ground turkey
- 6 whole wheat hamburger buns, split

1. In a small bowl, combine the egg, bread crumbs, celery, onion, parsley, Worcestershire sauce and seasonings. Crumble turkey over mixture and mix well. Shape into six patties.

2. Moisten a paper towel with cooking oil; using long-handled tongs, lightly coat grill rack. Grill, covered, over medium heat or broil 4 in. from the heat for 5-6 minutes on each side or until a thermometer reads 165° and the juices run clear. Serve on hamburger buns.

PER SERVING *293 cal., 11 g fat (3 g sat. fat), 110 mg chol., 561 mg sodium, 27 g carb., 4 g fiber, 22 g pro.* **Diabetic Exchanges:** *3 lean meat, 2 starch.*

Pork Medallions with Cranberry Sauce ⊂

Birthdays and other festive events don't always happen on the weekend, so it's nice to have quick but special weekday recipes like this cranberry pork.

—CATHERINE HIGGINS BOUNTIFUL, UT

START TO FINISH: 25 MIN.
MAKES: 4 SERVINGS

- 1 pork tenderloin (1 pound), cut into 1-inch slices
- ⅛ teaspoon salt
- ⅛ teaspoon pepper
- ½ cup whole-berry cranberry sauce
- 2 tablespoons barbecue sauce
- 1 tablespoon water
- 2 garlic cloves, minced
- ½ teaspoon Chinese five-spice powder

1. Sprinkle the pork with salt and pepper. In a large nonstick skillet coated with cooking spray, cook the pork in batches over medium heat for 3-5 minutes on each side or until juices run clear. Remove and keep warm.

2. Add the cranberry sauce, barbecue sauce, water, garlic and five-spice powder to the skillet. Bring to a boil. Reduce heat; simmer, uncovered, for 1-2 minutes or until thickened. Serve with the pork.

PER SERVING *190 cal., 4 g fat (1 g sat. fat), 63 mg chol., 198 mg sodium, 15 g carb., 1 g fiber, 23 g pro.* **Diabetic Exchanges:** *3 lean meat, 1 starch.*

GRILLED TURKEY BURGERS

96

97

101

Slow Cooker

"I live in Georgia, but I appreciate the tangy, sweet and slightly spicy taste of Carolina vinegar chicken. I make my version in the slow cooker, and when you walk in the door after being gone all day, the tempting aroma will stoke your appetite."

—RAMONA PARRIS ACWORTH, GA
about her recipe, Carolina-Style Vinegar BBQ Chicken, on page 105

SLOW-COOKED
COCONUT CHICKEN

Slow-Cooked Coconut Chicken C

One of my favorite things about this recipe is how incredible it makes the house smell. Everyone who comes by asks, "What are you cooking?" And anyone who tastes it goes home with the recipe.
—**ANN SMART** NORTH LOGAN, UT

PREP: 10 MIN. • **COOK:** 4 HOURS
MAKES: 6 SERVINGS

- ½ cup light coconut milk
- 2 tablespoons brown sugar
- 2 tablespoons reduced-sodium soy sauce
- 2 garlic cloves, minced
- ⅛ teaspoon ground cloves
- 6 boneless skinless chicken thighs (about 1½ pounds)
- 6 tablespoons flaked coconut, toasted
  Minced fresh cilantro

In a large bowl, combine the first five ingredients. Place chicken in a 3-qt. slow cooker. Pour coconut milk mixture over top. Cook, covered, on low 4-5 hours or until chicken is tender. Sprinkle each serving with coconut and cilantro.

NOTE *To toast coconut, spread in a 15x10x1-in. baking pan. Bake at 350° for 5-10 minutes or until golden brown, stirring frequently.*

PER SERVING *201 cal., 10 g fat (3 g sat. fat), 76 mg chol., 267 mg sodium, 6 g carb., trace fiber, 21 g pro.* **Diabetic Exchanges:** *3 lean meat, ½ starch, ½ fat.*

Slow Cooker Beef Bourguignonne C

PREP: 30 MIN. + MARINATING
COOK: 8 HOURS • **MAKES:** 12 SERVINGS

- 3 pounds beef stew meat
- 1¾ cups dry red wine
- 3 tablespoons olive oil
- 3 tablespoons dried minced onion
- 2 tablespoons dried parsley flakes
- 1 bay leaf
- 1 teaspoon dried thyme
- ¼ teaspoon pepper
- 8 bacon strips, chopped
- 1 pound whole fresh mushrooms, quartered
- 24 pearl onions, peeled (about 2 cups)
- 2 garlic cloves, minced
- ⅓ cup all-purpose flour
- 1 teaspoon salt
  Hot cooked whole wheat egg noodles, optional

1. Place beef in a large resealable plastic bag; add wine, oil and the seasonings. Seal bag and turn to coat. Refrigerate overnight.

2. In a large skillet, cook bacon over medium heat until crisp, stirring occasionally. Remove with a slotted spoon; drain on paper towels. Discard drippings, reserving 1 tablespoon in the pan.

3. Add mushrooms and onions to drippings; cook and stir over medium-high heat until tender. Add garlic; cook 1 minute longer.

4. Drain beef, reserving marinade; transfer beef to a 4- or 5-qt. slow cooker. Sprinkle beef with flour and salt; toss to coat. Top with bacon and mushroom mixture. Add reserved marinade.

5. Cook, covered, on low 8-10 hours or until beef is tender. Remove bay leaf. If desired, serve stew with noodles.

PER SERVING *⅔ cup stew equals 289 cal., 15 g fat (5 g sat. fat), 77 mg chol., 350 mg sodium, 8 g carb., 1 g fiber, 25 g pro.* **Diabetic Exchanges:** *3 lean meat, 1½ fat, 1 vegetable.*

I've wanted to make beef Burgundy ever since I got one of Julia Child's cookbooks, but I wanted to find a way to fix it in a slow cooker. My version of the popular stew is still rich, hearty and delicious, but without all the steps. It's also delightful served with mashed potatoes. —**CRYSTAL JO BRUNS** ILIFF, CO

SLOW COOKER BEEF BOURGUIGNONNE

SOUTHERN PULLED PORK

Southern Pulled Pork C

With molasses and brown sugar, this sweet and tangy pork takes just a few minutes of prep. It's even more rewarding served with a traditional accompaniment of sweet potatoes.

—**KATIE KORNITSKY** WEST BOYLSTON, MA

PREP: 20 MIN. • **COOK:** 6½ HOURS
MAKES: 10 SERVINGS

- 1 **boneless pork shoulder butt roast (3 pounds)**
- ⅓ **cup spicy brown mustard**
- ⅓ **cup molasses**
- ¼ **cup packed brown sugar**
- 1½ **teaspoons soy sauce**
- 1 **tablespoon cornstarch**
- ¼ **cup cold water**
  Baked sweet potatoes, optional

1. Place pork in a 3- or 4-qt. slow cooker. Combine the mustard, molasses, brown sugar and soy sauce; pour over roast. Cover and cook on low for 6-8 hours or until meat is tender.
2. Remove meat; cool slightly. Skim fat from cooking juices; transfer to a large saucepan. Bring to a boil. Combine cornstarch and water until smooth; gradually stir into juices. Return to a boil; cook and stir for 2 minutes or until thickened.
3. Shred meat with two forks; return to the slow cooker. Stir in sauce. Cover and cook for 15 minutes or until heated through. Serve with sweet potatoes if desired.
PER SERVING *282 cal., 14 g fat (5 g sat. fat), 81 mg chol., 240 mg sodium, 14 g carb., trace fiber, 23 g pro. **Diabetic Exchanges:** 3 medium-fat meat, 1 starch.*

Meaty Slow-Cooked Jambalaya

This recipe makes a big batch. Stash some away in the freezer for days you don't feel like cooking.

—**DIANE SMITH** PINE MOUNTAIN, GA

PREP: 25 MIN. • **COOK:** 7¼ HOURS
MAKES: 12 SERVINGS (3½ QUARTS)

- 1 **can (28 ounces) diced tomatoes, undrained**
- 1 **cup reduced-sodium chicken broth**
- 1 **large green pepper, chopped**
- 1 **medium onion, chopped**
- 2 **celery ribs, sliced**
- ½ **cup white wine or additional reduced-sodium chicken broth**
- 4 **garlic cloves, minced**
- 2 **teaspoons Cajun seasoning**
- 2 **teaspoons dried parsley flakes**
- 1 **teaspoon dried basil**
- 1 **teaspoon dried oregano**
- ¾ **teaspoon salt**
- ½ to 1 **teaspoon cayenne pepper**
- 2 **pounds boneless skinless chicken thighs, cut into 1-inch pieces**
- 1 **package (12 ounces) fully cooked andouille or other spicy chicken sausage links**
- 2 **pounds uncooked medium shrimp, peeled and deveined**
- 8 **cups hot cooked brown rice**

1. In a large bowl, combine the first 13 ingredients. Place chicken and sausage in a 6-qt. slow cooker. Pour tomato mixture over top. Cook, covered, on low for 7-9 hours or until the chicken is tender.
2. Stir in shrimp. Cook, covered, 15-20 minutes longer or until shrimp turn pink. Serve with rice.
PER SERVING *387 cal., 10 g fat (3 g sat. fat), 164 mg chol., 674 mg sodium, 37 g carb., 4 g fiber, 36 g pro. **Diabetic Exchanges:** 3 lean meat, 2½ starch.*

MEATY SLOW-COOKED JAMBALAYA

Grandma Edna's Cajun Pork C

My grandmother used to make this every year as part of our Christmas dinner. These days, I make it for my family at the holidays. We love to carry on the delicious tradition of Grandma's Cajun pork.

—TONYA CLINE GREENVILLE, OH

PREP: 35 MIN. • **COOK:** 6 HOURS
MAKES: 12 SERVINGS (2¼ CUPS SAUCE)

- 1 **small onion**
- 1 **celery rib**
- 1 **small green pepper**
- 3 **tablespoons butter**
- 3 **garlic cloves, minced**
- 2 **teaspoons dried thyme**
- 1 **teaspoon paprika**
- ½ **teaspoon each salt, white pepper and pepper**
- ½ **teaspoon ground mustard**
- ½ **teaspoon hot pepper sauce**
- 1 **boneless pork loin roast (4 pounds)**
- 2 **tablespoons cornstarch**
- 2 **tablespoons cold water**

1. Finely chop vegetables. In a large skillet, saute vegetables in butter until tender. Add garlic; cook 1 minute longer. Stir in seasonings and hot pepper sauce.

2. Cut several slits in roast to within ½ in. of bottom. Place in a 5-qt. slow cooker. Spoon onion mixture between slits and over the top of meat. Cover and cook on low for 6-8 hours or until pork is tender.

3. Transfer roast to a serving platter; keep warm. Pour cooking juices into a small saucepan. Combine cornstarch and water until smooth; stir into the pan. Bring to a boil; cook and stir for 2 minutes or until thickened. Serve with roast.

PER SERVING *225 cal., 10 g fat (4 g sat. fat), 83 mg chol., 167 mg sodium, 3 g carb., 1 g fiber, 29 g pro.* **Diabetic Exchanges:** *4 lean meat, ½ fat.*

CHICKEN THIGHS WITH GINGER-PEACH SAUCE

Chicken Thighs with Ginger-Peach Sauce

This slightly sweet Asian chicken has become one of my favorite recipes to prepare on Sunday. It's easy to make, requires very little cleanup and leaves me plenty of time to do other things.

—LISA RENSHAW KANSAS CITY, MO

PREP: 15 MIN. • **COOK:** 4 HOURS
MAKES: 10 SERVINGS

- 10 **boneless skinless chicken thighs (about 2½ pounds)**
- 1 **cup sliced peeled fresh or frozen peaches**
- 1 **cup golden raisins**
- 1 **cup peach preserves**
- ⅓ **cup chili sauce**
- 2 **tablespoons minced crystallized ginger**
- 1 **tablespoon reduced-sodium soy sauce**
- 1 **tablespoon minced garlic**
  Hot cooked rice, optional

1. Place chicken in a 4-qt. slow cooker coated with cooking spray. Top with peaches and raisins. In a small bowl, combine the preserves, chili sauce, ginger, soy sauce and garlic. Spoon over top.

2. Cover and cook on low for 4-5 hours or until chicken is tender. Serve with rice if desired.

PER SERVING *314 cal., 8 g fat (2 g sat. fat), 76 mg chol., 250 mg sodium, 39 g carb., 1 g fiber, 22 g pro.*

GRANDMA EDNA'S CAJUN PORK

Meat Loaf with Chili Sauce C

I used to serve this meat loaf in my cafe, and many customers asked for the recipe. I adapted it for my slow cooker at home, where it's quite popular, too.

—**ROBERT COX** LAS CRUCES, NM

PREP: 20 MIN.
COOK: 3 HOURS + STANDING
MAKES: 8 SERVINGS

- 1 large onion, finely chopped
- ½ cup seasoned bread crumbs
- 1 small green pepper, chopped
- 2 eggs, lightly beaten
- ½ cup chili sauce
- 2 tablespoons spicy brown mustard
- 3 to 4 garlic cloves, minced
- ¾ teaspoon salt
- ¼ teaspoon dried oregano
- ¼ teaspoon dried basil
- 2 pounds lean ground beef (90% lean)
  Additional chili sauce, optional

1. Cut four 20x3-in. strips of heavy-duty foil; crisscross so they resemble spokes of a wheel. Place strips on bottom and up sides of a 5-qt. slow cooker. Coat strips with cooking spray.

2. In a large bowl, combine the first 10 ingredients. Add beef; mix lightly but thoroughly. Shape into a 9-in. round loaf. Place loaf in center of strips in slow cooker.

3. Cook, covered, on low 3-4 hours or until a thermometer reads at least 160°. If desired, spoon additional chili sauce over meat loaf; let stand 10 minutes. Using foil strips as handles, remove meat loaf to a platter.

PER SERVING *253 cal., 11 g fat (4 g sat. fat), 123 mg chol., 686 mg sodium, 12 g carb., 1 g fiber, 25 g pro.* **Diabetic Exchanges:** *3 lean meat, 1 starch.*

Chicken with Beans and Potatoes C

This all-in-one entree is great to make when your afternoon is going to be busy. The veggies and a little onion soup mix give the broth lots of flavor.

—*TASTE OF HOME* TEST KITCHEN

PREP: 20 MIN. • **COOK:** 4 HOURS
MAKES: 10 SERVINGS

- 2 pounds boneless skinless chicken breasts, cut into 1-inch cubes
- ½ teaspoon lemon-pepper seasoning
- 1 tablespoon canola oil

CHICKEN WITH BEANS AND POTATOES

- 1 pound fresh green beans, trimmed
- 1 pound small red potatoes, quartered
- ½ pound medium fresh mushrooms, halved
- ½ cup thinly sliced sweet onion
- 2 cans (14½ ounces each) chicken broth
- 2 tablespoons onion soup mix
- 2 teaspoons Worcestershire sauce
- 1 teaspoon grated lemon peel
- ½ teaspoon salt
- ½ teaspoon pepper
- ¼ teaspoon garlic powder

1. Sprinkle chicken with lemon-pepper. In a large skillet, cook chicken in oil over medium heat for 4-5 minutes or until lightly browned.

2. In a 5- or 6-qt. slow cooker, layer the green beans, potatoes, mushrooms and onion. In a small bowl, combine the remaining ingredients; pour over vegetables. Top with chicken.

3. Cover and cook on low for 4-5 hours or until vegetables are tender. Serve with a slotted spoon.

PER SERVING *209 cal., 5 g fat (1 g sat. fat), 63 mg chol., 324 mg sodium, 15 g carb., 3 g fiber, 26 g pro.* **Diabetic Exchanges:** *3 lean meat, 1 vegetable, ½ starch.*

? Did you know?

Using lean ground beef in the meat loaf instead of beef that's 80% lean saves 45 calories per 4-ounce serving of beef. Lean ground beef is also 29% lower in saturated fat.

MEAT LOAF WITH CHILI SAUCE

Round Steak Italiano

My mom used to make this wonderful dish, and it's always been one that I've enjoyed. I especially like how the thick, flavorful gravy drapes over the meat.

—DEANNE STEPHENS MCMINNVILLE, OR

PREP: 15 MIN. • **COOK:** 7 HOURS
MAKES: 8 SERVINGS

- 2 **pounds beef top round steak**
- 1 **can (8 ounces) tomato sauce**
- 2 **tablespoons onion soup mix**
- 2 **tablespoons canola oil**
- 2 **tablespoons red wine vinegar**
- 1 **teaspoon ground oregano**
- ½ **teaspoon garlic powder**
- ¼ **teaspoon pepper**
- 8 **medium potatoes (7 to 8 ounces each)**
- 1 **tablespoon cornstarch**
- 1 **tablespoon cold water**

1. Cut steak into serving-size pieces; place in a 5-qt. slow cooker. In a large bowl, combine the tomato sauce, soup mix, oil, vinegar, oregano, garlic powder and pepper; pour over meat. Scrub and pierce potatoes; place over meat. Cover and cook on low for 7 to 8 hours or until meat and potatoes are tender.

2. Remove meat and potatoes; keep warm. For gravy, pour cooking juices into a small saucepan; skim fat. Combine cornstarch and water until smooth; gradually stir into juices. Bring to a boil; cook and stir for 2 minutes or until thickened. Serve with meat and potatoes.

PER SERVING *357 cal., 7 g fat (2 g sat. fat), 64 mg chol., 329 mg sodium, 42 g carb., 4 g fiber, 31 g pro.* **Diabetic Exchanges:** *3 lean meat, 2½ starch, ½ fat.*

Moroccan Chicken

This autumn-perfect dish with chickpeas, olives and sweet-savory spices is sure to delight. Most of the ingredients are pantry staples, but they combine to make something really special.

—LILY JULOW LAWRENCEVILLE, GA

PREP: 25 MIN. • **COOK:** 6 HOURS
MAKES: 8 SERVINGS

- 1½ **pounds butternut squash, peeled, seeded and cut into 2-inch cubes**
- 1 **can (15 ounces) garbanzo beans or chickpeas, rinsed and drained**
- 1 **medium onion, chopped**
- 1 **cup chicken broth**
- ⅓ **cup raisins**
- 2 **garlic cloves, minced**
- 2 **teaspoons ground coriander**
- 2 **teaspoons ground cumin**
- ½ **teaspoon ground cinnamon**
- ½ **teaspoon salt**
- ¼ **teaspoon pepper**
- 8 **bone-in chicken thighs (about 3 pounds), skin removed**
- 2 **medium tomatoes, chopped**
- ½ **cup pitted green olives**
- 1 **tablespoon cornstarch**
- 1 **tablespoon cold water**
  Hot cooked couscous

1. In a 6-qt. slow cooker, place the squash, beans, onion, broth, raisins and garlic. Combine the coriander, cumin, cinnamon, salt and pepper; rub over chicken. Place in slow cooker.

2. Cover and cook on low for 6-8 hours or until chicken is tender, adding tomatoes and olives during the last 20 minutes of cooking.

3. Remove chicken and vegetables to a serving platter; keep warm. Skim fat from cooking juices; transfer to a small saucepan. Bring to a boil. Combine cornstarch and water until smooth; gradually stir into cooking juices. Return to a boil; cook and stir for 2 minutes or until thickened. Serve with chicken, vegetables and couscous.

PER SERVING *330 cal., 13 g fat (3 g sat. fat), 88 mg chol., 599 mg sodium, 27 g carb., 6 g fiber, 28 g pro.* **Diabetic Exchanges:** *4 lean meat, 2 starch, ½ fat.*

MOROCCAN CHICKEN

SIMPLE POACHED SALMON

Simple Poached Salmon S C

I love this recipe because it's healthy and almost effortless. And the salmon always cooks to perfection!

—**ERIN CHILCOAT** CENTRAL ISLIP, NY

PREP: 10 MIN. • **COOK:** 1½ HOURS
MAKES: 4 SERVINGS

- 2 **cups water**
- 1 **cup white wine**
- 1 **medium onion, sliced**
- 1 **celery rib, sliced**
- 1 **medium carrot, sliced**
- 2 **tablespoons lemon juice**
- 3 **fresh thyme sprigs**
- 1 **fresh rosemary sprig**
- 1 **bay leaf**
- ½ **teaspoon salt**
- ¼ **teaspoon pepper**
- 4 **salmon fillets (1¼ inches thick and 6 ounces each)**
  Lemon wedges

1. In a 3-qt. slow cooker, combine the first 11 ingredients. Cook, covered, on low 45 minutes.

2. Carefully place fillets in liquid; add additional warm water (120° to 130°) to cover if needed. Cook, covered, 45-55 minutes or just until fish flakes easily with a fork (a thermometer inserted into fish should read at least 145°). Remove fish from cooking liquid. Serve warm or cold with lemon wedges.

PER SERVING *272 cal., 16 g fat (3 g sat. fat), 85 mg chol., 115 mg sodium, 1 g carb., trace fiber, 29 g pro.* **Diabetic Exchange:** *4 lean meat.*

Spicy Shredded Chicken C

PREP: 40 MIN. • **COOK:** 4¼ HOURS
MAKES: 8 SERVINGS

- 2 **tablespoons olive oil**
- 1 **pound boneless skinless chicken thighs**
- 1 **pound boneless skinless chicken breasts**
- 3 **cups reduced-sodium chicken broth, divided**
- 6 **green onions, chopped**
- 1 **medium green pepper, chopped**
- 2 **tablespoons ground cumin**
- 1 **tablespoon garlic powder**
- 1 **tablespoon chili powder**
- 1 **tablespoon paprika**
- 1 **teaspoon cayenne pepper**
- ½ **teaspoon salt**
- ¼ **teaspoon pepper**
- 1 **plum tomato, chopped**

1. In a large skillet, heat oil over medium-high heat. Brown the chicken in batches. Transfer to a 3- or 4-qt. slow cooker. Add 1 cup broth to pan. Cook, stirring to loosen browned bits from pan.

2. Stir in onions and green pepper; cook and stir 3-5 minutes or until vegetables are tender. Stir in seasonings; cook 1-2 minutes. Add tomato and remaining broth; pour over chicken. Cook, covered, on low 4-5 hours or until chicken is tender.

3. When cool enough to handle, shred meat with two forks; return to slow cooker. Cook, covered, on low 15-20 minutes or until heated through. Serve with a slotted spoon.

PER SERVING *202 cal., 10 g fat (2 g sat. fat), 69 mg chol., 436 mg sodium, 5 g carb., 2 g fiber, 24 g pro.* **Diabetic Exchanges:** *3 lean meat, 1 fat.*

I love Mexican food, but not the high calorie count that often comes with it. This easy dish is healthy, delicious and a definite crowd-pleaser! I like to serve the chicken with warm tortillas, rice, beans and salsa. —**HEATHER WALKER** SCOTTSDALE, AZ

SPICY SHREDDED CHICKEN

Tropical Pulled Pork Sliders

I used what I had in my cupboard to make this pork, and the results were fantastic! I enjoy transforming an inexpensive cut of meat into something extraordinary .

—**SHELLY MITCHELL** GRESHAM, OR

PREP: 15 MIN. • **COOK:** 8 HOURS
MAKES: 12 SERVINGS

- 1 boneless pork shoulder butt roast (3 pounds)
- 2 garlic cloves, minced
- ½ teaspoon lemon-pepper seasoning
- 1 can (20 ounces) unsweetened crushed pineapple, undrained
- ½ cup orange juice
- 1 jar (16 ounces) mango salsa
- 24 whole wheat dinner rolls, split

1. Rub roast with garlic and lemon-pepper. Transfer to a 4-qt. slow cooker; top with pineapple and orange juice. Cook, covered, on low 8-10 hours or until meat is tender.

2. Remove roast; cool slightly. Skim fat from cooking juices. Shred pork with two forks. Return pork and cooking juices to slow cooker. Stir in salsa; heat through. Serve with rolls.

PER SERVING *422 cal., 15 g fat (5 g sat. fat), 67 mg chol., 674 mg sodium, 47 g carb., 6 g fiber, 26 g pro.* **Diabetic Exchanges:** *3 medium-fat meat, 2 starch, 1 fruit.*

Lime-Chipotle Carnitas Tostadas C

Here's a fabulous party recipe! Set out various toppings and garnishes so guests can custom-make their own tostadas with the lime-kissed shredded pork.

—**JAN VALDEZ** CHICAGO, IL

PREP: 20 MIN. • **COOK:** 8 HOURS
MAKES: 16 SERVINGS

- ½ cup chicken broth
- 4 teaspoons ground chipotle pepper
- 4 teaspoons ground cumin
- 1 teaspoon salt
- 1 boneless pork shoulder roast (4 to 5 pounds), halved
- 1 large onion, peeled and halved
- 8 garlic cloves, peeled
- 1 to 2 limes, halved
- 16 tostada shells
   Optional toppings: refried beans, salsa, sour cream, lettuce, avocado, queso fresco and cilantro
   Lime wedges

1. Add broth to a 5-qt. slow cooker. Mix seasonings; rub over all sides of pork. Place in slow cooker. Add onion and garlic cloves. Cook, covered, on low 8-10 hours or until meat is tender.

2. Remove pork; cool slightly. Strain cooking juices, reserving garlic; discard onion. Skim fat from cooking juices. Mash garlic with a fork. Shred pork with two forks.

3. Return cooking juices, garlic and pork to slow cooker. Squeeze lime juice over pork; stir to combine. Layer tostada shells with pork mixture and toppings. Serve with lime wedges.

PER SERVING *269 cal., 15 g fat (5 g sat. fat), 76 mg chol., 279 mg sodium, 9 g carb., 1 g fiber, 23 g pro.* **Diabetic Exchanges:** *3 medium-fat meat, ½ starch.*

top tip Pork Shoulder

This flavorful cut has plenty of fatty marbling throughout. The meat needs a long cooking time to become tender, making it ideal for the slow cooker.

TROPICAL PULLED PORK SLIDERS

LIME-CHIPOTLE CARNITAS TOSTADAS

Italian Sausage and Vegetables

This complete meal-in-a-pot is both healthy and delicious. It's wonderful served with a slice of hot garlic bread. I found the recipe in a magazine and made just a few adjustments to suit myself. Enjoy!

—**GINNY STUBY** ALTOONA, PA

PREP: 20 MIN. • **COOK:** 5½ HOURS • **MAKES:** 6 SERVINGS

- 1¼ pounds sweet or hot Italian turkey sausage links
- 1 can (28 ounces) diced tomatoes, undrained
- 2 medium potatoes, cut into 1-inch pieces
- 4 small zucchini, cut into 1-inch slices
- 1 medium onion, cut into wedges
- ½ teaspoon garlic powder
- ¼ teaspoon crushed red pepper flakes
- ¼ teaspoon dried oregano
- ¼ teaspoon dried basil
- 1 tablespoon dry bread crumbs
- ¾ cup shredded pepper jack cheese

1. In a nonstick skillet, brown sausages over medium heat. Place in a 5-qt. slow cooker. Add vegetables and seasonings. Cover and cook on low for 5½ to 6½ hours or until a thermometer reads 165°.

2. Remove sausages and cut into 1-in. pieces; return to slow cooker. Stir in bread crumbs. Serve in bowls; sprinkle with cheese.

PER SERVING *304 cal., 13 g fat (4 g sat. fat), 71 mg chol., 838 mg sodium, 26 g carb., 5 g fiber, 22 g pro.*

CHICKEN CACCIATORE

Chicken Cacciatore C

My husband and I milk 125 cows. There are days when there's just no time left for cooking! It's really nice to be able to come into the house at night and smell this wonderful dinner simmering.

—**AGGIE ARNOLD-NORMAN** LIBERTY, PA

PREP: 15 MIN. • **COOK:** 6 HOURS • **MAKES:** 6 SERVINGS

- 2 medium onions, thinly sliced
- 1 broiler/fryer chicken (3 to 4 pounds), cut up and skin removed
- 2 garlic cloves, minced
- 1 to 2 teaspoons dried oregano
- 1 teaspoon salt
- ½ teaspoon dried basil
- ¼ teaspoon pepper
- 1 bay leaf
- 1 can (14½ ounces) diced tomatoes, undrained
- 1 can (8 ounces) tomato sauce
- 1 can (4 ounces) mushroom stems and pieces, drained, or 1 cup sliced fresh mushrooms
- ¼ cup white wine or water
  Hot cooked pasta

1. Place onions in a 5-qt. slow cooker. Add the chicken, seasonings, tomatoes, tomato sauce, mushrooms and wine.

2. Cover and cook on low for 6-8 hours or until chicken is tender. Discard bay leaf. Serve chicken and sauce over pasta.

PER SERVING *207 cal., 6 g fat (2 g sat. fat), 73 mg chol., 787 mg sodium, 11 g carb., 3 g fiber, 27 g pro.* **Diabetic Exchanges:** *4 lean meat, 2 vegetable.*

ITALIAN SAUSAGE AND VEGETABLES

Fiesta Beef Bowls

This easy entree will knock your socks off. Zesty ingredients turn round steak, beans and rice into a phenomenal meal.

—**DEBORAH LINN** VALDEZ, AK

PREP: 25 MIN. • **COOK:** 8½ HOURS • **MAKES:** 6 SERVINGS

- 1½ **pounds boneless beef top round steak**
- 1 **can (10 ounces) diced tomatoes and green chilies**
- 1 **medium onion, chopped**
- 2 **garlic cloves, minced**
- 1 **teaspoon dried oregano**
- 1 **teaspoon chili powder**
- 1 **teaspoon ground cumin**
- ¼ **teaspoon salt**
- ¼ **teaspoon pepper**
- 2 **cans (15 ounces each) pinto beans, rinsed and drained**
- 3 **cups hot cooked rice**
- ½ **cup shredded cheddar cheese**
- 6 **tablespoons sliced ripe olives**
- 6 **tablespoons thinly sliced green onions**
- 6 **tablespoons guacamole**

1. Place round steak in a 3-qt. slow cooker. In a small bowl, combine the tomatoes, onion, garlic and seasonings; pour over steak. Cover and cook on low for 8-9 hours or until meat is tender.

2. Remove meat from slow cooker. Add beans to tomato mixture. Cover and cook on high for 30 minutes or until beans are heated through. When cool enough to handle, slice meat. In individual bowls, layer the rice, meat and bean mixture. Top with cheese, olives, onions and guacamole.

PER SERVING *460 cal., 11 g fat (4 g sat. fat), 74 mg chol., 720 mg sodium, 52 g carb., 9 g fiber, 38 g pro.*

CAROLINA-STYLE VINEGAR BBQ CHICKEN

Carolina-Style Vinegar BBQ Chicken F C

I live in Georgia, but I appreciate the tangy, sweet and slightly spicy taste of Carolina vinegar chicken. I make my version in the slow cooker, and when you walk in the door after being gone all day, the tempting aroma will stoke your appetite.

—**RAMONA PARRIS** ACWORTH, GA

PREP: 10 MIN. • **COOK:** 4 HOURS • **MAKES:** 6 SERVINGS

- 2 **cups water**
- 1 **cup white vinegar**
- ¼ **cup sugar**
- 1 **tablespoon reduced-sodium chicken base**
- 1 **teaspoon crushed red pepper flakes**
- ¾ **teaspoon salt**
- 1½ **pounds boneless skinless chicken breasts**
- 6 **whole wheat hamburger buns, split, optional**

1. In a small bowl, mix the first six ingredients. Place chicken in a 3-qt. slow cooker; add vinegar mixture. Cook, covered, on low 4-5 hours or until chicken is tender.

2. Remove chicken; cool slightly. Reserve 1 cup cooking juices; discard remaining juices. Shred chicken with two forks. Return meat and reserved cooking juices to slow cooker; heat through. If desired, serve chicken mixture on buns.

NOTE *Look for chicken base near the broth and bouillon.*
PER SERVING *134 cal., 3 g fat (1 g sat. fat), 63 mg chol., 228 mg sodium, 3 g carb., trace fiber, 23 g pro.* **Diabetic Exchange:** *3 lean meat.*

FIESTA BEEF BOWLS

110

113

117

Beef Entrees

❝It's amazing what a little coffee and cocoa can do to add bold flavor and richness to your steaks. This simple recipe is one you'll remember the next time you want to treat the family.❞

—**GINA MYERS** SPOKANE, WA
about her recipe, Cocoa-Crusted Beef Tenderloin, on page 112

GRILLED FLANK STEAK

Sirloin in Wine Sauce C

This family-favorite recipe is an easy, welcome option for company, too. Coated in a hearty mushroom-wine sauce, the tender sirloin is fantastic over pasta.

—BARBARA KAMM WILMINGTON, DE

START TO FINISH: 30 MIN.
MAKES: 4 SERVINGS

- 2 tablespoons all-purpose flour
- ⅛ teaspoon ground mustard
- 1 pound beef top sirloin steak, thinly sliced
- 2 tablespoons butter
- 1 can (10½ ounces) condensed beef consomme, undiluted
- ½ cup dry red wine or beef broth
- 1 jar (4½ ounces) sliced mushrooms, drained
- ¼ cup chopped green onions
- 1 teaspoon Worcestershire sauce
  Hot cooked linguine

1. In a large resealable plastic bag, combine flour and mustard. Add beef, a few pieces at a time, and shake to coat. In a large skillet, brown the beef in butter.
2. Add consomme and wine. Stir in the mushrooms, onions and Worcestershire sauce. Bring to a boil. Reduce heat; simmer, uncovered, for 10-15 minutes or until sauce is thickened. Serve with linguine.
PER SERVING *258 cal., 10 g fat (5 g sat. fat), 61 mg chol., 748 mg sodium, 7 g carb., 1 g fiber, 28 g pro.* **Diabetic Exchanges:** *3 lean meat, 1½ fat, ½ starch.*

Grilled Flank Steak C

The marinade for this steak requires only four ingredients, but that's not why it will be your new favorite dinner. The flavors are spot-on, and the meat turns out fork-tender every time. If you don't have a grill, you can easily broil the steaks instead.

—HEATHER AHRENS COLUMBUS, OH

PREP: 10 MIN. + MARINATING
COOK: 20 MIN.
MAKES: 6 SERVINGS

- 1 cup reduced-sodium soy sauce
- ¼ cup lemon juice
- ¼ cup honey
- 6 garlic cloves, minced
- 1 beef flank steak (1½ pounds)

1. In a large resealable plastic bag, combine the soy sauce, lemon juice, honey and garlic; add steak. Seal bag and turn to coat; refrigerate for 6-8 hours.

2. Drain and discard marinade. Broil steak 4-6 in. from the heat or grill over medium heat for 8-10 minutes on each side or until meat reaches desired doneness (for medium-rare, a thermometer should read 145°; medium, 160°; well-done, 170°). Thinly slice steak across the grain.
PER SERVING *186 cal., 8 g fat (4 g sat. fat), 54 mg chol., 471 mg sodium, 4 g carb., trace fiber, 23 g pro.* **Diabetic Exchange:** *3 lean meat.*

top tip **Measuring Honey**

For easy cleanup, spritz the measuring cup with cooking spray before measuring sticky ingredients like honey.

SIRLOIN IN WINE SAUCE

PEPPERED FILETS WITH TOMATO-MUSHROOM SALSA

Peppered Filets with Tomato-Mushroom Salsa **C**

The secret to these marvelous filets is in the salsa. It's full of fresh veggies and seasonings that bring a true taste of summer at any time of the year.

—**ANN HILLMEYER** SANDIA PARK, NM

PREP: 30 MIN. • **COOK:** 15 MIN.
MAKES: 6 SERVINGS

- 6 plum tomatoes, seeded and chopped
- 1 cup chopped fresh mushrooms
- ¼ cup minced fresh Italian parsley
- 2 tablespoons finely chopped shallot
- 2 teaspoons minced garlic, divided
- 5 teaspoons olive oil, divided
- 1 tablespoon lime juice
- ½ teaspoon salt
- ¼ teaspoon pepper
- 6 beef tenderloin steaks (4 ounces each)
- 2 teaspoons lemon-pepper seasoning
- ⅓ cup balsamic vinegar
- ¼ cup beef broth
- 4 teaspoons butter
- 6 lime slices

1. For salsa, in a small bowl, combine the tomatoes, mushrooms, parsley, shallot, 1 teaspoon garlic, 3 teaspoons oil, lime juice, salt and pepper; set aside.

2. Sprinkle steaks with lemon-pepper. In a large skillet, cook steaks in remaining oil for 4-5 minutes on each side or until meat reaches desired doneness (for medium-rare, a thermometer should read 145°; medium, 160°; well-done, 170°). Remove and keep warm.

3. Combine the vinegar, broth and remaining garlic; add to pan, stirring to loosen browned bits. Cook until liquid is reduced by half, about 2-3 minutes. Stir in butter.

4. Spoon sauce over steaks. Serve with salsa. Garnish with lime slices.
PER SERVING *251 cal., 13 g fat (5 g sat. fat), 56 mg chol., 414 mg sodium, 7 g carb., 1 g fiber, 26 g pro.* **Diabetic Exchanges:** *3 lean meat, 1½ fat, ½ starch.*

Chili Beef Pasta

Right after I got married, my aunt gave me her recipe for skillet spaghetti and told me it was ideal for a quick weeknight meal. Over the years, I've tinkered with the ingredients and played with the seasonings to make it a healthier dish that my family truly loves.

—**KRISTEN KILLIAN** DEPEW, NY

START TO FINISH: 30 MIN.
MAKES: 6 SERVINGS

- 1 pound lean ground beef (90% lean)
- 2 tablespoons dried minced onion
- 2 teaspoons dried oregano
- 2 teaspoons chili powder
- ½ teaspoon garlic powder
- ⅛ teaspoon salt
- 3 cups tomato juice
- 2 cups water
- 1 can (6 ounces) tomato paste
- 1 teaspoon sugar
- 8 ounces uncooked whole wheat spiral pasta
  Chopped tomatoes and minced fresh oregano, optional

1. In a Dutch oven, cook beef over medium heat 6-8 minutes or until no longer pink, breaking into crumbles; drain. Stir in seasonings.

2. Add tomato juice, water, tomato paste and sugar to pan; bring to a boil. Stir in pasta. Reduce heat; simmer, covered, 20-22 minutes or until pasta is tender, stirring occasionally. If desired, top with tomatoes and fresh oregano.
PER SERVING *319 cal., 7 g fat (2 g sat. fat), 47 mg chol., 442 mg sodium, 41 g carb., 6 g fiber, 24 g pro.* **Diabetic Exchanges:** *3 lean meat, 2 starch, 1 vegetable.*

CHILI BEEF PASTA

Mexican Stuffed Peppers

This nutritious yet economical summer meal makes the most of my homegrown peppers. I like to top it with sour cream and serve it alongside chips and salsa, but it's wonderful on its own, too.
—**KIM COLEMAN** COLUMBIA, SC

PREP: 25 MIN. • **BAKE:** 30 MIN. • **MAKES:** 8 SERVINGS

- 8 **medium green peppers**
- 1 **pound lean ground beef (90% lean)**
- 1 **can (14½ ounces) diced tomatoes and green chilies, undrained**
- 1½ **cups water**
- 1 **envelope (5.4 ounces) Mexican-style rice and pasta mix**
- 2 **cups (8 ounces) shredded Mexican cheese blend**

1. Preheat oven to 375°. Cut tops off peppers and remove seeds. In a Dutch oven, cook peppers in boiling water 3-5 minutes. Drain and rinse in cold water; set aside.

2. In a large skillet, cook beef over medium heat until no longer pink; drain. Add diced tomatoes, water and pasta mix. Bring to a boil. Reduce heat; cover and simmer 6-8 minutes or until liquid is absorbed.

3. Place ⅓ cup meat mixture in each pepper; sprinkle each with 2 tablespoons cheese. Top with remaining rice mixture. Place in a greased 13x9-in. baking dish. Cover and bake 25 minutes. Sprinkle with remaining cheese; bake 5-10 minutes longer or until the cheese is melted and peppers are tender.

PER SERVING *301 cal., 14 g fat (8 g sat. fat), 61 mg chol., 797 mg sodium, 23 g carb., 3 g fiber, 20 g pro.*

MEXICAN STUFFED PEPPERS

BRAISED HANUKKAH BRISKET

Braised Hanukkah Brisket **C**

To make this recipe, my mother always used the most marbled brisket she could find so she'd get the most flavor. When she added carrots to the pan, she threw in some potatoes, too. The best thing about this dish is that it's even tastier the next day.
—**ELLEN RUZINSKY** YORKTOWN HEIGHTS, NY

PREP: 25 MIN. • **COOK:** 2¾ HOURS
MAKES: 12 SERVINGS (4 CUPS VEGETABLES)

- 2 **tablespoons canola oil**
- 1 **fresh beef brisket (4 to 5 pounds)**
- 3 **celery ribs, cut into 1-inch pieces**
- 3 **large carrots, cut into ¼-inch slices**
- 2 **large onions, sliced**
- 1 **pound medium fresh mushrooms**
- ¾ **cup cold water**
- ¾ **cup tomato sauce**
- 3 **tablespoons Worcestershire sauce**
- 1 **tablespoon prepared horseradish**

1. In a Dutch oven, heat oil over medium heat. Brown brisket on both sides. Remove from pan.

2. Add celery, carrots and onions to pan; cook and stir 4-6 minutes or until crisp-tender. Stir in remaining ingredients.

3. Return brisket to pan, fat side up. Bring mixture to a boil. Reduce heat; simmer, covered, 2½ to 3 hours or until meat is tender. Remove beef and vegetables; keep warm. Skim fat from pan juices. If desired, thicken juices.

4. Cut brisket diagonally across the grain into thin slices. Serve with vegetables and pan juices.

NOTE *This is a fresh beef brisket, not corned beef.*

PER SERVING *247 cal., 9 g fat (3 g sat. fat), 64 mg chol., 189 mg sodium, 8 g carb., 2 g fiber, 33 g pro.* **Diabetic Exchanges:** *4 lean meat, 1 vegetable, ½ fat.*

Gingered Beef and Asparagus Stir-Fry

A friend who owns a bed-and-breakfast in Maryland shared this recipe with me. It's a delicious and different way to cook asparagus. The zesty Asian flavors come through but aren't at all overpowering.

—SONJA BLOW NIXA, MO

PREP: 20 MIN. + MARINATING • **COOK:** 20 MIN. • **MAKES:** 4 SERVINGS

- 3 tablespoons reduced-sodium soy sauce, divided
- 1 tablespoon sherry
- ¼ teaspoon minced fresh gingerroot or dash ground ginger
- ½ pound beef flank steak, cut into thin strips
- 1 teaspoon cornstarch
- ½ cup beef broth
- 1½ teaspoons hoisin sauce
- ⅛ teaspoon sugar
- 2 tablespoons canola oil, divided
- 2 pounds fresh asparagus, cut into 1-inch lengths
- 1 garlic clove, minced
- 3 cups hot cooked rice

1. In a large resealable plastic bag, combine 2 tablespoons soy sauce, sherry and ginger; add beef. Seal bag and turn to coat; refrigerate 30 minutes.

2. In a small bowl, combine cornstarch, broth, hoisin sauce, sugar and remaining soy sauce until smooth; set aside.

3. In a large skillet or wok, stir-fry beef in 1 tablespoon oil until no longer pink. Remove and set aside. Stir-fry asparagus in remaining oil until crisp-tender. Add the garlic; cook 1 minute.

4. Stir cornstarch mixture and add to the pan. Bring to a boil; cook and stir 2 minutes or until thickened. Return beef to the pan; heat through. Serve with rice.

PER SERVING 347 cal., 12 g fat (2 g sat. fat), 27 mg chol., 645 mg sodium, 41 g carb., 2 g fiber, 18 g pro. **Diabetic Exchanges:** 2 starch, 2 fat, 1 lean meat, 1 vegetable.

GINGERED BEEF AND ASPARAGUS STIR-FRY

GRILLED SIRLOIN WITH CHILI-BEER BARBECUE SAUCE

Grilled Sirloin with Chili-Beer Barbecue Sauce C

We came up with this recipe as a tasty way to cook with beer, but the combination of seasonings in the sauce is what makes this recipe a standout.

—TASTE OF HOME TEST KITCHEN

PREP: 40 MIN. • **GRILL:** 20 MIN. • **MAKES:** 8 SERVINGS

- 1½ cups beer or nonalcoholic beer
- 1 small onion, chopped
- ¾ cup chili sauce
- 2 tablespoons soy sauce
- 1 tablespoon brown sugar
- 2 teaspoons chili powder
- 2 garlic cloves, minced
- ¼ teaspoon cayenne pepper
- ¼ teaspoon ground mustard
- ⅛ teaspoon ground cumin
- 2 beef top sirloin steaks (1½ pounds each)
- ½ teaspoon salt
- ½ teaspoon pepper

1. In a small saucepan, combine the first ten ingredients. Bring to a boil. Reduce heat; simmer, uncovered, for 25-30 minutes or until thickened. Set aside ¾ cup and keep warm.

2. Sprinkle steaks with salt and pepper. Grill steaks, covered, over medium heat or broil 4 in. from the heat for 9-13 minutes on each side or until meat reaches desired doneness (for medium-rare, a thermometer should read 145°; medium 160°; well-done 170°), basting occasionally with remaining sauce. Serve with reserved sauce.

PER SERVING 263 cal., 7 g fat (3 g sat. fat), 69 mg chol., 807 mg sodium, 10 g carb., trace fiber, 37 g pro.

Cocoa-Crusted Beef Tenderloin C

It's amazing what a little coffee and cocoa can do to add bold flavor and richness to your steaks. This simple recipe is one you'll remember the next time you want to treat the family.

—GINA MYERS SPOKANE, WA

START TO FINISH: 30 MIN.
MAKES: 4 SERVINGS

- 4 **beef tenderloin steaks (1½ inches thick and 6 ounces each)**
- ½ **teaspoon salt**
- ½ **teaspoon coarsely ground pepper**
- 3 **tablespoons baking cocoa**
- 3 **tablespoons finely ground coffee**

1. Preheat broiler. Sprinkle steaks with salt and pepper. In a shallow bowl, mix cocoa and coffee. Dip steaks in cocoa mixture to coat all sides; shake off excess.

2. Place steaks on a rack of a broiler pan. Broil 3-4 in. from heat for 9-11 minutes on each side or until the meat reaches desired doneness (for medium-rare, a thermometer should read 145°; medium, 160°; well-done, 170°).

PER SERVING *252 cal., 10 g fat (4 g sat. fat), 75 mg chol., 296 mg sodium, 1 g carb., trace fiber, 37 g pro.* **Diabetic Exchange:** *5 lean meat.*

SIZZLING BEEF KABOBS

Sizzling Beef Kabobs C

A mild soy sauce marinade lends an appealing flavor to these tender beef and veggie kabobs. With colorful chunks of yellow squash and bell peppers, they're perfect for parties!

—KATHY SPANG MANHEIM, PA

PREP: 20 MIN. + MARINATING
GRILL: 10 MIN. • **MAKES:** 8 SERVINGS

- ⅓ **cup canola oil**
- ¼ **cup soy sauce**
- 2 **tablespoons red wine vinegar**
- 2 **teaspoons garlic powder**
- 2 **pounds beef top sirloin steak, cut into 1-inch pieces**
- 2 **medium yellow summer squash, cut into ½-inch slices**
- 1 **large onion, cut into 1-inch chunks**
- 1 **large green pepper, cut into 1-inch pieces**
- 1 **large sweet red pepper, cut into 1-inch pieces**

1. In a large resealable plastic bag, combine the oil, soy sauce, vinegar and garlic powder; add beef. Seal bag and turn to coat; refrigerate for at least 1 hour.

2. Drain and discard marinade. On eight metal or soaked wooden skewers, alternately thread beef and vegetables. Grill, covered, over medium-high heat or broil 4-6 in. from the heat for 8-10 minutes or until meat reaches desired doneness, turning kabobs occasionally.

PER SERVING *227 cal., 12 g fat (3 g sat. fat), 63 mg chol., 326 mg sodium, 6 g carb., 2 g fiber, 23 g pro.* **Diabetic Exchanges:** *3 lean meat, 1 vegetable, 1 fat.*

COCOA-CRUSTED BEEF TENDERLOIN

Beef & Spinach Lo Mein

I discovered this dish at an international luncheon, and it became an instant favorite. It really satisfies.

—DENISE PATTERSON BAINBRIDGE, OH

START TO FINISH: 30 MIN.
MAKES: 5 SERVINGS

- ¼ cup hoisin sauce
- 2 tablespoons soy sauce
- 1 tablespoon water
- 2 teaspoons sesame oil
- 2 garlic cloves, minced
- ¼ teaspoon crushed red pepper flakes
- 1 pound beef top round steak, thinly sliced
- 6 ounces uncooked spaghetti
- 4 teaspoons canola oil, divided
- 1 can (8 ounces) sliced water chestnuts, drained
- 2 green onions, sliced
- 1 package (10 ounces) fresh spinach, coarsely chopped
- 1 red chili pepper, seeded and thinly sliced

1. In a small bowl, mix the first six ingredients. Remove ¼ cup mixture to a large bowl; add beef and toss to coat. Let stand 10 minutes.
2. Cook spaghetti according to package directions. Meanwhile, in a large skillet, heat 1½ teaspoons canola oil. Add half of the beef mixture; stir-fry 1-2 minutes or until no longer pink. Remove from pan. Repeat with an additional 1½ teaspoons oil and remaining beef mixture.
3. Stir-fry water chestnuts and green onions in remaining canola oil for 30 seconds. Add spinach and remaining hoisin mixture; cook until spinach is wilted. Return beef to pan; heat through.
4. Drain spaghetti; add to the beef mixture and toss to combine. Sprinkle with chili pepper.

NOTE *Wear disposable gloves when cutting hot peppers; the oils can burn skin. Avoid touching your face.*

PER SERVING *363 cal., 10 g fat (2 g sat. fat), 51 mg chol., 652 mg sodium, 40 g carb., 4 g fiber, 28 g pro.* **Diabetic Exchanges:** *3 lean meat, 2 vegetable, 1½ starch, 1 fat.*

OLD-FASHIONED SWISS STEAK

Old-Fashioned Swiss Steak

My husband and I have enjoyed this recipe for years. The comforting sauce is wonderful, and the dish always brings back memories.

—VERA KLEIBER RALEIGH, NC

PREP: 20 MIN. • **BAKE:** 1½ HOURS
MAKES: 4 SERVINGS

- 2 tablespoons all-purpose flour
- ½ to 1 teaspoon salt
- ¼ teaspoon pepper
- 1½ pounds beef top round steak
- 2 tablespoons canola oil
- 2 medium onions, chopped
- 2 cans (5½ ounces each) tomato juice
- 1 cup diced tomatoes
- 4 teaspoons lemon juice
- 4 teaspoons Worcestershire sauce
- 2 to 3 teaspoons packed brown sugar
- 1 teaspoon prepared mustard

1. In a large resealable plastic bag, combine the flour, salt and pepper. Cut steak into four pieces. Add beef to bag, a few pieces at a time, and shake to coat. Remove meat from bag and pound with a mallet to tenderize.
2. In a large skillet, brown meat in oil on both sides. Place in a shallow 2-qt. baking dish coated with cooking spray.
3. In the same skillet, saute onions in drippings until tender. Stir in the remaining ingredients. Pour over meat. Cover and bake at 350° for 1½ hours or until tender.

PER SERVING *359 cal., 12 g fat (2 g sat. fat), 96 mg chol., 721 mg sodium, 20 g carb., 3 g fiber, 41 g pro.* **Diabetic Exchanges:** *5 lean meat, 2 vegetable, 1½ fat, ½ starch.*

BEEF & SPINACH LO MEIN

Not your average burgers, these Middle Eastern patties are seasoned with fresh herbs and warm spices such as cinnamon, pepper and nutmeg. Serving them with tzatziki sauce is optional, but you won't regret it if you do. —ANNE HENRY TORONTO, ON

JUICY & DELICIOUS MIXED SPICE BURGERS

Juicy & Delicious Mixed Spice Burgers c

START TO FINISH: 30 MIN.
MAKES: 6 SERVINGS

- 1 medium onion, finely chopped
- 3 tablespoons minced fresh parsley
- 2 tablespoons minced fresh mint
- 1 garlic clove, minced
- ¾ teaspoon ground allspice
- ¾ teaspoon pepper
- ½ teaspoon ground cinnamon
- ½ teaspoon salt
- ¼ teaspoon ground nutmeg
- 1½ pounds lean ground beef (90% lean)
  Refrigerated tzatziki sauce, optional

1. In a large bowl, combine the first nine ingredients. Add beef; mix lightly but thoroughly. Shape into six 4x2-in. oblong patties.

2. Grill patties, covered, over medium heat or broil 4 in. from the heat 4-6 minutes on each side or until a thermometer reads 160°. If desired, serve with sauce.

PER SERVING *192 cal., 9 g fat (4 g sat. fat), 71 mg chol., 259 mg sodium, 3 g carb., 1 g fiber, 22 g pro.* **Diabetic Exchange:** *3 lean meat.*

Chipotle-Rubbed Beef Tenderloin c

Go ahead, rub it in! Coating beef tenderloin with lively, peppery flavors gives it a south-of-the-border twist. Your family or dinner guests will be impressed.

—*TASTE OF HOME* TEST KITCHEN

PREP: 10 MIN. + CHILLING
BAKE: 45 MIN. + STANDING
MAKES: 8 SERVINGS

- 1 beef tenderloin roast (2 pounds)
- 2 teaspoons canola oil
- 3 teaspoons coarsely ground pepper
- 3 garlic cloves, minced
- 2½ teaspoons brown sugar
- 1 teaspoon salt
- 1 teaspoon ground coriander
- ½ teaspoon ground chipotle pepper
- ¼ teaspoon cayenne pepper

1. Brush beef with oil. Combine the remaining ingredients; rub over meat. Cover and refrigerate for 2 hours.

2. Place on a rack coated with cooking spray in a shallow roasting pan. Bake, uncovered, at 400° for 45-55 minutes or until meat reaches desired doneness (for medium-rare, a thermometer should read 145°; medium, 160°; well-done, 170°). Let stand for 10 minutes before slicing.

PER SERVING *195 cal., 9 g fat (3 g sat. fat), 71 mg chol., 351 mg sodium, 2 g carb., trace fiber, 24 g pro.* **Diabetic Exchange:** *3 lean meat.*

Zesty Orange Beef

I put this recipe together in the morning before I leave for work. In the evening, the pleasing aroma hits me as soon as I open the door. All I have to do is quickly cook some rice, and dinner is served.

—**DEBORAH PUETTE** LILBURN, GA

PREP: 15 MIN. • **COOK:** 5 HOURS
MAKES: 5 SERVINGS

- 1 beef top sirloin steak (1½ pounds), cut into ¼-inch strips
- 2½ cups sliced fresh shiitake mushrooms
- 1 medium onion, cut into wedges
- 3 dried hot chilies
- ¼ cup packed brown sugar
- ¼ cup orange juice
- ¼ cup reduced-sodium soy sauce
- 3 tablespoons cider vinegar
- 1 tablespoon cornstarch
- 1 tablespoon minced fresh gingerroot
- 1 tablespoon sesame oil
- 2 garlic cloves, minced
- 1¾ cups fresh snow peas
- 1 tablespoon grated orange peel
  Hot cooked rice

1. Place beef in a 4-qt. slow cooker. Add the mushrooms, onion, and chilies. In a small bowl, combine the brown sugar, orange juice, soy sauce, vinegar, cornstarch, ginger, oil and garlic. Pour over meat.

2. Cover and cook on high for 5-6 hours or until meat is tender, adding snow peas during the last 30 minutes of cooking. Stir in orange peel. Serve with rice.

PER SERVING *310 cal., 8 g fat (3 g sat. fat), 55 mg chol., 554 mg sodium, 24 g carb., 3 g fiber, 33 g pro.* **Diabetic Exchanges:** *4 lean meat, 1½ starch, ½ fat.*

ZESTY ORANGE BEEF

Moroccan Beef Kabobs S C

My grandmother's homemade marinade adds tang and tenderness to beef kabobs. Her unique blend of herbs, spices, lemon and ginger really punches up the flavor without adding lots of calories.

—JENNIFER SHAW DORCHESTER, MA

PREP: 25 MIN. + MARINATING
GRILL: 10 MIN. • **MAKES:** 8 SERVINGS

- 1 cup chopped fresh parsley
- 1 cup chopped fresh cilantro
- ¼ cup grated onion
- 3 tablespoons lemon juice
- 2 tablespoons olive oil
- 1 tablespoon ground cumin
- 1 tablespoon ground coriander
- 1 tablespoon paprika
- 1 tablespoon cider vinegar
- 1 tablespoon ketchup
- 2 garlic cloves, minced
- 1 teaspoon minced fresh gingerroot
- 1 teaspoon Thai red chili paste

  Dash salt and pepper
- 2 pounds beef top sirloin steak, cut into 1-inch pieces

1. In a large resealable plastic bag, combine the parsley, cilantro, onion, lemon juice, oil, cumin, coriander, paprika, vinegar, ketchup, garlic, ginger, chili paste, salt and pepper; add beef. Seal bag and turn to coat; refrigerate for 8 hours or overnight.

2. Drain and discard marinade. On eight metal or soaked wooden skewers, thread beef cubes. Moisten a paper towel with cooking oil; using long-handled tongs, lightly coat the grill rack.

3. Grill beef, covered, over medium-high heat or broil 4 in. from the heat for 8-12 minutes or until meat reaches desired doneness, turning occasionally.

PER SERVING *185 cal., 9 g fat (3 g sat. fat), 63 mg chol., 91 mg sodium, 3 g carb., 1 g fiber, 22 g pro.* **Diabetic Exchanges:** *3 lean meat, ½ fat.*

BLUE CHEESE FLANK STEAK

Blue Cheese Flank Steak C

While having a house built, we lived with my parents for a few months, where I sifted through my mother's recipe files. One of the many treasures I collected is this tasty steak.

—LAURIE NUDO THE WOODLANDS, TX

PREP: 10 MIN. + MARINATING
GRILL: 10 MIN. • **MAKES:** 4 SERVINGS

- 1 medium onion, sliced
- 1 garlic clove, peeled and sliced
- ⅓ cup water
- ⅓ cup white wine vinegar
- 2 tablespoons reduced-sodium soy sauce
- ½ teaspoon coarsely ground pepper
- 1 beef flank steak (1 pound)
- ½ cup crumbled blue cheese

1. In a large resealable plastic bag, combine the first six ingredients. Add the steak; seal bag and turn to coat. Refrigerate overnight, turning occasionally.

2. Drain and discard marinade. Moisten a paper towel with cooking oil; using long-handled tongs, lightly coat the grill rack.

3. Grill beef, covered, over medium-high heat for 5-7 minutes on each side or until meat reaches desired doneness (for medium-rare, a thermometer should read 145°; medium, 160°; well-done, 170°).

4. Let stand for 5 minutes; thinly slice across the grain. Sprinkle steak with blue cheese.

PER SERVING *239 cal., 12 g fat (6 g sat. fat), 65 mg chol., 367 mg sodium, 5 g carb., 1 g fiber, 26 g pro.* **Diabetic Exchanges:** *3 lean meat, 1 fat.*

MOROCCAN BEEF KABOBS

Beef Brisket Marinara C

Marinara sauce and tender meat are real comfort food, especially when served with mashed potatoes, rice or pasta.

—DONNA MARIE RYAN TOPSFIELD, MA

PREP: 10 MIN. • **COOK:** 3¾ HOURS
MAKES: 10 SERVINGS

- 1 fresh beef brisket (4 pounds)
- ½ teaspoon salt
- ¼ teaspoon pepper
- 2 tablespoons olive oil
- 2 celery ribs, finely chopped
- 1 medium carrot, finely chopped
- ½ cup dry red wine or beef broth
- 1 jar (24 ounces) marinara sauce

1. Sprinkle brisket with salt and pepper. In a large Dutch oven, heat oil over medium heat. Brown brisket on both sides. Remove from pan.
2. Add celery and carrot to same pan; cook and stir 2-3 minutes or until crisp-tender. Add wine; cook, stirring to loosen browned bits from pan. Stir in marinara sauce.
3. Return brisket to pan; bring to a boil. Reduce heat; simmer, covered, 3½ to 4 hours or until meat is tender.
4. Remove brisket from pan. Skim fat from sauce. Cut brisket diagonally across the grain into thin slices; serve with sauce.

PER SERVING *295 cal., 11 g fat (3 g sat. fat), 77 mg chol., 307 mg sodium, 9 g carb., 1 g fiber, 38 g pro.* **Diabetic Exchanges:** *5 lean meat, ½ starch, ½ fat.*

BEEF BRISKET MARINARA

SOUTHWEST STEAK & POTATOES

Southwest Steak & Potatoes

Bold seasonings give meat and potatoes a Southwestern twist. Feel free to adjust the heat factor by using more or less chili powder and cayenne.

—KENNY FISHER CIRCLEVILLE, OH

START TO FINISH: 30 MIN.
MAKES: 4 SERVINGS

- 4 medium Yukon Gold potatoes
- 2 teaspoons cider vinegar
- 1 teaspoon Worcestershire sauce
- 1 beef top round steak (1 inch thick and about 1½ pounds)
- 1 tablespoon brown sugar
- 1 tablespoon chili powder
- 1½ teaspoons ground cumin
- 1 teaspoon garlic powder
- 1 teaspoon salt, divided
- ⅛ teaspoon cayenne pepper
- ⅛ teaspoon pepper

1. Pierce potatoes; place on a microwave-safe plate. Microwave, uncovered, on high 4-5 minutes or until almost tender, turning once. Cool slightly.
2. Meanwhile, mix vinegar and Worcestershire sauce; brush over steak. Mix brown sugar, chili powder, cumin, garlic powder, ½ teaspoon salt and cayenne until blended; sprinkle over both sides of steak.
3. Cut potatoes into ½-in. slices. Sprinkle with pepper and remaining salt. Grill potatoes and steak, covered, over medium heat 12-17 minutes or until potatoes are tender and a thermometer inserted in beef reads 145° for medium-rare, turning occasionally.
4. Cut steak into thin slices. Serve with potatoes.

PER SERVING *360 cal., 6 g fat (2 g sat. fat), 96 mg chol., 681 mg sodium, 34 g carb., 3 g fiber, 41 g pro.* **Diabetic Exchanges:** *5 lean meat, 2 starch.*

124

131

132

Chicken Favorites

66 With two young boys who are constantly on the go, I'm always trying to simplify. This one-skillet dish is great when I have only half an hour to make dinner. *99*

—SARA RICHARDSON LITTLETON, CO
about her recipe, Rosemary Chicken with Spinach & Beans, on page 121

Bruschetta-Topped Chicken & Spaghetti

My family needs recipes that are lower in cholesterol. Whenever we have a craving for Italian food, this fuss-free but delicious main course really hits the spot.

—**SUSAN WHOLLEY** FAIRFIELD, CT

START TO FINISH: 30 MIN.
MAKES: 4 SERVINGS

- 8 **ounces uncooked whole wheat spaghetti**
- 4 **boneless skinless chicken breast halves (5 ounces each)**
- ½ **teaspoon pepper**
- 1 **cup prepared bruschetta topping**
- ⅓ **cup shredded Italian cheese blend**
- 2 **tablespoons grated Parmesan cheese**

1. Preheat broiler. Cook whole wheat spaghetti according to the package directions; drain. Pound the chicken breasts with a meat mallet to ½-in. thickness. Sprinkle with pepper. In a large nonstick skillet coated with cooking spray, cook the chicken over medium heat 5-6 minutes on each side or until no longer pink.

2. Transfer to an 8-in.-square baking pan. Spoon the bruschetta topping over the chicken; sprinkle with Italian cheese blend and Parmesan cheese. Broil 3-4 in. from the heat 5-6 minutes or until cheese is golden brown. Serve with spaghetti.

PER SERVING *431 cal., 10 g fat (4 g sat. fat), 87 mg chol., 641 mg sodium, 47 g carb., 8 g fiber, 40 g pro.* **Diabetic Exchanges:** *4 lean meat, 3 starch, ½ fat.*

Saucy BBQ Chicken Thighs c

Love classic barbecued chicken? Give it a makeover that fits your eating plan—and savor the flavor without the guilt! You're sure to enjoy the zippy taste.

—**SHARON FRITZ** MORRISTOWN, TN

PREP: 15 MIN. • **COOK:** 5 HOURS
MAKES: 6 SERVINGS

- 6 **boneless skinless chicken thighs (about 1½ pounds)**
- ½ **teaspoon poultry seasoning**
- 1 **medium onion, chopped**
- 1 **can (14½ ounces) diced tomatoes, undrained**
- 1 **can (8 ounces) tomato sauce**
- ½ **cup barbecue sauce**
- ¼ **cup orange juice**
- 1 **teaspoon garlic powder**
- ¾ **teaspoon dried oregano**
- ½ **teaspoon hot pepper sauce**
- ¼ **teaspoon pepper**
  Hot cooked brown rice, optional

1. Place the chicken thighs in a 3-qt. slow cooker; sprinkle with the poultry seasoning. Top with the onion and diced tomatoes. In a small bowl, mix tomato sauce, barbecue sauce, orange juice and seasonings; pour over top.

2. Cook, covered, on low 5-6 hours or until the chicken is tender. If desired, serve with rice.

FREEZE OPTION *Place the cooked chicken mixture in freezer containers. Cool and freeze. To use, partially thaw the chicken mixture in the refrigerator overnight. Microwave, covered, on high in a microwave-safe dish until heated through, gently stirring and adding a little water if necessary.*

PER SERVING *221 cal., 9 g fat (2 g sat. fat), 76 mg chol., 517 mg sodium, 12 g carb., 2 g fiber, 23 g pro.* **Diabetic Exchanges:** *3 lean meat, 2 starch.*

SAUCY BBQ CHICKEN THIGHS

BRUSCHETTA-TOPPED CHICKEN & SPAGHETTI

Saucy Peach-Balsamic Chicken

START TO FINISH: 30 MIN.
MAKES: 4 SERVINGS

- 4 **boneless skinless chicken breast halves (4 ounces each)**
- ½ **teaspoon salt**
- ¼ **teaspoon pepper**
- 2 **tablespoons butter**
- ¼ **cup reduced-sodium chicken broth**
- ¼ **cup sherry or additional reduced-sodium chicken broth**
- ⅓ **cup peach preserves**
- 2 **garlic cloves, thinly sliced**
- 2 **teaspoons minced fresh tarragon**
- 1 **tablespoon balsamic vinegar**

1. Sprinkle the chicken breast halves with salt and pepper. In a large skillet, brown the chicken on both sides in butter. Remove from the skillet and keep warm.

2. Add broth and sherry to skillet, stirring to loosen browned bits from the pan. Stir in preserves, garlic and tarragon. Bring to a boil. Reduce heat; simmer, uncovered, for 5 minutes, stirring occasionally. Stir in vinegar.

3. Return the chicken to the skillet; cover and cook over medium heat for 8-10 minutes or until a thermometer reads 165°.

PER SERVING *249 cal., 8 g fat (4 g sat. fat), 78 mg chol., 427 mg sodium, 19 g carb., trace fiber, 23 g pro.* **Diabetic Exchanges:** *3 lean meat, 1½ fat, 1 starch.*

ROSEMARY CHICKEN WITH SPINACH & BEANS

Rosemary Chicken with Spinach & Beans

With two young boys who are constantly on the go, I'm always trying to simplify. This one-skillet dish is great when I have only half an hour to make dinner.
—SARA RICHARDSON LITTLETON, CO

START TO FINISH: 30 MIN.
MAKES: 4 SERVINGS

- 1 **can (14½ ounces) stewed tomatoes**
- 4 **boneless skinless chicken breast halves (6 ounces each)**
- 2 **teaspoons dried rosemary, crushed**
- ½ **teaspoon salt**
- ½ **teaspoon pepper**
- 4 **teaspoons olive oil, divided**
- 1 **package (6 ounces) fresh baby spinach**
- 2 **garlic cloves, minced**
- 1 **can (15 ounces) white kidney or cannellini beans, rinsed and drained**

1. Drain tomatoes, reserving juice; coarsely chop tomatoes. Pound chicken with a meat mallet to ¼-in. thickness. Rub with rosemary, salt and pepper. In a large skillet, heat 2 teaspoons oil over medium heat. Add chicken; cook 5-6 minutes on each side or until no longer pink. Remove and keep warm.

2. In same pan, heat the remaining oil over medium-high heat. Add spinach and garlic; cook and stir 2-3 minutes or until spinach is wilted. Stir in beans, tomatoes and the reserved juice; heat through. Serve with chicken.

PER SERVING *348 cal., 9 g fat (2 g sat. fat), 94 mg chol., 729 mg sodium, 25 g carb., 6 g fiber, 41 g pro.* **Diabetic Exchanges:** *5 lean meat, 2 vegetable, 1 starch, 1 fat.*

I can throw this sweet and savory entree together in just 30 minutes. Add some rice and broccoli on the side for a healthy weekday meal that pleases everyone.
—TRISHA KRUSE EAGLE, ID

SAUCY PEACH-BALSAMIC CHICKEN

Chicken & Vegetable Kabobs C

My husband and I love to grill—especially veggies. These colorful five-ingredient kabobs taste as good as they look.

—**TINA OLES** NASHWAUK, MN

START TO FINISH: 30 MIN. • **MAKES:** 4 SERVINGS

- 1 **pound boneless skinless chicken breasts, cut into 1½ inch cubes**
- 1 **medium sweet red pepper, cut into 1½ inch pieces**
- 1 **medium zucchini, cut into 1½ inch pieces**
- 1 **medium red onion, cut into thick wedges**
- ⅔ **cup sun-dried tomato salad dressing, divided**

1. In a large bowl, combine the chicken and vegetables. Drizzle with ⅓ cup dressing and toss to coat. Alternately thread chicken and vegetables onto four metal or soaked wooden skewers.

2. Grill kabobs, covered, over medium heat or broil 4 in. from heat 8-10 minutes or until chicken is no longer pink, turning occasionally and basting with remaining dressing during the last 3 minutes.

PER SERVING *228 cal., 10 g fat (1 g sat. fat), 63 mg chol., 515 mg sodium, 11 g carb., 2 g fiber, 24 g pro. **Diabetic Exchanges:** 3 lean meat, 1 vegetable, 1 fat.*

Indian Baked Chicken

Cumin and turmeric give chicken thighs just the right amount of Indian flavor. Even picky eaters at the table will like it!

—**STEPHANIE KURIN** MUNCIE, IN

PREP: 15 MIN. • **BAKE:** 1 HOUR • **MAKES:** 6 SERVINGS

- 1 **pound small red potatoes, quartered**
- 4 **medium carrots, cut into 1-inch pieces**
- 1 **large onion, cut into 1-inch pieces**
- 6 **boneless skinless chicken thighs (about 1½ pounds)**
- 1 **can (14½ ounces) chicken broth**
- 1 **can (6 ounces) tomato paste**
- 2 **tablespoons olive oil**
- 1 **tablespoon ground turmeric**
- 1 **teaspoon chili powder**
- 1 **teaspoon ground cumin**
- ½ **teaspoon salt**
- ½ **teaspoon garlic powder**
- ½ **teaspoon pepper**

1. Place potatoes, carrots and onion in a greased 13x9x2-in. baking dish; add the chicken. In a small bowl, combine the remaining ingredients and pour over the top.

2. Cover and bake at 400° for 1 to 1¼ hours or until a meat thermometer inserted into the chicken reads 180° and the vegetables are tender.

PER SERVING *323 cal., 13 g fat (3 g sat. fat), 77 mg chol., 612 mg sodium, 25 g carb., 4 g fiber, 25 g pro. **Diabetic Exchanges:** 3 lean meat, 2 vegetable, 1 starch, 1 fat.*

Citrus-Marinated Chicken C

Here's a recipe that stars in many of our summertime menus. While there are a million ways to dress up poultry, I find myself turning to this juicy, zesty entree again and again.

—**DEBORAH GRETZINGER** GREEN BAY, WI

PREP: 10 MIN. + MARINATING • **GRILL:** 10 MIN. • **MAKES:** 6 SERVINGS

- ½ cup lemon juice
- ½ cup orange juice
- 6 garlic cloves, minced
- 2 tablespoons canola oil
- 1 teaspoon salt
- 1 teaspoon ground ginger
- 1 teaspoon dried tarragon
- ¼ teaspoon pepper
- 6 boneless skinless chicken breast halves (6 ounces each)

1. Combine the first eight ingredients in a large resealable plastic bag. Add the chicken; seal the bag and turn to coat. Refrigerate for at least 4 hours.

2. Drain and discard marinade. Grill chicken, covered, over medium heat or broil 4 in. from the heat for 5-7 minutes on each side or until a thermometer reads 170°.

PER SERVING *195 cal., 5 g fat (1 g sat. fat), 94 mg chol., 161 mg sodium, 1 g carb., trace fiber, 34 g pro.* **Diabetic Exchange:** *5 lean meat.*

Tangy Chicken & Peppers

I created my chicken-and-pepper dish during the workweek when I was short on time. A frozen stir-fry blend really speeds up the prep work. For a change of pace, replace the rice with noodles.

—**DONNA MCLEOD** BENTONVILLE, AR

START TO FINISH: 30 MIN. • **MAKES:** 6 SERVINGS

- 6 boneless skinless chicken breast halves (6 ounces each)
- ½ teaspoon salt
- ¼ teaspoon pepper
- 1 package (16 ounces) frozen pepper and onion stir-fry blend
- 1 jar (16 ounces) pineapple salsa
- 1 can (11 ounces) mandarin oranges, drained
- 4½ cups hot cooked brown rice or hot cooked rice

1. Sprinkle the chicken with salt and pepper. Heat a large nonstick skillet coated with cooking spray over medium heat. Brown chicken in batches; remove from pan.

2. In same pan, add stir-fry blend and salsa; bring to a boil, stirring occasionally. Return chicken to pan; reduce heat. Simmer, covered, 12-15 minutes or until a thermometer inserted into chicken reads 165°. Stir in the oranges; heat through. Serve with rice.

PER SERVING *422 cal., 5 g fat (1 g sat. fat), 94 mg chol., 519 mg sodium, 50 g carb., 6 g fiber, 39 g pro.*

Cherry-Chicken Lettuce Wraps

When I had a lot of sweet cherries, I used them in chicken lettuce wraps. My family asked for the same meal the next day!
—MELISSA BARLOW FRUIT HEIGHTS, UT

START TO FINISH: 25 MIN.
MAKES: 4 SERVINGS

- ¾ pound boneless skinless chicken breasts, cut into ¾-inch cubes
- 1 teaspoon ground ginger
- ¼ teaspoon salt
- ¼ teaspoon pepper
- 2 teaspoons olive oil
- 1½ cups shredded carrots
- 1¼ cups coarsely chopped pitted fresh sweet cherries
- 4 green onions, chopped
- ⅓ cup coarsely chopped almonds
- 2 tablespoons rice vinegar
- 2 tablespoons reduced-sodium teriyaki sauce
- 1 tablespoon honey
- 8 Bibb or Boston lettuce leaves

1. Sprinkle the chicken with ginger, salt and pepper. In a large nonstick skillet coated with cooking spray, heat the oil over medium-high heat. Add the chicken; cook and stir 3-5 minutes or until no longer pink.

2. Remove from heat. Stir in carrots, cherries, green onions and almonds. In a small bowl, mix the rice vinegar, teriyaki sauce and honey; stir into the chicken mixture. Divide among lettuce leaves; fold the lettuce over the filling.

PER SERVING *257 cal., 10 g fat (1 g sat. fat), 47 mg chol., 381 mg sodium, 22 g carb., 4 g fiber, 21 g pro.* **Diabetic Exchanges:** *3 lean meat, 1 vegetable, ½ fruit, ½ fat.*

Spinach Chicken Manicotti

This authentic-tasting Italian dish was a hit when I prepared it for my husband on our first Valentine's Day together.
—AMY LUCE DALLAS, TX

PREP: 1 HOUR • **BAKE:** 35 MIN.
MAKES: 6 SERVINGS

- 1 large onion, chopped
- 1 teaspoon olive oil
- 1 garlic clove, minced
- 2½ cups diced cooked chicken breast
- 1 package (10 ounces) frozen chopped spinach, thawed and squeezed dry
- ¾ cup diced fully cooked lean ham
- ¼ cup grated Parmesan cheese
- 2 egg whites
- ½ teaspoon dried basil
- ⅛ teaspoon pepper
   Dash ground nutmeg
- 12 uncooked manicotti shells

SAUCE
- ¾ cup all-purpose flour
- 3 cups reduced-sodium chicken broth
- 1 cup fat-free milk
- ¼ teaspoon salt
- ⅛ teaspoon ground nutmeg
- ⅛ teaspoon pepper
   Dash cayenne pepper
- ¼ cup grated Parmesan cheese

1. In a small skillet, saute onion in oil until tender. Add garlic; cook 1 minute longer. In a large bowl, combine the onion mixture, chicken, spinach, ham, cheese, egg whites, basil, pepper and nutmeg; set aside.

2. Cook shells according to package directions. Meanwhile, for the sauce, combine the flour and broth in a large saucepan until smooth; gradually stir in the milk, salt, nutmeg, pepper and cayenne. Bring to a boil over medium heat; cook and stir for 2 minutes or until thickened. Spoon 1 cup into the chicken mixture. Add the cheese to the remaining sauce.

3. Spread 1 cup cheese sauce into a 13x9x2-in. baking dish coated with cooking spray. Drain shells; stuff with chicken mixture. Arrange over sauce. Drizzle with remaining sauce. Cover and bake at 375° for 35-40 minutes or until bubbly and heated through.

PER SERVING *372 cal., 7 g fat (2 g sat. fat), 58 mg chol., 866 mg sodium, 43 g carb., 3 g fiber, 35 g pro.* **Diabetic Exchanges:** *4 lean meat, 2 starch, 2 vegetable, ½ fat.*

CHERRY-CHICKEN LETTUCE WRAPS

top tip Nutmeg

Nutmeg is the secret seasoning in many savory recipes. It's commonly used in white sauces, pastas and potato dishes. Be careful not to overdo it—a small amount of the spice goes a long way.

SPINACH CHICKEN MANICOTTI

ORANGE-SPICED CHICKEN

Orange-Spiced Chicken F

Love the orange chicken served at Chinese restaurants? Stay home and enjoy a terrific grilled version. It's bound to become your family's most-requested dinner.

—DEBRA STEVENS LUTZ, FL

PREP: 10 MIN. + MARINATING
GRILL: 10 MIN. • **MAKES:** 4 SERVINGS

- ½ cup thawed orange juice concentrate
- ¼ cup honey
- ¼ cup soy sauce
- 1 teaspoon Chinese five-spice powder
- ½ teaspoon garlic powder
- 4 boneless skinless chicken breast halves (5 ounces each)

1. In a small bowl, combine the first five ingredients. Pour ½ cup marinade into a large resealable plastic bag; add the chicken breasts. Seal the bag and turn to coat; refrigerate for 2 hours. Cover and refrigerate the remaining marinade.

2. Drain chicken and discard the marinade. Moisten a paper towel with cooking oil; using long-handled tongs, lightly coat the grill rack. Grill chicken, covered, over medium heat or broil 4 in. from the heat for 5-7 minutes on each side or until a thermometer reads 170°, basting frequently with reserved marinade.

PER SERVING *234 cal., 3 g fat (1 g sat. fat), 78 mg chol., 643 mg sodium, 19 g carb., trace fiber, 30 g pro.* **Diabetic Exchanges:** *4 lean meat, 1 starch, ½ fruit.*

Thai Chicken Peanut Noodles

START TO FINISH: 30 MIN.
MAKES: 6 SERVINGS

- ¼ cup creamy peanut butter
- ½ cup reduced-sodium chicken broth
- ¼ cup lemon juice
- ¼ cup reduced-sodium soy sauce
- 4 teaspoons Sriracha Asian hot chili sauce
- ¼ teaspoon crushed red pepper flakes
- 12 ounces uncooked multigrain spaghetti
- 1 pound lean ground chicken
- 1½ cups julienned carrots
- 1 medium sweet red pepper, chopped
- 1 garlic clove, minced
- ½ cup finely chopped unsalted peanuts
- 4 green onions, chopped

1. In a small bowl, whisk the first six ingredients until blended. Cook the multigrain spaghetti according to the package directions; drain.

2. Meanwhile, in a large skillet, cook the ground chicken, carrots, sweet red pepper and garlic over medium heat 5-6 minutes or until the chicken is no longer pink, breaking up the chicken into crumbles; drain.

3. Stir in the peanut butter mixture; bring to a boil. Reduce heat; simmer, uncovered, 3-5 minutes or until the sauce is slightly thickened. Serve with the spaghetti. Top with peanuts and green onions.

PER SERVING *475 cal., 17 g fat (3 g sat. fat), 54 mg chol., 711 mg sodium, 51 g carb., 7 g fiber, 33 g pro.*

My husband just can't get enough of the spicy Asian flavors in this lightened-up Thai classic. As soon as I get it cooking, he breaks out the chopsticks!

—JENNIFER FISHER AUSTIN, TX

THAI CHICKEN PEANUT NOODLES

PECAN-CRUSTED CHICKEN NUGGETS

Pecan-Crusted Chicken Nuggets C

When I was a kid, I was a big fan of chicken nuggets. This baked variation coated with nuts is healthier than the original.
—**HAILI CARROLL** VALENCIA, CA

START TO FINISH: 30 MIN.
MAKES: 6 SERVINGS

- 1½ cups cornflakes
- 1 tablespoon dried parsley flakes
- ½ teaspoon garlic powder
- ½ cup panko (Japanese) bread crumbs
- ½ cup finely chopped pecans
- 3 tablespoons 2% milk
- 1½ pounds boneless skinless chicken breasts, cut into 1-inch pieces
- ½ teaspoon salt
- ¼ teaspoon pepper
  Cooking spray

1. Preheat oven to 400°. Place the cornflakes, parsley and garlic powder in a blender; cover and pulse until finely ground. Transfer to a shallow bowl; stir in panko bread crumbs and pecans. Place milk in another shallow bowl. Sprinkle chicken with salt and pepper; dip in milk, then roll in crumb mixture to coat.
2. Place on a greased baking sheet; spritz the chicken with cooking spray. Bake 12-16 minutes or until chicken is no longer pink, turning once halfway through cooking.
PER SERVING *206 cal., 9 g fat (1 g sat. fat), 63 mg chol., 290 mg sodium, 6 g carb., 1 g fiber, 24 g pro. Diabetic Exchanges: 3 lean meat, 1 fat, ½ starch.*

Mango-Pineapple Chicken Tacos

I lived in the Caribbean as a child. Featuring the tangy burst of fresh tropical fruits, my slow-cooked taco filling always brings back special memories of that time.
—**LISSA NELSON** PROVO, UT

PREP: 25 MIN. • **COOK:** 5 HOURS
MAKES: 16 SERVINGS

- 2 medium mangoes, peeled and chopped
- 1½ cups cubed fresh pineapple or canned pineapple chunks, drained
- 2 medium tomatoes, chopped
- 1 medium red onion, finely chopped
- 2 small Anaheim peppers, seeded and chopped
- 2 green onions, finely chopped
- 1 tablespoon lime juice
- 1 teaspoon sugar
- 4 pounds bone-in chicken breast halves, skin removed
- 3 teaspoons salt
- ¼ cup packed brown sugar
- 32 taco shells, warmed
- ¼ cup minced fresh cilantro

1. In a large bowl, combine the first eight ingredients. Place the chicken in a 6-qt. slow cooker; sprinkle with salt and brown sugar. Top with the mango mixture. Cover and cook on low for 5-6 hours or until chicken is tender.
2. Remove the chicken; cool slightly. Strain cooking juices, reserving mango mixture and ½ cup juices. Discard the remaining juices. When cool enough to handle, remove chicken from bones; discard bones.
3. Shred the chicken with two forks. Return chicken and reserved mango mixture and cooking juices to slow cooker; heat through. Serve in taco shells; sprinkle with cilantro.
FREEZE OPTION *Freeze the cooled chicken mixture in freezer containers. To use, partially thaw in refrigerator overnight. Heat through in a saucepan, stirring occasionally and adding a little broth if necessary.*
PER SERVING *246 cal., 7 g fat (2 g sat. fat), 51 mg chol., 582 mg sodium, 25 g carb., 2 g fiber, 21 g pro. Diabetic Exchanges: 3 lean meat, 1½ starch.*

MANGO-PINEAPPLE CHICKEN TACOS

Coconut-Lime Chicken

Sweet coconut and tongue-tingling lime come together for an entree that takes you to the tropics. I serve fragrant jasmine rice as an exotic accompaniment.
—**TRISHA KRUSE** EAGLE, ID

PREP: 20 MIN. • **COOK:** 15 MIN.
MAKES: 4 SERVINGS

- 1 cup uncooked jasmine rice
- 1 cup water
- ¾ cup light coconut milk
- ½ teaspoon sugar
- ½ teaspoon salt
- ¼ cup lime juice
- 2 tablespoons reduced-sodium soy sauce
- 1 tablespoon grated lime peel
- 1 tablespoon minced fresh gingerroot
- 1 tablespoon rice vinegar
- 1 tablespoon honey
- 1 pound boneless skinless chicken breasts, cut into 1-inch cubes
- 2 teaspoons canola oil
- 1 teaspoon sesame oil
- ¼ cup flaked coconut
- 1 tablespoon minced fresh cilantro

1. In a large saucepan, bring the rice, water, coconut milk, sugar and salt to a boil. Reduce heat; cover and simmer for 15-20 minutes or until the liquid is absorbed and the rice is tender.

2. Meanwhile, in a small bowl, combine lime juice, soy sauce, lime peel, ginger, vinegar and honey; set aside. In a large skillet, saute chicken in the canola and sesame oils until no longer pink. Add lime mixture to the pan. Bring to a boil; cook and stir for 2 minutes. Sprinkle with coconut and cilantro. Fluff the rice with a fork and serve with chicken mixture.
PER SERVING *415 cal., 11 g fat (5 g sat. fat), 63 mg chol., 671 mg sodium, 48 g carb., 1 g fiber, 27 g pro.*

Savory Braised Chicken with Vegetables

Pair this hearty dish with a fresh baguette. You'll want to use it to soak up every last drop of the savory broth!
—**MICHELLE COLLINS** LAKE ORION, MI

PREP: 15 MIN. • **COOK:** 40 MIN.
MAKES: 6 SERVINGS

- ½ cup seasoned bread crumbs
- 6 boneless skinless chicken breast halves (4 ounces each)
- 2 tablespoons olive oil
- 1 can (14½ ounces) beef broth
- 2 tablespoons tomato paste
- 1 teaspoon poultry seasoning
- ½ teaspoon salt
- ½ teaspoon pepper
- 1 pound fresh baby carrots
- 1 pound sliced fresh mushrooms
- 2 medium zucchini, sliced
  Sliced French bread baguette, optional

1. Place the bread crumbs in a shallow bowl. Dip the chicken in bread crumbs to coat both sides; shake off excess.
2. In a Dutch oven, heat the oil over medium heat. Add chicken in batches; cook 2-4 minutes on each side or until browned. Remove chicken from pan.
3. Add the beef broth, tomato paste and seasonings to the same pan; cook over medium-high heat, stirring to loosen the browned bits from the pan. Add vegetables and chicken; bring to a boil. Reduce heat; simmer, covered, 25-30 minutes or until vegetables are tender and a thermometer inserted into chicken reads 165°. If desired, serve with baguette.
PER SERVING *247 cal., 8 g fat (1 g sat. fat), 63 mg chol., 703 mg sodium, 16 g carb., 3 g fiber, 28 g pro.* **Diabetic Exchanges:** *3 lean meat, 2 vegetable, 1 fat, ½ starch.*

SAVORY BRAISED CHICKEN WITH VEGETABLES

COCONUT-LIME CHICKEN

Peanut Chicken Stir-Fry

Here's a comforting stir-fry with a hint of heat from crushed red pepper.

—LISA ERICKSON RIPON, WI

START TO FINISH: 30 MIN.
MAKES: 6 SERVINGS

- 8 **ounces uncooked thick rice noodles**
- ⅓ **cup water**
- ¼ **cup reduced-sodium soy sauce**
- ¼ **cup peanut butter**
- 4½ **teaspoons brown sugar**
- 1 **tablespoon lemon juice**
- 2 **garlic cloves, minced**
- ½ **teaspoon crushed red pepper flakes**
- 1 **pound boneless skinless chicken breasts, cut into ½-inch strips**
- 2 **tablespoons canola oil, divided**
- 1 **bunch broccoli, cut into florets**
- ½ **cup shredded carrot**

1. Cook the rice noodles according to the package directions. Meanwhile, in a small bowl, combine the water, soy sauce, peanut butter, brown sugar, lemon juice, garlic and crushed red pepper flakes; set aside.

2. In a large skillet or wok, stir-fry the chicken strips in 1 tablespoon oil until chicken strips are no longer pink. Remove and keep warm. Stir-fry the broccoli and carrot in the remaining oil for 4-6 minutes or until vegetables are crisp-tender.

3. Stir the sauce mixture; add the sauce and chicken to skillet. Return the chicken to skillet. Drain noodles; toss with chicken mixture.

PER SERVING *361 cal., 13 g fat (2 g sat. fat), 42 mg chol., 525 mg sodium, 40 g carb., 5 g fiber, 24 g pro.* **Diabetic Exchanges:** *2 starch, 2 lean meat, 2 fat, 1 vegetable.*

 Did you know?

It's safe to freeze leftover buttermilk, but make sure to use it within 3 months for the best flavor. Instead of buying buttermilk, you can combine 1 tablespoon of vinegar or lemon juice with enough milk to measure 1 cup. Stir and let stand 5 minutes before using.

Popcorn & Pretzel Chicken Tenders F

My daughter, Alivia, thought of coating chicken tenders with two of our favorite movie-watching snacks: popcorn and pretzels. Crunchy and crispy, these strips bring even more raves when I include the creamy mustard sauce for dipping.

—SUZANNE CLARK PHOENIX, AZ

PREP: 25 MIN. + MARINATING
BAKE: 20 MIN.
MAKES: 6 SERVINGS (2 TBSP. SAUCE EACH)

- 1½ **pounds chicken tenderloins**
- 1 **cup buttermilk**
- 2 **teaspoons garlic powder**
- 1 **teaspoon salt**
- 1 **teaspoon onion powder**
- ½ **teaspoon pepper**
- ¾ **cup fat-free plain Greek yogurt**
- ¼ **cup peach preserves**
- 1 **tablespoon prepared mustard**
- 4 **cups miniature pretzels, crushed**
- 2 **cups air-popped popcorn, crushed**
  Cooking spray

1. In a large bowl, combine the first six ingredients; toss to coat. Refrigerate, covered, at least 30 minutes. In a small bowl, mix the yogurt, peach preserves and mustard; refrigerate until serving.

2. Preheat oven to 400°. In a large shallow dish, combine the crushed pretzels and popcorn. Remove the chicken from marinade, discarding marinade. Dip both sides of chicken in the pretzel mixture, patting to help coating adhere. Place on a parchment paper-lined baking sheet; spritz with cooking spray.

3. Bake 20-25 minutes or until the coating is golden brown and chicken is no longer pink. Serve with sauce.

PER SERVING *296 cal., 3 g fat (trace sat. fat), 67 mg chol., 636 mg sodium, 36 g carb., 2 g fiber, 33 g pro.* **Diabetic Exchanges:** *3 lean meat, 2 starch.*

POPCORN & PRETZEL CHICKEN TENDERS

SAUSAGE & PEPPERS
WITH CHEESE POLENTA

Chicken in Tomato-Caper Sauce

Sit down to an Italian-style feast any night of the week. Pasta and a green salad round out the meal perfectly. If you don't have capers, try diced green olives.

—SHEMAINE ROHRBACH ALLENTOWN, PA

PREP: 20 MIN. • **COOK:** 15 MIN.
MAKES: 4 SERVINGS

- 4 **boneless skinless chicken breast halves (6 ounces each)**
- ¼ **teaspoon pepper**
- 2 **tablespoons olive oil, divided**
- 1 **medium onion, chopped**
- 3 **garlic cloves, minced**
- 2 **cans (14½ ounces each) no-salt-added diced tomatoes, undrained**
- 1 **package (6 ounces) fresh baby spinach**
- 2 **tablespoons drained capers**
- 2 **tablespoons minced fresh basil or 2 teaspoons dried basil**
- ¼ **teaspoon cayenne pepper**
- ½ **cup shredded part-skim mozzarella cheese**
- ½ **cup grated Parmesan cheese**

1. Pound chicken breasts with a meat mallet to ¼-in. thickness; sprinkle with pepper. In a large nonstick skillet, heat 1 tablespoon oil over medium heat. Brown chicken on both sides; remove from pan.
2. In same skillet, heat remaining oil over medium-high heat. Add onion; cook and stir until tender. Add garlic; cook 1 minute longer. Stir in tomatoes, spinach, capers, basil and cayenne. Return chicken to pan. Cook, covered, 8-10 minutes or until the chicken is no longer pink.
3. Sprinkle with the cheeses. Remove from heat; let stand, covered, until the cheese is melted.
PER SERVING *392 cal., 16 g fat (5 g sat. fat), 111 mg chol., 545 mg sodium, 17 g carb., 5 g fiber, 45 g pro.* **Diabetic Exchanges:** *6 lean meat, 1 starch, 1½ fat.*

Sausage & Peppers with Cheese Polenta

Who'd have thought that sausage could be light? Creamy homemade polenta flavored with Asiago cheese makes a wonderful backdrop for the sauteed meat mixture.

—HOLLY GOMEZ SEABROOK, NH

PREP: 20 MIN. • **COOK:** 20 MIN.
MAKES: 6 SERVINGS

- 3 **cups reduced-sodium chicken broth, divided**
- 1½ **cups water**
- 1 **cup cornmeal**
- 2 **teaspoons olive oil**
- 1 **package (12 ounces) fully cooked Italian chicken sausage links, cut into ½-inch slices**
- 1 **medium green pepper, sliced**
- 1 **medium sweet red pepper, sliced**
- 1 **medium onion, sliced**
- 1 **garlic clove, minced**
- ½ **cup shredded Asiago cheese**
- ½ **cup fat-free milk**
- 1 **teaspoon butter**

1. In a large heavy saucepan, bring 2½ cups broth and water to a boil. Reduce heat to a gentle boil; slowly whisk in the cornmeal. Cook and stir with a wooden spoon 15-20 minutes or until polenta is thickened and pulls away cleanly from sides of pan.
2. Meanwhile, in a large skillet, heat oil over medium heat. Add sausage, peppers and onion; cook and stir 5-7 minutes or until vegetables are tender. Add garlic; cook 1 minute longer. Add remaining broth, stirring to loosen browned bits from pan; heat through.
3. Remove polenta from heat; stir in cheese, milk and butter until cheese is melted. Serve with sausage mixture.
PER SERVING *269 cal., 10 g fat (4 g sat. fat), 54 mg chol., 647 mg sodium, 27 g carb., 2 g fiber, 17 g pro.* **Diabetic Exchanges:** *2 lean meat, 1½ starch, 1 vegetable, 1 fat.*

GREEK-STYLE
CHICKEN SKEWERS

Greek-Style Chicken Skewers F S C

This is the only chicken my son doesn't put ketchup on, so I know it's good!

—KATHY LEWIS-MARTINEZ
SPRING VALLEY, CA

START TO FINISH: 30 MIN.
MAKES: 4 SERVINGS

- ¾ cup reduced-fat plain yogurt
- 1 tablespoon lemon juice
- 1 tablespoon olive oil
- 1 teaspoon poultry seasoning
- 1 teaspoon dried oregano
- ½ teaspoon salt
- ½ teaspoon grated lemon peel
- ¼ teaspoon onion powder
- ¼ teaspoon pepper
- 1 pound boneless skinless chicken breasts, cut into strips

1. In a large bowl, combine all ingredients, tossing lightly. Refrigerate chicken for 10 minutes or up to 8 hours.
2. Remove chicken from marinade; discard marinade. Thread chicken onto eight metal or soaked wooden skewers. Moisten a paper towel with cooking oil; using long-handled tongs, lightly coat the grill rack.
3. Grill the chicken, covered, over medium heat or broil 4 in. from the heat 5-7 minutes or until chicken is no longer pink, turning once.
PER SERVING *134 cal., 3 g fat (1 g sat. fat), 63 mg chol., 120 mg sodium, 1 g carb., trace fiber, 23 g pro.* **Diabetic Exchange:** *3 lean meat.*

Italian Chicken Chardonnay

PREP: 20 MIN. • **COOK:** 5 HOURS
MAKES: 6 SERVINGS

- 2 teaspoons paprika
- 1 teaspoon salt
- 1 teaspoon pepper
- ¼ teaspoon cayenne pepper
- 3 pounds bone-in chicken breast halves, skin removed
- ½ pound baby portobello mushrooms, quartered
- 1 medium sweet red pepper, chopped
- 1 medium onion, chopped
- 1 can (14 ounces) water-packed artichoke hearts, rinsed and drained
- 1½ cups chardonnay
- 1 can (6 ounces) tomato paste
- 3 garlic cloves, minced
- 2 tablespoons minced fresh thyme or 2 teaspoons dried thyme
- ¼ cup minced fresh parsley
  Hot cooked pasta
  Shredded Romano cheese

1. Combine the paprika, salt, pepper and cayenne pepper; sprinkle over the chicken. Place the chicken, portobello mushrooms, red pepper, onion and artichokes in a 5-qt. slow cooker. In a small bowl, combine the chardonnay, tomato paste, garlic and thyme; pour over vegetables.
2. Cover and cook on low for 5-6 hours or until chicken is tender. Stir in the parsley. Serve with pasta and cheese.
PER SERVING *282 cal., 5 g fat (2 g sat. fat), 103 mg chol., 550 mg sodium, 16 g carb., 5 g fiber, 43 g pro.* **Diabetic Exchanges:** *5 lean meat, 3 vegetable.*

One day when I needed to have dinner ready as soon as we got home from work and school, I tweaked a skillet recipe and put it in my slow cooker. I loved the result, and now I even serve it to company.

—JUDY ARMSTRONG PRAIRIEVILLE, LA

ITALIAN CHICKEN CHARDONNAY

Parmesan Chicken Couscous

My two children love Parmesan couscous, so I created a version that can make a one-dish meal on busy nights. Spinach lends extra nutrition, and the toasted walnuts add crunch.

—**LISA ABBOTT** NEW BERLIN, WI

START TO FINISH: 20 MIN. • **MAKES:** 4 SERVINGS

- ½ cup chopped walnuts
- 2 teaspoons olive oil, divided
- 3 garlic cloves, minced
- 2 cups chopped fresh spinach
- 1½ cups cubed cooked chicken
- 1¼ cups water
- 2 teaspoons dried basil
- ¼ teaspoon pepper
- 1 package (5.9 ounces) Parmesan couscous
- ¼ cup grated Parmesan cheese

1. In a large saucepan, cook the walnuts over medium heat in 1 teaspoon oil for 2-3 minutes or until toasted. Remove and set aside.

2. In the same pan, saute the garlic in the remaining oil for 1 minute. Add the spinach, chicken, water, basil and pepper. Bring to a boil. Stir in the couscous. Remove from the heat; cover and let stand for 5-10 minutes or until the water is absorbed. Fluff with a fork. Stir in walnuts and sprinkle with Parmesan cheese.

PER SERVING *391 cal., 18 g fat (3 g sat. fat), 51 mg chol., 490 mg sodium, 34 g carb., 3 g fiber, 25 g pro.* **Diabetic Exchanges:** *3 lean meat, 2 starch, 2 fat.*

GRILLED BROWN SUGAR-MUSTARD CHICKEN

Grilled Brown Sugar-Mustard Chicken C

When I was a college student, I came up with this easy grilled recipe. The sweetness of the brown sugar contrasts with the zip of the mustard, allspice and crushed red pepper flakes.

—**KENDRA DOSS** COLORADO SPRINGS, CO

START TO FINISH: 20 MIN. • **MAKES:** 8 SERVINGS

- ½ cup yellow or Dijon mustard
- ⅓ cup packed brown sugar
- ½ teaspoon ground allspice
- ¼ teaspoon crushed red pepper flakes
- 8 boneless skinless chicken thighs (about 2 pounds)

1. In a large bowl, mix the mustard, brown sugar, allspice and pepper flakes. Remove ¼ cup mixture for serving. Add chicken to remaining mixture; toss to coat.

2. Grill chicken, covered, over medium heat or broil 4 in. from heat 6-8 minutes on each side or until a thermometer reads 170°. Serve with reserved mustard mixture.

PER SERVING *224 cal., 9 g fat (2 g sat. fat), 76 mg chol., 597 mg sodium, 13 g carb., 1 g fiber, 22 g pro.* **Diabetic Exchanges:** *3 lean meat, 1 starch.*

PARMESAN CHICKEN COUSCOUS

Herbed Chicken and Rice ⑤

Marjoram, thyme, rosemary and sage make this main dish taste like Thanksgiving. And chopped walnuts add a nice crunch. For an even nuttier taste, I sometimes use instant brown rice.

—CINDY REAMS PHILIPSBURG, PA

START TO FINISH: 30 MIN. • **MAKES:** 5 SERVINGS

- ½ **pound boneless skinless chicken breasts, cut into 1-inch strips**
- 1 **tablespoon butter**
- 2 **large carrots, shredded**
- 1 **small onion, chopped**
- 2 **cups hot water**
- ¼ **teaspoon dried marjoram**
- ¼ **teaspoon dried thyme**
- ⅛ **teaspoon dried rosemary, crushed**
- ⅛ **teaspoon rubbed sage**
- 2 **cups uncooked instant rice**
- ½ **cup chopped walnuts**

1. In a large skillet, saute chicken in butter for 3-4 minutes. Add the carrots and onion; saute until tender.

2. Add water and seasonings; bring to a boil. Stir in the rice. Cover and remove from the heat; let stand for 5 minutes. Garnish with walnuts.

PER SERVING *299 cal., 11 g fat (2 g sat. fat), 31 mg chol., 66 mg sodium, 35 g carb., 3 g fiber, 16 g pro.* **Diabetic Exchanges:** *2 starch, 1 lean meat, 1 vegetable, 1 fat.*

HERBED CHICKEN AND RICE

SPICY APRICOT-GLAZED CHICKEN

Spicy Apricot-Glazed Chicken ⒡

Combine your favorite chili sauce, apricot preserves and just three other ingredients to transform plain chicken breasts into a spicy, fruity and fabulous entree. You'll appreciate the fact that it's ready to enjoy in only 20 minutes, too.

—SONYA LABBE WEST HOLLYWOOD, CA

START TO FINISH: 20 MIN. • **MAKES:** 4 SERVINGS

- ⅓ **cup apricot preserves**
- ¼ **cup chili sauce**
- 1 **tablespoon hot mustard**
- ¼ **teaspoon salt**
- ⅛ **teaspoon pepper**
- 4 **boneless skinless chicken breast halves (4 ounces each)**

1. Preheat broiler. In a small saucepan, combine the first five ingredients; cook and stir over medium heat until heated through.

2. Place chicken in a 15x10x1-in. baking pan coated with cooking spray. Broil 3-4 in. from heat 6-8 minutes on each side or until a thermometer reads 165°. Brush occasionally with the apricot preserves mixture during the last 5 minutes of cooking.

PER SERVING *209 cal., 3 g fat (1 g sat. fat), 63 mg chol., 476 mg sodium, 23 g carb., trace fiber, 23 g pro.*

139

140

145

Turkey Specialties

❝As a frugal mom, I try to use leftovers in a way that provides good nutrition. This recipe does just that, and it's also a great way for my children to learn to enjoy the flavors of their Mexican heritage.❞

—AIMEE DAY FERNDALE, WA
about her recipe, Chipotle Turkey Chilaquiles, on page 141

BUFFALO SLOPPY JOES

Buffalo Sloppy Joes 🇫

Lean ground turkey makes this a lighter sloppy joe than the standard ground beef version. A big splash of hot sauce and optional blue cheese provide that authentic Buffalo-style flavor.

—**MARIA REGAKIS** SAUGUS, MA

START TO FINISH: 30 MIN.
MAKES: 8 SERVINGS

- 2 **pounds extra-lean ground turkey**
- 2 **celery ribs, chopped**
- 1 **medium onion, chopped**
- 1 **medium carrot, grated**
- 3 **garlic cloves, minced**
- 1 **can (8 ounces) tomato sauce**
- ½ **cup reduced-sodium chicken broth**
- ¼ **cup Louisiana-style hot sauce**
- 2 **tablespoons brown sugar**
- 2 **tablespoons red wine vinegar**
- 1 **tablespoon Worcestershire sauce**
- ¼ **teaspoon pepper**
- 8 **hamburger buns, split**
  Crumbled blue cheese, optional

1. Cook the first five ingredients in a Dutch oven over medium heat until turkey is no longer pink. Stir in the tomato sauce, broth, hot sauce, brown sugar, vinegar, Worcestershire sauce and pepper; heat through.
2. Serve on buns; sprinkle with cheese if desired.
PER SERVING *279 cal., 3 g fat (trace sat. fat), 45 mg chol., 475 mg sodium, 30 g carb., 2 g fiber, 33 g pro.* **Diabetic Exchanges:** *4 lean meat, 2 starch.*

Mediterranean Turkey Skillet

I've always heard that it's important to eat a rainbow of colors to get all of the nutrients we need. Thanks to my garden-grown veggies, this dish certainly fits the bill.

—**NICOLE EHLERT** BURLINGTON, WI

START TO FINISH: 30 MIN.
MAKES: 6 SERVINGS

- 1 **tablespoon olive oil**
- 1 **package (20 ounces) lean ground turkey**
- 2 **medium zucchini, quartered lengthwise and cut into ½-inch slices**
- 1 **medium onion, chopped**
- 2 **banana peppers, seeded and chopped**
- 3 **garlic cloves, minced**
- ½ **teaspoon dried oregano**
- 1 **can (15 ounces) black beans, rinsed and drained**
- 1 **can (14½ ounces) diced tomatoes, undrained**
- 1 **tablespoon balsamic vinegar**
- ½ **teaspoon salt**

1. In a large skillet, heat oil over medium-high heat. Add turkey, vegetables, garlic and oregano; cook 10-12 minutes or until turkey is no longer pink and vegetables are tender, breaking up turkey into crumbles.
2. Stir in remaining ingredients; heat through, stirring occasionally.
PER SERVING *259 cal., 10 g fat (2 g sat. fat), 65 mg chol., 504 mg sodium, 20 g carb., 6 g fiber, 24 g pro.* **Diabetic Exchanges:** *3 lean meat, 1 vegetable, ½ starch, ½ fat.*

MEDITERRANEAN TURKEY SKILLET

PEAR & TURKEY
SAUSAGE RIGATONI

Pear & Turkey Sausage Rigatoni

The sweet pear, salty sausage and creamy blue cheese are a wonderful combination in this one-pot supper. Now we don't have to go to an elegant restaurant to get something similar.

—DEBBY HARDEN WILLIAMSTON, MI

START TO FINISH: 30 MIN.
MAKES: 6 SERVINGS

- 8 **ounces uncooked rigatoni or large tube pasta**
- 2 **Italian turkey sausage links (4 ounces each), casings removed**
- 2 **medium pears, sliced**
- 2 **cups fresh baby spinach**
- ½ **cup half-and-half cream**
- ½ **cup crumbled blue cheese, divided**
  Toasted sliced almonds, optional

1. Cook the rigatoni according to package directions.
2. Meanwhile, in a Dutch oven, cook sausage over medium heat 6-8 minutes or until no longer pink, breaking into large crumbles. Add pears; cook and stir 3-5 minutes or until lightly browned.
3. Drain rigatoni; add to sausage mixture. Add spinach, cream and ¼ cup cheese; cook 3-4 minutes or until spinach is wilted, stirring occasionally. Top with remaining cheese. If desired, sprinkle with toasted almonds.
PER SERVING *273 cal., 9 g fat (4 g sat. fat), 32 mg chol., 333 mg sodium, 37 g carb., 3 g fiber, 13 g pro.* **Diabetic Exchanges:** *2½ starch, 2 medium-fat meat.*

Sesame Turkey Stir-Fry

START TO FINISH: 25 MIN.
MAKES: 4 SERVINGS

- 1 **teaspoon cornstarch**
- ½ **cup water**
- 2 **tablespoons reduced-sodium soy sauce**
- 1 **tablespoon honey**
- 2 **teaspoons curry powder**
- ⅛ **teaspoon crushed red pepper flakes**
- 2 **teaspoons sesame or canola oil**
- 1 **medium sweet red pepper, julienned**
- 1 **small onion, cut into thin wedges**
- 1 **garlic clove, minced**
- 2 **cups shredded cooked turkey breast**
- 1 **green onion, sliced**
- 2 **cups hot cooked brown rice**
  Thinly sliced serrano pepper and toasted sesame seeds, optional

1. In a small bowl, mix the first six ingredients until blended. In a large skillet, heat oil over medium-high heat. Add red pepper and onion; stir-fry until crisp-tender. Add garlic; cook 1 minute longer.
2. Stir cornstarch mixture and add to pan. Bring to a boil; cook and stir 2 minutes or until sauce is thickened. Add turkey; heat through. Stir in green onion. Serve with rice. If desired, top with serrano pepper and sesame seeds.
NOTE *Wear disposable gloves when cutting hot peppers; the oils can burn skin. Avoid touching your face.*
PER SERVING *269 cal., 4 g fat (1 g sat. fat), 60 mg chol., 349 mg sodium, 32 g carb., 3 g fiber, 25 g pro.* **Diabetic Exchanges:** *3 lean meat, 2 starch, ½ fat.*

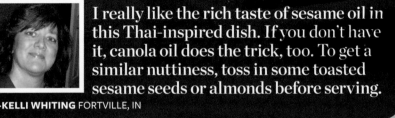

I really like the rich taste of sesame oil in this Thai-inspired dish. If you don't have it, canola oil does the trick, too. To get a similar nuttiness, toss in some toasted sesame seeds or almonds before serving.

—KELLI WHITING FORTVILLE, IN

SESAME TURKEY STIR-FRY

Portobello Turkey Bolognese

This sauce tastes better the longer it simmers, which allows the flavors to fully develop. In fact, it tastes best the second day after a night in the refrigerator.

—DARRELL KAU EUGENE, OR

PREP: 15 MIN. • **COOK:** 1¼ HOURS
MAKES: 8 SERVINGS

- 1 tablespoon olive oil
- 1½ pounds lean ground turkey
- ½ pound sliced baby portobello mushrooms
- 2 large onions, chopped
- 1 cup chopped carrots
- 6 garlic cloves, minced
- 1 can (14½ ounces) reduced-sodium beef broth
- 1 cup dry red wine or additional reduced-sodium beef broth
- 1 cup water
- 1 can (6 ounces) tomato paste
- ½ cup minced fresh basil
- 1 tablespoon minced fresh oregano
- 2 teaspoons minced fresh rosemary
- 2 teaspoons fennel seed
- ¾ teaspoon salt
- ½ teaspoon crushed red pepper flakes
- ½ teaspoon pepper
- 1 teaspoon sugar
- 12 ounces uncooked penne pasta
- ½ cup shredded Parmesan cheese

1. In a Dutch oven coated with cooking spray, heat oil over medium heat. Add turkey, mushrooms, onions, carrots and garlic; cook 10-12 minutes or until turkey is no longer pink and vegetables are tender.

2. Stir in broth, wine, water, tomato paste, herbs, seasonings and sugar; bring to a boil. Reduce heat; simmer, uncovered, 1 hour or until thickened, stirring occasionally.

3. Cook pasta according to package directions; drain. Serve with sauce. Sprinkle with cheese.

PER SERVING *380 cal., 11 g fat (3 g sat. fat), 72 mg chol., 508 mg sodium, 44 g carb., 5 g fiber, 25 g pro.* **Diabetic Exchanges:** *2 starch, 2 lean meat, 2 vegetable, 1 fat.*

Curry-Apple Turkey Loaf

I came up with this tender turkey loaf to help my husband and me stick to our healthy-eating goals. Leftover slices make satisfying lunch box take-alongs the next day.

—MARY GUDENKAUF HARRISONVILLE, MO

PREP: 30 MIN. • **BAKE:** 50 MIN.
MAKES: 6 SERVINGS

- 2 cups soft bread crumbs
- 1 medium apple, finely chopped
- 1 cup finely chopped fresh mushrooms
- 1 small red onion, finely chopped
- 2 egg whites, lightly beaten
- 1 egg, lightly beaten
- 1 to 2 teaspoons curry powder
- 1 teaspoon salt
- 1 pound lean ground turkey

TOPPING

- 2 tablespoons butter
- 2 medium apples, finely chopped
- 1 small red onion, finely chopped
- ½ cup unsweetened apple juice
- 1 teaspoon curry powder
- ¼ teaspoon salt

1. In a large bowl, combine the bread crumbs, apple, mushrooms, onion, egg whites, egg, curry and salt. Crumble turkey over mixture and mix well. Pat into a greased 9x5-in. loaf pan.

2. Bake, uncovered, at 350° for 50-60 minutes or until no pink remains and a thermometer reads 165°.

3. For topping, in a small saucepan, melt the butter. Add the apples, onion, apple juice, curry and salt; bring to a boil. Reduce heat; simmer, uncovered, for 12-15 minutes or until apples and onion are tender.

4. Let the meat loaf stand for 5-10 minutes before slicing. Serve with warm topping.

PER SERVING *264 cal., 12 g fat (5 g sat. fat), 105 mg chol., 725 mg sodium, 23 g carb., 3 g fiber, 18 g pro.* **Diabetic Exchanges:** *2 lean meat, 1 fruit, 1 fat, ½ starch.*

PORTOBELLO TURKEY BOLOGNESE

Grilled Turkey Tenderloin C

When they taste my grilled specialty, guests say, "This turkey melts in your mouth—the flavor is fantastic!" The recipe includes a tangy marinade that was developed for our turkey producers' booth at the state fair one summer.
—DENISE NEBEL WAYLAND, IA

PREP: 5 MIN. + MARINATING • **GRILL:** 20 MIN.
MAKES: 4 SERVINGS

- ¼ cup apple juice
- ¼ cup reduced-sodium soy sauce
- ¼ cup canola oil
- 2 tablespoons lemon juice
- 2 tablespoons dried minced onion
- 1 teaspoon vanilla extract
- ¼ teaspoon ground ginger
- Dash each garlic powder and pepper
- 2 turkey breast tenderloins (½ pound each)

1. In a large resealable plastic bag, combine the apple juice, soy sauce, oil, lemon juice, onion, vanilla, ginger, garlic powder and pepper; add the turkey. Seal bag and turn to coat. Refrigerate for at least 2 hours.
2. Drain and discard marinade. Grill turkey, covered, over medium heat for 8-10 minutes on each side or until a thermometer reads 170°.
PER SERVING *157 cal., 5 g fat (1 g sat. fat), 56 mg chol., 211 mg sodium, 1 g carb., trace fiber, 27 g pro.* **Diabetic Exchanges:** *3 lean meat, ½ fat.*

SKILLET CASSOULET

Skillet Cassoulet

Here's a light and simple take on the French comfort-food classic. Serve it with crisp artisan bread for a fast and fabulous dinner any time.
—BARBARA BRITTAIN SANTEE, CA

START TO FINISH: 30 MIN.
MAKES: 3 SERVINGS

- 2 teaspoons canola oil
- ¼ pound smoked turkey kielbasa, cut into ½-inch slices
- ¼ pound fully cooked boneless ham, cubed
- 2 medium carrots, sliced
- 1 celery rib, sliced
- ½ medium red onion, sliced
- 2 garlic cloves, minced
- 1 can (15 ounces) no-salt-added white kidney or cannellini beans, rinsed and drained
- 1 can (14½ ounces) no-salt-added diced tomatoes, undrained
- ¾ teaspoon dried thyme
- ⅛ teaspoon pepper

1. In a large skillet, heat oil over medium-high heat. Add kielbasa, ham, carrots, celery and onion; cook and stir until sausage is browned and the vegetables are tender. Stir in garlic; cook 1 minute longer.
2. Stir in the remaining ingredients. Bring to a boil. Reduce heat; simmer, uncovered, 4-5 minutes or until heated through.
PER SERVING *282 cal., 8 g fat (1 g sat. fat), 43 mg chol., 901 mg sodium, 33 g carb., 10 g fiber, 22 g pro.*

GRILLED TURKEY TENDERLOIN

Confetti Kielbasa Skillet

Here's one of my husband's favorite dishes. When it's in season, substitute fresh corn for frozen. Add a dash of cayenne pepper if you like a little heat.

—SHEILA GOMEZ SHAWNEE, KS

START TO FINISH: 30 MIN. • **MAKES:** 4 SERVINGS

- 1 tablespoon canola oil
- 7 ounces smoked turkey kielbasa, cut into ¼-inch slices
- 1 medium onion, halved and sliced
- ½ cup sliced baby portobello mushrooms
- 2 garlic cloves, minced
- ½ cup reduced-sodium chicken broth
- ¾ teaspoon Mrs. Dash Garlic & Herb seasoning blend
- 1 can (15 ounces) no-salt-added black beans, rinsed and drained
- 1 package (8.8 ounces) ready-to-serve brown rice
- 1 cup frozen corn
- ½ cup chopped roasted sweet red peppers
- 4 teaspoons minced fresh cilantro

1. In a large skillet, heat oil over medium-high heat. Add the kielbasa, onion and mushrooms; cook and stir for 4-6 minutes or until vegetables are tender. Add garlic; cook 1 minute longer.

2. Add broth and seasoning blend, stirring to loosen browned bits from pan. Bring to a boil; cook 2-3 minutes or until liquid is almost evaporated. Stir in remaining ingredients; heat through.

PER SERVING *347 cal., 9 g fat (1 g sat. fat), 31 mg chol., 692 mg sodium, 45 g carb., 7 g fiber, 18 g pro.* **Diabetic Exchanges:** *3 starch, 2 lean meat, ½ fat.*

CONFETTI KIELBASA SKILLET

STUFFED PIZZA BURGERS

Stuffed Pizza Burgers

For years, I used this recipe to make pizza meat loaf, which was absolutely killer. I decided to try it as burgers for a party, and they were a smashing success. Everyone left with the recipe.

—DENNIS BARTER REEDSBURG, WI

PREP: 30 MIN. • **GRILL:** 10 MIN. • **MAKES:** 8 SERVINGS

- 2 eggs, lightly beaten
- 1 medium onion, finely chopped
- 1 medium green pepper, finely chopped
- ½ cup crushed cornflakes
- ½ cup chopped fresh mushrooms
- 1 tablespoon minced fresh basil or 1 teaspoon dried basil
- 1 tablespoon minced fresh oregano or 1 teaspoon dried oregano
- 2 garlic cloves, minced
- 2 pounds lean ground turkey
- 1 cup pizza sauce, divided
- ½ cup finely chopped turkey pepperoni
- ½ cup shredded part-skim mozzarella cheese
- 8 hamburger buns, split

1. In a large bowl, combine the first eight ingredients. Crumble turkey over mixture and mix well. Shape into 16 patties. Layer 1 tablespoon pizza sauce, the pepperoni and cheese onto the center of each of eight patties. Top with remaining patties and press edges firmly to seal.

2. Moisten a paper towel with cooking oil; using long-handled tongs, lightly coat the grill rack. Grill burgers, covered, over medium heat or broil 4 in. from the heat for 4-6 minutes on each side or until a thermometer reads 165° and juices run clear. Serve on buns with remaining pizza sauce.

PER SERVING *385 cal., 14 g fat (4 g sat. fat), 155 mg chol., 613 mg sodium, 32 g carb., 2 g fiber, 31 g pro.* **Diabetic Exchanges:** *4 lean meat, 2 starch, 1 fat.*

Chipotle Turkey Chilaquiles

PREP: 30 MIN. • **BAKE:** 25 MIN. • **MAKES:** 8 SERVINGS

- 15 corn tortillas (6 inches), torn into 1½-inch pieces
- 3 cups shredded cooked turkey or chicken
- 1 large onion, chopped
- 4 garlic cloves, minced
- ⅓ cup lime juice
- 2 chipotle peppers in adobo sauce
- 2 cans (15 ounces each) black beans, rinsed and drained
- 3 cups (12 ounces) crumbled queso fresco or shredded part-skim mozzarella cheese
- 3 cups turkey or chicken broth
  Chopped fresh cilantro
  Sour cream and hot cooked rice, optional

1. Preheat oven to 400°. In batches, arrange tortilla pieces in a single layer on an ungreased baking sheet and bake 6-8 minutes or until crisp.

2. Toss turkey with onion and garlic; set aside. Place lime juice and chipotles in a blender; process until blended. Arrange half of the tortilla pieces in a greased 13x9-in. baking dish. Layer with turkey, beans, 1½ cups cheese and chipotle mixture. Top with remaining tortillas and cheese.

3. Pour broth over top. Bake, uncovered, 25-30 minutes or until cheese is melted. Sprinkle with cilantro. If desired, serve with sour cream and rice.

PER SERVING *364 cal., 8 g fat (3 g sat. fat), 56 mg chol., 766 mg sodium, 44 g carb., 7 g fiber, 29 g pro.*

As a frugal mom, I try to use leftovers in a way that provides good nutrition. This recipe does just that, and it's also a great way for my children to learn to enjoy the flavors of their Mexican heritage.
—**AIMEE DAY** FERNDALE, WA

CHIPOTLE TURKEY CHILAQUILES

TURKEY CUTLETS IN LEMON WINE SAUCE

Turkey Cutlets in Lemon Wine Sauce **S C**

After I enjoyed something like this at a local Italian restaurant, I figured out how to make it at home for my family. Now I serve it a lot since it's so quick to make—and they're so happy I do.
—**KATHIE WILSON** WARRENTON, VA

START TO FINISH: 25 MIN. • **MAKES:** 4 SERVINGS

- ½ cup all-purpose flour
- ½ teaspoon salt
- ½ teaspoon paprika
- ¼ teaspoon pepper
- 4 turkey breast cutlets (2½ ounces each)
- 1 tablespoon olive oil
- 1 cup white wine or chicken broth
- ¼ cup lemon juice

1. In a shallow bowl, mix flour, salt, paprika and pepper. Dip turkey in flour mixture to coat both sides; shake off excess.

2. In a large skillet, heat oil over medium heat. Add turkey and cook in batches 1-2 minutes on each side or until no longer pink. Remove from pan.

3. Add wine and lemon juice to skillet, stirring to loosen browned bits. Bring to a boil; cook until liquid is reduced by half. Return cutlets to pan; turn to coat and heat through.

PER SERVING *145 cal., 4 g fat (1 g sat. fat), 44 mg chol., 110 mg sodium, 5 g carb., trace fiber, 18 g pro.* **Diabetic Exchanges:** *2 lean meat, 1 fat.*

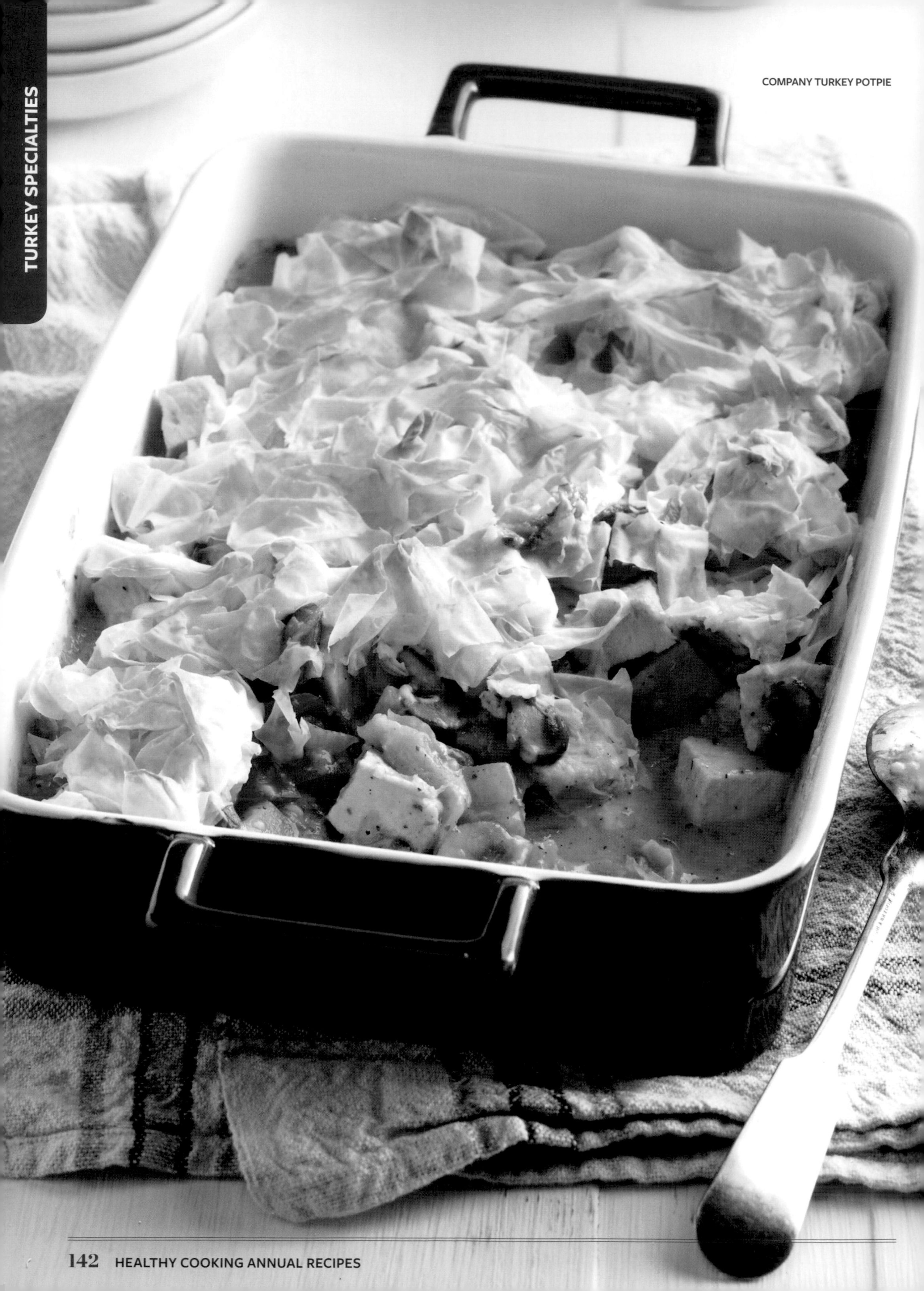

COMPANY TURKEY POTPIE

Company Turkey Potpie

Do you enjoy serving friends and family comfort food? If so, you'll want to make this indulgent potpie loaded with turkey and autumn vegetables. And, there's no crust to make—just top with phyllo dough. Easy!

—*TASTE OF HOME* TEST KITCHEN

PREP: 1 HOUR • **BAKE:** 10 MIN.
MAKES: 6 SERVINGS

- ½ pound sliced baby portobello mushrooms
- 2 shallots, chopped
- 2 teaspoons olive oil
- 2 cups cubed peeled butternut squash
- 1 cup chopped sweet red pepper
- ½ cup sliced fennel bulb
- 2 cups reduced-sodium chicken broth, divided
- ⅓ cup all-purpose flour
- ½ cup 2% milk
- 3 cups cubed cooked turkey breast
- 2 tablespoons sherry or additional reduced-sodium chicken broth
- 1 teaspoon rubbed sage
- ½ teaspoon salt
- ½ teaspoon dried thyme
- ¼ teaspoon pepper
- 10 sheets phyllo dough (14x9-inch size)
  Refrigerated butter-flavored spray

1. In a large skillet, saute mushrooms and shallots in oil until tender. Add the squash, red pepper and fennel; saute 5 minutes longer. Add ¼ cup broth. Cover and cook over medium-low heat until vegetables are tender, about 15 minutes.

2. Sprinkle flour over the vegetables; cook and stir for 1 minute. Gradually add milk and remaining broth. Bring to a boil; cook and stir for 1-2 minutes or until thickened. Stir in the turkey, sherry and seasonings; heat through. Transfer mixture to a 2-qt. baking dish coated with cooking spray.

3. Stack all 10 phyllo sheets. Roll up, starting with a long side; cut into ½-in. strips. Place strips in a large bowl and toss to separate; spritz with butter-flavored spray. Arrange over turkey mixture; spritz again. Bake, uncovered, at 425° for 10-15 minutes or until golden brown.

GREEK STUFFED BANANA PEPPERS

PER SERVING *275 cal., 4 g fat (1 g sat. fat), 62 mg chol., 544 mg sodium, 33 g carb., 5 g fiber, 28 g pro.* **Diabetic Exchanges:** *3 lean meat, 2 starch.*

Greek Stuffed Banana Peppers

If you're looking for a ground turkey recipe that delivers, this is the one! The filling is flavorful and the peppers add some nice heat. You can easily stuff them ahead of time and bake them up when you're ready.

—OLA SNOW POWELL, OH

PREP: 40 MIN. • **BAKE:** 45 MIN.
MAKES: 4 SERVINGS

- 8 large banana peppers
- ½ teaspoon olive oil
- 1 small onion, chopped
- 2 garlic cloves, minced
- 3 tablespoons minced fresh basil or 1 tablespoon dried basil
- 8 pitted Greek olives, sliced
- ⅓ cup crumbled feta cheese
- ¼ cup dry bread crumbs
- ¼ cup water
- ¼ cup egg substitute
- ¼ teaspoon pepper
- ¾ pound lean ground turkey
- 2 cans (8 ounces each) no-salt-added tomato sauce

1. Preheat oven to 350°. Cut and discard tops from banana peppers; remove seeds. In a Dutch oven, cook peppers in boiling water 2 minutes. Drain and rinse in cold water; pat dry.

2. In a small skillet coated with cooking spray, heat oil over medium-high heat. Add onion; cook and stir until tender. Add garlic; cook 1 minute longer. Stir in basil; transfer to a large bowl. Stir in olives, cheese, bread crumbs, water, egg substitute and pepper. Add turkey; mix lightly but thoroughly.

3. Spoon mixture into banana peppers. Place in a 13x9-in. baking dish coated with cooking spray; top with tomato sauce. Bake, covered, 45-50 minutes or until a thermometer inserted into turkey mixture reads 165° and peppers are tender.

PER SERVING *298 cal., 12 g fat (3 g sat. fat), 72 mg chol., 431 mg sodium, 24 g carb., 7 g fiber, 22 g pro.* **Diabetic Exchanges:** *2 lean meat, 1½ starch, 1 fat.*

Lemon-Basil Turkey Breast F C

Transform turkey into a season-spanning dish that's great for company with this fresh and citrusy version. It roasts up golden brown, super-moist and tender.

—SHARON DELANEY-CHRONIS
SOUTH MILWAUKEE, WI

PREP: 20 MIN. • **BAKE:** 2 HOURS
MAKES: 12 SERVINGS

- 6 medium carrots
- 3 celery ribs
- 2 medium onions
- 2 cups reduced-sodium chicken broth
- 1 cup water
- 1 cup minced fresh basil
- 2 tablespoons grated lemon peel
- 4 garlic cloves, minced
- ½ teaspoon salt
- ½ teaspoon pepper
- 1 bone-in turkey breast (5 to 6 pounds)
- 2 medium lemons, sliced

1. Cut carrots and celery into 2-in. lengths; cut onions into wedges. Place in a roasting pan; add broth and water.
2. Combine basil, lemon peel, garlic, salt and pepper. With fingers, carefully loosen skin from turkey breast; rub mixture under the skin. Secure skin to underside of breast with toothpicks. Place turkey breast over carrot mixture. Place lemon slices over skin.
3. Bake, uncovered, at 325° for 2 to 2½ hours or until a thermometer reads 170°, basting every 30 minutes. Cover loosely with foil if turkey browns too quickly. Cover and let stand for 15 minutes before slicing turkey. Serve with vegetables.
PER SERVING 192 cal., 1 g fat (trace sat. fat), 98 mg chol., 290 mg sodium, 7 g carb., 2 g fiber, 37 g pro. *Diabetic Exchanges: 5 lean meat, 1 vegetable.*

Did you know?
When preparing meat loaf, burgers or meatballs, combine the other ingredients first, then crumble the meat on top. Mix just until combined. This ensures a tender finished product.

Just-Like-Thanksgiving Turkey Meat Loaf

For a holiday-esque meal any time of year, this tender turkey meat loaf is perfect. Complemented with a cranberry glaze, it's a mouthwatering dish.

—MOLLIE BROWN LOS ANGELES, CA

PREP: 30 MIN. + STANDING • **BAKE:** 45 MIN.
MAKES: 6 SERVINGS

- 1 cup seasoned stuffing cubes
- ½ cup milk
- 1 egg, beaten
- 1 celery rib, finely chopped
- 1 small onion, grated
- 1 small carrot, grated
- ¼ cup dried cranberries
- ½ teaspoon salt
- ¼ teaspoon pepper
- 3 to 4½ teaspoons minced fresh sage
- 3 teaspoons minced fresh rosemary
- 1½ pounds lean ground turkey
- ½ cup whole-berry cranberry sauce
- ½ cup ketchup
- ⅛ teaspoon hot pepper sauce

1. Preheat oven to 375°. In a large bowl, combine stuffing cubes and milk. Let stand 10 minutes; break up stuffing cubes with a fork. Stir in egg, celery, onion, carrot, cranberries, salt and pepper. Combine the sage and rosemary; add half to the mixture. Crumble turkey over mixture; mix lightly but thoroughly. Pat into an ungreased 9x5-in. loaf pan.
2. Bake, uncovered, 25 minutes; drain if necessary. Combine the cranberry sauce, ketchup, pepper sauce and remaining herbs; spread over meat loaf. Bake 20-25 minutes or until no pink remains and a thermometer reads 165°.
PER SERVING 303 cal., 11 g fat (3 g sat. fat), 127 mg chol., 712 mg sodium, 28 g carb., 2 g fiber, 23 g pro.

JUST-LIKE-THANKSGIVING TURKEY MEAT LOAF

SAUSAGE PIZZA PASTA

Sausage Pizza Pasta

It's pizza in a bowl! Here's a terrific (and tasty) way to make sure your kids get the whole grains and vegetables they need to grow up big and strong

—**DANNA HOLT** SHOALS, IN

START TO FINISH: 30 MIN.
MAKES: 6 SERVINGS

- 1 pound Italian turkey sausage links, casings removed
- 2 cups sliced fresh mushrooms
- 1 medium green pepper, chopped
- 1 medium onion, chopped
- 3 cups uncooked whole grain spiral pasta
- 1 can (15 ounces) pizza sauce
- 1½ cups water
- 1½ teaspoons Italian seasoning
- ¼ teaspoon salt
- ¾ cup shredded part-skim mozzarella cheese

1. In a Dutch oven, cook sausage, mushrooms, green pepper and onion over medium heat 5-6 minutes or until sausage is no longer pink and vegetables are tender, breaking up sausage into crumbles; drain.
2. Stir in pasta, pizza sauce, water, Italian seasoning and salt; bring to a boil. Reduce heat; simmer, covered, 10-15 minutes or until pasta is tender. Remove from heat; sprinkle with cheese. Let stand, covered, 5 minutes or until cheese is melted.
PER SERVING *358 cal., 8 g fat (3 g sat. fat), 36 mg chol., 577 mg sodium, 52 g carb., 4 g fiber, 21 g pro.*

Light Turkey Cutlets Stroganoff C

PREP: 20 MIN. • **COOK:** 25 MIN.
MAKES: 4 SERVINGS

- ¼ cup all-purpose flour
- ½ teaspoon salt, divided
- ¼ teaspoon plus ⅛ teaspoon pepper, divided
- 1 package (17.6 ounces) turkey breast cutlets
- 2 tablespoons butter, divided
- 2½ cups quartered fresh mushrooms
- 1 large onion, chopped
- ¾ cup reduced-sodium chicken broth
- ¼ cup sherry or additional reduced-sodium chicken broth
- ½ cup reduced-fat sour cream
- 1½ teaspoons minced fresh tarragon

1. In a shallow bowl, mix flour and ¼ teaspoon each salt and pepper. Dip cutlets in flour mixture to coat both sides; shake off excess.

2. Place a large nonstick skillet coated with cooking spray over medium heat. In batches, cook turkey in 1 tablespoon butter 2-3 minutes on each side or until meat is no longer pink. Remove from pan; keep warm. Wipe pan clean if necessary.
3. In same skillet, heat remaining butter over medium-high heat. Add mushrooms and onion; cook and stir until tender. Stir in broth and sherry. Bring to a boil; cook just until liquid is almost evaporated. Stir in sour cream, tarragon and the remaining salt and pepper; heat through (do not allow to boil). Serve with turkey.
PER SERVING *290 cal., 9 g fat (5 g sat. fat), 102 mg chol., 493 mg sodium, 12 g carb., 1 g fiber, 36 g pro.* **Diabetic Exchanges:** *4 lean meat, 1½ fat, ½ starch.*

My husband, who's a real red-meat man, loves this lighter version of classic beef Stroganoff. I like to serve traditional egg noodles on the side.
—**DONNA LINDECAMP** MORGANTON, NC

LIGHT TURKEY CUTLETS STROGANOFF

149

152

157

Pork Entrees

❝Over the years, we've adapted this roast to give it tropical flair. The fresh, zippy chutney is great on just about any meat. You might want to make an extra batch for tacos the next night. Delicious!❞

—**PAMELA VITTI KNOWLES** HENDERSONVILLE, NC
about her recipe, Mango Chutney Pork Roast, on page 158

Pork Medallions with Pomegranate Sauce

The richly colored pomegranate glaze draped over this pork is the perfect blend of sweet, tangy and savory. I think it's best served with a generous helping of wild rice to soak up every last drop of sauce.

—**ELIZABETH DUMONT** BOULDER, CO

PREP: 45 MIN. • **COOK:** 5 MIN./BATCH
MAKES: 4 SERVINGS

- 2½ cups water
- 1 cup uncooked wild rice
- 1 pork tenderloin (1 pound)
- ¼ cup all-purpose flour
- ¼ cup cornmeal
- 2 teaspoons grated lemon peel
- 1 tablespoon olive oil
- 1 cup reduced-sodium chicken broth
- 1 cup pomegranate juice
- 2 tablespoons brown sugar
- 2 garlic cloves, minced
- ½ teaspoon pepper
- ¼ teaspoon salt
- ¼ teaspoon ground ginger
- ⅛ teaspoon cayenne pepper
- 1 tablespoon cornstarch
- 2 tablespoons cold water

1. In a large saucepan, bring the water and rice to a boil. Reduce heat; cover and simmer for 45-60 minutes or until rice is tender.

2. Meanwhile, cut the pork tenderloin into eight slices; flatten slightly. In a large resealable plastic bag, combine the flour, cornmeal and lemon peel. Add tenderloin, a few pieces at a time, and shake to coat.

3. In a large skillet coated with cooking spray, cook the tenderloin in olive oil in batches for 2-3 minutes on each side or until tender. Remove and keep warm.

4. In the same skillet, combine the chicken broth, pomegranate juice, brown sugar, garlic and seasonings. Bring to a boil. Reduce heat; simmer, uncovered, for 5 minutes.

5. Combine the cornstarch and cold water until smooth; gradually stir into the pan. Bring to a boil; cook and stir for 1 minute or until thickened. Serve with pork and rice.

PER SERVING *425 cal., 8 g fat (2 g sat. fat), 63 mg chol., 346 mg sodium, 57 g carb., 2 g fiber, 30 g pro.*

Pork & Potato Supper

Looking for a comforting dinner that's easy enough for a weeknight? Here it is! The Worcestershire and minced garlic add mouthwatering flavor. After just one taste, my husband wanted to put the recipe on our list of regular family meals.

—**MACEY ALLEN** GREEN FOREST, AR

START TO FINISH: 30 MIN.
MAKES: 4 SERVINGS

- 2 tablespoons butter, divided
- 1 pork tenderloin (1 pound), cut into ¼-inch slices
- 1 cup sliced fresh mushrooms
- 2 garlic cloves, minced
- 8 small red potatoes, quartered
- 1 can (14½ ounces) reduced-sodium chicken broth, divided
- 2 teaspoons Worcestershire sauce
- ¼ teaspoon salt
- ¼ teaspoon pepper
- 2 tablespoons all-purpose flour
- 4 green onions, sliced

1. In a 12-in. skillet, heat 1 tablespoon butter over medium heat. Cook pork 2-4 minutes on each side or until tender. Remove from pan.

2. In same pan, heat the remaining butter over medium-high heat. Add mushrooms; cook and stir until almost tender. Add the garlic; cook 1 minute longer. Stir in potatoes, 1½ cups broth, Worcestershire sauce, salt and pepper. Bring to a boil. Reduce heat; simmer, covered, 10-15 minutes or until the potatoes are tender.

3. In a small bowl, mix the flour and remaining broth until smooth. Stir into the mushroom mixture. Bring to a boil; cook and stir until the sauce is thickened. Stir in the green onions. Return pork to pan and heat through.

PER SERVING *282 cal., 10 g fat (5 g sat. fat), 78 mg chol., 565 mg sodium, 21 g carb., 2 g fiber, 27 g pro.* ***Diabetic Exchanges:*** *3 lean meat, 1½ fat, 1 starch.*

PORK & POTATO SUPPER

SHREDDED PORK BARBECUE

Shredded Pork Barbecue

Well seasoned before going on the grill, this roast develops a crispy exterior that's lip-smacking good. Enjoy the shredded meat all by itself or top it off with some of your favorite barbecue sauce.

—**AMANDA MCLEMORE** MARYVILLE, TN

PREP: 15 MIN.
GRILL: 3½ HOURS + STANDING
MAKES: 16 SERVINGS

- 1½ **teaspoons each white pepper, paprika and black pepper**
- 1 **teaspoon each onion powder, garlic powder and cayenne pepper**
- 1 **teaspoon dried thyme**
- ½ **teaspoon salt**
- 1 **boneless pork shoulder roast (4 to 5 pounds)**
- 16 **hard rolls, split**
   Barbecue sauce, optional

1. Combine the seasonings; rub over roast. Prepare grill for indirect heat, using a drip pan with 1 in. of water. Grill roast, covered, over medium-low heat for 3½ to 4 hours or until the meat is tender.
2. When cool enough to handle, shred the meat with two forks. Spoon ½ cup onto each bun; serve with barbecue sauce if desired.
PER SERVING *354 cal., 14 g fat (4 g sat. fat), 67 mg chol., 454 mg sodium, 31 g carb., 2 g fiber, 25 g pro.* **Diabetic Exchanges:** *3 medium-fat meat, 2 starch.*

Southwest Pork Tenderloin [C]

PREP: 10 MIN. • **BAKE:** 25 MIN. + STANDING
MAKES: 8 SERVINGS

- 2 **pork tenderloins (1 pound each)**
- 2 **tablespoons canola oil**
- 1 **envelope taco seasoning**
- 3 **medium limes, cut into wedges**

1. Preheat oven to 425°. Rub the tenderloins with oil; sprinkle with taco seasoning. Place on a rack in a shallow roasting pan.
2. Roast 25-30 minutes or until a thermometer reads 145°. Remove tenderloins from oven; tent with foil. Let stand 10 minutes before slicing. Squeeze lime wedges over pork.
PER SERVING *184 cal., 7 g fat (2 g sat. fat), 63 mg chol., 446 mg sodium, 6 g carb., 1 g fiber, 22 g pro.* **Diabetic Exchanges:** *3 lean meat, ½ starch, ½ fat.*

> While living in Europe, I really missed Southwestern cooking. I used what I had on hand to create a spicy tenderloin, and it's been one of my staples ever since.
> —**JOHN COX** SEGUIN, TX

SOUTHWEST PORK TENDERLOIN

Salsa Skillet Pork Chops

START TO FINISH: 30 MIN.
MAKES: 6 SERVINGS

- 6 **boneless pork loin chops (6 ounces each)**
- ½ **teaspoon salt**
- ¼ **teaspoon pepper**
- 2 **cups fresh whole kernel corn**
- 1 **can (15 ounces) pinto beans, rinsed and drained**
- 1¼ **cups chunky salsa**
- 2 **tablespoons water**
- 1 **teaspoon ground cumin**

1. Sprinkle the pork chops with salt and pepper. Heat a large nonstick skillet coated with cooking spray over medium heat. Brown pork chops on both sides in batches.

2. Return all pork chops to the pan. Add remaining ingredients; bring to a boil. Reduce heat; simmer, covered, 6-8 minutes or until a thermometer inserted in pork reads 145°. Let stand 5 minutes before serving.

PER SERVING *366 cal., 11 g fat (4 g sat. fat), 82 mg chol., 548 mg sodium, 29 g carb., 4 g fiber, 38 g pro.* **Diabetic Exchanges:** *5 lean meat, 2 starch.*

Apple-Stuffed Pork Tenderloins C

To dress up my stuffed tenderloins for guests, I add a special garnish of apple slices and fresh parsley.

—**SUZANNE EARL** SPRING, TX

PREP: 25 MIN. • **BAKE:** 25 MIN. + STANDING
MAKES: 8 SERVINGS

- 1 **medium apple, peeled and chopped**
- 1 **small onion, chopped**
- 1 **tablespoon olive oil**
- 1 **garlic clove, minced**
- ½ **teaspoon salt**
- ¼ **teaspoon pepper**
- 2 **pork tenderloins (1 pound each)**

SAUCE

- 1 **cup unsweetened apple juice**
- 1 **cup pomegranate juice**
- 1 **tablespoon Dijon mustard**
- 2 **tablespoons cornstarch**
- 2 **tablespoons cold water**
- 1 **tablespoon minced fresh parsley**

1. In a small skillet, saute the apple and onion in oil until tender. Add the garlic, salt and pepper; cook 1 minute longer. Remove from the heat.

2. Make a lengthwise slit down the center of each tenderloin to within ½ in. of bottom. Open tenderloins so they lie flat; cover with plastic wrap. Flatten to ¾-in. thickness.

3. Remove plastic wrap; spread the apple mixture over the meat. Close tenderloins; tie with kitchen string and secure ends with toothpicks. Place in an ungreased 13x9x2-in. baking dish. Bake, uncovered, at 425° for 15 minutes.

4. Meanwhile, in a small saucepan, combine the juices and mustard. Bring to a boil; cook for 5 minutes, stirring occasionally. Combine the cornstarch and cold water until smooth; gradually stir into juice mixture. Bring to a boil; cook and stir for 2 minutes or until thickened. Stir in parsley.

5. Pour ¾ cup sauce over tenderloins. Bake 10-15 minutes longer or until a meat thermometer reads 160°. Let stand for 10 minutes before slicing. Serve with remaining sauce.

PER SERVING *200 cal., 6 g fat (2 g sat. fat), 63 mg chol., 243 mg sodium, 13 g carb., trace fiber, 23 g pro.* **Diabetic Exchanges:** *3 lean meat, 1 fruit.*

When cooking for my family, I'm satisfied if I can serve up a quick meal that pleases everyone. This south-of-the-border pork chop recipe is definitely a keeper!
—**DEANNA ELLETT** BOYNTON BEACH, FL

SALSA SKILLET PORK CHOPS

APPLE-STUFFED PORK TENDERLOINS

Bacon-Swiss Pork Chops C

I'm always looking for quick and easy recipes that are impressive enough to serve to company. With a topping of bacon, onion and Swiss cheese, this one certainly fills the bill.
—**KEITH MILLER** FORT GRATIOT, MI

START TO FINISH: 25 MIN. • **MAKES:** 4 SERVINGS

- 2 **bacon strips, chopped**
- 1 **medium onion, chopped**
- 4 **boneless pork loin chops (4 ounces each)**
- ½ **teaspoon garlic powder**
- ¼ **teaspoon salt**
- 2 **slices reduced-fat Swiss cheese, halved**

1. In a nonstick skillet coated with cooking spray, cook bacon and onion over medium heat until bacon is crisp, stirring occasionally. Remove with a slotted spoon; drain on paper towels. Discard drippings.

2. Sprinkle pork chops with garlic powder and salt. Add pork to the same pan; cook over medium heat 3-4 minutes on each side or until a thermometer reads 145°. Top pork with the bacon mixture and Swiss cheese. Cook, covered, on low heat for 1-2 minutes or until cheese is melted. Let stand 5 minutes before serving.

PER SERVING *218 cal., 10 g fat (4 g sat. fat), 64 mg chol., 268 mg sodium, 4 g carb., 1 g fiber, 27 g pro.* **Diabetic Exchanges:** *4 lean meat, ½ fat.*

Pork & Vegetable Stir-Fry

When I have leftovers from a roast, I use the extra meat to fix a saucy stir-fry the next night. Just add rice and dinner's done!
—**JEANNIE KLUGH** LANCASTER, PA

START TO FINISH: 20 MIN. • **MAKES:** 4 SERVINGS

- 1 **tablespoon cornstarch**
- ¼ **cup unsweetened apple juice**
- 2 **tablespoons sherry or additional unsweetened apple juice**
- 2 **tablespoons soy sauce**
- 1 **package (16 ounces) frozen stir-fry vegetable blend, thawed**
- 1 **garlic clove, minced**
- 1 **tablespoon canola oil**
- 2 **cups cubed cooked pork**
- ¼ **cup slivered almonds, toasted**
  Hot cooked rice

1. In a small bowl, combine the cornstarch, apple juice, sherry and soy sauce until smooth; set aside.

2. Stir-fry vegetable blend and garlic in oil for 1-2 minutes or until the vegetables are crisp-tender. Stir the cornstarch mixture and add to the pan. Bring to a boil; cook and stir for 1-2 minutes or until thickened. Add pork; heat through. Sprinkle with almonds. Serve with rice.

PER SERVING *306 cal., 13 g fat (3 g sat. fat), 63 mg chol., 552 mg sodium, 20 g carb., 5 g fiber, 25 g pro.* **Diabetic Exchanges:** *3 lean meat, 2 vegetable, 1 fat, ½ starch.*

Caramelized Pork Tenderloin ⓒ

Four everyday ingredients—brown sugar, steak seasoning, garlic and butter—really enhance this standout tenderloin. It's a skillet entree that tastes like it came from the grill.

—**DEBRA ARONE** FORT COLLINS, CO

START TO FINISH: 20 MIN. • **MAKES:** 4 SERVINGS

- 1 **pork tenderloin (1 pound)**
- ¼ **cup packed brown sugar**
- 4 **garlic cloves, minced**
- 1 **tablespoon Montreal steak seasoning**
- 2 **tablespoons butter**

1. Cut pork into four pieces and pound with a meat mallet to ¼-in. thickness. In a shallow bowl, mix the brown sugar, garlic and steak seasoning. Dip the pork in brown sugar mixture, patting to help coating adhere.

2. In a large skillet, heat butter over medium-high heat. Add pork; cook 2-3 minutes on each side or until tender.

PER SERVING *236 cal., 10 g fat (5 g sat. fat), 78 mg chol., 585 mg sodium, 14 g carb., trace fiber, 23 g pro.*

Chipotle-Orange Pork Chops

Want to get your family excited about pork chops? Try these! Maple syrup and orange juice concentrate add a one-two punch of sweetness that contrasts wonderfully with zippy chipotles.

—**BILLY HENSLEY** MOUNT CARMEL, TN

START TO FINISH: 30 MIN. • **MAKES:** 8 SERVINGS

- ½ **cup maple syrup**
- ½ **cup thawed orange juice concentrate**
- 3 **tablespoons chopped chipotle peppers in adobo sauce**
- 1 **teaspoon salt**
- 1 **teaspoon pepper**
- 8 **bone-in pork loin chops (8 ounces each and ¾ inch thick)**

1. In a small bowl, combine the first five ingredients. Set aside ⅓ cup for serving.

2. Moisten a paper towel with cooking oil; using long-handled tongs, lightly coat the grill rack. Grill pork chops, covered, over medium heat or broil 4-5 in. from the heat for 4-5 minutes on each side or until a thermometer reads 145°, basting frequently with orange mixture. Let chops stand for 5 minutes before serving with reserved sauce.

PER SERVING *289 cal., 9 g fat (3 g sat. fat), 86 mg chol., 398 mg sodium, 21 g carb., trace fiber, 31 g pro.*

Apple-Cinnamon Pork Loin

I love to make my slow-cooked roast and homemade mashed potatoes for dinner on chilly autumn days. The comforting apple-cinnamon aroma spreads through the entire house.

—**RACHEL SCHULTZ** LANSING, MI

PREP: 20 MIN. • **COOK:** 6 HOURS • **MAKES:** 6 SERVINGS

- 1 **boneless pork loin roast (2 to 3 pounds)**
- ½ **teaspoon salt**
- ¼ **teaspoon pepper**
- 1 **tablespoon canola oil**
- 3 **medium apples, peeled and sliced, divided**
- ¼ **cup honey**
- 1 **small red onion, halved and sliced**
- 1 **tablespoon ground cinnamon**
  Minced fresh parsley, optional

1. Sprinkle roast with salt and pepper. In a large skillet, brown roast in oil on all sides; cool slightly. With a paring knife, cut about sixteen 3-in.-deep slits in sides of roast; insert one apple slice into each slit.

2. Place half of the remaining apples in a 4-qt. slow cooker. Place roast over apples. Drizzle with honey; top with onion and remaining apples. Sprinkle with cinnamon.

3. Cover and cook on low for 6-8 hours or until the meat is tender. Remove pork and apple mixture; keep warm.

4. Transfer cooking juices to a small saucepan. Bring to a boil; cook until liquid is reduced by half. Serve with pork and apple mixture. Sprinkle with parsley if desired.

PER SERVING *290 cal., 10 g fat (3 g sat. fat), 75 mg chol., 241 mg sodium, 22 g carb., 2 g fiber, 29 g pro. **Diabetic Exchanges:** 4 lean meat, 1 starch, ½ fruit, ½ fat.*

PORK MEDALLIONS WITH RASPBERRY-BALSAMIC SAUCE

Pork Medallions with Raspberry-Balsamic Sauce S

When I entertain, I prefer to keep my cooking to a minimum so I have more time to spend with guests. This 30-minute main dish gives me a company-worthy entree without the fuss.

—**LISA VARNER** EL PASO, TX

START TO FINISH: 30 MIN. • **MAKES:** 4 SERVINGS

- 1 **pork tenderloin (1 pound), cut into 1-inch slices**
- 1 **teaspoon garlic powder**
- 1 **tablespoon olive oil**
- ½ **cup seedless raspberry jam**
- 2 **tablespoons balsamic vinegar**
- 2 **teaspoons Dijon mustard**

1. Flatten the pork tenderloin slices to ½-in. thickness; sprinkle with garlic powder.

2. In a large skillet over medium heat, cook pork in oil for 3-5 minutes on each side or until no longer pink. Remove and keep warm. Add the raspberry jam, balsamic vinegar and mustard to the pan. Cook and stir for 2-3 minutes or until thickened. Serve with pork.

PER SERVING *271 cal., 7 g fat (2 g sat. fat), 63 mg chol., 107 mg sodium, 28 g carb., trace fiber, 23 g pro.*

APPLE-CINNAMON PORK LOIN

? Did you know?

Balsamic vinegar is made from sweet white grapes and gets its dark color from aging in wooden barrels. The longer it ages, the more thick and sweet it becomes. Highly aged vinegars are expensive and best enjoyed drizzled over cheese or used for dipping with oil and bread. Moderately priced vinegar works fine for preparing sauces and reductions. If needed, add a little sugar to taste.

Pork Tenderloin with Marsala Mushroom Sauce C

This special tenderloin became a family favorite after I served it on Christmas Eve. My husband likes having leftovers to use for sandwiches.

—**KAREN LATIMER** WINNIPEG, MB

PREP: 15 MIN. • **COOK:** 25 MIN.
MAKES: 6 SERVINGS

- 1 package (½ ounce) dried chanterelle mushrooms
- ½ cup hot water
- 1 teaspoon dried parsley flakes
- ½ teaspoon dried marjoram
- ½ teaspoon dried rosemary, crushed
- ½ teaspoon dried sage leaves
- ½ teaspoon dried savory
- ½ teaspoon garlic powder
- ¾ teaspoon salt, divided
- ¼ teaspoon pepper
- 2 pork tenderloins (¾ pound each)
- 3 tablespoons canola oil, divided
- ½ pound sliced baby portobello mushrooms
- ½ pound sliced fresh button mushrooms
- 4 ounces pearl onions, trimmed and peeled
- 1 cup marsala wine
- 1 cup chicken broth
- 2 tablespoons cornstarch
- 2 tablespoons cold water
  Minced fresh parsley, optional

1. In a small bowl, combine the dried chanterelle mushrooms and hot water; set aside. In another bowl, combine the dried herbs, garlic powder, ¼ teaspoon salt and pepper. Sprinkle over the pork tenderloins.
2. In a large skillet, brown the pork in 2 tablespoons oil on all sides. Remove from pan and keep warm.
3. In same skillet, saute the portobello mushrooms, button mushrooms and pearl onions in the remaining oil until mushrooms are browned. Add marsala wine, chicken broth and remaining salt. Drain chanterelle mushrooms; add to the pan. Bring to a boil. Reduce the heat; add pork.
4. Cover and cook for 15-20 minutes or until a thermometer reads 145°. Remove pork; let stand for 5 minutes before slicing.

5. Combine cornstarch and cold water until smooth; gradually stir into the pan. Bring to a boil; cook and stir for 2 minutes or until thickened.
6. Slice the pork and serve with sauce. Garnish with parsley if desired.
PER SERVING *306 cal., 11 g fat (2 g sat. fat), 64 mg chol., 414 mg sodium, 15 g carb., 2 g fiber, 26 g pro.* **Diabetic Exchanges:** *3 lean meat, 1½ fat, 1 starch.*

Pork Chops with Mushroom-Tarragon Sauce C

In a white wine sauce loaded with fresh mushrooms, pork chops seem decadent. Garlic salt and pepper boost the flavor even more without piling on calories.

—**MELISSA JELINEK** APPLE VALLEY, MN

START TO FINISH: 30 MIN.
MAKES: 4 SERVINGS

- 4 boneless pork loin chops (¾ inch thick and 6 ounces each)
- ¼ teaspoon garlic salt
- ¼ teaspoon pepper
- 2 teaspoons olive oil, divided
- ¾ pound sliced fresh mushrooms
- 1 medium onion, chopped
- 2 garlic cloves, minced
- ⅓ cup white wine or reduced-sodium chicken broth
- ¼ cup all-purpose flour
- 1 cup reduced-sodium chicken broth
- 2 teaspoons minced fresh tarragon or ½ teaspoon dried tarragon
- 2 teaspoons butter

1. Sprinkle pork chops with garlic salt and pepper. In a large nonstick skillet coated with cooking spray, brown pork chops in 1 teaspoon oil. Remove and keep warm. In the same pan, saute the mushrooms and onion in remaining oil until almost tender. Add the garlic; cook 1 minute longer.
2. Stir in white wine. Bring to a boil; cook until liquid is almost evaporated. Combine the flour and chicken broth until smooth; stir into the pan. Bring to a boil; cook and stir for 2 minutes or until thickened.
3. Return the pork chops to the pan and add tarragon. Cover and cook for 6-8 minutes or until a thermometer reads 145°. Stir in butter.
PER SERVING *342 cal., 14 g fat (5 g sat. fat), 87 mg chol., 322 mg sodium, 14 g carb., 2 g fiber, 37 g pro.* **Diabetic Exchanges:** *5 lean meat, 1 vegetable, 1 fat, ½ starch.*

PORK CHOPS WITH MUSHROOM-TARRAGON SAUCE

WALSH FAMILY GRILLED PORK TENDERLOINS

Walsh Family Grilled Pork Tenderloins **C**

This fantastic grilled recipe has been a longtime favorite in my friend's family. When I served the marinated tenderloins to my own family, they understood why!

—LISA FINNEGAN FORKED RIVER, NJ

PREP: 10 MIN. + MARINATING
GRILL: 20 MIN. • **MAKES:** 8 SERVINGS

- ⅓ **cup water**
- ⅓ **cup molasses**
- ⅓ **cup reduced-sodium soy sauce**
- 2 **tablespoons minced fresh gingerroot**
- 2 **garlic cloves, minced**
- ¼ **teaspoon salt**
- ¼ **teaspoon pepper**
- 2 **pork tenderloins (1 pound each)**

1. Combine the first seven ingredients in a large resealable plastic bag. Add the pork tenderloins; seal the bag and turn to coat. Refrigerate for at least 8 hours or overnight.
2. Drain and discard the marinade. Moisten a paper towel with cooking oil; using long-handled tongs, lightly coat the grill rack. Grill pork, covered, over indirect medium-hot heat for 20-25 minutes or until a thermometer reads 145°. Let stand for 5 minutes before slicing.
PER SERVING *143 cal., 4 g fat (1 g sat. fat), 63 mg chol., 165 mg sodium, 3 g carb., trace fiber, 23 g pro. **Diabetic Exchange:** 3 lean meat.*

Citrus-Herb Pork Roast **C**

Here's a wonderful way to prepare a roast. The citrus and herbs lend terrific flavor.

—LAURA BRODINE COLORADO SPRINGS, CO

PREP: 25 MIN. • **COOK:** 8 HOURS
MAKES: 8 SERVINGS

- 1 **boneless pork sirloin roast (3 to 4 pounds)**
- 1 **teaspoon dried oregano**
- ½ **teaspoon ground ginger**
- ½ **teaspoon pepper**
- 2 **medium onions, cut into thin wedges**
- 1 **cup plus 3 tablespoons orange juice, divided**
- 1 **tablespoon sugar**
- 1 **tablespoon white grapefruit juice**
- 1 **tablespoon steak sauce**
- 1 **tablespoon reduced-sodium soy sauce**
- 1 **teaspoon grated orange peel**
- ½ **teaspoon salt**
- 3 **tablespoons cornstarch**
  Hot cooked egg noodles

1. Cut roast in half. In a small bowl, combine oregano, ginger and pepper; rub over roast. In a large nonstick skillet coated with cooking spray, brown roast on all sides. Transfer to a 4-qt. slow cooker; add onions.
2. In a small bowl, combine 1 cup orange juice, sugar, grapefruit juice, steak sauce and soy sauce; pour over the top. Cover and cook on low for 8-10 hours or until the meat is tender. Remove meat and onions to a serving platter; keep warm.
3. Skim the fat from the cooking juices; transfer to a small saucepan. Add the orange peel and salt. Bring to a boil. Combine the cornstarch and remaining orange juice until smooth. Gradually stir into the pan. Bring to a boil; cook and stir for 2 minutes or until thickened. Serve with pork roast and egg noodles.
PER SERVING *289 cal., 10 g fat (4 g sat. fat), 102 mg chol., 326 mg sodium, 13 g carb., 1 g fiber, 35 g pro. **Diabetic Exchanges:** 5 lean meat, 1 starch.*

CITRUS-HERB PORK ROAST

Pork Satay with Rice Noodles

I love adding peanut butter to savory fare, including this Thai-inspired dish. For extra appeal, sprinkle minced fresh cilantro and chopped peanuts on top.

—**STEPHANIE ANDERSON** HORSEHEADS, NY

PREP: 20 MIN. • **COOK:** 4 HOURS
MAKES: 6 SERVINGS

- 1½ **pounds boneless pork loin chops, cut into 2-inch pieces**
- ¼ **teaspoon pepper**
- 1 **medium onion, halved and sliced**
- ⅓ **cup creamy peanut butter**
- ¼ **cup reduced-sodium soy sauce**
- ½ **teaspoon onion powder**
- ½ **teaspoon garlic powder**
- ½ **teaspoon hot pepper sauce**
- 1 **can (14½ ounces) reduced-sodium chicken broth**
- 3 **tablespoons cornstarch**
- 3 **tablespoons water**
- 9 **ounces uncooked thick rice noodles**
  Minced fresh cilantro and chopped peanuts, optional

1. Sprinkle pork with pepper. Place in a 3-qt. slow cooker; top with the onion. In a small bowl, mix peanut butter, soy sauce, onion powder, garlic powder and pepper sauce; gradually add broth. Pour over onion. Cook, covered, on low 4-6 hours or until pork is tender.
2. Remove the pork from slow cooker and keep warm. Skim fat from cooking juices; transfer the cooking juices to a large skillet. Bring to a boil. In a small bowl, mix cornstarch and water until smooth and add to pan. Return to a boil; cook and stir 2 minutes or until thickened. Add pork; heat through.
3. Meanwhile, cook noodles according to the package directions; drain. Serve with pork mixture. If desired, sprinkle with cilantro and peanuts.
NOTE *Reduced-fat peanut butter is not recommended for this recipe.*
PER SERVING *411 cal., 14 g fat (4 g sat. fat), 55 mg chol., 700 mg sodium, 41 g carb., 2 g fiber, 30 g pro.* **Diabetic Exchanges:** *3 lean meat, 2½ starch, 1 fat.*

With a slightly spicy-sweet glaze that requires just four ordinary ingredients, these chops are not only tasty. They're super-quick and easy to fix, too!

—**LILY JULOW** LAWRENCEVILLE, GA

CHILI-APRICOT PORK CHOPS

Chili-Apricot Pork Chops

START TO FINISH: 20 MIN.
MAKES: 4 SERVINGS

- ¼ **cup apricot preserves**
- ¼ **cup chili sauce**
- 1 **tablespoon spicy brown mustard**
- 1 **tablespoon water**
- 4 **bone-in pork loin chops (7 ounces each)**
- ¼ **teaspoon salt**
- ¼ **teaspoon pepper**

1. In a small bowl, combine the preserves, chili sauce, mustard and water. Sprinkle pork chops with salt and pepper. Spoon glaze over both sides of pork.
2. Broil 4-5 in. from the heat for 4-5 minutes on each side or until a thermometer reads 145°. Let stand for 5 minutes before serving.
PER SERVING *271 cal., 8 g fat (3 g sat. fat), 86 mg chol., 497 mg sodium, 17 g carb., trace fiber, 30 g pro.* **Diabetic Exchanges:** *4 lean meat, 1 starch.*

Mango Chutney Pork Roast C

Over the years, we've adapted this roast to give it tropical flair. The fresh, zippy chutney is great on just about any meat. You might want to make an extra batch for tacos the next night. Delicious!

—PAMELA VITTI KNOWLES
HENDERSONVILLE, NC

PREP: 15 MIN. • **BAKE:** 1 HOUR + STANDING
MAKES: 6 SERVINGS (2 CUPS CHUTNEY)

- 1 tablespoon butter
- 1 boneless pork loin roast (2 to 3 pounds)
- ½ teaspoon each salt, pepper and ground ginger

MANGO CHUTNEY

- 2 medium mangoes, peeled and cubed
- ¼ cup finely chopped red onion
- ¼ cup finely chopped sweet red pepper
- 1 jalapeno pepper, seeded and minced
- 2 tablespoons white vinegar
- 1 tablespoon grated fresh gingerroot
- ⅛ teaspoon each salt, ground turmeric and ground cloves

1. In a large skillet, heat the butter over medium-high heat. Brown the pork roast on all sides. Sprinkle with the salt, pepper and ginger.

2. Place the pork roast on a rack in a shallow roasting pan. Bake at 350° for 1 to 1½ hours or until a thermometer reads 145°. Remove roast from oven; tent with foil. Let stand for 10 minutes before slicing.

3. Meanwhile, in a large saucepan, combine all chutney ingredients. Cook, uncovered, over medium heat for 8-10 minutes to allow the flavors to blend, stirring occasionally. Serve with pork.

PER SERVING *256 cal., 9 g fat (4 g sat. fat), 80 mg chol., 305 mg sodium, 13 g carb., 2 g fiber, 30 g pro.* **Diabetic Exchanges:** *4 lean meat, 1 fruit, ½ fat.*

HONEY-GLAZED
PORK TENDERLOINS

Honey-Glazed Pork Tenderloins

Enjoy a flavor-packed tenderloin and skip the fuss. With veggies or rice on the side, you'll have an easy weekday meal.

—DIANE COTTON FRANKLIN, NC

PREP: 15 MIN. • **BAKE:** 20 MIN.
MAKES: 6 SERVINGS

- ½ teaspoon garlic powder
- ½ teaspoon ground chipotle pepper
- ½ teaspoon pepper
- 2 pork tenderloins (1 pound each)
- 1 tablespoon canola oil
- ½ cup honey
- 2 tablespoons reduced-sodium soy sauce
- 1 tablespoon balsamic vinegar
- 1 teaspoon sesame oil

1. Preheat oven to 350°. Combine the first three ingredients; rub over pork. In a large ovenproof skillet, brown pork in canola oil on all sides.

2. In a small bowl, combine honey, soy sauce, vinegar and sesame oil; spoon over the pork. Bake, uncovered, 20-25 minutes or until a thermometer reads 145°, basting occasionally with the pan juices. Let stand 5 minutes before slicing.

PER SERVING *288 cal., 8 g fat (2 g sat. fat), 84 mg chol., 265 mg sodium, 24 g carb., trace fiber, 31 g pro.*

MANGO CHUTNEY
PORK ROAST

Roasted Pork Loin with Fig Sauce

Fruit is a classic accompaniment for pork. I like to change things up using tender figs in a honey-sweetened orange gravy.

—RIAN MACDONALD POWDER SPRINGS, GA

PREP: 1 HOUR • **BAKE:** 1½ HOURS
MAKES: 16 SERVINGS (6¼ CUPS SAUCE)

- 1 **pound dried figs, quartered**
- 1 **cup sherry or reduced-sodium chicken broth**
- 1 **medium lemon, sliced**
- 1 **cinnamon stick (3 inches)**
- 2 **whole cloves**
- 1 **boneless rolled pork loin roast (4 to 5 pounds)**
- 1 **teaspoon salt**
- ¼ **teaspoon ground cinnamon**
- ¼ **teaspoon pepper**
- ½ **cup orange juice**
- ¼ **cup honey**
- 2 **tablespoons cornstarch**
- 2 **cups reduced-sodium chicken broth**

1. In a saucepan, combine the first five ingredients. Bring to a boil. Reduce heat; simmer, uncovered, for 10 minutes. Remove from heat. Cover and steep for 1 hour. Strain the figs, discarding lemon, cinnamon stick and cloves. Reserve the liquid and set aside.

2. Sprinkle the roast with salt, ground cinnamon and pepper. Place roast on a rack in a shallow roasting pan. Bake, uncovered, at 350° for 1 hour. In a small bowl, combine the orange juice, honey and reserved liquid; brush over pork. Bake 30-60 minutes longer or until a meat thermometer reads 160°, basting occasionally.

3. Remove meat to a platter; keep warm. Skim fat from cooking juices; transfer to a large saucepan. Add figs. Combine cornstarch and broth until smooth. Gradually stir into pan. Bring to a boil; cook and stir for 2 minutes or until thickened. Serve with pork.

PER SERVING *249 cal., 5 g fat (2 g sat. fat), 56 mg chol., 256 mg sodium, 25 g carb., 4 g fiber, 23 g pro.* **Diabetic Exchanges:** *3 lean meat, 1 fruit, ½ starch.*

ROASTED PORK LOIN WITH FIG SAUCE

173

164

172

Fish & Seafood

❝I came up with this recipe for my family because they love grilled shrimp. I especially like that it's quick, delicious and good for us.❞

—**LISA SPEER** PALM BEACH, FL
about her recipe, Lemony Shrimp & Tomatoes, on page 175

Mediterranean Shrimp Linguine

To save time, you can do most of the prep work for this dish in advance. But even if you don't, it's a very simple recipe with lots of Mediterranean flavors and a little kick of heat from red pepper flakes.

—MEGAN HIDALGO QUARRYVILLE, PA

PREP: 20 MIN. • **COOK:** 20 MIN.
MAKES: 8 SERVINGS

- 1 package (16 ounces) linguine
- 2 pounds uncooked medium shrimp, peeled and deveined
- 1 medium onion, chopped
- 6 tablespoons olive oil
- 4 garlic cloves, minced
- 1 cup chopped roasted sweet red peppers
- 2 cans (2¼ ounces each) sliced ripe olives, drained
- ½ cup minced fresh parsley
- ½ cup white wine or chicken broth
- ½ teaspoon crushed red pepper flakes
- ½ teaspoon kosher salt
- ½ teaspoon dried oregano
- ½ teaspoon pepper
- ¾ cup crumbled feta cheese
- 2 tablespoons lemon juice

1. Cook linguine according to package directions.
2. Meanwhile, in a large skillet, saute shrimp and onion in oil until shrimp turn pink. Add garlic; cook 1 minute longer. Stir in the red peppers, olives, parsley, wine, pepper flakes, salt, oregano and pepper. Reduce heat.
3. Drain linguine, reserving ½ cup cooking water. Add linguine and reserved water to the skillet. Stir in cheese and lemon juice; cook and stir until cheese is melted.
PER SERVING *462 cal., 16 g fat (3 g sat. fat), 144 mg chol., 610 mg sodium, 48 g carb., 3 g fiber, 28 g pro.*

Sprigs in a Snip

Place parsley in a small glass container and snip the sprigs with kitchen shears until minced. No need for a cutting board!

Fish & Chips with Dipping Sauce

My husband and I really like fish and chips, just not all the grease that typically comes along with it. I decided to give the classic dinner a makeover. Turns out the pickle dip is healthier than tartar sauce, and we like it a lot better—who knew?

—MICHELLE LUCAS COLD SPRING, KY

PREP: 30 MIN. • **BAKE:** 30 MIN.
MAKES: 4 SERVINGS

- ½ cup reduced-fat sour cream
- 2 tablespoons chopped dill pickle
- 1 tablespoon dill pickle juice
- ⅛ teaspoon pepper

FRIES
- 4 large potatoes (about 2 pounds)
- 2 tablespoons olive oil
- ½ teaspoon salt
- ¼ teaspoon pepper

FISH
- 1½ cups panko (Japanese) bread crumbs
- 1 teaspoon garlic powder
- 1 teaspoon onion powder
- ½ teaspoon salt
- ½ teaspoon pepper
- 2 egg whites, beaten
- 4 cod fillets (4 ounces each)
  Cooking spray
  Lemon wedges

1. Arrange one oven rack at lowest rack setting; place second rack in middle of oven. Preheat oven to 425°. In a small bowl, mix sour cream, chopped pickle, pickle juice and pepper. Refrigerate, covered, until serving.
2. Cut potatoes into ¼-in. julienne strips. Rinse well and pat dry. In a large bowl, toss with oil, salt and pepper; transfer to a baking sheet coated with cooking spray. Bake on bottom oven rack 30-35 minutes or until golden brown and tender, turning once.
3. For fish, in a shallow bowl, mix bread crumbs, garlic powder, onion powder, salt and pepper. Place egg whites in a separate shallow bowl. Dip fish in egg whites, then in crumb mixture, patting to help coating adhere.
4. Transfer to a baking sheet coated with cooking spray. Spritz fish with cooking spray. Bake on top oven rack 14-16 minutes or until fish just begins to flake easily with a fork. Serve with fries, sour cream mixture and lemon wedges.
PER SERVING *402 cal., 11 g fat (3 g sat. fat), 53 mg chol., 667 mg sodium, 48 g carb., 4 g fiber, 27 g pro.* **Diabetic Exchanges:** *3 starch, 3 lean meat, 2 fat.*

FISH & CHIPS WITH DIPPING SAUCE

GRILLED PISTACHIO-LEMON PESTO SHRIMP

PER SERVING *236 cal., 18 g fat (3 g sat. fat), 105 mg chol., 241 mg sodium, 3 g carb., 1 g fiber, 16 g pro.*

Oven-Barbecued Salmon C

START TO FINISH: 25 MIN.
MAKES: 5 SERVINGS

- 5 **salmon fillets (6 ounces each)**
- 3 **tablespoons orange juice**
- 2 **tablespoons lemon juice**
- 2 **tablespoons brown sugar**
- 1 **tablespoon chili powder**
- 1 **tablespoon paprika**
- ½ **teaspoon salt**
- ½ **teaspoon garlic powder**
- ½ **teaspoon ground cumin**

1. Preheat oven to 425°. Place salmon in a greased 15x10x1-in. baking pan; drizzle with orange and lemon juices.
2. In a small bowl, mix remaining ingredients; sprinkle over fillets. Bake 13-15 minutes or until fish flakes easily with a fork.

PER SERVING *301 cal., 16 g fat (3 g sat. fat), 85 mg chol., 340 mg sodium, 9 g carb., 1 g fiber, 29 g pro.* **Diabetic Exchanges:** *4 lean meat, 1 fat, ½ starch.*

Grilled Pistachio-Lemon Pesto Shrimp C

Not your ordinary pesto, this one is made with arugula and pistachios. It's excellent on more than shrimp, too. Try spreading it on crostini or toss it with pasta.
—AMY DALE LONG BEACH, CA

PREP: 15 MIN. + CHILLING • **GRILL:** 5 MIN.
MAKES: 8 SERVINGS

- ¾ **cup fresh arugula**
- ½ **cup minced fresh parsley**
- ⅓ **cup shelled pistachios**
- 2 **tablespoons lemon juice**
- 1 **garlic clove, peeled**
- ¼ **teaspoon grated lemon peel**
- ½ **cup olive oil**
- ¼ **cup shredded Parmesan cheese**
- ¼ **teaspoon salt**
- ⅛ **teaspoon pepper**
- 1½ **pounds uncooked jumbo shrimp, peeled and deveined**

1. Place the first six ingredients in a food processor; pulse until finely chopped. Continue processing while gradually adding oil in a steady stream. Add Parmesan cheese, salt and pepper; pulse just until combined. Transfer ⅓ cup pesto to a large bowl. Add shrimp; toss to coat. Refrigerate, covered, 30 minutes.
2. Moisten a paper towel with cooking oil; using long-handled tongs, rub on grill rack to coat lightly. Thread shrimp onto eight metal or soaked wooden skewers. Grill, covered, over medium heat 5-6 minutes or until shrimp turn pink, turning once. Serve with the remaining pesto.

Late last summer, the South Carolina heat drove me indoors and away from my grill. So I changed my favorite over-the-coals recipe to be baked in the oven. I'm happy to say it's just as tasty.
—MANDY RIVERS LEXINGTON, SC

OVEN-BARBECUED SALMON

Tilapia Tacos

I absolutely love fish tacos and wanted to create a slimmed-down recipe so I could enjoy them anytime I wanted. The compliments come in when I serve these for dinner.

—JADE PETERSON PORTLAND, OR

START TO FINISH: 30 MIN.
MAKES: 4 SERVINGS

- 1 egg
- 1 tablespoon fat-free milk
- ½ teaspoon green hot pepper sauce
- ½ cup cornmeal
- 2 tablespoons all-purpose flour
- ¼ teaspoon ground cumin
- ¼ teaspoon pepper
- 4 tilapia fillets (4 ounces each), cut lengthwise in half
- 4 teaspoons olive oil
- 1 can (15 ounces) Southwestern black beans
- 8 corn tortillas (6 inches), warmed
- 3 plum tomatoes, chopped
- 2 cups shredded cabbage
- ½ cup salsa verde
- ¼ cup minced fresh cilantro
- 1 medium lime, cut into 8 wedges

1. Preheat oven to 375°. In a shallow bowl, whisk egg, milk and pepper sauce. In another shallow bowl, mix cornmeal, flour, cumin and pepper. Dip tilapia in egg mixture, then in cornmeal mixture, patting to help coating adhere. Place on a baking sheet coated with cooking spray. Drizzle tops with oil. Bake 15-20 minutes or until fish flakes easily with a fork.

2. Meanwhile, place beans in a small saucepan; heat through over medium-low heat, stirring occasionally. Serve tilapia in tortillas; top with beans, tomatoes, cabbage, salsa verde and cilantro. Serve with lime wedges.

PER SERVING *438 cal., 9 g fat (2 g sat. fat), 87 mg chol., 567 mg sodium, 57 g carb., 12 g fiber, 34 g pro.*

SOUTHWESTERN
SCALLOPS

Southwestern Scallops 🄲

My saucy sea scallops are popular at dinner parties, and they're in my collection of easy weekday meals. The seasoning gives the sweet shellfish a pleasant kick.

—MAGGIE FONTENOT THE WOODLANDS, TX

START TO FINISH: 20 MIN.
MAKES: 4 SERVINGS

- 2 teaspoons chili powder
- ½ teaspoon ground cumin
- ¼ teaspoon salt
- ⅛ teaspoon pepper
- 12 sea scallops (1 to 1½ pounds)
- 2 tablespoons butter, divided
- ½ cup white wine or chicken broth

1. In a small bowl, mix seasonings. Pat scallops dry with paper towels; sprinkle with seasonings, pressing to coat.

2. In a large skillet, heat 1 tablespoon butter over medium-high heat. Add scallops; cook 2-3 minutes on each side or until golden brown and firm. Remove from pan; keep warm.

3. Add wine to pan. Cook over medium heat, stirring to loosen browned bits from pan. Bring to a boil; cook until liquid is reduced by half. Stir in remaining butter until melted. Serve with scallops.

PER SERVING *180 cal., 7 g fat (4 g sat. fat), 52 mg chol., 386 mg sodium, 4 g carb., 1 g fiber, 19 g pro.* **Diabetic Exchanges:** *3 lean meat, 1½ fat.*

TILAPIA TACOS

Shrimp & Chicken Sausage with Grits

I'm originally from Tennessee and had never had shrimp and grits until I moved to South Carolina several years ago. I think my version is just as delicious as the original...but easier on the waistline.
—**ATHENA RUSSELL** FLORENCE, SC

START TO FINISH: 30 MIN.
MAKES: 5 SERVINGS

- 3 **cups water**
- 1 **cup quick-cooking grits**
- 4 **ounces reduced-fat cream cheese, cubed**
- 3 **fully cooked spicy chicken sausage links (3 ounces each), cut into ½-inch slices**
- 2 **teaspoons canola oil, divided**
- 2 **garlic cloves, minced**
- 2 **green onions, chopped, divided**
- 4 **teaspoons whole wheat flour**
- 1½ **cups chicken broth**
- ¼ **cup fat-free evaporated milk**
- 1 **pound uncooked medium shrimp, peeled and deveined**
- 1 **medium tomato, chopped**

1. In a large saucepan, bring water to a boil. Slowly stir in grits. Reduce heat; cook and stir for 5-7 minutes or until thickened. Stir in cream cheese until melted.

2. Meanwhile, in a large skillet, brown sausage in 1 teaspoon oil. Remove and keep warm.

3. In the same pan, heat remaining oil over medium-high heat. Add garlic and half of the green onions; cook and stir for 1 minute. Stir in flour until blended; gradually whisk in broth and milk. Bring to a boil, stirring constantly; cook and stir for 2 minutes or until thickened.

4. Stir in shrimp and sausage; cook for 3-5 minutes or until shrimp turn pink. Serve with grits; top with tomato and remaining green onion.

PER SERVING *367 cal., 13 g fat (5 g sat. fat), 161 mg chol., 810 mg sodium, 30 g carb., 2 g fiber, 31 g pro.* **Diabetic Exchanges:** *4 lean meat, 2 starch, ½ fat.*

SALMON WITH TANGY RASPBERRY SAUCE

Salmon with Tangy Raspberry Sauce C

We love salmon at our house and are always finding new ways to make it. This one turned out so well; the raspberry sauce adds a nice sweetness. My son calls it salmon candy!
—**ANNA-MARIE WILLIAMS** LEAGUE CITY, TX

START TO FINISH: 25 MIN.
MAKES: 4 SERVINGS

- 1 **teaspoon smoked paprika**
- ¼ **teaspoon salt**
- ¼ **teaspoon pepper**
- 4 **salmon fillets (6 ounces each)**
- 2 **tablespoons olive oil**
- 2 **tablespoons red raspberry preserves**
- 1 **tablespoon white vinegar**
- 1 **tablespoon honey**

1. Combine the paprika, salt and pepper; sprinkle over salmon. Drizzle with oil. Moisten a paper towel with cooking oil; using long-handled tongs, lightly coat the grill rack. Place salmon skin side down on grill rack.

2. Grill, covered, over medium heat or broil 4 in. from the heat for 10-12 minutes or until fish flakes easily with a fork. In a small bowl, whisk the preserves, vinegar and honey; spoon over fillets.

PER SERVING *367 cal., 23 g fat (4 g sat. fat), 85 mg chol., 233 mg sodium, 11 g carb., trace fiber, 29 g pro.* **Diabetic Exchanges:** *5 lean meat, 1½ fat, 1 starch.*

SHRIMP & CHICKEN SAUSAGE WITH GRITS

ZUCCHINI PESTO WITH
SHRIMP AND FARFALLE

Zucchini Pesto with Shrimp and Farfalle

Wonderful zucchini-basil pesto takes advantage of summer's best produce and adds fantastic flavor to this simple pasta toss. You'll feel like you're dining in a fine restaurant, but the seasonal ingredients make it easy on your wallet.

—AMBER MASSEY ARGYLE, TX

PREP: 25 MIN. • **COOK:** 15 MIN. • **MAKES:** 6 SERVINGS

 8 **ounces uncooked multigrain bow tie pasta**
 1 **pound zucchini, sliced**
 2 **tablespoons olive oil, divided**
 1 **cup loosely packed basil leaves**
 ½ **cup shredded Parmigiano-Reggiano or Parmesan cheese, divided**
 3 **tablespoons pine nuts, toasted**
 4 **garlic cloves, peeled and halved**
 1 **large sweet onion, chopped**
 1 **pound peeled and deveined cooked medium shrimp**
 ½ **cup reduced-fat evaporated milk**
 1 **teaspoon lemon juice**
 1¾ **teaspoons kosher salt**
 ½ **teaspoon grated lemon peel**
 ½ **teaspoon coarsely ground pepper**

1. Cook pasta according to package directions. Meanwhile, in a Dutch oven, saute zucchini in 1 tablespoon oil until tender. Remove from the pan and cool slightly.
2. Drain pasta, reserving ⅓ cup cooking liquid. In a food processor, combine the basil, ¼ cup cheese, pine nuts, garlic, reserved cooking liquid and ⅔ cup cooked zucchini. Cover and process until pureed.
3. In the same Dutch oven, cook onion in remaining oil until tender. Stir in the shrimp, pasta and remaining zucchini. Add the pureed mixture, milk, lemon juice, salt, lemon peel and pepper; toss to coat. Heat through. Sprinkle with remaining cheese.
PER SERVING *368 cal., 12 g fat (3 g sat. fat), 121 mg chol., 827 mg sodium, 37 g carb., 5 g fiber, 29 g pro.* **Diabetic Exchanges:** *2 starch, 2 lean meat, 1½ fat, 1 vegetable.*

Hoisin & Honey Glazed Salmon

Now that I have this recipe, my husband and I always look forward to the fresh wild salmon season. You can find hoisin sauce in the international foods aisle at the grocery store.

—CHERYL REIN ORLANDO, FL

START TO FINISH: 20 MIN. • **MAKES:** 4 SERVINGS

 3 **tablespoons hoisin sauce**
 3 **tablespoons honey**
 1 **tablespoon unsweetened pineapple juice**
 4 **salmon fillets (6 ounces each)**

1. Preheat broiler. Mix the hoisin sauce, honey and pineapple juice.
2. Place salmon in a foil-lined 15x10x1-in. baking pan. Broil 4-5 in. from heat 12-14 minutes or until fish just begins to flake easily with a fork. Baste occasionally with ¼ cup hoisin mixture during the last 6 minutes of cooking. Serve with remaining sauce.
PER SERVING *341 cal., 16 g fat (3 g sat. fat), 86 mg chol., 280 mg sodium, 19 g carb., trace fiber, 29 g pro.* **Diabetic Exchanges:** *4 lean meat, 1 starch.*

HOISIN & HONEY GLAZED SLAMON

Savory Tomato-Braised Tilapia C

When I shared this recipe with a few friends, it was a huge hit! One friend makes it often now, which I think is a testament to how good it is.

—**NANCY SHIVELY** SHOREWOOD, IL

START TO FINISH: 30 MIN. • **MAKES:** 4 SERVINGS

- 4   tilapia fillets (6 ounces each)
- ¼   teaspoon seasoned salt
- 1   tablespoon lemon juice
- 2   tablespoons olive oil
- 1   small red onion, chopped
- 1   can (10 ounces) diced tomatoes and green chilies, undrained
- ¾   cup chopped roasted sweet red peppers
- ½   cup chicken broth
- ¼   cup tomato paste
- 1   teaspoon garlic powder
- 1   teaspoon dried oregano
      Hot cooked pasta, optional

1. Sprinkle fillets with seasoned salt; drizzle with lemon juice. In a large skillet, heat oil over medium-high heat. Add onion; cook and stir until tender. Add tomatoes, peppers, broth, tomato paste, garlic powder and oregano; cook and stir 2-3 minutes longer.

2. Place fillets over tomato mixture; cook, covered, 6-8 minutes or until fish flakes easily with a fork. If desired, serve with pasta.

PER SERVING 254 cal., 8 g fat (2 g sat. fat), 83 mg chol., 740 mg sodium, 10 g carb., 2 g fiber, 34 g pro. *Diabetic Exchanges: 5 lean meat, 1½ fat, 1 vegetable.*

> I like this Asian-inspired tuna because it's easy to prepare, appetizing and healthy. It's a popular dish with my friends.
> —**DIANE HALFERTY** CORPUS CHRISTI, TX

TUNA WITH CITRUS PONZU SAUCE

Tuna with Citrus Ponzu Sauce C

START TO FINISH: 20 MIN. • **MAKES:** 4 SERVINGS

- ½   teaspoon Chinese five-spice powder
- ¼   teaspoon salt
- ¼   teaspoon cayenne pepper
- 4   tuna steaks (6 ounces each)
- 1   tablespoon canola oil
- ¼   cup orange juice
- 2   green onions, thinly sliced
- 1   tablespoon lemon juice
- 1   tablespoon reduced-sodium soy sauce
- 2   teaspoons rice vinegar
- 1   teaspoon brown sugar
- ¼   teaspoon minced fresh gingerroot

1. Combine the five-spice powder, salt and cayenne; sprinkle over tuna steaks. In a large skillet, cook tuna in oil over medium heat for 2-3 minutes on each side for medium-rare or until slightly pink in the center; remove and keep warm.

2. Combine the orange juice, green onions, lemon juice, soy sauce, vinegar, brown sugar and ginger; pour into skillet. Cook for 1-2 minutes or until slightly thickened. Serve with tuna.

PER SERVING 234 cal., 5 g fat (1 g sat. fat), 77 mg chol., 364 mg sodium, 5 g carb., trace fiber, 40 g pro. *Diabetic Exchanges: 5 lean meat, ½ fat.*

SAVORY TOMATO-BRAISED TILAPIA

PINEAPPLE SHRIMP STIR-FRY

Pineapple Shrimp Stir-Fry

I came up with this recipe for a luau-themed party and served it with sliced papaya, mango and avocado. Delish! If you don't care for coconut, sprinkle with chopped macadamia nuts instead.

—TRISHA KRUSE EAGLE, ID

START TO FINISH: 30 MIN.
MAKES: 4 SERVINGS

- 1 **can (20 ounces) unsweetened pineapple tidbits**
- 2 **tablespoons cornstarch**
- 1 **cup chicken broth**
- 1 **tablespoon brown sugar**
- 1 **tablespoon orange juice**
- 1 **tablespoon reduced-sodium soy sauce**
- 1 **tablespoon sesame or canola oil**
- 1 **medium sweet red pepper, thinly sliced**
- 1 **medium green pepper, thinly sliced**
- 1 **medium sweet onion, thinly sliced**
- 1 **pound uncooked shrimp (31-40 per pound), peeled and deveined**
- ¼ **cup flaked coconut, toasted Hot cooked rice**

1. Drain pineapple, reserving juice. In a small bowl, mix cornstarch, broth, brown sugar, orange juice, soy sauce and reserved pineapple juice until smooth.
2. In a large skillet, heat oil over medium-high heat. Add peppers and onion; stir-fry 1-2 minutes or just until crisp-tender. Add shrimp; stir-fry 2-3 minutes longer or until shrimp turn pink. Remove from pan.
3. Place pineapple in skillet. Stir cornstarch mixture and add to pan. Bring to a boil; cook and stir 4-5 minutes or until sauce is thickened. Return shrimp mixture to pan; heat through, stirring to combine. Sprinkle with coconut; serve with rice.
PER SERVING *301 cal., 7 g fat (3 g sat. fat), 139 mg chol., 568 mg sodium, 38 g carb., 3 g fiber, 20 g pro.*

Peppered Tuna Kabobs **F** **S**

When we barbecue, we like to wow our guests, so hot dogs and burgers are out! We make tuna skewers topped with salsa instead. My five kids like to help me put the skewers together.

—JENNIFER INGERSOLL HERNDON, VA

START TO FINISH: 30 MIN.
MAKES: 4 SERVINGS

- ½ **cup frozen corn, thawed**
- 4 **green onions, chopped**
- 1 **jalapeno pepper, seeded and chopped**
- 2 **tablespoons coarsely chopped fresh parsley**
- 2 **tablespoons lime juice**
- 1 **pound tuna steaks, cut into 1-inch cubes**
- 1 **teaspoon coarsely ground pepper**
- 2 **large sweet red peppers, cut into 2x1-inch pieces**
- 1 **medium mango, peeled and cut into 1-inch cubes**

1. For salsa, in a small bowl, combine the first five ingredients; set aside.
2. Moisten a paper towel with cooking oil; using long-handled tongs, rub on grill rack to coat lightly. Rub tuna with pepper. On four metal or soaked wooden skewers, alternately thread red peppers, tuna and mango.
3. Grill, covered, over medium heat 10-12 minutes for medium-rare or until slightly pink in the center and peppers are tender, turning occasionally. Serve with salsa.
NOTE *Wear disposable gloves when cutting hot peppers; the oils can burn skin. Avoid touching your face.*
PER SERVING *205 cal., 2 g fat (trace sat. fat), 51 mg chol., 50 mg sodium, 20 g carb., 4 g fiber, 29 g pro. Diabetic Exchanges: 3 lean meat, 1 starch.*

PEPPERED TUNA KABOBS

Skillet Sea Scallops C

You'll want to slip this recipe into the front of your "last-minute meals" file. Pasta and mixed greens nicely complement the tender, citrusy shellfish and it cooks up in 10 minutes.

—MARGARET E. LOWENBERG KINGMAN, AZ

START TO FINISH: 25 MIN.
MAKES: 4 SERVINGS

- ½ cup dry bread crumbs
- ½ teaspoon salt
- 1 pound sea scallops
- 2 tablespoons butter
- 1 tablespoon olive oil
- ¼ cup white wine or reduced-sodium chicken broth
- 2 tablespoons lemon juice
- 1 teaspoon minced fresh parsley
- 1 garlic clove, minced

1. In a large resealable plastic bag, combine bread crumbs and salt. Add scallops, a few at a time, and shake to coat.

2. In a large skillet over medium-high heat, brown scallops in butter and oil for 1½ to 2 minutes on each side or until firm and opaque. Remove and keep warm. Add the wine, lemon juice, parsley and garlic to the skillet; bring to a boil. Pour over scallops. Serve immediately.

PER SERVING *249 cal., 11 g fat (4 g sat. fat), 52 mg chol., 618 mg sodium, 14 g carb., 1 g fiber, 21 g pro.* **Diabetic Exchanges:** *3 lean meat, 2 fat, 1 starch.*

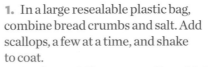

CAJUN SHRIMP & CUCUMBER WRAPS

Cajun Shrimp & Cucumber Wraps

Spicy Cajun shrimp get a cool contrast when you wrap them up with cucumbers, lettuce and parsley. Serve these handheld wraps on an alfresco dinner night.

—CHANTEL BEAUREGARD
LAKE ARROWHEAD, CA

START TO FINISH: 20 MIN.
MAKES: 4 SERVINGS

- ¼ cup lemon juice
- 4 tablespoons olive oil, divided
- 1½ teaspoons Cajun seasoning, divided
- ⅛ teaspoon pepper
- 1 pound uncooked large shrimp, peeled and deveined (tails removed)
- 8 Bibb or Boston lettuce leaves
- 4 flatbread wraps
- 2 small cucumbers, cut lengthwise into quarters
- 4 thin slices red onion
- ¼ cup fresh parsley leaves

1. In a small bowl, whisk lemon juice, 3 tablespoons oil, 1 teaspoon Cajun seasoning and pepper. Toss shrimp with remaining Cajun seasoning. In a large skillet, heat remaining oil over medium-high heat. Add shrimp mixture; cook and stir until shrimp turn pink.

2. Place lettuce on flatbread wraps; top with cucumbers, onion, parsley and shrimp. Drizzle with dressing; roll up and, if desired, secure with toothpicks.

PER SERVING *365 cal., 17 g fat (2 g sat. fat), 138 mg chol., 670 mg sodium, 29 g carb., 4 g fiber, 26 g pro.*

SKILLET SEA SCALLOPS

Fish & Vegetable Packets C

Try this traditional cooking technique to keep the contents extra moist. I like to serve fish still wrapped in the parchment paper for each person to open.

—JILL ANDERSON SLEEPY EYE, MN

START TO FINISH: 25 MIN.
MAKES: 4 SERVINGS

- 1½ cups julienned carrots
- 1½ cups fresh snow peas
- 2 green onions, cut into 2-inch pieces
- 4 cod fillets (6 ounces each)
- 2 teaspoons lemon juice
- ¼ teaspoon salt
- ¼ teaspoon dried thyme
- ¼ teaspoon crushed red pepper flakes
- ¼ teaspoon pepper
- 4 teaspoons butter

1. Preheat oven to 450°. In a small bowl, combine carrots, snow peas and green onions. Cut parchment paper or heavy-duty foil into four 18x12-in. pieces; place a fish fillet off center on each. Drizzle with lemon juice and top with carrot mixture. Sprinkle with seasonings; dot with butter.

2. Fold parchment paper over fish. Bring edges of paper together on all sides and crimp to seal, forming a large packet. Repeat for remaining packets. Place on baking sheets.

3. Bake 10-15 minutes or until fish just begins to flake easily with a fork. Open packets carefully to allow steam to escape.

PER SERVING *206 cal., 5 g fat (3 g sat. fat), 75 mg chol., 301 mg sodium, 10 g carb., 3 g fiber, 29 g pro.* **Diabetic Exchanges:** *3 lean meat, 1 vegetable, 1 fat.*

Fish Facts

If you are using fresh cod for Fish & Vegetable Packets, be sure to prepare the fish within a day or two of bringing it home from the market. If you use frozen cod, look for packages that are free of freezer burn and odor.

FISH & VEGETABLE PACKETS

Crunchy Tuna Salad with Tomatoes C

On a hot summer day, there's nothing more refreshing than fresh tomatoes with sweet onion tuna. I grow a few tomato plants in my garden and the homegrown taste makes the recipe even more of a treat.

—**DIANE SELICH** VASSAR, MI

START TO FINISH: 20 MIN. • **MAKES:** 4 SERVINGS

- ⅔ cup reduced-fat mayonnaise
- ½ cup chopped sweet onion
- 1 celery rib, chopped
- 1 teaspoon minced fresh parsley or ¼ teaspoon dried parsley flakes
- ¾ teaspoon pepper
- 1 can (12 ounces) albacore white tuna in water, drained and flaked
- 4 medium tomatoes, cut into wedges

In a small bowl, combine mayonnaise, onion, celery, parsley and pepper. Stir in tuna. Serve with tomato wedges.
PER SERVING *280 cal., 16 g fat (3 g sat. fat), 50 mg chol., 656 mg sodium, 12 g carb., 2 g fiber, 22 g pro.* **Diabetic Exchanges:** *3 lean meat, 2 fat, 1 vegetable.*

Herb-Roasted Salmon Fillets C

Roasted salmon is simple but elegant enough to serve to company. I make it on days when I have less than an hour to cook.
—**LUANNE ASTA** NEW YORK, NY

START TO FINISH: 30 MIN. • **MAKES:** 4 SERVINGS

- 4 salmon fillets (6 ounces each)
- 4 garlic cloves, minced
- 1 tablespoon minced fresh rosemary or 1 teaspoon dried rosemary, crushed
- 1 tablespoon olive oil
- 2 teaspoons minced fresh thyme or ½ teaspoon dried thyme
- ¾ teaspoon salt
- ½ teaspoon pepper

Preheat oven to 425°. Place salmon in a greased 15x10x1-in. baking pan, skin side down. Combine remaining ingredients; spread over fillets. Roast 15-18 minutes or until desired doneness.
PER SERVING *301 cal., 19 g fat (4 g sat. fat), 85 mg chol., 529 mg sodium, 1 g carb., trace fiber, 29 g pro.* **Diabetic Exchanges:** *4 lean meat, 1 fat.*

Sesame Noodles with Shrimp & Snap Peas

Stir-fries and busy nights are a mealtime match made in heaven. For a boost of vibrant color and freshness, I sometimes stir in chopped cilantro just before I serve it from the pan.
—**NEDRA SCHELL** FORT WORTH, TX

START TO FINISH: 25 MIN. • **MAKES:** 4 SERVINGS

- 8 **ounces uncooked whole wheat linguine**
- 1 **tablespoon canola oil**
- 1 **pound uncooked medium shrimp, peeled and deveined**
- 2 **cups fresh sugar snap peas, trimmed**
- ⅛ **teaspoon salt**
- ⅛ **teaspoon crushed red pepper flakes**
- ¾ **cup reduced-fat Asian toasted sesame salad dressing**

1. Cook linguine according to package directions for al dente.
2. Meanwhile, in a large skillet, heat oil over medium-high heat. Add shrimp, peas, salt and pepper flakes; stir-fry 2-3 minutes or until shrimp turn pink and peas are crisp-tender. Drain linguine, reserving ¼ cup pasta water. Add pasta, pasta water and salad dressing to shrimp mixture; toss to combine.
PER SERVING *418 cal., 10 g fat (1 g sat. fat), 138 mg chol., 646 mg sodium, 60 g carb., 8 g fiber, 29 g pro.*

Blackened Halibut C

Try serving the spicy fillets with garlic mashed potatoes, crusty bread and a crisp salad on the side. This is what my family eats when we have a special occasion.
—**BRENDA WILLIAMS** SANTA MARIA, CA

START TO FINISH: 25 MIN. • **MAKES:** 4 SERVINGS

- 2 **tablespoons garlic powder**
- 1 **tablespoon salt**
- 1 **tablespoon onion powder**
- 1 **tablespoon dried oregano**
- 1 **tablespoon dried thyme**
- 1 **tablespoon cayenne pepper**
- 1 **tablespoon pepper**
- 2½ **teaspoons paprika**
- 4 **halibut fillets (4 ounces each)**
- 2 **tablespoons butter**

1. In a large resealable plastic bag, combine the first eight ingredients. Add fillets, two at a time, and shake to coat.
2. In a large cast-iron skillet, cook fillets in butter over medium heat for 3-4 minutes on each side or until fish flakes easily with a fork.
PER SERVING *189 cal., 8 g fat (4 g sat. fat), 51 mg chol., 758 mg sodium, 3 g carb., 1 g fiber, 24 g pro.* **Diabetic Exchanges:** *3 lean meat, 1 fat.*

HALIBUT SOFT TACOS

Broiled Fish with Tarragon Sauce F

The delicate taste of this fish pairs perfectly with the tangy sauce. A delicious hint of honey comes through. Serve the fish with warm bread, mixed vegetables or rice to help soak up the sauce.
—**ROBIN PRATT** ATHENS, GA

START TO FINISH: 25 MIN.
MAKES: 8 SERVINGS

- 2 **pounds cod or red snapper fillets**
- 1 **tablespoon cornstarch**
- ½ **cup cold water**
- ½ **cup honey**
- ¼ **cup white wine or chicken broth**
- ¼ **cup lemon juice**
- 1 **teaspoon garlic salt**
- ½ **teaspoon grated lemon peel**
- 1 **tablespoon minced fresh tarragon**

1. Place fish on a lightly greased 15x10x1-in. baking pan. Broil 4 in. from the heat for 8-10 minutes or until fish flakes easily with a fork.
2. Meanwhile, in a small saucepan, whisk cornstarch and water until smooth. Stir in the honey, wine, lemon juice, garlic salt and lemon peel. Bring to a boil. Cook and stir for 3-5 minutes or until thickened. Remove from the heat; stir in tarragon. Serve with fish.
PER SERVING *186 cal., 1 g fat (trace sat. fat), 40 mg chol., 276 mg sodium, 19 g carb., trace fiber, 23 g pro.* **Diabetic Exchanges:** *3 lean meat, 1 starch.*

BROILED FISH WITH TARRAGON SAUCE

Halibut Soft Tacos

I sometimes serve the fish wrapped in lettuce instead of tortillas. Either way, the mango salsa tastes amazing with grilled halibut. This warm-weather favorite is quick, colorful and full of nutrients.
—**KRISTIN KOSSAK** BOZEMAN, MT

START TO FINISH: 25 MIN.
MAKES: 4 SERVINGS

- 1 **medium mango, peeled and cubed**
- ½ **cup cubed avocado**
- ¼ **cup chopped red onion**
- 2 **tablespoons chopped seeded jalapeno pepper**
- 1 **tablespoon minced fresh cilantro**
- 3 **teaspoons olive oil, divided**
- 1 **teaspoon lemon juice**
- 1 **teaspoon honey**
- 1 **pound halibut steaks (¾ inch thick)**
- ½ **teaspoon salt**
- ¼ **teaspoon pepper**
- 4 **Bibb lettuce leaves**
- 4 **flour tortillas (6 inches), warmed**
- 4 **teaspoons sweet Thai chili sauce**

1. In a small bowl, combine the mango, avocado, onion, jalapeno, cilantro, 2 teaspoons oil, lemon juice and honey; set aside. Brush halibut with remaining oil; sprinkle with salt and pepper.
2. Moisten a paper towel with cooking oil; using long-handled tongs, lightly coat the grill rack. Grill halibut, covered, over high heat or broil 3-4 in. from the heat for 3-5 minutes on each side or until the fish flakes easily with a fork.
3. Place lettuce leaves on tortillas; top with fish and mango mixture. Drizzle with chili sauce.
NOTE *Wear disposable gloves when cutting hot peppers; the oils can burn skin. Avoid touching your face.*
PER SERVING *330 cal., 12 g fat (1 g sat. fat), 36 mg chol., 648 mg sodium, 28 g carb., 2 g fiber, 28 g pro.* **Diabetic Exchanges:** *3 lean meat, 2 starch, 1 fat.*

BROWN-SUGAR SALMON
WITH STRAWBERRIES

Brown-Sugar Salmon with Strawberries

I first tried strawberries and cucumber together when living in the UK; now they make a delightful relish for salmon.

—JUDITH FOREMAN ALEXANDRIA, VA

PREP: 20 MIN. + CHILLING • **GRILL:** 10 MIN.
MAKES: 4 SERVINGS (2 CUPS RELISH)

- ⅓ **cup packed brown sugar**
- 1 **tablespoon canola oil**
- 1 **teaspoon ground mustard**
- 1 **teaspoon ground allspice**
- ½ **teaspoon salt**
- 4 **salmon fillets (5 ounces each)**

RELISH

- 1 **tablespoon minced fresh mint**
- 1 **tablespoon canola oil**
- 1 **tablespoon lemon juice**
- 2 **teaspoons grated lemon peel**
- ⅛ **teaspoon sugar**
- 1 **cup finely chopped fresh strawberries**
- 1 **small cucumber, finely chopped**

1. In a small bowl, mix the first five ingredients; rub over flesh side of salmon. Refrigerate, covered, 1 hour.
2. For relish, in another bowl, mix mint, oil, lemon juice, lemon peel and sugar. Add the strawberries and cucumber; toss to coat.
3. Moisten a paper towel with cooking oil; using long-handled tongs, rub on grill rack to coat lightly. Place salmon on grill rack, skin side down. Grill, covered, over medium heat 8-10 minutes or until fish flakes easily with a fork. Serve with relish.

PER SERVING *375 cal., 20 g fat (3 g sat. fat), 71 mg chol., 375 mg sodium, 23 g carb., 1 g fiber, 25 g pro.* **Diabetic Exchanges:** *3 lean meat, 1½ fat, 1½ starch.*

Lemony Shrimp & Tomatoes **C**

PREP: 20 MIN. + MARINATING • **GRILL:** 5 MIN.
MAKES: 4 KABOBS (½ CUP SAUCE)

- ⅓ **cup lemon juice**
- 2 **tablespoons olive oil**
- 2 **garlic cloves, minced**
- ½ **teaspoon grated lemon peel**
- 1 **pound uncooked jumbo shrimp, peeled and deveined**
- ⅔ **cup fresh arugula**
- 2 **green onions, sliced**
- ¼ **cup plain yogurt**
- 2 **teaspoons 2% milk**
- 1 **teaspoon cider vinegar**
- 1 **teaspoon Dijon mustard**
- ½ **teaspoon sugar**
- ½ **teaspoon salt, divided**
- 12 **cherry tomatoes**
- ¼ **teaspoon pepper**

1. In a large bowl, whisk lemon juice, oil, garlic and lemon peel until blended. Add shrimp; toss to coat. Let stand 10 minutes.
2. Place arugula, green onions, yogurt, milk, vinegar, mustard, sugar and ¼ teaspoon salt in a food processor; process until smooth.
3. On four metal or soaked wooden skewers, alternately thread shrimp and tomatoes. Sprinkle with pepper and remaining salt.
4. Grill, covered, over medium-high heat or broil 3-4 in. from heat 2-3 minutes on each side or until shrimp are no longer pink. Serve with sauce.

PER SERVING *147 cal., 5 g fat (1 g sat. fat), 140 mg chol., 475 mg sodium, 6 g carb., 1 g fiber, 20 g pro.* **Diabetic Exchanges:** *3 lean meat, ½ starch, ½ fat.*

I came up with this recipe for my family because they love grilled shrimp. I especially like that it's quick, delicious and good for us. **—LISA SPEER** PALM BEACH, FL

LEMONY SHRIMP & TOMATOES

184

186

187

Meatless Mains

❝I spread creamy baked sweet potatoes inside the whole wheat flour tortillas of my black bean quesadillas. Perfect as an easy lunch or dinner, they'd even make a great Southwestern breakfast.❞

—**BRITTANY HUBBARD** ST. PAUL, MN
about her recipe, Sweet Potato & Bean Quesadillas, on page 185

Asian Veggie Glass Noodles M

My mom immigrated from the Philippines and often served Filipino Pancit, a noodle dish. Here is my easier, healthier version.
—JASMIN BARON LIVONIA, NY

PREP: 30 MIN. + STANDING • **COOK:** 15 MIN.
MAKES: 4 SERVINGS

- 5 **ounces uncooked bean thread noodles**
- 2 **tablespoons canola oil**
- ⅓ **cup finely chopped onion**
- 2 **garlic cloves, minced**
- 1½ **teaspoons minced fresh gingerroot**
- 1½ **cups thinly sliced fresh mushrooms**
- 4 **cups coleslaw mix**
- 1 **cup fresh snow peas, trimmed and halved diagonally**
- ½ **cup thinly sliced sweet red pepper**
- 1¼ **cups vegetable broth**
- 3 **tablespoons reduced-sodium soy sauce**
- ¼ **teaspoon pepper**
- 3 **green onions, thinly sliced**
- 3 **tablespoons minced fresh cilantro**
- 3 **hard-cooked eggs, sliced**
  Lime or lemon wedges, optional

1. Place the bean thread noodles in a large bowl; cover with water. Let stand 30 minutes or until the noodles are translucent and softened.

2. In a large skillet, heat the oil over medium-high heat. Add the onion, garlic and ginger; stir-fry 2 minutes. Add mushrooms; stir-fry 2 minutes. Add coleslaw mix, snow peas and red pepper; stir-fry 1-2 minutes or until crisp-tender. Remove from pan.

3. Drain the bean thread noodles. Using scissors, cut the noodles into 4-in. lengths. In same pan, combine vegetable broth, soy sauce and pepper; bring to a boil. Add the noodles; cook and stir until the noodles are tender. Add the vegetable mixture, green onions and cilantro; heat through, stirring occasionally.

4. Transfer to a serving plate. Top with hard-cooked eggs; if desired, serve with lime wedges.

PER SERVING *321 cal., 11 g fat (2 g sat. fat), 159 mg chol., 817 mg sodium, 46 g carb., 4 g fiber, 9 g pro.* **Diabetic Exchanges:** *2 starch, 2 vegetable, 1½ fat, 1 medium-fat meat.*

ASIAN VEGGIE GLASS NOODLES

FRESH CORN & TOMATO FETTUCCINE

Fresh Corn & Tomato Fettuccine M

Tender pasta tossed with fresh veggies and feta cheese? It's a surefire winner!
—ANGELA SPENGLER MECHANICSBURG, PA

START TO FINISH: 30 MIN.
MAKES: 4 SERVINGS

- 8 **ounces uncooked whole wheat fettuccine**
- 2 **medium ears sweet corn, husks removed**
- 2 **teaspoons plus 2 tablespoons olive oil, divided**
- ½ **cup chopped sweet red pepper**
- 4 **green onions, chopped**
- 2 **medium tomatoes, chopped**
- ½ **teaspoon salt**
- ½ **teaspoon pepper**
- 1 **cup crumbled feta cheese**
- 2 **tablespoons minced fresh parsley**

1. In a Dutch oven, cook the fettuccine according to package directions, adding corn during last 8 minutes of cooking.

2. Meanwhile, in a small skillet, heat 2 teaspoons oil over medium-high heat. Add the red pepper and green onions; cook and stir until tender.

3. Drain pasta and corn; transfer pasta to a large bowl. Cool corn slightly; cut corn from cob and add to pasta. Add tomatoes, salt, pepper, remaining oil and pepper mixture; toss to combine. Sprinkle with cheese and parsley.

PER SERVING *422 cal., 15 g fat (4 g sat. fat), 15 mg chol., 580 mg sodium, 56 g carb., 10 g fiber, 17 g pro.*

Rosemary Butternut Squash Lasagna ⓜ

I came up with a lasagna recipe when our garden had an excess of butternut squash. This is now our favorite way to use it.

—CHRISTINE WOOD TIPTON, IA

PREP: 30 MIN. • **BAKE:** 50 MIN. + STANDING
MAKES: 8 SERVINGS

- 9 uncooked whole grain lasagna noodles
- 1 medium butternut squash (about 3 pounds), peeled and cut crosswise into ¼-inch slices
- 2 tablespoons olive oil
- 1 teaspoon salt, divided
- 6 tablespoons all-purpose flour
- 4 cups fat-free milk
- 6 garlic cloves, minced
- 1 tablespoon minced fresh rosemary
- 1⅓ cups shredded Parmesan cheese

1. Preheat oven to 425°. Cook noodles according to package directions; drain.
2. In a large bowl, combine the squash, oil and ½ teaspoon salt; toss to coat.

Transfer to a 15x10x1-in. baking pan coated with cooking spray. Bake 10-15 minutes or until tender; remove from oven. Reduce heat to 375°.
3. Place the flour and remaining salt in a large saucepan; gradually whisk in the milk. Bring to a boil, stirring constantly. Cook and stir 1-2 minutes or until thickened. Stir in the garlic and rosemary.
4. Spread 1 cup sauce into a 13x9x2-in. baking dish coated with cooking spray. Layer with three lasagna noodles, ⅓ cup Parmesan cheese, a third of the squash and 1 cup sauce. Repeat the layers twice. Sprinkle with remaining Parmesan cheese.
5. Cover and bake 40 minutes. Uncover; bake 10 minutes or until bubbly and top is lightly browned. Let stand 10 minutes before serving.
PER SERVING *275 cal., 8 g fat (3 g sat. fat), 12 mg chol., 577 mg sodium, 40 g carb., 6 g fiber, 14 g pro.* **Diabetic Exchanges:** *2½ starch, ½ fat-free milk, ½ fat.*

PORTOBELLO PIZZA BURGERS

Portobello Pizza Burgers ⓜ

Enjoy tasty pizza burgers in less than half an hour. Broiling the mushrooms gives them a wonderful smoky flavor.

—SALLY LAUF WEST DEPTFORD, NJ

START TO FINISH: 25 MIN.
MAKES: 4 SERVINGS

- 4 large portobello mushrooms (4 to 4½ inches)
- 4 teaspoons plus 1 tablespoon olive oil, divided
- 1½ cups finely chopped plum tomatoes
- ¾ cup shredded part-skim mozzarella cheese
- 1½ teaspoons Italian seasoning
- 4 hamburger buns, split

1. Preheat broiler. Remove and discard stems from the portobello mushrooms; with a spoon, scrape and remove the gills. Brush the caps with 4 teaspoons oil. Place in an ungreased 15x10x1-in. baking pan, stem side down. Broil 4 in. from heat 5 minutes.
2. In a small bowl, mix the plum tomatoes, mozzarella cheese, Italian seasoning and remaining oil. Remove the mushrooms from the broiler; turn over and fill the caps with the plum tomato mixture.
3. Broil 4-6 minutes longer or until the mushrooms are tender and the mozzarella cheese is melted. Serve on hamburger buns.
PER SERVING *284 cal., 13 g fat (4 g sat. fat), 12 mg chol., 314 mg sodium, 29 g carb., 3 g fiber, 12 g pro.* **Diabetic Exchanges:** *2 starch, 1½ fat, 1 medium-fat meat, 1 vegetable.*

ROSEMARY BUTTERNUT SQUASH LASAGNA

Pizza has been a weekend staple at our house since my sons, now grown, were young boys. We laughingly call pizza an art form because each one is an original!
—**RACHEL BARTON** AUSTIN, TX

MAMA RACHEL'S TOMATO & KALAMATA PIZZAS

Mama Rachel's Tomato & Kalamata Pizzas M

PREP: 35 MIN. + RISING • **BAKE:** 20 MIN.
MAKES: 2 PIZZAS (6 SLICES EACH)

- 1 tablespoon active dry yeast
- 1 cup warm water (110° to 115°)
- 1 tablespoon sugar
- 1 tablespoon olive oil
- ½ teaspoon salt
- 2½ to 3 cups all-purpose flour
- 2 tablespoons cornmeal

TOPPINGS

- 2 tablespoons olive oil
- 3 garlic cloves, peeled and thinly sliced
- 2 cups (8 ounces) shredded part-skim mozzarella cheese
- 2 large tomatoes, thinly sliced
- ⅓ cup pitted kalamata olives, thinly sliced
- ½ cup shredded Parmesan cheese
- ¼ teaspoon crushed red pepper flakes
- 6 fresh basil leaves, thinly sliced

1. In a small bowl, dissolve yeast in warm water. In a large bowl, combine sugar, oil, salt, yeast mixture and 1 cup flour; beat on medium speed until smooth. Stir in enough remaining flour to form a stiff dough.
2. Turn dough onto a floured surface; knead until smooth and elastic, about 6-8 minutes. Place in a greased bowl, turning once to grease the top. Cover with plastic wrap and let rise in a warm place until doubled, about 45 minutes.
3. Preheat oven to 400°. Grease two 12-in. pizza pans; sprinkle with the cornmeal. Punch down dough; divide in half. Press to fit pans. Pinch edges to form a rim. Cover; let rest 10 minutes. Bake 8-10 minutes or until edges are lightly browned.
4. Increase oven setting to 450°. Brush the crusts with oil; top with garlic, mozzarella cheese, tomatoes, olives and Parmesan cheese. Bake 10-12 minutes or until crust is golden and cheese is melted. Sprinkle with pepper flakes and basil.
PER SERVING *216 cal., 9 g fat (3 g sat. fat), 13 mg chol., 307 mg sodium, 25 g carb., 1 g fiber, 9 g pro.* **Diabetic Exchanges:** *1½ starch, 1 medium-fat meat, 1 fat.*

CORN, RICE & BEAN BURRITOS

Corn, Rice & Bean Burritos M

Even meat lovers will gobble up these burritos loaded with a fresh-tasting filling. Serve them with a bowl of your family's favorite salsa on the side.

—**SHARON BICKETT** CHESTER, SC

START TO FINISH: 30 MIN.
MAKES: 8 SERVINGS

- 1 tablespoon canola oil
- 1⅓ cups fresh or frozen corn, thawed
- 1 medium onion, chopped
- 1 medium green pepper, sliced
- 2 garlic cloves, minced
- 1½ teaspoons chili powder
- ½ teaspoon ground cumin
- 1 can (15 ounces) black beans, rinsed and drained
- 1½ cups cooked brown rice
- 8 flour tortillas (8 inches), warmed
- ¾ cup shredded reduced-fat cheddar cheese
- ½ cup reduced-fat plain yogurt
- 2 green onions, sliced
- ½ cup salsa

1. In a large skillet, heat the oil over medium-high heat. Add corn, onion and pepper; cook and stir until tender. Add garlic, chili powder and cumin; cook 1 minute longer. Add beans and rice; heat through.
2. Spoon ½ cup filling across the center of each flour tortilla; top with the cheddar cheese, plain yogurt and green onions. Fold bottom and sides of tortilla over the filling and roll up. Serve with salsa.
PER SERVING *326 cal., 8 g fat (2 g sat. fat), 8 mg chol., 500 mg sodium, 52 g carb., 4 g fiber, 13 g pro.*

Basil Polenta with Ratatouille M

For our wedding reception, we wanted to provide a vegan menu for our guests. Everyone raved about the polenta topped with colorful ratatouille—our version of the classic stewed vegetable dish.
—**KIMBERLY HAMMOND** KINGWOOD, TX

PREP: 25 MIN. + CHILLING • **COOK:** 40 MIN.
MAKES: 4 SERVINGS

- 4 **cups water**
- ½ **teaspoon salt, divided**
- 1 **cup cornmeal**
- ½ **cup minced fresh basil**
- 1 **medium eggplant, peeled and cut into ½-inch cubes**
- 1 **medium onion, halved and sliced**
- 1 **medium green pepper, julienned**
- 5 **tablespoons olive oil, divided**
- 4 **garlic cloves, minced**
- 1 **can (14½ ounces) diced tomatoes, drained**
- ½ **cup pitted Greek olives, sliced**
- 1 **teaspoon dried oregano**
- ¼ **teaspoon pepper**
  Fresh basil leaves

1. In a large heavy saucepan, bring water and ¼ teaspoon salt to a boil. Reduce heat to a gentle boil; slowly whisk in cornmeal. Cook and stir with a wooden spoon for 15-20 minutes or until polenta is thickened and pulls away cleanly from the sides of the pan. Stir in basil.

2. Spread polenta into an 8-in. square baking dish coated with cooking spray. Refrigerate for 30 minutes.

3. Meanwhile, in a large skillet, saute the eggplant, onion and green pepper in 2 tablespoons oil until crisp-tender. Add the garlic; cook 1 minute longer. Stir in the tomatoes, Greek olives, oregano, pepper and remaining salt. Cook and stir over medium heat for 10-12 minutes or until the vegetables are tender.

4. Cut the polenta into four squares. In another large skillet, cook polenta in the remaining oil in batches for 7-8 minutes on each side or until golden brown. Serve with ratatouille; garnish with basil leaves.

PER SERVING *400 cal., 22 g fat (3 g sat. fat), 0 chol., 709 mg sodium, 46 g carb., 10 g fiber, 6 g pro.*

Tropical Fusion Salad with Spicy Tortilla Ribbons M

The fresh taste of this colorful medley makes it the perfect choice for spring or summer meals. Served with spicy tortilla strips, it's special enough for company.
—**JENNIFER FISHER** AUSTIN, TX

START TO FINISH: 30 MIN.
MAKES: 4 SERVINGS

- 2 **cups cubed peeled papaya**
- 1 **can (15 ounces) black beans, rinsed and drained**
- 1 **medium ripe avocado, peeled and cubed**
- 1 **cup frozen corn, thawed**
- ½ **cup golden raisins**
- ¼ **cup minced fresh cilantro**
- ¼ **cup orange juice**
- 2 **serrano peppers, seeded and chopped**
- 2 **tablespoons lime juice**
- 1 **tablespoon cider vinegar**
- 2 **garlic cloves, minced**
- 2 **teaspoons ground ancho chili pepper, divided**
- ¼ **teaspoon sugar**
- ¼ **teaspoon salt**
- 2 **corn tortillas (6 inches), cut into ¼-inch strips**
  Cooking spray

1. Preheat oven to 350°. In a large bowl, combine papaya, black beans, avocado, corn, golden raisins, cilantro, orange juice, serrano peppers, lime juice, vinegar, garlic, ½ teaspoon chili pepper, sugar and salt.

2. Place tortilla strips on a greased baking sheet; spritz with cooking spray. Sprinkle with remaining chili pepper. Bake 8-10 minutes or until crisp. Top salad with tortilla strips.

NOTE *Wear disposable gloves when cutting hot peppers; the oils can burn skin. Avoid touching your face.*

PER SERVING *321 cal., 8 g fat (1 g sat. fat), 0 chol., 380 mg sodium, 58 g carb., 11 g fiber, 9 g pro.*

TROPICAL FUSION SALAD WITH SPICY TORTILLA RIBBONS

AVOCADO & TOMATO SANDWICHES

Stir-Fry Rice Bowl M

START TO FINISH: 30 MIN.
MAKES: 4 SERVINGS

- 1 **tablespoon canola oil**
- 2 **medium carrots, julienned**
- 1 **medium zucchini, julienned**
- ½ **cup sliced baby portobello mushrooms**
- 1 **cup bean sprouts**
- 1 **cup fresh baby spinach**
- 1 **tablespoon water**
- 1 **tablespoon reduced-sodium soy sauce**
- 1 **tablespoon chili garlic sauce**
- 4 **eggs**
- 3 **cups hot cooked brown rice**
- 1 **teaspoon sesame oil**

1. In a large skillet, heat canola oil over medium-high heat. Add carrots, zucchini and portobello mushrooms; cook and stir 3-5 minutes or until carrots are crisp-tender. Add bean sprouts, spinach, water, soy sauce and chili sauce; cook and stir just until the spinach is wilted. Remove from heat; keep warm.

2. Place 2-3 in. of water in a large skillet with high sides. Bring to a boil; adjust the heat to maintain a gentle simmer. Break the cold eggs, one at a time, into a small bowl; holding the bowl close to the surface of the water, slip the egg into the water.

3. Cook, uncovered, 3-5 minutes or until the whites are completely set and the yolks begin to thicken but are not hard. Using a slotted spoon, lift eggs out of the water.

4. Serve the rice in bowls; top with vegetables. Drizzle with sesame oil. Top each serving with a poached egg.
PER SERVING *305 cal., 11 g fat (2 g sat. fat), 186 mg chol., 364 mg sodium, 40 g carb., 4 g fiber, 12 g pro.* **Diabetic Exchanges:** *2 starch, 1 medium-fat meat, 1 vegetable, 1 fat.*

Avocado & Tomato Sandwiches M

I'm a vegetarian, and this is my go-to sandwich because it's a combo I never get tired of. I call it "HATS" for hummus, avocado, tomato and shallots.
—SARAH JARAHA MOORESTOWN, NJ

START TO FINISH: 10 MIN.
MAKES: 2 SERVINGS

- ½ **medium ripe avocado, peeled and mashed**
- 4 **slices whole wheat bread, toasted**
- 1 **medium tomato, sliced**
- 2 **tablespoons finely chopped shallot**
- ¼ **cup hummus**

Spread the avocado over two slices of toast. Top with the tomato and shallot. Spread the hummus over remaining toasts; place over tops.
PER SERVING *278 cal., 11 g fat (2 g sat. fat), 0 chol., 379 mg sodium, 35 g carb., 9 g fiber, 11 g pro.* **Diabetic Exchanges:** *2 starch, 2 fat.*

 Did you know?
You can quickly ripen an avocado by placing it in a paper bag with an apple. Make holes in the bag by poking it with a toothpick in several spots, then let the bag sit at room temperature. The avocado should be ripe and ready to use in 1 to 3 days.

My meatless version of Korean bibimbap is easy to tweak for different spice levels. I skip the usual addition of beef and top each serving with a poached egg.
—**DEVON DELANEY** WESTPORT, CT

STIR-FRY RICE BOWL

Makeover Creamy Mac & Cheese M

Macaroni and cheese just might be the king of all comfort foods. This irresistible version is bubbling with tasty goodness but is lower in calories.

—**APRIL TAYLOR** HOLCOMB, KS

PREP: 30 MIN. • **BAKE:** 25 MIN.
MAKES: 10 SERVINGS

- 1 package (16 ounces) elbow macaroni
- ⅓ cup all-purpose flour
- ½ teaspoon garlic powder
- ½ teaspoon pepper
- ¼ teaspoon salt
- 2 cups fat-free half-and-half
- 2 tablespoons butter
- 2 cups fat-free milk
- 3 cups (12 ounces) shredded reduced-fat sharp cheddar cheese

OPTIONAL TOPPING

- 2 tablespoons butter
- 1 medium onion, chopped
- 5 cups cubed bread
- ½ cup shredded reduced-fat cheddar cheese

1. Preheat oven to 350°. Cook the macaroni according to the package directions; drain.
2. Meanwhile, in small bowl, whisk the flour, seasonings and half-and-half until smooth. In a large saucepan, melt the butter over medium heat. Stir in half-and-half mixture. Add milk. Bring to a gentle boil, stirring constantly; remove from the heat. Add the cheese; stir until melted. Stir in the macaroni. Transfer to a 13x9x2-in. baking dish coated with cooking spray.
3. For the optional topping, in a large skillet, heat butter over medium-high heat. Add the onion; cook and stir until tender. Add the cubed bread; cook and stir 2 minutes longer. Sprinkle over the macaroni mixture; top with cheese.
4. Bake, uncovered, 25-30 minutes or until heated through.

PER SERVING *343 cal., 11 g fat (6 g sat. fat), 31 mg chol., 354 mg sodium, 45 g carb., 2 g fiber, 18 g pro.*

MAKEOVER CREAMY MAC & CHEESE

COCONUT-GINGER CHICKPEAS & TOMATOES

Coconut-Ginger Chickpeas & Tomatoes M

Here's my go-to dish when I need a quick entree. I garnish it with extra cilantro for even more color and flavor.

—**MALA UDAYAMURTHY** SAN JOSE, CA

START TO FINISH: 30 MIN.
MAKES: 6 SERVINGS

- 2 tablespoons canola oil
- 2 medium onions, chopped (about 1⅓ cups)
- 3 large tomatoes, seeded and chopped (about 2 cups)
- 1 jalapeno pepper, seeded and chopped
- 1 tablespoon minced fresh gingerroot
- 2 cans (15 ounces each) chickpeas or garbanzo beans, rinsed and drained
- ¼ cup water
- 1 teaspoon salt
- 1 cup light coconut milk
- 3 tablespoons minced fresh cilantro
- 4½ cups hot cooked brown rice
  Additional minced fresh cilantro, optional

1. In a large skillet, heat the oil over medium-high heat. Add the onions; cook and stir until crisp-tender. Add the tomatoes, jalapeno and ginger; cook and stir 2-3 minutes longer or until tender.
2. Stir in the chickpeas, water and salt; bring to a boil. Reduce heat; simmer, uncovered, 4-5 minutes or until the liquid is almost evaporated. Remove from the heat; stir in the coconut milk and cilantro.
3. Serve with brown rice; sprinkle with additional cilantro if desired.
NOTE *Wear disposable gloves when cutting hot peppers; the oils can burn skin. Avoid touching your face.*
PER SERVING *402 cal., 12 g fat (3 g sat. fat), 0 chol., 590 mg sodium, 65 g carb., 10 g fiber, 11 g pro.*

Butternut Squash Enchiladas M

Squash adds a slight sweetness and tender texture to a meatless enchilada filling.

—RACHEL ERDSTEIN ANN ARBOR, MI

PREP: 1¼ HOURS • **BAKE:** 25 MIN.
MAKES: 8 SERVINGS

- 1 **medium butternut squash (3½ to 4 pounds)**
- 1 **medium sweet red pepper, chopped**
- ½ **cup chopped onion**
- 1 **garlic clove, minced**
- 1 **teaspoon canola oil**
- 1 **teaspoon ground cumin**
- ½ **teaspoon chili powder**
- ½ **teaspoon pepper**
- ¼ **teaspoon salt**
- 1 **package (12 ounces) frozen vegetarian meat crumbles, thawed**
- 1 **can (10 ounces) enchilada sauce, divided**
- 8 **flour tortillas (8 inches), warmed**
- 1 **cup (4 ounces) shredded reduced-fat Mexican cheese blend, divided**

1. Cut the butternut squash in half; discard the seeds. Place the squash cut side down in a 15x10x1-in. baking pan coated with cooking spray. Bake at 350° for 55-65 minutes or until tender. Cool slightly; scoop out flesh and set aside.
2. In a large nonstick skillet coated with cooking spray, cook red pepper, onion and garlic in oil until tender. Stir in cumin, chili powder, pepper and salt; cook 1 minute longer. Stir in crumbles and reserved squash; heat through.
3. Spread ¼ cup enchilada sauce into a 13x9x2-in. baking dish coated with cooking spray. Place about ¾ cup squash mixture down center of each tortilla; top with 1 tablespoon cheese. Roll up; place seam side down in baking dish. Pour remaining sauce over the top; sprinkle with remaining cheese.
4. Bake, uncovered, at 350° for 25-35 minutes or until heated through.
NOTE *Vegetarian meat crumbles are a nutritious protein source made from soy. Look for them in the natural foods freezer section.*
PER SERVING *346 cal., 9 g fat (2 g sat. fat), 10 mg chol., 801 mg sodium, 53 g carb., 9 g fiber, 19 g pro.*

Sweet Potato & Bean Quesadillas M

I spread creamy baked sweet potatoes inside the whole wheat flour tortillas of my black bean quesadillas. Perfect as an easy lunch or dinner, they'd even make a great Southwestern breakfast.

—BRITTANY HUBBARD ST. PAUL, MN

START TO FINISH: 30 MIN.
MAKES: 4 SERVINGS

- 2 **medium sweet potatoes**
- 4 **whole wheat tortillas (8 inches)**
- ¾ **cup canned black beans, rinsed and drained**
- ½ **cup shredded pepper jack cheese**
- ¾ **cup salsa**

1. Scrub the sweet potatoes; pierce several times with a fork. Place on a microwave-safe plate. Microwave, uncovered, on high 7-9 minutes or until very tender, turning once.
2. When cool enough to handle, cut each potato lengthwise in half. Scoop out flesh. Spread onto one half of each tortilla; top with the beans and cheese. Fold other half of tortilla over filling.
3. Heat a griddle or skillet over medium heat. Cook quesadillas 2-3 minutes on each side or until golden brown and cheese is melted. Serve with salsa.
PER SERVING *306 cal., 8 g fat (3 g sat. fat), 15 mg chol., 531 mg sodium, 46 g carb., 6 g fiber, 11 g pro.*

SWEET POTATO & BEAN QUESADILLAS

PASTA WITH EGGPLANT SAUCE

Pasta with Eggplant Sauce M

My mom discovered a great way to incorporate eggplant into a meal. Her thick, chunky sauce is fantastic! I round out the menu with crusty Italian bread and a tossed salad.
—JEAN LAWRENCE ROCHESTER, NY

PREP: 15 MIN. • **COOK:** 25 MIN. • **MAKES:** 6 SERVINGS

- 1 large eggplant, cut into 1-inch cubes
- ½ cup finely chopped onion
- 2 tablespoons minced fresh parsley
- 1 garlic clove, chopped
- ¼ cup olive oil
- 1 can (14½ ounces) Italian stewed tomatoes, cut up
- ½ cup dry red wine or chicken broth
- 1 can (6 ounces) Italian tomato paste
- 1 can (4½ ounces) sliced mushrooms, drained
- 1 teaspoon sugar
- 1 teaspoon dried oregano
- ½ teaspoon salt
- ¾ pound thin spaghetti
  Grated Parmesan cheese

1. In a Dutch oven, saute the eggplant, onion, parsley and garlic in oil until tender.

2. Stir in the tomatoes, wine, tomato paste, mushrooms, sugar, oregano and salt. Bring to a boil. Reduce the heat; simmer, uncovered, for 10-15 minutes or until thickened, stirring occasionally.

3. Meanwhile, cook spaghetti according to the package directions. Drain spaghetti. Serve with the sauce. Sprinkle with Parmesan cheese.

PER SERVING *385 cal., 11 g fat (1 g sat. fat), 0 chol., 782 mg sodium, 61 g carb., 7 g fiber, 11 g pro.*

Garden Quinoa Salad M

This recipe is delicious as well as wholesome. Serve it hot or cold and enjoy the leftovers while they're fresh.
—PATRICIA NIEH PORTOLA VALLEY, CA

START TO FINISH: 30 MIN. • **MAKES:** 4 SERVINGS

- 1½ cups quinoa, rinsed and well drained
- 3 cups water
- 1 pound fresh asparagus, cut into 2-inch pieces
- ½ pound fresh sugar snap peas
- ½ pound fresh green beans, trimmed
- 2 tablespoons olive oil
- 2 tablespoons lemon juice
- 2 tablespoons minced fresh parsley
- 1 teaspoon grated lemon peel
- ¾ teaspoon salt
- 1 cup cherry tomatoes, halved
- 3 tablespoons salted pumpkin seeds or pepitas

1. In a large saucepan, cook and stir the quinoa over medium-high heat 3-5 minutes or until toasted. Add the water; bring to a boil. Reduce the heat; simmer, covered, 12-15 minutes or until the liquid is absorbed. Transfer to a large bowl.

2. Meanwhile, in a large saucepan, bring 4 cups water to a boil. Add the asparagus and snap peas; cook, uncovered, 2-4 minutes or just until crisp-tender. Remove vegetables and immediately drop into ice water.

3. Return the water to a boil. Add the green beans; cook 3-4 minutes or until crisp-tender. Remove the beans and drop into ice water. Drain vegetables; pat dry.

4. In a small bowl, whisk oil, lemon juice, parsley, lemon peel and salt. Add the tomatoes and blanched vegetables to the quinoa; drizzle with the dressing and toss to combine. Top with pumpkin seeds.

PER SERVING *417 cal., 15 g fat (2 g sat. fat), 0 chol., 533 mg sodium, 58 g carb., 9 g fiber, 16 g pro.*

GARDEN QUINOA SALAD

> I put a vegetarian spin on my favorite turkey burger. Using black beans instead of meat boosts the fiber.
> —JENNY LEIGHTY WEST SALEM, OH

SALSA BEAN BURGERS

Salsa Bean Burgers M

PREP: 15 MIN. + CHILLING • **COOK:** 10 MIN. • **MAKES:** 4 SERVINGS

- 1 can (15 ounces) black beans, rinsed and drained
- ¾ cup panko (Japanese) bread crumbs
- 1 cup salsa, divided
- 1 egg, lightly beaten
- 2 tablespoons minced fresh cilantro
- 1 garlic clove, minced
- 2 teaspoons canola oil
- 4 whole wheat hamburger buns, split

1. In a large bowl, mash beans. Mix in bread crumbs, ½ cup salsa, egg, cilantro and garlic. Shape bean mixture into four patties; refrigerate 30 minutes.

2. In a large skillet, heat the oil over medium heat. Cook the burgers 3-5 minutes on each side or until a thermometer reads 160°. Serve on buns with remaining salsa.

PER SERVING *299 cal., 6 g fat (1 g sat. fat), 53 mg chol., 696 mg sodium, 49 g carb., 8 g fiber, 12 g pro.* **Diabetic Exchanges:** *3 starch, 1 lean meat, ½ fat.*

Grilled Artichoke-Mushroom Pizza M

We live on a lake and frequently entertain our family and friends. This special pizza is one of our most popular summer meals.
—**BRENDA WATERS** CLARKESVILLE, GA

PREP: 20 MIN. • **GRILL:** 15 MIN. • **MAKES:** 6 SERVINGS

- 1 prebaked 12-inch pizza crust
- ½ teaspoon olive oil
- ⅔ cup tomato and basil spaghetti sauce
- 2 plum tomatoes, sliced
- ¼ cup sliced fresh mushrooms
- ¼ cup water-packed artichoke hearts, rinsed, drained and chopped
- 2 tablespoons sliced ripe olives, optional
- 1 cup (4 ounces) shredded part-skim mozzarella cheese
- ½ cup crumbled tomato and basil feta cheese
- 1½ teaspoons minced fresh basil or ½ teaspoon dried basil
- 1½ teaspoons minced fresh rosemary or ½ teaspoon dried rosemary, crushed
- 1½ teaspoons minced chives

1. Brush the pizza crust with oil. Spread the spaghetti sauce over the crust to within 1 in. of edges. Top with tomatoes, mushrooms, artichokes and ripe olives if desired. Sprinkle with cheeses.

2. Prepare grill for indirect heat. Grill the pizza, covered, over medium indirect heat for 12-15 minutes or until the cheese is melted and the crust is lightly browned. Sprinkle with herbs during the last 5 minutes of cooking. Let stand for 5 minutes before slicing.

PER SERVING *283 cal., 10 g fat (3 g sat. fat), 17 mg chol., 712 mg sodium, 34 g carb., 1 g fiber, 14 g pro.* **Diabetic Exchanges:** *2 starch, 1½ fat, 1 lean meat.*

GRILLED ARTICHOKE-MUSHROOM PIZZA

191

192

196

The Bread Basket

66Hearty and dense, this Boston brown bread features hazelnuts for a delightfully nutty taste. Thick slices pair well with just about anything, from soups and stews to roasts and casseroles.99

—LORRAINE CALAND SHUNIAH, ON
about her recipe, A Bit Nutty Boston Brown Bread, on page 196

FLAKY WHOLE WHEAT BISCUITS

Pecan Bread F S M

I have this bread on hand most of the time. It is delicious for morning toast with berry jams and jellies, and also as a base for French toast.

—**CARYL MILLER** MUSCODA, WI

PREP: 25 MIN. + RISING
BAKE: 45 MIN. + COOLING
MAKES: 1 LOAF (12 SLICES)

- 1⅛ teaspoons active dry yeast
- ½ cup warm water (110° to 115°)
- ½ cup warm milk (110° to 115°)
- 4 teaspoons honey
- 1 tablespoon olive oil
- 1½ cups whole wheat flour
- 1 cup all-purpose flour
- ½ teaspoon salt
- ¼ teaspoon pepper, optional
- 1 tablespoon cornmeal
- 3 tablespoons chopped pecans, toasted
- 1 tablespoon milk

1. In a large bowl, dissolve yeast in warm water. Add the warm milk, honey and oil. Combine the flours, salt and pepper if desired; add 1½ cups to yeast mixture. Beat on medium speed for 3 minutes. Stir in pecans and remaining flour mixture to form a stiff dough.
2. Turn onto a floured surface; knead until smooth and elastic, about 6-8 minutes. Place in a greased bowl, turning once to grease top. Cover and let rise in a warm place until doubled, about 1 hour.
3. Sprinkle cornmeal over a greased baking sheet. Punch dough down. Shape into a round loaf; place on prepared baking sheet. Cover and let rise until doubled, about 30 minutes.
4. Brush milk over loaf. Bake at 350° for 45-50 minutes or until bread sounds hollow when tapped. Remove from pan to a wire rack to cool.
PER SERVING *129 cal., 3 g fat (1 g sat. fat), 1 mg chol., 104 mg sodium, 22 g carb., 2 g fiber, 4 g pro.* **Diabetic Exchanges:** *1½ starch, ½ fat.*

Flaky Whole Wheat Biscuits M

Whole wheat flour gives these biscuits a nutty flavor. Since I've started making these, white flour biscuits just don't taste as good! Pair these with soup or slather them with whipped cream and sweetened berries for a dessert treat.

—**TRISHA KRUSE** EAGLE, ID

START TO FINISH: 25 MIN.
MAKES: 10 BISCUITS

- 1 cup all-purpose flour
- 1 cup whole wheat flour
- 3 teaspoons baking powder
- 1 tablespoon brown sugar
- 1 teaspoon baking soda
- ½ teaspoon salt
- ¼ cup cold butter
- 1 cup 2% milk

1. In a large bowl, combine the first six ingredients. Cut in butter until mixture resembles coarse crumbs. Stir in milk just until moistened. Turn onto a lightly floured surface; knead 8-10 times.
2. Pat or roll out dough to ½-in. thickness; cut with a floured 2½-in. biscuit cutter. Place 2 in. apart on an ungreased baking sheet. Bake at 425° for 8-10 minutes or until biscuits are golden brown.
PER SERVING *144 cal., 6 g fat (3 g sat. fat), 14 mg chol., 417 mg sodium, 21 g carb., 2 g fiber, 4 g pro.* **Diabetic Exchanges:** *1½ starch, 1 fat.*

LIME MUFFINS WITH
COCONUT STREUSEL

Lime Muffins with Coconut Streusel M

Looking for a way to dazzle Easter brunch guests? A dozen of these tempting gems should do the trick. The macadamia-coconut streusel is the perfect complement to the muffin's fresh lime flavor.

—TERESA GRISSOM ZIONSVILLE, IN

PREP: 30 MIN. • **BAKE:** 20 MIN.
MAKES: 1 DOZEN

- 2 cups all-purpose flour
- ¾ cup sugar
- 1 teaspoon baking powder
- ¾ teaspoon baking soda
- ½ teaspoon salt
- ¾ cup buttermilk
- ¾ cup (6 ounces) key lime yogurt
- 1 egg
- ¼ cup butter, melted
- 2 teaspoons key lime juice
- 1 teaspoon grated lime peel
- 1 teaspoon vanilla extract

TOPPING
- 3 tablespoons sugar
- 2 tablespoons all-purpose flour
- 2 tablespoons flaked coconut
- 2 tablespoons finely chopped macadamia nuts
- 2 tablespoons butter, melted

1. In a large bowl, combine the first five ingredients. In another bowl, combine the buttermilk, yogurt, egg, butter, lime juice, lime peel and vanilla. Stir into dry ingredients just until moistened. Fill greased muffin cups three-fourths full.

2. In a small bowl, combine topping ingredients; sprinkle over muffins.

Bake at 375° for 18-22 minutes or until a toothpick inserted in muffin comes out clean. Cool for 5 minutes before removing from pan to a wire rack. Serve warm.

PER SERVING *234 cal., 8 g fat (4 g sat. fat), 34 mg chol., 287 mg sodium, 37 g carb., 1 g fiber, 4 g pro.*

Granola Blueberry Muffins M

PREP: 20 MIN. • **BAKE:** 15 MIN.
MAKES: 1 DOZEN

- 1½ cups whole wheat flour
- ½ cup all-purpose flour
- ¼ cup packed brown sugar
- 2 teaspoons baking powder
- ½ teaspoon salt
- ½ teaspoon baking soda
- 1 cup granola without raisins, divided
- 1 egg
- 1 cup buttermilk
- ¼ cup canola oil
- 2 tablespoons orange juice
- 1 tablespoon lemon juice
- 1 cup fresh or frozen unsweetened blueberries

1. Preheat oven to 400°. In a small bowl, whisk flours, brown sugar, baking powder, salt and baking soda. Stir in ½ cup granola. In another bowl, whisk egg, buttermilk, oil and juices until blended. Add to the flour mixture; stir just until moistened. Fold in blueberries.

2. Fill greased muffin cups three-fourths full; sprinkle remaining granola over batter. Bake 12-15 minutes or until a toothpick inserted in center comes out clean. Cool 5 minutes before removing from pan to a wire rack.

NOTE *If using frozen blueberries, use without thawing to avoid discoloring the batter.*

PER SERVING *188 cal., 7 g fat (1 g sat. fat), 18 mg chol., 251 mg sodium, 28 g carb., 4 g fiber, 6 g pro.* **Diabetic Exchanges:** *2 starch, 1 fat.*

I wanted to put a new spin on muffins, so I mixed in some granola. I brought a batch to work the next morning—success. The granola I used contained lots of nuts, pumpkin seeds and shredded coconut.

—MEGAN WEISS MENOMONIE, WI

GRANOLA BLUEBERRY MUFFINS

JALAPENO BUTTERMILK CORN BREAD

Jalapeno Buttermilk Corn Bread M

If you're from the South, you have to have a good corn bread recipe. Here's a healthier version of my mom's traditional corn bread.

—**DEBI MITCHELL** FLOWER MOUND, TX

PREP: 15 MIN. • **BAKE:** 20 MIN.
MAKES: 8 SERVINGS

- 1 **cup self-rising flour**
- 1 **cup yellow cornmeal**
- 1 **cup buttermilk**
- ¼ **cup egg substitute**
- 3 **tablespoons canola oil, divided**
- 2 **tablespoons honey**
- 1 **tablespoon reduced-fat mayonnaise**
- ¼ **cup fresh or frozen corn, thawed**
- 3 **tablespoons shredded reduced-fat cheddar cheese**
- 3 **tablespoons finely chopped sweet red pepper**
- ½ **to 1 jalapeno pepper, seeded and finely chopped**

1. Preheat oven to 425°. In a large bowl, whisk flour and cornmeal. In another bowl, whisk buttermilk, egg substitute, 2 tablespoons oil, honey and mayonnaise. Pour remaining oil into an 8-in. ovenproof skillet; place skillet in oven 4 minutes.
2. Meanwhile, add buttermilk mixture to flour mixture; stir just until moistened. Fold in the corn, cheese and peppers.
3. Carefully tilt and rotate skillet to coat bottom with oil; add batter. Bake 20-25 minutes or until a toothpick inserted in center comes out clean. Serve warm.
PER SERVING *180 cal., 4 g fat (1 g sat. fat), 4 mg chol., 261 mg sodium, 32 g carb., 2 g fiber, 6 g pro.* **Diabetic Exchanges:** *2 starch, 1 fat.*

Thin Crust Pizza Dough F S C M

My family loves pizza, and this crust is our go-to recipe. It's healthier and less expensive than delivery and tastes so much better.

—**THERESA ROHDE** SCOTTVILLE, MI

PREP: 10 MIN.+ STANDING
MAKES: 2 POUNDS (ENOUGH FOR 4 PIZZAS)

- 3½ **cups bread flour**
- 1 **cup whole wheat flour**
- 5 **teaspoons quick-rise yeast**
- 1 **teaspoon salt**
- 1 **teaspoon honey**
- 1½ **to 1⅔ cups warm water (120° to 130°)**

1. Place flours, yeast and salt in a food processor; pulse until blended. Add honey. While processing, gradually add water until a ball forms. Continue processing 60 seconds to knead dough.
2. Turn dough onto floured surface; shape into a ball. Cover; let rest 10 minutes. Divide dough into quarters. Use immediately or securely wrap and freeze for later use.
TO MAKE PIZZA *Grease a 12-in. pizza pan; sprinkle with cornmeal. On a lightly floured surface, stretch and shape one portion of dough to form a 12-in. crust; transfer to prepared pan. Top as desired. Bake at 450° for 15-20 minutes or until crust is lightly browned. If using frozen dough, thaw in the refrigerator overnight. Proceed as directed.*
PER SERVING *1 ounce dough equals 59 cal., trace fat (trace sat. fat), 0 chol., 89 mg sodium, 13 g carb., 1 g fiber, 3 g pro.*

? Did you know?

Frozen pizza can be high in trans fat, which raises LDL (the "bad" cholesterol). Manufacturers often add hydrogenated oils to pizza crusts, refrigerated doughs and the buns used in convenient grab-and-go sandwiches. Half of Americans' consumption of trans fat comes from processed foods; the rest is from meat and dairy.

Cranberry Orange Muffins ⓜ

These cranberry-studded muffins have a splash of orange flavor. They're so simple to fix, my husband and I enjoy one for breakfast almost every morning.

—SARA EICHENLAUB BURLINGTON, ON

PREP: 20 MIN. • **BAKE:** 15 MIN.
MAKES: 1 DOZEN

- 2 cups whole wheat flour
- ⅓ cup sugar
- 2 teaspoons baking powder
- ½ teaspoon baking soda
- ¼ teaspoon salt
- 1 egg
- 1½ cups orange juice
- ¼ cup canola oil
- 1 cup fresh or frozen cranberries, halved

1. Preheat oven to 400°. In a large bowl, whisk flour, sugar, baking powder, baking soda and salt. In another bowl, whisk egg, orange juice and oil until blended. Add to flour mixture; stir just until moistened. Fold in cranberries.

2. Coat muffin cups with cooking spray or use paper liners; fill three-fourths full. Bake 15-20 minutes or until a toothpick inserted in center comes out clean. Cool 5 minutes before removing from pan to a wire rack. Serve warm.

PER SERVING *153 cal., 5 g fat (1 g sat. fat), 18 mg chol., 175 mg sodium, 24 g carb., 3 g fiber, 3 g pro.* **Diabetic Exchanges:** *1½ starch, 1 fat.*

SUNFLOWER SEED WHEAT BREAD

Sunflower Seed Wheat Bread ⓜ

I've tried other bread recipes, but this one is a staple in our home. I won $50 in a baking contest with a loaf that I had stored in the freezer.

—MICKEY TURNER GRANTS PASS, OR

PREP: 40 MIN. + RISING
BAKE: 35 MIN. + COOLING
MAKES: 3 LOAVES (12 SLICES EACH)

- 2 packages (¼ ounce each) active dry yeast
- 3¾ cups warm water (110° to 115°)
- ¼ cup bread flour
- ⅓ cup canola oil
- ⅓ cup honey
- 3 teaspoons salt
- 6½ to 7½ cups whole wheat flour
- ½ cup sunflower kernels
- 3 tablespoons butter, melted

1. In a large bowl, dissolve yeast in warm water. Add the bread flour, oil, honey, salt and 4 cups whole wheat flour. Beat until smooth. Stir in sunflower kernels and enough remaining flour to form a firm dough.

2. Turn onto a floured surface; knead until smooth and elastic, about 6-8 minutes. Place in a greased bowl, turning once to grease the top. Cover and let rise in a warm place until doubled, about 1 hour.

3. Punch dough down; divide into three portions. Shape into loaves; place in three greased 8x 4-in. loaf pans. Cover and let rise until doubled, about 30 minutes.

4. Bake at 350° for 35-40 minutes or until golden brown. Brush with melted butter. Remove from pans to wire racks to cool.

PER SERVING *125 cal., 4 g fat (1 g sat. fat), 3 mg chol., 212 mg sodium, 19 g carb., 3 g fiber, 4 g pro.* **Diabetic Exchanges:** *1 starch, 1 fat.*

CRANBERRY ORANGE MUFFINS

SWIRLED PUMPKIN YEAST BREAD

Swirled Pumpkin Yeast Bread S M

I call this my hostess-gift bread, but it's fantastic for any occasion at all. Swirls of cinnamon-sugar make every slice irresistible.

—SHIRLEY RUNKLE ST. PARIS, OH

PREP: 45 MIN. + RISING • **BAKE:** 55 MIN. + COOLING
MAKES: 2 LOAVES (16 SLICES EACH)

- 4½ to 5 cups all-purpose flour
- 3 cups whole wheat flour
- 2 cups quick-cooking oats
- ⅔ cup packed brown sugar
- 2½ teaspoons pumpkin pie spice
- 1½ teaspoons salt
- 1 teaspoon sugar
- 2 packages (¼ ounce each) active dry yeast
- 1½ cups warm water (120° to 130°)
- 1 cup canned pumpkin
- ⅓ cup unsweetened applesauce
- ⅓ cup canola oil
- 2 eggs, lightly beaten
- ½ cup raisins

FILLING
- ¼ cup butter, softened
- ½ cup packed brown sugar
- 1 teaspoon ground cinnamon

1. In a large bowl, combine 2 cups all-purpose flour, whole wheat flour, oats, brown sugar, pumpkin pie spice, salt, sugar and yeast. Beat in the warm water, pumpkin, applesauce and oil just until moistened. Add the eggs; beat until smooth. Stir in raisins. Add enough remaining all-purpose flour to form a firm dough.

2. Turn onto a lightly floured surface; knead until smooth and elastic, about 6-8 minutes. Place in a greased bowl, turning once to grease top. Cover and let rise in a warm place until doubled, about 1 hour.

3. Punch dough down. Turn onto a lightly floured surface; divide in half. Roll each portion into an 18x 9-in. rectangle; brush with butter to within ½ in. of edges. Combine brown sugar and cinnamon; sprinkle over dough. Roll up jelly-roll style, starting with a short side; pinch seam to seal.

4. Place seam side down in two greased 9x 5-in. loaf pans. Cover and let rise until doubled, about 30 minutes.

5. Bake at 350° 55-65 minutes or until golden brown. Cool 10 minutes before removing from pans to wire racks.
PER SERVING *201 cal., 5 g fat (1 g sat. fat), 17 mg chol., 130 mg sodium, 36 g carb., 3 g fiber, 5 g pro.*

Honey Wheat Loaves F S M

This bread bakes up tender and chewy with a hint of sweetness. It's great to give as a gift or to bring along to a potluck dinner.

—ROGER HAWLEY VALLEY PARK, MO

PREP: 45 MIN. + RISING • **BAKE:** 30 MIN. + COOLING
MAKES: 4 LOAVES (16 SLICES EACH)

- 3 packages (¼ ounce each) active dry yeast
- 5 cups warm water (110° to 115°), divided
- 1 tablespoon plus ⅔ cup honey, divided
- ⅔ cup canola oil
- ½ cup sugar
- 2 teaspoons salt
- 4 cups whole wheat flour
- 1 cup toasted wheat germ
- 6 to 8 cups bread flour

1. In a large bowl, dissolve yeast in ¾ cup warm water and 1 tablespoon honey. Add the remaining water and honey, the oil, sugar, salt, whole wheat flour, wheat germ and 3 cups bread flour. Beat until smooth. Stir in enough remaining bread flour to form a soft dough (dough will be sticky).

2. Turn onto a lightly floured surface; knead until smooth and elastic, about 6-8 minutes. Place in a bowl coated with cooking spray, turning once to coat the top. Cover and let rise in a warm place until doubled, about 1 hour.

3. Punch dough down. Shape into four loaves. Place in 9x5-in. loaf pans coated with cooking spray. Cover and let rise until nearly doubled, about 30 minutes.

4. Bake at 350° for 30-35 minutes or until golden brown. Remove from pans to wire racks to cool.
PER SERVING *108 cal., 3 g fat (trace sat. fat), 0 chol., 75 mg sodium, 19 g carb., 1 g fiber, 3 g pro.* **Diabetic Exchanges:** *1½ starch, ½ fat.*

HONEY WHEAT LOAVES

Oats & Honey Yeast Bread F M

This recipe meets my three most important criteria: It's easy, healthy and kid-approved! A friend of my husband's shared the directions for this fabulous multigrain bread.

—LISA BEDORD POWER, MT

PREP: 30 MIN. + RISING
BAKE: 25 MIN. + COOLING
MAKES: 1 LOAF (12 WEDGES)

- ½ cup water
- 6½ teaspoons butter, divided
- ½ cup old-fashioned oats
- ½ cup unsweetened applesauce
- ¼ cup honey
- 1 teaspoon salt
- 2 teaspoons active dry yeast
- 2 tablespoons warm water (110° to 115°)
- 1 egg
- 1½ cups whole wheat flour
- 1¼ to 1¾ cups all-purpose flour

1. In a small saucepan, bring water and 4½ teaspoons butter just to a boil. In a small bowl, pour boiling liquid over oats. Add the applesauce, honey and salt. Let stand until mixture cools to 110°-115°, stirring occasionally.

2. In a large bowl, dissolve yeast in warm water. Add the oatmeal mixture, egg, whole wheat flour and 1 cup all-purpose flour. Beat until smooth. Stir in enough remaining all-purpose flour to form a soft dough (dough will be sticky).

3. Turn onto a floured surface; knead until dough is smooth and elastic, about 6-8 minutes. Place in a greased bowl, turning once to grease the top. Cover and let rise in a warm place until doubled, about 1 hour.

4. Punch dough down. Shape into an 8-in. round loaf on a greased baking sheet. Cover and let rise in a warm place until doubled, about 30 minutes.

5. Melt remaining butter; brush over loaf. Bake at 375° for 25-30 minutes or until golden brown. Cool on wire rack.

PER SERVING *162 cal., 3 g fat (2 g sat. fat), 23 mg chol., 219 mg sodium, 30 g carb., 3 g fiber, 5 g pro.* **Diabetic Exchanges:** *2 starch, ½ fat.*

A Bit Nutty Boston Brown Bread F M

PREP: 30 MIN. • **BAKE:** 45 MIN. + COOLING
MAKES: 2 LOAVES (12 SLICES EACH)

- 3 **cups whole wheat flour**
- 1 **cup all-purpose flour**
- 2½ **teaspoons baking soda**
- 1 **teaspoon salt**
- 2½ **cups buttermilk**
- 1 **cup molasses**
- 1 **cup golden raisins**
- ¾ **cup chopped hazelnuts**

1. In a large bowl, combine the flours, baking soda and salt. In a small bowl, whisk buttermilk and molasses. Stir into dry ingredients just until moistened. Fold in raisins and nuts. Transfer to two greased 8x4-in. loaf pans.

2. Bake at 350° for 45-50 minutes or until a toothpick inserted near the center comes out clean. Cool for 10 minutes before removing from pans to wire racks.

NOTE *To toast nuts, spread in a 15x10x1-in. baking pan. Bake at 350° for 5-10 minutes or until lightly browned, stirring occasionally. Or, spread in a dry nonstick skillet and heat over low heat until lightly browned, stirring occasionally.*

PER SERVING *159 cal., 3 g fat (trace sat. fat), 1 mg chol., 263 mg sodium, 31 g carb., 3 g fiber, 4 g pro.*

Hearty and dense, this Boston brown bread features hazelnuts for a delightfully nutty taste. Thick slices pair well with just about anything, from soups and stews to roasts and casseroles.

—**LORRAINE CALAND** SHUNIAH, ON

A BIT NUTTY BOSTON BROWN BREAD

Cranberry Whole Wheat Bagels F M

The bagel recipes I saw in a magazine inspired me to try creating my own. I've been making them like crazy ever since! My whole wheat version dotted with cranberries is a favorite.

—**TAMI KUEHL** LOUP CITY, NE

PREP: 30 MIN. + RISING
BAKE: 15 MIN. + COOLING
MAKES: 1 DOZEN

- 1¼ **cups water (70° to 80°)**
- ⅓ **cup honey**
- 2 **tablespoons butter, softened**
- 1½ **teaspoons salt**
- 1 **teaspoon dried orange peel**
- ¼ **teaspoon ground mace**
- 2 **cups all-purpose flour**
- 1¼ **cups whole wheat flour**
- 2¾ **teaspoons active dry yeast**
- ½ **cup dried cranberries**
- 1 **egg white**
- 1 **tablespoon water**

1. In bread machine pan, place the first nine ingredients in order suggested by manufacturer. Select dough setting. Check dough after 5 minutes of mixing; add 1-2 tablespoons water or flour if needed. Just before the final kneading (your machine may audibly signal this), add cranberries.

2. Preheat oven to 400°. When cycle is completed, turn dough onto a lightly floured surface. Divide and shape into 12 balls. Push thumb through center of each, stretching and shaping to form an even ring with a 1½-in. hole. Place on a floured surface. Cover with kitchen towels; let rest 10 minutes. Flatten bagels slightly.

3. Fill a Dutch oven two-thirds full with water; bring to a boil. Drop bagels, two at a time, into boiling water. Cook 45 seconds; turn and cook 45 seconds longer. Remove with a slotted spoon; drain well on paper towels.

4. Place bagels 2 in. apart on parchment paper-lined baking sheets. Whisk egg white and water; brush over bagels. Bake 15-20 minutes or until golden brown. Remove from pans to wire racks to cool.

PER SERVING *184 cal., 2 g fat (1 g sat. fat), 5 mg chol., 315 mg sodium, 38 g carb., 3 g fiber, 5 g pro.*

CRANBERRY WHOLE WHEAT BAGELS

MULTIGRAIN BREAD

Multigrain Bread M

This attractive loaf studded with flaxseed couldn't be easier to make—you just combine the ingredients in a bread machine and let it do the rest of the work! It's delicious and healthy.

—**RUTH SKAFTE** FORT ST. JOHN, BC

PREP: 15 MIN. • **BAKE:** 3 HOURS
MAKES: 1 LOAF (2 POUNDS, 16 SLICES)

- 1⅓ cups water (70° to 80°)
- 2 tablespoons shortening
- 2 tablespoons honey
- ½ cup seven-grain cereal
- ⅓ cup flaxseed
- 2 tablespoons nonfat dry milk powder
- 2 tablespoons unsalted sunflower kernels
- 1 tablespoon sesame seeds
- 1 teaspoon salt
- 2 cups all-purpose flour
- 1 cup whole wheat flour
- 1 package (¼ ounce) active dry yeast

In bread machine pan, place all the ingredients in order suggested by manufacturer. Select basic bread setting. Choose crust color and loaf size if available. Bake according to bread machine directions (check dough after 5 minutes of mixing; add 1 to 2 tablespoons of water or flour if needed).

PER SERVING *148 cal., 4 g fat (1 g sat. fat), trace chol., 155 mg sodium, 24 g carb., 3 g fiber, 5 g pro.* **Diabetic Exchanges:** *1½ starch, ½ fat.*

Pumpkin Dinner Rolls F M

Serve these spicy-sweet dinner rolls and get ready to hear a chorus of "yums" in your house!

—**LINNEA REIN** TOPEKA, KS

PREP: 20 MIN. + RISING • **BAKE:** 20 MIN.
MAKES: 20 ROLLS

- ¾ cup milk
- ⅓ cup packed brown sugar
- 5 tablespoons butter, divided
- 1 teaspoon salt
- 2 packages (¼ ounce each) active dry yeast
- ½ cup warm water (110° to 115°)
- 2 to 2½ cups all-purpose flour
- 1½ cups whole wheat flour
- ½ cup canned pumpkin
- ½ teaspoon ground cinnamon
- ¼ teaspoon ground ginger
- ¼ teaspoon ground nutmeg

1. In a small saucepan, heat the milk, brown sugar, 4 tablespoons butter and salt to 110°-115°; set aside.

2. In a large bowl, dissolve yeast in warm water. Stir in milk mixture. Add 1½ cups all-purpose flour, wheat flour, pumpkin, cinnamon, ginger and nutmeg. Beat until smooth. Add enough remaining all-purpose flour to form a soft dough.

3. Turn onto a floured surface; knead until dough is smooth and elastic, about 6-8 minutes. Place in a greased bowl, turning once to grease top. Cover and let rise in a warm place until doubled, about 1 hour.

4. Punch dough down. Divide into 20 pieces; shape into balls. Place in a greased 13x9-in. baking pan. Cover and let rise for 30 minutes or until dough is doubled.

5. Preheat oven to 375°. Melt remaining butter; brush over dough. Bake 20-25 minutes or until golden brown. Remove from pan to a wire rack. Serve warm.

PER SERVING *124 cal., 3 g fat (2 g sat. fat), 9 mg chol., 154 mg sodium, 21 g carb., 2 g fiber, 3 g pro.* **Diabetic Exchanges:** *1½ starch, ½ fat.*

These tender rolls are a welcome addition to any meal. Whole wheat flour and oats make them nutritious, too.

—**ARLENE BUTLER** OGDEN, UT

HONEY-OAT PAN ROLLS

Honey-Oat Pan Rolls F S M

PREP: 45 MIN. + RISING • **BAKE:** 20 MIN. • **MAKES:** 2 DOZEN

- 2½ to 2¾ cups all-purpose flour
- ¾ cup whole wheat flour
- ½ cup old-fashioned oats
- 2 packages (¼ ounce each) active dry yeast
- 1 teaspoon salt
- 1 cup water
- ¼ cup honey
- 5 tablespoons butter, divided
- 1 egg

1. In a large bowl, mix 1 cup all-purpose flour, whole wheat flour, oats, yeast and salt. In a small saucepan, heat water, honey and 4 tablespoons butter to 120°-130°. Add to dry ingredients; beat on medium speed 2 minutes. Add egg; beat on high 2 minutes. Stir in enough remaining all-purpose flour to form a soft dough (dough will be sticky).

2. Turn dough onto a floured surface; knead until smooth and elastic, about 6-8 minutes. Place in a greased bowl, turning once to grease the top. Cover with plastic wrap and let rise in a warm place until doubled, about 1 hour.

3. Punch down dough. Turn onto a lightly floured surface; divide and shape into 24 balls. Place in a greased 13x9-in.

baking pan. Cover with a kitchen towel; let rise in a warm place until doubled, about 30 minutes.

4. Preheat oven to 375°. Bake 20-22 minutes or until golden brown. Melt remaining butter; brush over rolls. Remove from pan to a wire rack.

PER SERVING *103 cal., 3 g fat (2 g sat. fat), 15 mg chol., 126 mg sodium, 17 g carb., 1 g fiber, 3 g pro.* **Diabetic Exchanges:** *1 starch, ½ fat.*

Favorite Irish Soda Bread F M

My best friend shared this traditional soda bread recipe with me. It bakes up high with a golden brown top and tantalizing combo of sweet and savory flavors.

—**JAN ALFANO** PRESCOTT, AZ

PREP: 20 MIN. • **BAKE:** 45 MIN. + COOLING
MAKES: 1 LOAF (12 WEDGES)

- 3 cups all-purpose flour
- ⅔ cup sugar
- 3 teaspoons baking powder
- 1 teaspoon salt
- 1 teaspoon baking soda
- 1 cup raisins
- 2 eggs, beaten
- 1½ cups buttermilk
- 1 tablespoon canola oil

1. Preheat oven to 350°. In a large bowl, combine first five ingredients. Stir in raisins. Set aside 1 tablespoon beaten egg. In a bowl, combine buttermilk, oil and remaining eggs; stir into flour mixture just until moistened (dough will be sticky). Transfer to a greased 9-in. round baking pan; brush top with reserved egg.

2. Bake 45-50 minutes or until a toothpick inserted near the center comes out clean. Cool 10 minutes before removing from pan to a wire rack to cool. Cut into wedges.

PER SERVING *227 cal., 3 g fat (1 g sat. fat), 36 mg chol., 447 mg sodium, 46 g carb., 1 g fiber, 6 g pro.*

FAVORITE IRISH SODA BREAD

Chocolate Banana Bran Muffins M

So easy to make, these healthy treats still satisfy my chocolate-loving family. Stir in raisin bran instead of bran flakes if that's what you have. It adds a little extra fun.

—TRACY CHAPPELL HAMIOTA, MB

START TO FINISH: 25 MIN.
MAKES: 1 DOZEN

- 1   cup all-purpose flour
- ½   cup sugar
- 2   tablespoons baking cocoa
- 1   teaspoon baking powder
- 1   teaspoon baking soda
- ½   teaspoon salt
- 1   cup bran flakes
- 2   eggs
- 1   cup mashed ripe bananas (about 2 medium)
- ⅓   cup canola oil
- ¼   cup buttermilk

1. Preheat oven to 400°. In a large bowl, whisk the first six ingredients. Stir in bran flakes. In another bowl, whisk eggs, bananas, oil and buttermilk until blended. Add to flour mixture; stir just until moistened.

2. Fill foil-lined muffin cups three-fourths full. Bake 12-14 minutes or until a toothpick inserted in center comes out clean. Cool 5 minutes before removing from pan to a wire rack. Serve warm.

PER SERVING *169 cal., 7 g fat (1 g sat. fat), 35 mg chol., 278 mg sodium, 24 g carb., 2 g fiber, 3 g pro.* **Diabetic Exchanges:** *1½ starch, 1½ fat.*

Cinnamon-Pecan Swirl Bread M

This old-fashioned bread is a staple in our house. The recipe makes two loaves, and I like to freeze one for later.

—JANICE SHEPARD GLENDALE, OR

PREP: 45 MIN. + RISING
BAKE: 35 MIN. + COOLING
MAKES: 2 LOAVES (12 SLICES EACH)

- 2¼   cups whole wheat flour
- 2   to 2½ cups bread flour
- ½   cup ground flaxseed
- 2   tablespoons vital wheat gluten
- 3   teaspoons active dry yeast
- 2   teaspoons salt
- 1¼   cups water
- ⅓   cup canola oil
- ⅓   cup honey
- ½   teaspoon lemon juice
- 1   egg

CINNAMON NUT FILLING
- ¾   cup packed brown sugar
- ½   cup finely chopped pecans
- 2½   teaspoons ground cinnamon
- ¼   teaspoon ground nutmeg

1. In a large bowl, combine the whole wheat flour, 2 cups bread flour, flax, gluten, yeast and salt. In a small saucepan, heat the water, oil, honey and lemon juice to 120°-130°. Add to dry ingredients; beat just until moistened. Add egg; beat until smooth. Stir in enough remaining bread flour to form a stiff dough (dough will be sticky).

2. Turn onto a floured surface; knead until smooth and elastic, about 6-8 minutes. Place in a greased bowl, turning once to grease the top. Cover and let rise for 1 hour or until doubled.

3. Meanwhile, combine filling ingredients; set aside.

4. Punch dough down. Turn onto a lightly floured surface; divide dough in half. Roll each half into a 14-in. x 8-in. rectangle. Sprinkle half of the filling over each rectangle to within ½ in. of edges. Roll up, jelly-roll style, starting with a short side. Pinch to seal. Place each loaf seam-side down in a greased 9-in. x 5-in. loaf pan. Cover and let rise until doubled, about 1 hour.

5. Bake at 350° for 34-38 minutes or until golden brown. Remove from pans to wire racks to cool.

PER SERVING *188 cal., 7 g fat (1 g sat. fat), 9 mg chol., 205 mg sodium, 28 g carb., 3 g fiber, 5 g pro.*

CHOCOLATE BANANA BRAN MUFFINS

? Did you know?

Whole flaxseed is an attractive garnish in bread, but it doesn't contribute much nutritional value. The body more easily absorbs the nutrients in ground flax because it doesn't have to deal with the seeds' hard protective covers.

SEEDED WHOLE GRAIN LOAF

Seeded Whole Grain Loaf F M

My husband and I want whole grain bread, but we don't like the spongy store-bought whole wheat breads. I drastically altered a favorite batter bread recipe to create this simple bread-machine dream. The add-ins are just suggestions. Sometimes I use pepitas, sesame seeds or even ¼ cup of a multigrain hot cereal mix.

—AMBER RIFE COLUMBUS, OH

PREP: 20 MIN. • **BAKE:** 4 HOURS
MAKES: 1 LOAF (1½ POUNDS, 16 SLICES)

- 1⅓ cups warm 2% milk (70° to 80°)
- 3 tablespoons honey
- 2 tablespoons canola oil
- 1¼ teaspoons salt
- 2⅔ cups whole wheat flour
- 2 tablespoons old-fashioned oats
- 4 teaspoons vital wheat gluten
- 1 tablespoon millet
- 1 tablespoon sunflower kernels
- 1 tablespoon flaxseed
- 1 tablespoon cracked wheat or additional flaxseed
- 1 package (¼ ounce) active dry yeast

In bread machine pan, place all the ingredients in order suggested by manufacturer. Select basic bread setting. Choose crust color and loaf size if available. Bake according to bread machine directions (check dough after 5 minutes of mixing; add 1 to 2 tablespoons of water or flour if needed).
PER SERVING *128 cal., 3 g fat (1 g sat. fat), 2 mg chol., 199 mg sodium, 21 g carb., 3 g fiber, 5 g pro.* **Diabetic Exchanges:** *1 starch, ½ fat.*

Tomato-Herb Focaccia F M

With its medley of herbs and tomatoes, this rustic bread will liven up any occasion, from a family meal to a get-together on game day. And it never lasts long.

—JANET MILLER INDIANAPOLIS, IN

PREP: 30 MIN. + RISING • **BAKE:** 20 MIN.
MAKES: 1 LOAF (12 PIECES)

- 1 package (¼ ounce) active dry yeast
- 1 cup warm water (110° to 115°)
- 2 tablespoons olive oil, divided
- 1½ teaspoons salt
- 1 teaspoon sugar
- 1 teaspoon garlic powder
- 1 teaspoon each dried oregano, thyme and rosemary, crushed
- ½ teaspoon dried basil
  Dash pepper
- 2 to 2½ cups all-purpose flour
- 2 plum tomatoes, thinly sliced
- ¼ cup shredded part-skim mozzarella cheese
- 1 tablespoon grated Parmesan cheese

1. In a large bowl, dissolve yeast in warm water. Add 1 tablespoon oil, salt, sugar, garlic powder, herbs, pepper and 1½ cups flour. Beat until smooth. Stir in enough remaining flour to form a soft dough (dough will be sticky).

2. Turn onto a floured surface; knead until smooth and elastic, about 6-8 minutes. Place in a greased bowl, turning once to grease the top. Cover and let rise in a warm place until doubled, about 1 hour.

3. Punch dough down. Cover and let rest for 10 minutes. Shape into a 13x9-in. rectangle; place on a greased baking sheet. Cover and let rise until doubled, about 30 minutes. With fingertips, make several dimples over top of dough.

4. Brush dough with remaining oil; arrange tomatoes over the top. Sprinkle with cheeses. Bake at 400° for 20-25 minutes or until golden brown. Remove to a wire rack.
PER SERVING *111 cal., 3 g fat (1 g sat. fat), 2 mg chol., 314 mg sodium, 17 g carb., 1 g fiber, 3 g pro.* **Diabetic Exchanges:** *1 starch, ½ fat.*

TOMATO-HERB FOCACCIA

206

210

213

Table for Two

"These sundaes are an easy way to add fruit and calcium to your diet. Berries star in the dish, which I like as a simple breakfast or healthy dessert for two."

—EDIE DESPAIN LOGAN, UT
about her recipe, Mixed Berry Sundaes for 2, on page 205

VEGGIE
SALMON CHOWDER

Veggie Salmon Chowder F

This dish came about as a way to use up odds and ends in my fridge. I thought other readers might enjoy a recipe that began as an experiment but became a mainstay for me.

—LIV VORS PETERBOROUGH, ON

START TO FINISH: 30 MIN.
MAKES: 2 SERVINGS

- 1 medium sweet potato, peeled and cut into ½-inch cubes
- 1 cup reduced-sodium chicken broth
- ½ cup fresh or frozen corn
- ½ small onion, chopped
- 2 garlic cloves, minced
- 1½ cups fresh spinach, torn
- ½ cup flaked smoked salmon fillet
- 1 teaspoon pickled jalapeno slices, chopped
- 1 tablespoon cornstarch
- ½ cup 2% milk
- 1 tablespoon minced fresh cilantro
  Dash pepper

1. In a large saucepan, combine the first five ingredients; bring to a boil. Reduce heat; simmer, covered, for 8-10 minutes or until potato is tender.
2. Stir in spinach, salmon and jalapeno; cook 1-2 minutes or until spinach is wilted. In a small bowl, mix cornstarch and milk until smooth; stir into soup. Bring to a boil; cook and stir 2 minutes or until thickened. Stir in cilantro and pepper.
PER SERVING *202 cal., 3 g fat (1 g sat. fat), 12 mg chol., 645 mg sodium, 32 g carb., 4 g fiber, 13 g pro.* **Diabetic Exchanges:** *2 starch, 1 lean meat, 1 vegetable.*

Grilled Chipotle Tenderloin C

For Easter, I served this recipe with au gratin potatoes and a green salad. If you prefer not to grill, you can bake the tenderloin in the oven.

—KELLY TOWNSEND SYRACUSE, NE

PREP: 20 MIN. + MARINATING
GRILL: 20 MIN. • **MAKES:** 2 SERVINGS

- ¼ cup orange juice
- ¼ cup reduced-sodium teriyaki sauce
- 2 tablespoons olive oil
- 1 tablespoon chipotle hot pepper sauce
- 2 teaspoons chili powder
- 2 teaspoons Worcestershire sauce
- 1 teaspoon garlic salt
- 1 teaspoon Dijon mustard
- 1 pork tenderloin (¾ pound)
GLAZE
- 2 tablespoons brown sugar
- 1½ teaspoons cornstarch
- ½ cup orange juice
- ¼ cup cold water
- 2 teaspoons reduced-sodium soy sauce
- 1 teaspoon chipotle hot pepper sauce
- ½ teaspoon chili powder

1. In a large resealable plastic bag, combine the first eight ingredients; add pork. Seal bag and turn to coat; refrigerate for up to 2 hours.
2. For glaze, in a small saucepan, combine brown sugar and cornstarch. Stir in orange juice, water, soy sauce, hot pepper sauce and chili powder until smooth. Bring to a boil; cook and stir for 1-2 minutes or until thickened.
3. Drain pork, discarding marinade in bag. Grill pork, covered, over medium heat for 18-22 minutes or until a thermometer reads 145°, turning occasionally and brushing with glaze during the last 10 minutes. Let stand 5 minutes before slicing.
PER SERVING *285 cal., 11 g fat (3 g sat. fat), 95 mg chol., 666 mg sodium, 11 g carb., trace fiber, 35 g pro.* **Diabetic Exchanges:** *5 lean meat, 1 starch, 1 fat.*

GRILLED CHIPOTLE TENDERLOIN

PENNE WITH VEGGIES 'N' BLACK BEANS

Penne with Veggies 'n' Black Beans M

Chock-full of zucchini, tomato, sweet pepper and carrot, this hearty pasta dish puts your garden harvest to good use.

—VICKIE SPOERLE CARMEL, IN

START TO FINISH: 25 MIN.
MAKES: 2 SERVINGS

- ¾ cup uncooked penne pasta
- ⅓ cup sliced zucchini
- ⅓ cup sliced fresh carrot
- 4 medium fresh mushrooms, sliced
- ½ small green pepper, thinly sliced
- ½ small onion, thinly sliced
- 1 small garlic clove, minced
- ¼ teaspoon each dried basil, oregano and thyme
- ¼ teaspoon salt
- ⅛ teaspoon pepper
- 2 teaspoons olive oil, divided
- 1 cup canned black beans, rinsed and drained
- ¼ cup chopped seeded tomato
- 2 tablespoons shredded Parmesan cheese
- 2 teaspoons minced fresh parsley

1. Cook pasta according to package directions. Meanwhile, in a large nonstick skillet, saute zucchini, carrot, mushrooms, green pepper, onion, garlic and seasonings in 1 teaspoon oil until crisp-tender. Stir in the beans.
2. Drain pasta; add to vegetable mixture. Add tomato and remaining olive oil; toss gently. Sprinkle with Parmesan cheese and parsley.

PER SERVING *300 cal., 7 g fat (2 g sat. fat), 4 mg chol., 643 mg sodium, 47 g carb., 8 g fiber, 14 g pro. **Diabetic Exchanges:** 2½ starch, 1 lean meat, 1 vegetable, 1 fat.*

Mixed Berry Sundaes for 2 S M

START TO FINISH: 10 MIN.
MAKES: 2 SERVINGS

- ¼ cup halved fresh strawberries
- ¼ cup each fresh raspberries, blueberries and blackberries
- 3 teaspoons honey, divided
- ½ cup fat-free plain Greek yogurt
- 2 tablespoons pomegranate juice
- 2 tablespoons chopped walnuts, toasted

1. In a small bowl, combine berries and 1 teaspoon honey; spoon mixture into two dessert dishes.
2. Combine the yogurt, pomegranate juice and remaining honey; spoon over berries. Sprinkle with walnuts.
PER SERVING *160 cal., 5 g fat (trace sat. fat), 0 chol., 33 mg sodium, 22 g carb., 3 g fiber, 10 g pro. **Diabetic Exchanges:** 1 starch, 1 fat, ½ fruit.*

These sundaes are an easy way to add fruit and calcium to your diet. Berries star in the dish, which I like as a simple breakfast or healthy dessert for two.
—EDIE DESPAIN LOGAN, UT

MIXED BERRY SUNDAES FOR 2

Beef Barley Soup

Here's a delicious soup that's brimming with satisfying ingredients. It's true comfort food for a cool day.

—SUE JURACK MEQUON, WI

START TO FINISH: 30 MIN.
MAKES: 2 SERVINGS

- 2 **tablespoons each chopped carrot, celery and onion**
- 1 **teaspoon butter**
- 1 **cup water**
- 1 **cup reduced-sodium beef broth**
- ½ **cup cubed cooked roast beef**
- ½ **cup canned diced tomatoes**
- ¼ **cup quick-cooking barley**
- 2 **tablespoons frozen peas**
- ¼ **teaspoon salt**
- ¼ **teaspoon dried basil**
- ¼ **teaspoon dried oregano**
- ¼ **teaspoon pepper**

In a small saucepan, saute the carrot, celery and onion in butter until tender. Add the remaining ingredients; bring to a boil. Reduce heat; cover and simmer for 15-20 minutes or until barley is tender, stirring occasionally.

PER SERVING *206 cal., 4 g fat (2 g sat. fat), 40 mg chol., 650 mg sodium, 24 g carb., 6 g fiber, 18 g pro.* **Diabetic Exchanges:** *2 lean meat, 1½ starch, ½ fat.*

GREEK SALAD PITAS

BEEF BARLEY SOUP

Greek Salad Pitas M

Veggie lovers, rejoice! This hearty meatless pita is full of flavor, thanks to plenty of chopped veggies and savory Greek accents.

—ALEXIS WORCHESKY-LASEK
WEST FRIENDSHIP, MD

START TO FINISH: 20 MIN.
MAKES: 2 SERVINGS

- ⅔ **cup chopped seeded cucumber**
- ⅔ **cup chopped sweet red pepper**
- ⅔ **cup chopped tomato**
- ⅔ **cup chopped zucchini**
- ¼ **cup crumbled feta cheese**
- 2 **tablespoons chopped ripe olives**
- 2 **teaspoons red wine vinegar**
- 2 **teaspoons lemon juice**
- ¾ **teaspoon dried oregano**
- ⅛ **teaspoon salt**
- ⅛ **teaspoon pepper**
- 4 **lettuce leaves**
- 4 **pita pocket halves**

In a small bowl, combine the cucumber, red pepper, tomato, zucchini, feta cheese and olives. In another bowl, whisk the vinegar, lemon juice, oregano, salt and pepper. Pour over vegetables and toss to coat. Spoon into lettuce-lined pita halves.

PER SERVING *255 cal., 4 g fat (2 g sat. fat), 8 mg chol., 688 mg sodium, 45 g carb., 5 g fiber, 10 g pro.* **Diabetic Exchanges:** *2 starch, 2 vegetable, ½ fat.*

Flaxseed Oatmeal Pancakes M

I came up with this healthy and really tasty recipe because my husband loves pancakes. They have a pleasing texture and a delightful touch of cinnamon.

—SHARON HANSEN PONTIAC, IL

START TO FINISH: 20 MIN.
MAKES: 4 PANCAKES

- ⅓ **cup whole wheat flour**
- 3 **tablespoons quick-cooking oats**
- 1 **tablespoon flaxseed**
- ½ **teaspoon baking powder**
- ¼ **teaspoon ground cinnamon**
- ⅛ **teaspoon baking soda**
  Dash salt
- 1 **egg, separated**
- ½ **cup buttermilk**
- 1 **tablespoon brown sugar**
- 1 **tablespoon canola oil**
- ½ **teaspoon vanilla extract**

1. In a large bowl, combine the first seven ingredients. In a small bowl, whisk the egg yolk, buttermilk, brown sugar, oil and vanilla; stir into dry ingredients just until moistened.
2. In a small bowl, beat egg white on medium speed until stiff peaks form. Fold into batter.
3. Pour batter by ¼ cupfuls onto a hot griddle coated with cooking spray; turn when bubbles form on top. Cook until the second side is golden brown.
PER SERVING *2 pancakes equals 273 cal., 13 g fat (2 g sat. fat), 108 mg chol., 357 mg sodium, 31 g carb., 5 g fiber, 10 g pro.* **Diabetic Exchanges:** *2 starch, 2 fat.*

BAKED FISH WITH CHEESE SAUCE FOR 2

Baked Fish with Cheese Sauce for 2 C

You can easily whip up this flaky fish and decadent cheese sauce. Go ahead: Turn a ho-hum weeknight into something special.

—KRISTIN REYNOLDS VAN BUREN, AR

START TO FINISH: 20 MIN.
MAKES: 2 SERVINGS

- 2 **flounder fillets (4 ounces each)**
- 1½ **teaspoons butter, melted**
- 1 **tablespoon dry bread crumbs**
- 1½ **teaspoons all-purpose flour**
- 6 **tablespoons 2% milk**
- ¼ **cup shredded cheddar cheese**
- ¾ **teaspoon Dijon mustard**

1. Place fish in a greased 11x 7-in. baking dish. Brush with butter; sprinkle with bread crumbs. Bake at 400° for 15-20 minutes or until fish flakes easily with a fork.
2. Meanwhile, in a small saucepan, combine flour and milk until smooth. Bring to a boil; cook and stir 2 minutes or until thickened. Stir in cheese and mustard until cheese is melted. Serve with fish.
PER SERVING *206 cal., 9 g fat (5 g sat. fat), 94 mg chol., 279 mg sodium, 7 g carb., trace fiber, 24 g pro.* **Diabetic Exchanges:** *3 lean meat, 1 fat, ½ starch.*

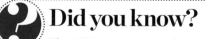

FLAXSEED OATMEAL PANCAKES

? Did you know?

The USDA recommends that adults eat 2 servings, or about 8 ounces, of seafood per week to help prevent heart disease. Choose a variety of fish and shellfish to meet your goal.

Southwest Tortilla Scramble M

Here's my version of a deconstructed breakfast burrito that's actually good for you. It has tons of flavor, and the protein keeps you going all morning long.
—**CHRISTINE SCHENHER** EXETER, CA

START TO FINISH: 15 MIN. • **MAKES:** 2 SERVINGS

- 4 **egg whites**
- 2 **eggs**
- ¼ **teaspoon pepper**
- 2 **corn tortillas (6 inches), halved and cut into strips**
- ¼ **cup chopped fresh spinach**
- 2 **tablespoons shredded reduced-fat cheddar cheese**
- ¼ **cup salsa**

1. In a large bowl, whisk egg whites, eggs and pepper. Stir in tortillas, spinach and cheese.
2. Heat a large skillet coated with cooking spray over medium heat. Pour in egg mixture; cook and stir until eggs are thickened and no liquid egg remains. Top with salsa.
PER SERVING *195 cal., 7 g fat (3 g sat. fat), 217 mg chol., 391 mg sodium, 16 g carb., 2 g fiber, 17 g pro.* **Diabetic Exchanges:** *2 lean meat, 1 starch.*

Citrus Fish for 2 C

One of my friends on the *tasteofhome.com* forums shared the basis for this easy recipe of delicately flavored fish, and I made some adjustments. The bonus? Cleanup is an absolute breeze.
—**BARBARA CARLUCCI** ORANGE PARK, FL

START TO FINISH: 30 MIN. • **MAKES:** 2 SERVINGS

- ¾ **pound haddock, cod or halibut fillets**
- ⅛ **teaspoon salt**
- ⅛ **teaspoon pepper**
- ½ **medium onion, chopped**
- 3 **tablespoons minced fresh parsley**
- 1 **teaspoon grated lemon peel**
- 1 **teaspoon grated orange peel**
- 2 **teaspoons canola oil**

1. Place a 15x12-in. piece of heavy-duty foil on a large baking sheet. Arrange fillets in a single layer on foil; sprinkle with salt and pepper. Top with onion, parsley, and lemon and orange peel. Drizzle with oil. Top with a second large piece of foil. Bring edges of foil together; crimp to seal, forming a large packet.
2. Bake at 450° for 15-20 minutes or until fish flakes easily with a fork. Open foil carefully to allow steam to escape.
PER SERVING *209 cal., 6 g fat (1 g sat. fat), 98 mg chol., 267 mg sodium, 4 g carb., 1 g fiber, 33 g pro.* **Diabetic Exchanges:** *5 lean meat, 1 fat.*

Peach Ice F S M

If the fresh peach is delicious, this recipe will be out of this world! It's a light dessert for those counting calories and perfect on a hot day or after a heavy meal.

—CARMA BLOSSER LIVERMORE, CO

PREP: 15 MIN. + FREEZING • **MAKES:** 2 SERVINGS

⅓ cup warm water (120° to 130°)
2 tablespoons sugar
1 small peach, peeled
2 teaspoons lemon juice

1. In a small bowl, stir water and sugar until sugar is dissolved. Place peach, lemon juice and sugar mixture in a blender. Cover and process 1 minute or until blended. Transfer to a freezer container; cover and freeze 3 hours or until almost firm.
2. Transfer to blender. Cover and process 30-40 seconds or until slushy. Return to freezer container; cover and freeze overnight.
3. Remove from freezer just before serving. Using a fork, scrape into two dessert dishes.
PER SERVING *65 cal., trace fat (trace sat. fat), 0 chol., trace sodium, 17 g carb., 1 g fiber, trace pro.* **Diabetic Exchange:** *1 starch.*

Southwest Grilled Chicken C

Lime juice, cumin and a splash of pepper sauce lend zesty flavor to my grilled chicken. It's so easy, you'll make it often.

—MOLLY SEIDEL EDGEWOOD, NM

PREP: 10 MIN. + MARINATING • **GRILL:** 10 MIN. • **MAKES:** 2 SERVINGS

¼ cup lime juice
1½ teaspoons olive oil
1 teaspoon hot pepper sauce
1 garlic clove, minced
½ teaspoon ground cumin
¼ teaspoon salt
2 boneless skinless chicken breast halves (5 ounces each)

1. In a large resealable plastic bag, combine the first six ingredients; add chicken. Seal bag and turn to coat; refrigerate for up to 1 hour.
2. Drain chicken, discarding marinade in bag. Grill, covered, over medium heat for 4-7 minutes on each side or until juices run clear.
PER SERVING *166 cal., 4 g fat (1 g sat. fat), 78 mg chol., 146 mg sodium, 1 g carb., trace fiber, 29 g pro.* **Diabetic Exchanges:** *4 lean meat, ½ fat.*

SKILLET PASTA

Skillet Pasta

This is always a good recipe to make when time is short. Accents of herbs delectably lace the simple one-pot spaghetti.

—**MARV SALTER** WEST HILLS, CA

PREP: 15 MIN. • **COOK:** 20 MIN. • **MAKES:** 2 SERVINGS

- ½ pound lean ground beef (90% lean)
- 1 cup sliced fresh mushrooms
- ⅓ cup chopped onion
- 1 garlic clove, minced
- 1 cup reduced-sodium beef broth
- ⅔ cup water
- ⅓ cup tomato paste
- ½ teaspoon dried basil
- ½ teaspoon dried oregano
- ⅛ teaspoon pepper
- 3 ounces uncooked spaghetti, broken in half
- 2 teaspoons grated Parmesan cheese

1. In a large skillet, cook the beef, mushrooms, onion and garlic over medium heat until meat is no longer pink and vegetables are tender; drain.
2. Stir in broth, water, tomato paste, seasonings and pasta. Bring to a boil. Reduce heat; cover and cook 15-20 minutes or until pasta is tender. Sprinkle with cheese.
PER SERVING *414 cal., 11 g fat (4 g sat. fat), 75 mg chol., 337 mg sodium, 45 g carb., 4 g fiber, 33 g pro.* **Diabetic Exchanges:** *3 lean meat, 2 starch, 2 vegetable.*

From the Web

Very good, not as fast as using jarred sauce, but it tastes 10 times better. I doubled the recipe and added half a bay leaf and a can of drained diced tomatoes. Using one pot to make the dish is a definite time-saver. —**SPYCE THYME** TASTEOFHOME.COM

Curried Apricot Pork Chops

A fresh fruit glaze that's both sweet and savory drapes these tender chops. They're pretty enough to serve for a special night in.

—**TRISHA KRUSE** EAGLE, ID

START TO FINISH: 30 MIN. • **MAKES:** 2 SERVINGS

- 2 tablespoons apricot nectar
- 1 tablespoon plus 1½ teaspoons apricot preserves
- 1 tablespoon Dijon mustard
- 1 tablespoon reduced-sodium soy sauce
- 1 teaspoon curry powder
- 2 boneless pork loin chops (5 ounces each)
- ⅛ teaspoon salt
- ⅛ teaspoon pepper
- 1½ teaspoons canola oil
- ½ cup sliced fresh apricots
- 2 green onions, sliced

1. In a small bowl, combine the first five ingredients; set aside.
2. Sprinkle pork chops with salt and pepper. In a small nonstick skillet, cook chops in oil for 4-5 minutes on each side or until a thermometer reads 145°. Remove pork chops and keep warm.
3. Add apricots and onions to the pan; saute until onions are tender. Stir in nectar mixture. Bring to a boil; cook and stir for 2 minutes or until slightly thickened. Serve with pork chops.
PER SERVING *306 cal., 12 g fat (3 g sat. fat), 68 mg chol., 679 mg sodium, 20 g carb., 2 g fiber, 29 g pro.* **Diabetic Exchanges:** *4 lean meat, 1 starch, 1 fat.*

CURRIED APRICOT PORK CHOPS

HONEY BALSAMIC CHICKEN

Sirloin on the Grill c

Marinated in onions, beer, mustard and chili sauce, this easy steak picks up a wonderful flavor on the grill.

—DEBBI JAHAASKI SAN DIEGO, CA

PREP: 15 MIN. + MARINATING • **GRILL:** 15 MIN. • **MAKES:** 2 SERVINGS

- ¾ **cup beer or nonalcoholic beer**
- 1 **small onion, chopped**
- ¼ **cup chili sauce**
- 2 **tablespoons canola oil**
- 1 **tablespoon reduced-sodium soy sauce**
- 1½ **teaspoons Dijon mustard**
- 1 **garlic clove, minced**
- ½ **teaspoon hot pepper sauce**
- ⅛ **teaspoon liquid smoke, optional**
- ¾ **pound beef top sirloin steak (1 inch thick)**

1. In a small bowl, combine the beer, onion, chili sauce, oil, soy sauce, mustard, garlic, pepper sauce and, if desired, liquid smoke. Pour 1 cup marinade into a large resealable plastic bag; add beef. Seal bag and turn to coat; refrigerate for at least 2 hours or overnight, turning occasionally. Cover and refrigerate remaining marinade for basting.

2. Drain beef, discarding marinade in bag. Moisten a paper towel with cooking oil; using long-handled tongs, lightly coat the grill rack. Grill steak, covered, over medium heat or broil 4 in. from the heat for 6-8 minutes on each side or until meat reaches desired doneness (for medium-rare, a thermometer should read 145°; medium, 160°; well-done, 170°), basting frequently with reserved marinade.

PER SERVING *263 cal., 12 g fat (4 g sat. fat), 94 mg chol., 284 mg sodium, 4 g carb., trace fiber, 32 g pro.* **Diabetic Exchanges:** *5 lean meat, 1½ fat.*

Here's a dish I adapted from a cookbook that featured quick and easy recipes. I adjusted the seasonings and added a bit more honey to better suit my tastes.
—LISA VARNER EL PASO, TX

Honey Balsamic Chicken c

START TO FINISH: 20 MIN. • **MAKES:** 2 SERVINGS

- 2 **boneless skinless chicken breast halves (5 ounces each)**
- ½ **teaspoon garlic salt**
- ⅛ **teaspoon coarsely ground pepper**
- 2 **teaspoons canola oil**
- 1 **tablespoon balsamic vinegar**
- 1 **tablespoon honey**
- ½ **teaspoon dried basil**

1. Sprinkle chicken with garlic salt and pepper. In a large skillet over medium heat, cook chicken in oil for 4-7 minutes on each side or until juices run clear. Remove and keep warm.

2. Add the vinegar, honey and basil to the pan; cook and stir for 1 minute. Return chicken to the pan; heat through, turning to coat with glaze.

PER SERVING *232 cal., 8 g fat (1 g sat. fat), 78 mg chol., 524 mg sodium, 10 g carb., trace fiber, 29 g pro.* **Diabetic Exchanges:** *4 lean meat, 1 fat, ½ starch.*

SIRLOIN ON THE GRILL

ZESTY SPINACH DIP

Zesty Spinach Dip [F][C][M]

I needed to take something healthy and low in fat to a get-together, so I experimented and came up with this dip. Packed full of flavorful veggies, it's always a hit whether served with bread, crackers or additional veggies. Somebody asks for the recipe every time.

—**NOELLE MYERS** GRAND FORKS, ND

PREP: 15 MIN. + CHILLING • **MAKES:** 1 CUP

- ½ **cup fat-free plain yogurt**
- 1 **ounce fat-free cream cheese**
- 2 **teaspoons thinly sliced green onion**
- 2 **teaspoons finely chopped sweet yellow pepper**
- 2 **teaspoons finely chopped sweet red pepper**
- 2 **teaspoons Italian salad dressing mix**
- ⅛ **teaspoon ground nutmeg**
- 1 **cup frozen leaf spinach, thawed and squeezed dry**
  Radishes and carrot sticks

In a small bowl, combine the first seven ingredients; stir in spinach. Chill for at least 1 hour before serving. Serve with vegetables.
PER SERVING *½ cup equals 62 cal., trace fat (trace sat. fat), 2 mg chol., 499 mg sodium, 9 g carb., 1 g fiber, 6 g pro.*

Apple Sundaes [F][S][M]

With just a few ingredients, these warm sundaes are perfect for indulging with a friend. They're guilt-free, too.

—**KERRY DINGWALL** PONTE VEDRA, FL

PREP: 10 MIN. • **COOK:** 25 MIN.
MAKES: 2 SERVINGS

- 2 **cups chopped peeled Golden Delicious apples**
- 2 **tablespoons water**
- 1 **tablespoon sugar**
- ¼ **teaspoon ground cinnamon**
- 8 **reduced-fat vanilla wafers, crumbled**
- 1 **cup low-fat vanilla frozen yogurt**

1. In a small saucepan, combine the apples, water, sugar and cinnamon. Bring to a boil. Reduce heat; cover and simmer for 15 minutes. Uncover; simmer 5-10 minutes longer or until apples are tender. Cool for 5 minutes.

2. Divide half of the vanilla wafer crumbs between two dessert dishes. Top with frozen yogurt and the apple mixture; sprinkle with remaining wafer crumbs. Serve immediately.
PER SERVING *249 cal., 3 g fat (1 g sat. fat), 5 mg chol., 112 mg sodium, 53 g carb., 2 g fiber, 5 g pro.*

Crispy Buffalo Chicken Roll-Ups for 2 [C]

These winning chicken rolls with a crispy crust are both impressive and easy to make. My family and friends absolutely love them!

—**LISA KEYS** KENNET SQUARE, PA

PREP: 15 MIN. • **BAKE:** 30 MIN.
MAKES: 2 SERVINGS

- 2 **boneless skinless chicken breast halves (6 ounces each)**
- ¼ **teaspoon salt**
- ¼ **teaspoon pepper**
- 2 **tablespoons crumbled blue cheese**
- 2 **tablespoons hot pepper sauce**
- 1 **tablespoon mayonnaise**
- ½ **cup crushed cornflakes**

1. Preheat oven to 400°. Flatten chicken breasts to ¼-in. thickness. Season with salt and pepper; sprinkle with blue cheese. Roll up each from a short side and secure with toothpicks.
2. In a shallow bowl, combine pepper sauce and mayonnaise. Place the cornflakes in a separate shallow bowl. Dip chicken in the pepper sauce mixture, then coat with cornflakes. Place seam side down in a greased 11x7-in. baking dish.
3. Bake, uncovered, 30-35 minutes or until chicken is no longer pink. Discard toothpicks.
PER SERVING *270 cal., 8 g fat (3 g sat. fat), 101 mg chol., 617 mg sodium, 10 g carb., trace fiber, 37 g pro.* **Diabetic Exchanges:** *5 lean meat, ½ starch, ½ fat.*

CRISPY BUFFALO CHICKEN ROLL-UPS FOR 2

Italian Steaks for 2 C

These tender steaks make a quick and flavorful entree. You'll love the pizza-flavored topping in this nutritious supper.

—**MARY HANKINS** KANSAS CITY, MO

START TO FINISH: 25 MIN.
MAKES: 2 SERVINGS

- 1 egg
- ¼ cup seasoned bread crumbs
- ¼ teaspoon dried basil
- ¼ teaspoon dried oregano
  Dash salt and pepper
- 1 beef top sirloin steak (½ pound)
- 1½ teaspoons canola oil
- ½ cup pizza sauce
- 2 tablespoons shredded Italian cheese blend

1. In a shallow bowl, whisk egg. In another shallow bowl, combine the bread crumbs, basil, oregano, salt and pepper. Cut steak in half; dip each piece in egg, then coat with bread crumb mixture.

2. In a large skillet, cook steaks in oil over medium-high heat for 2-4 minutes on each side or until meat reaches desired doneness (for medium-rare, a thermometer should read 145°; medium, 160°; well-done, 170°).

3. Meanwhile, heat sauce in a small saucepan. Spoon over steaks; sprinkle with cheese.

PER SERVING *282 cal., 12 g fat (4 g sat. fat), 157 mg chol., 416 mg sodium, 10 g carb., 1 g fiber, 31 g pro.* **Diabetic Exchanges:** *4 lean meat, 1 fat, ½ starch.*

HEALTHY GAZPACHO FOR 2

Healthy Gazpacho for 2 F M

Nutritious vegetables are the basis of this tasty chilled soup. We recommend using spicy V-8 juice for a spicier version.

—*TASTE OF HOME TEST KITCHEN*

PREP: 20 MIN. + CHILLING
MAKES: 2 SERVINGS

- 2 medium tomatoes, seeded and chopped
- ½ small green pepper, chopped
- ⅓ cup chopped peeled cucumber
- ⅓ cup chopped red onion
- 1⅓ cups reduced-sodium tomato juice
- ¼ teaspoon dried oregano
- ¼ teaspoon dried basil
- ⅛ teaspoon salt
- 1 small garlic clove, minced
  Dash pepper
  Dash hot pepper sauce
- 1 tablespoon minced chives
  Chopped sweet yellow pepper, optional

1. In a large bowl, combine the tomatoes, green pepper, cucumber and onion. In another bowl, combine the tomato juice, oregano, basil, salt, garlic, pepper and pepper sauce; pour over vegetables.

2. Cover and refrigerate for at least 4 hours or overnight. Just before serving, sprinkle with chives and, if desired, yellow pepper.

PER SERVING *81 cal., trace fat (trace sat. fat), 0 chol., 252 mg sodium, 17 g carb., 4 g fiber, 3 g pro.* **Diabetic Exchange:** *1 starch.*

KS FOR 2

Vegetable Omelet C M

I used to make this recipe with bacon, ham and regular cheese, but I found it's easy and satisfying to substitute low-fat or fat-free ingredients.

—**PAMELA SHANK** PARKERSBURG, WV

START TO FINISH: 20 MIN.
MAKES: 2 SERVINGS

- 2 **small red potatoes, diced**
- ¼ **cup sliced fresh mushrooms**
- 1 **tablespoon chopped green pepper**
- 1 **tablespoon chopped sweet red pepper**
- 1 **green onion, chopped**
- 1 **tablespoon olive oil**
- ⅔ **cup egg substitute**
- ¼ **cup shredded reduced-fat cheddar cheese, divided**
- 2 **tablespoons fat-free sour cream**
- ¼ **cup chopped tomato**

1. Place potatoes in a small saucepan and cover with water. Bring to a boil. Reduce heat; cover and cook for 5-7 minutes or until tender. Drain.
2. In a small skillet, saute the mushrooms, peppers, onion and potatoes in oil until tender. Coat a nonstick skillet with cooking spray and place over medium heat. Add egg substitute. As eggs set, push cooked edges toward the center, letting uncooked portion flow underneath. When the eggs are set, spoon vegetable mixture over the top; sprinkle with 2 tablespoons cheese.
3. Transfer to a serving plate. Top with sour cream, tomato and the remaining cheese.

PER SERVING *202 cal., 10 g fat (3 g sat. fat), 13 mg chol., 276 mg sodium, 15 g carb., 2 g fiber, 14 g pro.* **Diabetic Exchanges:** *2 lean meat, 1 starch, 1 fat.*

VEGETABLE OMELET

218

224

227

Cakes & Pies

66 My family adores sweets, and I like to serve treats like this that are good for them, too. It's spiced just right and has a creamy marshmallow topping spiked with orange juice and vanilla.99

—**LAYLA PAYTON** MIDWEST CITY, OK
about her recipe, Zucchini Carrot Spice Cake, on page 228

CAPPUCCINO CUPCAKES

Cappuccino Cupcakes M

Using reduced-fat whipped topping to frost these chocolatey cupcakes keeps them on the lighter side. If you prefer, you can substitute unsweetened applesauce for the prune puree.

—CAROL FORCUM MARION, IL

PREP: 15 MIN. • **BAKE:** 20 MIN. + COOLING
MAKES: 17 CUPCAKES

    2   cups all-purpose flour
    1½ cups sugar
    ½   cup baking cocoa
    1   teaspoon baking soda
    ½   teaspoon salt
    ¼   cup instant coffee granules
    ½   cup hot water
    2   eggs
    ½   cup prune baby food
    ¼   cup canola oil
    2   teaspoons vanilla extract
    1½ cups reduced-fat whipped topping
        Additional baking cocoa

1. In a bowl, combine the flour, sugar, cocoa, baking soda and salt. Dissolve coffee granules in hot water. In a large bowl, whisk the eggs, baby food, oil, vanilla and coffee mixture. Gradually stir into the dry ingredients just until moistened.

2. Fill paper-lined muffin cups two-thirds full with batter. Bake at 350° for 18-20 minutes or until a toothpick comes out clean. Cool for 10 minutes before removing from pans to wire racks to cool completely.

3. Just before serving, frost cooled cupcakes with whipped topping and sprinkle with cocoa.

PER SERVING 190 cal., 5 g fat (1 g sat. fat), 25 mg chol., 152 mg sodium, 34 g carb., 1 g fiber, 3 g pro. **Diabetic Exchanges:** 2 starch, 1 fat.

Pear Bundt Cake M

Next time you make cake from a mix, you should try my easy and delicious recipe. The chopped pears and syrup add sweet flavor and prevent the cake from drying out. And since there's no oil added to the batter, this tender fall-perfect cake is surprisingly low in fat.

—VERONICA ROSS COLUMBIA HEIGHTS, MN

PREP: 15 MIN. • **BAKE:** 50 MIN. + COOLING
MAKES: 16 SERVINGS

    1   can (15 ounces) reduced-sugar
        sliced pears
    1   package white cake mix
        (regular size)
    2   egg whites
    1   egg
    2   teaspoons confectioners' sugar

1. Drain pears, reserving the syrup; chop pears. Place pears and syrup in a large bowl; add the cake mix, egg whites and egg. Beat on low speed for 30 seconds. Beat on high for 4 minutes.

2. Coat a 10-in. fluted tube pan with cooking spray and dust with flour. Add batter.

3. Bake at 350° for 50-55 minutes or until a toothpick inserted near the center comes out clean. Cool for 10 minutes before removing from pan to a wire rack to cool completely. Dust with confectioners' sugar.

PER SERVING 163 cal., 4 g fat (1 g sat. fat), 13 mg chol., 230 mg sodium, 30 g carb., 1 g fiber, 2 g pro. **Diabetic Exchanges:** 2 starch, 1 fat.

PEAR BUNDT CAKE

MARSHMALLOW PUMPKIN PIE

Chunky Apple Snack Cake M

PREP: 30 MIN. • **BAKE:** 25 MIN. + COOLING
MAKES: 20 SERVINGS

- 2 eggs
- ½ cup packed brown sugar
- 6 tablespoons butter, melted
- ¼ cup sugar
- 2 teaspoons vanilla extract
- 2 cups all-purpose flour
- 2 teaspoons ground cinnamon
- 1 teaspoon baking powder
- 1 teaspoon baking soda
- ¼ teaspoon salt
- 4 medium Gala or Fuji apples, shredded (about 4 cups)
- ¾ cup chopped pecans

1. Preheat oven to 350°. Coat a 13x9-in. baking pan with cooking spray. In a large bowl, beat eggs, brown sugar, melted butter, sugar and vanilla until well blended. In another bowl, whisk flour, cinnamon, baking powder, baking soda and salt; gradually beat into the egg mixture. Stir in the apples and pecans.

2. Transfer to prepared pan. Bake 25-30 minutes or until a toothpick inserted in center comes out clean. Cool in pan on a wire rack.

PER SERVING *160 cal., 7 g fat (3 g sat. fat), 30 mg chol., 146 mg sodium, 22 g carb., 2 g fiber, 2 g pro.* **Diabetic Exchanges:** *1½ starch, 1 fat.*

Marshmallow Pumpkin Pie

This fluffy pie was one of my mother's favorites. It also tastes great in baked pastry crust or gingersnap crust. Mom was a wonderful cook and always generous about sharing her recipes.

—**RUTH FERRIS** BILLINGS, MT

PREP: 20 MIN. + CHILLING
MAKES: 8 SERVINGS

- 1 package (10 ounces) large marshmallows
- 1 cup canned pumpkin
- 1 teaspoon ground cinnamon
- ½ teaspoon salt
- ½ teaspoon ground ginger
- ½ teaspoon ground nutmeg
- 2 cups whipped topping
- 1 graham cracker crust (9 inches)
  Additional whipped topping, optional

1. In a large saucepan, combine the first six ingredients; cook and stir over medium heat 8-10 minutes or until marshmallows are melted. Remove from heat; cool to room temperature.

2. Fold in whipped topping. Spoon into crust. Refrigerate 3 hours or until set. If desired, serve with additional whipped topping.

PER SERVING *280 cal., 9 g fat (4 g sat. fat), 0 chol., 287 mg sodium, 49 g carb., 2 g fiber, 2 g pro.*

We enjoy this cake as a snack, packed in lunches or as a scrumptious dessert when warmed and topped with a scoop of low-fat ice cream. The best part about the recipe is that I always have the ingredients on hand! —**CINDY BEBERMAN** ORLAND PARK, IL

CHUNKY APPLE SNACK CAKE

LIGHT CHEESECAKE

Arctic Orange Pie M

This dessert is very easy to make. I have tried lemonade, mango and pineapple juice concentrates instead of orange, and my family loves each one.

—**MARIE PRZEPIERSKI** ERIE, PA

PREP: 20 MIN. + FREEZING
MAKES: 8 SERVINGS

- 1 **package (8 ounces) fat-free cream cheese**
- 1 **can (6 ounces) frozen orange juice concentrate, thawed**
- 1 **carton (8 ounces) frozen reduced-fat whipped topping, thawed**
- 1 **reduced-fat graham cracker crust (8 inches)**
- 1 **can (11 ounces) mandarin oranges, drained**

In a large bowl, beat cream cheese and orange juice concentrate until smooth. Fold in whipped topping; pour into crust. Cover and freeze for 4 hours or until firm. Remove from the freezer about 10 minutes before cutting. Garnish with oranges.
PER SERVING *241 cal., 7 g fat (4 g sat. fat), 2 mg chol., 251 mg sodium, 36 g carb., 1 g fiber, 6 g pro.* **Diabetic Exchanges:** *1½ fat, 1 starch, 1 fruit.*

Light Cheesecake M

Our family loves cheesecake, but I wanted to serve something healthier. I came up with this lighter version that I make for both holidays and everyday.

—**DIANE ROTH** ADAMS, WI

PREP: 25 MIN.
BAKE: 1 HOUR + CHILLING
MAKES: 12 SERVINGS

- 1¼ **cups crushed reduced-fat vanilla wafers (about 40 wafers)**
- 2 **tablespoons butter, melted**
- 1 **teaspoon plus 1¼ cups sugar, divided**
- 2 **packages (8 ounces each) reduced-fat cream cheese**
- 1 **package (8 ounces) fat-free cream cheese**
- 1 **cup (8 ounces) reduced-fat sour cream**
- 2 **tablespoons cornstarch**
- 1 **teaspoon vanilla extract**
- 2 **eggs, lightly beaten**
- 2 **egg whites, lightly beaten**
- 1 **cup sliced fresh strawberries**

1. Preheat oven to 350°. In a small bowl, combine wafer crumbs, butter and 1 teaspoon sugar. Press onto the bottom and ½ in. up sides of a greased 9-in. springform pan. Bake 8 minutes. Cool on a wire rack. Reduce oven setting to 325°.

2. In a large bowl, beat cream cheeses and remaining sugar until smooth. Beat in sour cream, cornstarch and vanilla. Add eggs and egg whites; beat on low speed just until blended. Pour into crust. Place pan on a baking sheet.

3. Bake 60-65 minutes or until center is almost set. Cool on a wire rack for 10 minutes. Loosen sides from pan with a knife. Cool 1 hour longer. Refrigerate overnight, covering cheesecake when completely cooled.

4. Remove rim from pan. Top cheesecake with strawberries.
PER SERVING *311 cal., 13 g fat (7 g sat. fat), 74 mg chol., 310 mg sodium, 39 g carb., trace fiber, 10 g pro.*

ARCTIC ORANGE PIE

Mocha-Hazelnut Glazed Angel Food Cake S M

Coffee, hazelnuts and cherries are three of my favorite flavors, and this cake has them all! The glaze alone is reason enough to try the recipe.

—**JOAN PECSEK** CHESAPEAKE, VA

PREP: 25 MIN. • **BAKE:** 30 MIN. + COOLING
MAKES: 16 SERVINGS

- 12 egg whites
- 1 cup cake flour
- ¼ teaspoon instant coffee granules
- 1 teaspoon cream of tartar
- 1 teaspoon almond extract
- ½ teaspoon salt
- 1¼ cups sugar

GLAZE

- 1 cup Nutella
- ½ cup confectioners' sugar
- ⅓ cup brewed coffee
- ¼ cup chopped hazelnuts
- 16 maraschino cherries with stems

1. Place egg whites in a large bowl; let stand at room temperature for 30 minutes.
2. Meanwhile, preheat oven to 350°. In a small bowl, mix flour and coffee granules until blended.
3. Add the cream of tartar, extract and salt to egg whites; beat on medium speed until soft peaks form. Gradually add sugar, 1 tablespoon at a time, beating on high after each addition until sugar is dissolved. Continue beating until soft glossy peaks form. Gradually fold in flour mixture, about ½ cup at a time.
4. Gently transfer to an ungreased 10-in. tube pan. Cut through batter with a knife to remove air pockets. Bake on the lowest oven rack 30-40 minutes or until top springs back when lightly touched. Immediately invert pan; cool cake in the pan, about 1½ hours.
5. Run a knife around sides and center tube of pan. Remove cake to a serving plate. In a small bowl, whisk Nutella, confectioners' sugar and coffee until smooth. Drizzle over cake; sprinkle with hazelnuts. Serve with cherries.
PER SERVING *234 cal., 7 g fat (1 g sat. fat), trace chol., 123 mg sodium, 41 g carb., 1 g fiber, 5 g pro.*

ALMOND PEAR TART

Almond Pear Tart S M

I had never seen a "pie without a pan" until my daughter brought back this wonderful recipe from a Rotary Club exchange program in Belgium. It's still a family favorite after all these years.

—**C. B. LAMAY** CAPITAN, NM

PREP: 15 MIN. • **BAKE:** 20 MIN. + COOLING
MAKES: 8 SERVINGS

- Pastry for single-crust pie (9 inches)
- ¾ cup plus 2 teaspoons sugar, divided
- 3 tablespoons all-purpose flour
- 4 cups sliced peeled fresh pears (about 4 medium)
- 3 tablespoons sliced almonds

1. On a lightly floured surface, roll dough into a 10-in. circle. Transfer to a parchment paper-lined baking sheet.
2. In a large bowl, combine ¾ cup sugar and flour; add pears and toss to coat. Spoon over the pastry to within 2 in. of edges. Fold up edges of pastry over filling, leaving center uncovered. Sprinkle with remaining sugar.
3. Bake at 450° for 15 minutes or until crust is golden and filling is bubbly. Sprinkle with almonds and bake 5 minutes longer. Using parchment, slide the tart onto a wire rack to cool.
Pastry for single-crust pie (9 inches): *Combine 1-¼ cups all-purpose flour and ¼ tsp. salt; cut in ½ cup cold butter until crumbly. Gradually add 3-5 Tbsp. ice water, tossing with a fork until dough holds together when pressed. Wrap in plastic wrap and refrigerate 1 hour.*
PER SERVING *269 cal., 8 g fat (3 g sat. fat), 5 mg chol., 100 mg sodium, 48 g carb., 2 g fiber, 2 g pro.*

? Did you know?

An informal free-form tart may be called a rustic tart or a galette, its French name. Sometimes, crushed cookies, graham cracker crumbs or bread crumbs are sprinkled over the pie pastry to absorb juices from the filling and keep the crust crisp.

Banana-Pecan Sheet Cake Ⓜ

A dear friend of mine gave me this recipe and I make it often, especially for potlucks. Sometimes I make it ahead and freeze the cake, then frost it before the party.
—**MERRILL POWERS** SPEARVILLE, KS

PREP: 35 MIN. • **BAKE:** 20 MIN. + COOLING
MAKES: 24 SERVINGS

- ½ cup butter, softened
- 1⅔ cups sugar
- 2 eggs
- 1½ cups mashed ripe bananas
- 2½ cups all-purpose flour
- 3 teaspoons baking powder
- 1 teaspoon salt
- ¼ teaspoon baking soda
- ⅔ cup buttermilk
- ½ cup chopped pecans

FROSTING
- ⅓ cup butter, softened
- 3 cups confectioners' sugar
- 1½ teaspoons vanilla extract
- 3 to 4 tablespoons fat-free milk
- ⅓ cup finely chopped pecans, toasted

1. Preheat oven to 350°. Coat a 15x10x1-in. baking pan with cooking spray.

2. In a large bowl, beat butter and sugar until blended. Add eggs, one at a time, beating well after each addition. Add bananas, mixing well (mixture will appear curdled).

3. In another bowl, whisk flour, baking powder, salt and baking soda; add to butter mixture alternately with buttermilk, beating well after each addition. Fold in pecans.

4. Transfer to prepared pan. Bake 20-25 minutes or until a toothpick inserted in center comes out clean. Cool completely in pan on a wire rack.

5. For frosting, in a large bowl, combine butter, confectioners' sugar and vanilla. Add enough milk to achieve desired consistency. Frost cake. Sprinkle with toasted pecans.

PER SERVING *267 cal., 10 g fat (4 g sat. fat), 35 mg chol., 240 mg sodium, 43 g carb., 1 g fiber, 3 g pro.*

Almond Fudge Cake Ⓕ Ⓜ

When it comes to decadent desserts, raspberries and chocolate make a winning combination. People are amazed that this cake has fewer than 250 calories per slice.
—**MIKE PICKEREL** COLUMBIA, MO

PREP: 20 MIN. • **BAKE:** 55 MIN. + COOLING
MAKES: 12 SERVINGS

- 4 egg whites
- 1 cup fat-free milk
- ¾ cup water
- ½ cup unsweetened applesauce
- 1 teaspoon almond extract
- 1¾ cups all-purpose flour
- 1½ cups sugar
- ¾ cup baking cocoa
- 1½ teaspoons baking powder
- 1½ teaspoons baking soda
- ½ teaspoon salt

ALMOND FUDGE CAKE

- ¼ cup miniature semisweet chocolate chips

RASPBERRY SAUCE
- 2 cups fresh or frozen raspberries, thawed
- 1 tablespoon sugar
- 1 teaspoon lemon juice
- ¾ cup reduced-fat whipped topping
- 12 fresh raspberries

1. In a large bowl, beat the egg whites, milk, water, applesauce and extract until well blended. In a small bowl, combine the flour, sugar, cocoa, baking powder, baking soda and salt; gradually beat into egg white mixture until blended (batter will be thin). Pour into a 9-in. springform pan coated with cooking spray. Sprinkle with chips. Place pan on a baking sheet.

2. Bake at 325° for 55-60 minutes or until a toothpick inserted near the center comes out clean. Cool cake for 30 minutes. Carefully run a knife around edge of pan to loosen; remove sides of pan. Cool completely.

3. For sauce, puree the raspberries in a blender; strain to remove seeds. Stir in sugar and lemon juice. Spoon sauce onto dessert plates; top with cake wedges. Garnish each serving with 1 tablespoon whipped topping and a raspberry.

PER SERVING *241 cal., 2 g fat (1 g sat. fat), 0 chol., 314 mg sodium, 51 g carb., 4 g fiber, 5 g pro.*

BANANA-PECAN SHEET CAKE

Moist Lemon Chiffon Cake F M

I think this cake is a real treat decorated with its attractive drizzle of sweet-tart lemon glaze. For brunch, a coffee break or dessert, this cake is great for guests.

—REBECCA BAIRD SALT LAKE CITY, UT

PREP: 15 MIN. • **BAKE:** 45 MIN. + COOLING
MAKES: 16 SERVINGS

- ½ cup fat-free evaporated milk
- ½ cup reduced-fat sour cream
- ¼ cup lemon juice
- 2 tablespoons canola oil
- 2 teaspoons vanilla extract
- 1 teaspoon grated lemon peel
- 1 teaspoon lemon extract
- 2 cups cake flour
- 1½ cups sugar
- 1 tablespoon baking powder
- ½ teaspoon salt
- 1 cup egg whites (about 7)
- ½ teaspoon cream of tartar

LEMON GLAZE

- 1¾ cups confectioners' sugar
- 3 tablespoons lemon juice

1. In a large bowl, combine the first seven ingredients. Sift together the flour, sugar, baking powder and salt; gradually beat into lemon mixture until smooth. In a small bowl, beat egg whites until foamy. Add cream of tartar; beat until stiff peaks form. Gently fold into the lemon mixture.

2. Pour into an ungreased 10-in. tube pan. Bake at 325° for 45-55 minutes or until the cake springs back when lightly touched. Immediately invert pan; cool completely.

3. Remove cake to a serving platter. Combine glaze ingredients; drizzle over cake.

PER SERVING *230 cal., 3 g fat (1 g sat. fat), 3 mg chol., 189 mg sodium, 47 g carb., trace fiber, 4 g pro.*

MOIST LEMON CIFFON CAKE

Strawberry Cream Cheese Pie S M

Cheesecake lovers will savor every bite of this creamy strawberry pie, even if they don't have to watch their diet. Everyone in my family is a fan.

—KIM MARIE VAN RHEENEN MENDOTA, IL

PREP: 20 MIN. + CHILLING • **BAKE:** 30 MIN. + COOLING
MAKES: 8 SERVINGS

    Pastry for a single-crust pie (9 inches)
1   package (8 ounces) reduced-fat cream cheese
½   cup egg substitute
3   tablespoons honey
1   teaspoon vanilla extract
3½ cups sliced fresh strawberries
1   tablespoon cornstarch
½   cup cold water
½   cup reduced-sugar strawberry preserves
    Fat-free whipped topping, optional

1. Roll out pastry to fit a 9-in. pie plate; transfer pastry to plate. Trim pastry to ½ in. beyond edge of plate; flute edges. Bake at 350° for 13-15 minutes or until lightly browned.
2. Meanwhile, in a large bowl, beat the cream cheese, egg substitute, honey and vanilla until smooth. Pour into crust. Bake 15-18 minutes longer or until center is almost set. Cool completely on a wire rack.
3. Arrange strawberries over filling. In a saucepan, combine cornstarch and water until smooth. Stir in preserves. Bring to a boil; cook and stir for 2 minutes or until thickened. Spoon or brush over the strawberries. Refrigerate for 2 hours before cutting. Garnish with whipped topping if desired.
PER SERVING *268 cal., 12 g fat (6 g sat. fat), 21 mg chol., 119 mg sodium, 34 g carb., 2 g fiber, 5 g pro.*

STRAWBERRY CREAM CHEESE PIE

CRANBERRY-PUMPKIN SPICE CAKE

Cranberry-Pumpkin Spice Cake M

Even though this is a light dessert, my kids love it! Since it's so popular, I stock up on canned pumpkin in the fall when it's on sale so I can make it all year long.

—CAMI LAFORGE MURRAY, UT

PREP: 20 MIN. • **BAKE:** 20 MIN. + COOLING • **MAKES:** 9 SERVINGS

1   egg
1   egg white
½   cup canned pumpkin
2   tablespoons butter, melted
1   tablespoon canola oil
1   teaspoon vanilla extract
1   cup all-purpose flour
¾   cup packed brown sugar
1   teaspoon baking powder
½   teaspoon ground cinnamon
¼   teaspoon baking soda
¼   teaspoon salt
⅓   cup dried cranberries
¼   cup chopped walnuts
2   teaspoons grated orange peel
1   teaspoon confectioners' sugar

1. Preheat oven to 350°. Coat a 9-in.-square baking pan with cooking spray.
2. In a large bowl, beat egg and egg white until foamy. Add pumpkin, melted butter, oil and vanilla; beat until well blended. In another bowl, whisk flour, brown sugar, baking powder, cinnamon, baking soda and salt; stir into egg mixture. Stir in cranberries, walnuts and orange peel. Transfer to prepared pan.
3. Bake 20-25 minutes or until a toothpick inserted in center comes out clean. Cool completely in pan on a wire rack. Sprinkle with confectioners' sugar before serving.
PER SERVING *208 cal., 7 g fat (2 g sat. fat), 30 mg chol., 192 mg sodium, 34 g carb., 1 g fiber, 4 g pro.* **Diabetic Exchanges:** *2 starch, 1½ fat.*

Orange Buttermilk Cupcakes M

Simple and delicious, this is our all-time favorite low-fat dessert. You'll be surprised how well the citrus flavor comes through in every bite.

—KIM CHESTER CARTERSVILLE, GA

PREP: 20 MIN. • **BAKE:** 20 MIN. + COOLING
MAKES: 9 SERVINGS

- 3 tablespoons butter, softened
- ⅓ cup packed brown sugar
- ¼ cup sugar blend
- 1 teaspoon grated orange peel
- 1 egg
- 1 egg white
- 2 tablespoons plus 2½ teaspoons orange juice, divided
- 1¼ cups cake flour
- ¾ teaspoon baking powder
- ¼ teaspoon baking soda
- ¼ teaspoon salt
- ¼ teaspoon ground ginger
- ⅔ cup buttermilk
- ½ cup confectioners' sugar

1. In a large bowl, beat the butter, brown sugar, sugar blend and orange peel. Beat in the egg, egg white and 2 tablespoons orange juice. Combine the flour, baking powder, baking soda, salt and ginger; gradually add to the butter mixture alternately with the buttermilk, beating well after each addition.

2. Coat muffin cups with cooking spray or use paper liners; fill three-fourths full with batter. Bake at 350° for 18-20 minutes or until a toothpick inserted near the center comes out clean. Cool for 5 minutes before removing from pan to a wire rack to cool completely.

3. In a small bowl, combine confectioners' sugar and remaining orange juice. Frost cupcakes.

NOTE *This recipe was tested with Splenda sugar blend.*

PER SERVING *201 cal., 5 g fat (3 g sat. fat), 35 mg chol., 208 mg sodium, 37 g carb., trace fiber, 3 g pro.*

Angel Food Cake with Berry Sauce F S M

Top this airy angel food cake with the accompanying berry sauce, and you'll have a heavenly dessert. It's the perfect light finale to a big meal.

—TASTE OF HOME TEST KITCHEN

PREP: 30 MIN. • **BAKE:** 50 MIN. + COOLING
MAKES: 16 SERVINGS (6 CUPS SAUCE)

- 12 egg whites
- 1 cup confectioners' sugar
- 1 cup cake flour
- 1 teaspoon cream of tartar
- 1 teaspoon vanilla extract
- ¼ teaspoon salt
- 1¼ cups sugar
- ⅓ cup blueberry vodka
- 1 tablespoon cornstarch
- 1 tablespoon cold water

SAUCE
- 2½ cups fresh raspberries, divided
- 2 cups fresh blueberries, divided
- ⅓ cup unsweetened pineapple juice
- 3 tablespoons raspberry liqueur
- 2 cups halved fresh strawberries
- 1 cup fresh blackberries

1. Place egg whites in a large bowl; let stand at room temperature for 30 minutes. Sift confectioners' sugar and flour together twice; set aside.

2. Add the cream of tartar, vanilla and salt to egg whites; beat on medium speed until soft peaks form. Gradually add sugar, about 2 tablespoons at a time, beating on high until stiff glossy peaks form and sugar is dissolved. Gradually fold in flour mixture, about ½ cup at a time.

3. Gently spoon into an ungreased 10-in. tube pan. Cut through the batter with a knife to remove air pockets. Bake on the lowest oven rack at 325° for 50-60 minutes or until lightly browned and entire top appears dry. Immediately invert pan; cool cake completely, about 1 hour.

4. Run a knife around side and center tube of pan. Remove cake to a serving plate. Brush top and sides of cake with vodka. Combine cornstarch and water; set aside.

5. For sauce, in a small saucepan, combine 1½ cups raspberries, 1 cup blueberries, pineapple juice and liqueur. Bring to a boil. Stir cornstarch mixture and add to the pan. Bring to a boil; cook and stir for 2 minutes or until thickened.

6. Remove from the heat; stir in the strawberries, blackberries and remaining raspberries and blueberries. Serve sauce with cake.

PER SERVING *189 cal., trace fat (trace sat. fat), 0 chol., 79 mg sodium, 39 g carb., 3 g fiber, 4 g pro.*

ANGEL FOOD CAKE WITH BERRY SAUCE

CHOCOLATE PEPPERMINT LOG

Chocolate Peppermint Log M

What a great make-ahead dessert! It's perfect for the holidays because you can make it when you have time, store it in the freezer and scratch dessert off of your to-do list.

—**BRENDA K. SINCLAIR** PRINCETON, MO

PREP: 35 MIN. + CHILLING
BAKE: 15 MIN. + COOLING
MAKES: 12 SERVINGS

- 3 eggs, separated
- ½ cup all-purpose flour
- ⅓ cup baking cocoa
- ½ teaspoon baking powder
- ¼ teaspoon baking soda
- ⅛ teaspoon salt
- ⅓ cup plus ½ cup sugar, divided
- ⅓ cup water
- 1 teaspoon vanilla extract

FILLING
- 1 package (8 ounces) reduced-fat cream cheese
- ½ cup sugar
- 1 carton (8 ounces) frozen reduced-fat whipped topping, thawed
- ¼ cup crushed peppermint candies

GLAZE
- 5 teaspoons butter
- 2 tablespoons baking cocoa
- 2 tablespoons water
- 1 cup confectioners' sugar
- ½ teaspoon vanilla extract
- 2 tablespoons crushed peppermint candies

1. Place egg whites in a small bowl; let stand at room temperature 30 minutes.

2. Meanwhile, preheat oven to 375°. Line bottom of a 15x10x1-in. baking pan with parchment paper. Sift flour, cocoa, baking powder, baking soda and salt twice.

3. In a large bowl, beat egg yolks until slightly thickened. Gradually add ⅓ cup sugar, beating on high speed until thick and lemon-colored. Beat in water and vanilla. Fold in flour mixture (batter will be very thick).

4. With clean beaters, beat egg whites on medium until soft peaks form. Gradually add remaining sugar, 1 tablespoon at a time, beating on high after each addition until sugar is dissolved. Continue beating until soft glossy peaks form. Fold a fourth of the whites into batter, then fold in remaining whites. Transfer to prepared pan, spreading evenly.

5. Bake 12-15 minutes or until top springs back when lightly touched. Cool 5 minutes. Invert onto a kitchen towel dusted with cocoa. Gently peel off paper. Roll up cake in the towel jelly-roll style, starting with a short side. Cool completely on a wire rack.

6. For filling, in a large bowl, beat cream cheese and sugar until smooth. Fold in whipped topping and peppermint candies.

7. Unroll cake; spread filling over cake to within ½ in. of edges. Roll up again, without towel. Place on a platter, seam side down. Refrigerate until cold.

8. For glaze, in a small saucepan, melt butter. Whisk in cocoa and water until blended. Bring to a boil. Remove from heat. Whisk in confectioners' sugar and vanilla until smooth. Cool slightly.

9. Spread glaze over cake. Sprinkle with peppermint candies. Refrigerate until set, about 10 minutes.

FREEZE OPTION *Securely wrap and freeze cake before glazing. To use, thaw wrapped cake in refrigerator overnight. Unwrap cake and glaze as directed.*

PER SERVING *286 cal., 9 g fat (6 g sat. fat), 70 mg chol., 178 mg sodium, 48 g carb., 1 g fiber, 5 g pro.*

Fudge Sundae Pie M

My son always asks for this frozen yogurt pie for his birthday. Complete with peanut butter, fudge topping and nuts, it tastes like an ice cream sundae.

—**MARGARET RILEY** TALLAHASSEE, FL

PREP: 20 MIN. + FREEZING
MAKES: 8 SERVINGS

- ¼ cup plus 3 tablespoons light corn syrup, divided
- 3 tablespoons reduced-fat butter
- 2 tablespoons brown sugar
- 2½ cups crisp rice cereal
- ¼ cup reduced-fat creamy peanut butter
- ¼ cup fat-free hot fudge ice cream topping, warmed
- ¼ cup chopped unsalted peanuts
- 4 cups fat-free vanilla frozen yogurt, softened

1. In a large saucepan, combine ¼ cup corn syrup, butter and brown sugar. Bring to a boil; cook and stir for 1 minute.

2. Remove from the heat; stir in cereal until blended. Press into a greased 9-in. pie plate.

3. In a small bowl, combine the peanut butter, hot fudge topping and remaining corn syrup. Set aside ⅓ cup for topping. Spread remaining mixture over crust; sprinkle with half of the peanuts. Top with frozen yogurt and remaining peanuts. Cover and freeze for 6 hours or until firm.

4. Warm reserved peanut butter mixture; drizzle over pie. Let stand at room temperature for 5 minutes before cutting.

NOTE *This recipe was tested with Land O'Lakes light stick butter.*
PER SERVING *300 cal., 7 g fat (2 g sat. fat), 7 mg chol., 253 mg sodium, 53 g carb., 1 g fiber, 9 g pro.*

FUDGE SUNDAE PIE

ZUCCHINI CARROT SPICE CAKE

Orange-Coconut Angel Food Cake M

Everyone who tries this luscious cake loves it, even those who aren't watching their weight. I have several cake recipes, but this is my favorite to make—and eat!
—**BETTY KINSER** ELIZABETHTON, TN

PREP: 25 MIN. • **BAKE:** 30 MIN. + COOLING
MAKES: 14 SERVINGS

- 1 **package (16 ounces) angel food cake mix**
- 1 **cup cold water**
- ⅓ **cup orange juice**
- 2 **teaspoons orange extract, divided**
- 1¾ **cups cold fat-free milk**
- 1 **package (1 ounce) sugar-free instant vanilla pudding mix**
- 1 **tablespoon grated orange peel**
- 1¼ **cups flaked coconut, divided**
- 1 **carton (8 ounces) frozen reduced-fat whipped topping, thawed, divided**

1. In a large bowl, combine the cake mix, water, orange juice and 1 teaspoon extract. Beat on low speed for 30 seconds. Beat on medium for 2 minutes. Spoon into an ungreased 10-in. tube pan.
2. Bake at 375° for 30-35 minutes or until lightly browned and entire top appears dry. Immediately invert pan onto a wire rack; cool completely, about 1 hour. Run a knife around sides of cake and remove from pan.
3. In a small bowl, whisk milk and pudding mix for 2 minutes. Stir in orange peel and remaining extract. Let stand for 2 minutes or until soft-set. Fold in ¾ cup coconut and ¾ cup whipped topping.
4. Split cake into three horizontal layers. Place bottom layer on a serving plate; top with half of the pudding mixture. Repeat layers. Top with remaining cake layer. Frost top and sides of cake with remaining whipped topping. Toast remaining coconut; sprinkle over top and sides of cake. Store in the refrigerator.
PER SERVING *222 cal., 5 g fat (4 g sat. fat), 1 mg chol., 361 mg sodium, 39 g carb., 1 g fiber, 4 g pro.*

Zucchini Carrot Spice Cake M

My family adores sweets, and I like to serve treats like this that are good for them, too. It's spiced just right and has a creamy marshmallow topping spiked with orange juice and vanilla.
—**LAYLA PAYTON** MIDWEST CITY, OK

PREP: 20 MIN. • **BAKE:** 30 MIN.
MAKES: 12 SERVINGS

- 1 **cup whole wheat flour**
- 1 **cup all-purpose flour**
- 2½ **teaspoons ground cinnamon**
- 2 **teaspoons baking soda**
- ¾ **teaspoon ground nutmeg**
- ¼ **teaspoon ground cloves**
- ½ **cup buttermilk**
- 1 **cup unsweetened applesauce**
- 1½ **cups shredded carrots**
- ½ **cup shredded zucchini**
- 1 **teaspoon vanilla extract**
- 6 **egg whites**
- 1⅓ **cups sugar**

FROSTING
- 1 **carton (8 ounces) reduced-fat cream cheese**
- 1 **jar (7½ ounces) marshmallow creme**
- 1 **teaspoon orange juice**
- ½ **teaspoon vanilla extract**

1. In a large bowl, combine the first six ingredients. Gradually add the buttermilk, applesauce, carrots, zucchini and vanilla. In a small bowl, beat egg whites until soft peaks form; gradually beat in sugar, 1 tablespoon at a time, until stiff peaks form. Gently fold into batter.
2. Pour into a 13x9-in. baking dish coated with cooking spray. Bake at 350° for 30-40 minutes or until a toothpick inserted in center comes out clean. Cool on a wire rack.
3. For frosting, in a large bowl, beat the cream cheese, marshmallow creme, orange juice and vanilla just until combined. Frost cake.
PER SERVING *291 cal., 4 g fat (2 g sat. fat), 11 mg chol., 325 mg sodium, 59 g carb., 3 g fiber, 7 g pro.*

Mocha Frosted Snack Cake M

Here's a lighter version of a chocolate mocha cake I've been baking for my family for over 30 years. I replaced part of the sugar with a lower-calorie sugar blend and some of the oil with applesauce. It turned out just as delicious.

—**DONNA ROBERTS** MANHATTAN, KS

PREP: 20 MIN. • **BAKE:** 35 MIN. + COOLING
MAKES: 9 SERVINGS

- 1 teaspoon instant coffee granules
- 1 cup boiling water
- 1¼ cups all-purpose flour
- ½ cup packed brown sugar
- ¼ cup cornstarch
- ¼ cup sugar blend
- 3 tablespoons baking cocoa
- 1 teaspoon baking soda
- ½ teaspoon salt
- ¼ cup unsweetened applesauce
- 2 tablespoons canola oil
- 1 tablespoon white vinegar
- ½ teaspoon vanilla extract

FROSTING
- ½ teaspoon instant coffee granules
- 1 tablespoon fat-free milk
- 1½ cups confectioners' sugar
- 2 tablespoons baking cocoa
- 3 tablespoons reduced-fat butter, softened
- ½ teaspoon vanilla extract

1. Preheat oven to 350°. In a small bowl, dissolve coffee granules in boiling water; cool slightly. Coat an 8-in.-square baking dish with cooking spray; set aside.
2. In a large bowl, whisk flour, brown sugar, cornstarch, sugar blend, cocoa, baking soda and salt. Whisk applesauce, oil, vinegar and vanilla into coffee mixture. Add to flour mixture; stir just until moistened.
3. Transfer batter to the prepared baking dish. Bake 35-40 minutes or until a toothpick inserted in the center comes out clean. Cool completely on a wire rack.
4. For frosting, in a small bowl, dissolve coffee granules in milk. In a large bowl, mix confectioners' sugar and cocoa until blended; beat in butter, vanilla and enough coffee mixture to reach a spreading consistency. Spread over cake.

NOTE *This recipe was tested with Splenda Sugar Blend for Baking and Land O'Lakes light stick butter.*
PER SERVING *280 cal., 6 g fat (2 g sat. fat), 7 mg chol., 301 mg sodium, 56 g carb., 1 g fiber, 3 g pro.*

Cranberry Pear Tart S M

It looks and tastes like a homey apple pie, except we used pears instead of apples— and each serving has half the calories of an average slice.

—*TASTE OF HOME* TEST KITCHEN

PREP: 15 MIN. • **BAKE:** 30 MIN. + COOLING
MAKES: 8 SERVINGS

- 1 sheet refrigerated pie pastry
- 4 cups sliced peeled fresh pears (about 4 medium)
- ⅓ cup dried cranberries
- ⅓ cup thawed apple juice concentrate
- 1 teaspoon apple pie spice

1. Press pastry into an ungreased 9-in. tart pan with removable bottom; trim edges. Generously prick the bottom with a fork; set aside.
2. In a large skillet, cook the remaining ingredients over medium heat until pears are tender. Pour into crust. Bake at 375° for 30-35 minutes or until the crust is golden brown. Cool on a wire rack.
PER SERVING *203 cal., 7 g fat (3 g sat. fat), 5 mg chol., 104 mg sodium, 35 g carb., 3 g fiber, 1 g pro.* **Diabetic Exchanges:** *1½ starch, 1½ fat, ½ fruit.*

CRANBERRY PEAR TART

238

241

242

Treat Yourself

"Anytime I can take a recipe that has been handed down two generations and lighten it up while keeping the delicious flavor memories intact, I'm a happy girl."

—**PATTI LAVELL** ISLAMORADA, FL
about her recipe, Lemony Cream Cheese Bars, on page 243

MANGO RICE PUDDIING

Peach Melba Trifle F M

This dream of a dessert tastes extra good on a busy day because you can make it ahead of time. If you don't have fresh peaches handy, use the canned ones.

—**CHRISTINA MOORE** CASAR, NC

PREP: 20 MIN. + CHILLING
MAKES: 12 SERVINGS

- 2 packages (12 ounces each) frozen unsweetened raspberries, thawed
- 1 tablespoon cornstarch
- 1½ cups (12 ounces) fat-free peach yogurt
- ⅛ teaspoon almond extract
- 1 carton (8 ounces) frozen reduced-fat whipped topping, thawed
- 2 prepared angel food cakes (8 to 10 ounces each), cut into 1-inch cubes (about 8 cups)
- 4 small peaches, peeled and sliced (about 2 cups)

1. In a large saucepan, mix raspberries and cornstarch until blended. Bring to a boil; cook and stir 1-2 minutes or until thickened. Strain seeds; cover and refrigerate.

2. In a large bowl, mix yogurt and extract; fold in whipped topping. In a 4-qt. bowl, layer half of the cake cubes, yogurt mixture and peaches. Repeat layers. Refrigerate, covered, at least 3 hours before serving. Serve with raspberry sauce.

PER SERVING *201 cal., 3 g fat (2 g sat. fat), 1 mg chol., 298 mg sodium, 41 g carb., 3 g fiber, 4 g pro.*

Mango Rice Pudding F M

Mangoes are my son's favorite fruit, so I was ecstatic to incorporate them into a healthy dessert. You can also use ripe bananas instead of mango, almond extract instead of vanilla, or regular milk in place of soy.

—**MELISSA MCCABE** LONG BEACH, CA

PREP: 5 MIN. • **COOK:** 50 MIN.
MAKES: 4 SERVINGS

- 2 cups water
- ¼ teaspoon salt
- 1 cup uncooked long grain brown rice
- 1 medium ripe mango
- 1 cup vanilla soy milk
- 2 tablespoons sugar
- ½ teaspoon ground cinnamon
- 1 teaspoon vanilla extract
  Chopped peeled mango, optional

1. In a large heavy saucepan, bring water and salt to a boil; stir in rice. Reduce heat; simmer, covered, 35-40 minutes or until water is absorbed and rice is tender.

2. Meanwhile, peel, seed and slice mango. Mash mango with a potato masher or fork.

3. Stir milk, sugar, cinnamon and mashed mango into rice. Cook, uncovered, on low 10-15 minutes longer or until liquid is almost absorbed, stirring occasionally.

4. Remove from heat; stir in vanilla. Serve warm or cold with chopped mango if desired.

PER SERVING *275 cal., 3 g fat (trace sat. fat), 0 chol., 176 mg sodium, 58 g carb., 3 g fiber, 6 g pro.*

PEACH MELBA TRIFLE

Lemon Meringue Pie Cookies F S C M

Here's a sweet way to have the refreshing flavor of lemon meringue pie in a cute handheld treat. Homemade lemon curd filling makes these crisp meringue cookies extra-special.

—*TASTE OF HOME* TEST KITCHEN

PREP: 25 MIN. + CHILLING
BAKE: 25 MIN. + STANDING
MAKES: 5 DOZEN

- 3 **egg whites**
- ½ **teaspoon vanilla extract**
- ¼ **teaspoon cream of tartar**
- ¾ **cup sugar**

LEMON CURD
- 4 **eggs**
- 1⅓ **cups sugar**
- ⅓ **cup lemon juice**
- 4 **teaspoons grated lemon peel**
- 3 **tablespoons butter**

1. Place egg whites in a large bowl; let stand at room temperature for 30 minutes. Add vanilla and cream of tartar; beat on medium speed until soft peaks form. Gradually beat in sugar, 1 tablespoon at a time, on high until stiff peaks form.

2. Cut a small hole in the corner of a pastry or plastic bag; insert a #24 star tip. Fill bag with meringue. Pipe 1-in. circles 2 in. apart onto parchment paper-lined baking sheets. Pipe one or two circles over the edge of the base, forming sides.

3. Bake at 300° for 25 minutes or until set and dry. Turn oven off; leave meringues in oven for 1 hour.

4. Meanwhile, in a small heavy saucepan over medium heat, whisk the eggs, sugar, lemon juice and peel until blended. Add butter; cook, whisking constantly, until mixture is thickened and coats the back of a metal spoon. Transfer to a small bowl; cool for 10 minutes. Cover and refrigerate until chilled.

5. Just before serving, spoon lemon curd into the center of cookies. Refrigerate leftovers.

PER SERVING *1 cookie equals 38 cal., 1 g fat (trace sat. fat), 16 mg chol., 11 mg sodium, 7 g carb., trace fiber, 1 g pro.*
***Diabetic Exchange:** ½ starch.*

Monkey Bars S M

To help manage my cravings, I record when I have them, where I am, how I feel, and the food I'm craving. These bars are a tasty and nutritious answer to even the most demanding craving.

—**TINA HAUPERT** WEYMOUTH, MA

PREP: 15 MIN. • **BAKE:** 25 MIN.
MAKES: 16 SERVINGS

- ½ **cup butter, softened**
- 1 **cup packed brown sugar**
- ½ **cup creamy peanut butter**
- 1 **egg**
- 1 **medium ripe banana, mashed**
- 1 **teaspoon vanilla extract**
- 1 **cup whole wheat flour**
- 1 **teaspoon baking powder**
- ⅛ **teaspoon salt**
  Confectioners' sugar, optional

1. Preheat oven to 350°. In a large bowl, beat butter, brown sugar and peanut butter until blended. Gradually beat in egg, banana and vanilla. In another bowl, whisk flour, baking powder and salt; gradually add to butter mixture, mixing well.

2. Spread into an 8-in.-square baking dish coated with cooking spray. Bake 25-30 minutes or until a toothpick inserted in center comes out clean. Cool on a wire rack. If desired, dust with confectioners' sugar.

PER SERVING *188 cal., 10 g fat (5 g sat. fat), 27 mg chol., 139 mg sodium, 22 g carb., 1 g fiber, 4 g pro.*

MONKEY BARS

Peanut Butter Cookies F S C M

When you bite into one of these yummy cookies, you'll never guess it's low in fat.

—MARIA REGAKIS SAUGUS, MA

PREP: 15 MIN. + FREEZING
BAKE: 10 MIN. + COOLING
MAKES: ABOUT 2 DOZEN

- 3 **tablespoons butter**
- 2 **tablespoons reduced-fat peanut butter**
- ½ **cup packed brown sugar**
- ¼ **cup sugar**
- 1 **egg white**
- 1 **teaspoon vanilla extract**
- 1 **cup all-purpose flour**
- ¼ **teaspoon baking soda**
- ⅛ **teaspoon salt**

1. In a large bowl, cream the butter, peanut butter and sugars until light and fluffy. Add egg white; beat until blended. Beat in vanilla. Combine the flour, baking soda and salt; gradually add to the creamed mixture and mix well. Shape into an 8-in. roll; wrap in plastic wrap. Freeze for 2 hours or until firm.

2. Unwrap and cut into slices, about ¼ in. thick. Place 2 in. apart on baking sheets coated with cooking spray. Flatten with a fork. Bake at 350° for 6-8 minutes for chewy cookies or 8-10 minutes for crisp cookies. Cool for 1-2 minutes before removing to wire racks; cool completely.

PER SERVING *1 cookie equals 62 cal., 2 g fat (1 g sat. fat), 4 mg chol., 64 mg sodium, 11 g carb., trace fiber, 1 g pro.* **Diabetic Exchanges:** *½ starch, ½ fat.*

Cranberry Pistachio Biscotti F S C M

Wonderful for dunking but just as delicious on its own, this crunchy Italian cookie features a classic holiday combo of cranberries and pistachios.

—RUTH KNOL ANNVILLE, PA

PREP: 40 MIN. • **BAKE:** 25 MIN. + COOLING
MAKES: 3½ DOZEN

- ½ **cup dried cranberries**
- ½ **cup boiling water**
- ½ **cup butter, softened**
- 1 **cup sugar**
- 3 **eggs**
- 2 **teaspoons vanilla extract**
- 3 **cups all-purpose flour**
- 2 **teaspoons baking powder**
- ½ **teaspoon salt**
- ½ **cup chopped pistachios**

TOPPING

- 1 **egg, beaten**
- 3 **tablespoons coarse sugar**

1. Place cranberries in a small bowl. Cover with boiling water; let stand for 5 minutes. Drain and set aside. In a large bowl, cream the butter and sugar until light and fluffy. Add eggs, one at a time, beating well after each addition. Stir in vanilla. Combine the flour, baking powder and salt; gradually add to creamed mixture and mix well. Stir in pistachios and cranberries with liquid.

2. Divide dough into three portions. On a parchment paper-lined baking sheet, shape each portion into a 12-in. x 1½-in. rectangle. Brush egg over rectangles and sprinkle with coarse sugar. Bake at 375° for 18-22 minutes or until set and lightly browned. Carefully remove to wire racks; cool for 15 minutes.

3. Transfer to a cutting board; cut diagonally with a serrated knife into ¾-in. slices. Place cut side down on ungreased baking sheets. Bake for 6-8 minutes on each side or until edges are browned. Remove to wire racks to cool completely. Store in an airtight container.

PER SERVING *1 cookie equals 93 cal., 3 g fat (2 g sat. fat), 23 mg chol., 74 mg sodium, 14 g carb., trace fiber, 2 g pro.* **Diabetic Exchanges:** *1 starch, ½ fat.*

PEANUT BUTTER COOKIES

Snow-Puffed Meringues F S C M

My family and friends like a nice pick-me-up dessert after a big holiday meal. These feather-light morsels fit the bill perfectly. To make 6 dozen, skip the Nutella and dust each cookie with cocoa instead.
—**LORRAINE CALAND** SHUNIAH, ON

PREP: 20 MIN. • **BAKE:** 45 MIN. + COOLING
MAKES: ABOUT 3 DOZEN

- 4 **egg whites**
- ½ **teaspoon vanilla extract**
- ¼ **teaspoon salt**
- ½ **cup sugar**
- 1 **cup confectioners' sugar**
- ⅓ **cup Nutella**

1. Place egg whites in a large bowl; let stand at room temperature 30 minutes.
2. Preheat oven to 225°. Add vanilla and salt to egg whites; beat on medium speed until foamy. Gradually add sugar, 1 tablespoon at a time, beating on high after each addition until sugar is dissolved. Continue beating until stiff glossy peaks form. Fold in confectioners' sugar.
3. Cut a small hole in the tip of a pastry bag or in a corner of a food-safe plastic bag; insert a #96 star tip. Transfer meringue to the bag. Pipe 1½-in.-diameter cookies 2 in. apart onto parchment paper-lined baking sheets.
4. Bake 45-50 minutes or until firm to the touch. Turn oven off (do not open oven door); leave meringues in oven for 1½ hours. Remove from oven; cool completely on baking sheets.
5. Remove meringues from paper. Spread Nutella on the bottoms of half the cookies; cover with remaining cookies. Store in airtight containers at room temperature.
PER SERVING *1 sandwich cookie equals 39 cal., 1 g fat (trace sat. fat), trace chol., 24 mg sodium, 8 g carb., trace fiber, 1 g pro.* **Diabetic Exchange:** *½ starch.*

FRESH PEAR GINGER CRISP

Fresh Pear Ginger Crisp M

Gingersnaps lend crunch to my heartwarming cool-weather classic, featuring the season's juiciest fruit—fresh pears.
—**LINDA ROBERTSON** COZAD, NE

PREP: 15 MIN. + CHILLING • **BAKE:** 35 MIN.
MAKES: 9 SERVINGS

- 1 **cup crushed gingersnap cookies (about 20 cookies)**
- ½ **cup old-fashioned oats**
- ½ **cup packed brown sugar**
- ¼ **teaspoon ground ginger**
- ¼ **teaspoon ground cloves**
- ⅛ **teaspoon salt**
- ⅓ **cup butter, softened**
- 7 **medium pears (about 2½ pounds), peeled and thinly sliced**
- 2 **tablespoons all-purpose flour**
  Vanilla ice cream, optional

1. In a small bowl, combine the first six ingredients. With clean hands, work butter into oat mixture until well combined. Refrigerate for 15 minutes.
2. Place pears in a small bowl; add flour and toss to coat. Transfer to a greased 8-in. square baking dish; sprinkle with oat mixture.
3. Bake, uncovered, at 350° for 35-40 minutes or until topping is golden brown and fruit is tender. Serve warm with ice cream if desired.
PER SERVING *268 cal., 9 g fat (5 g sat. fat), 18 mg chol., 189 mg sodium, 48 g carb., 5 g fiber, 2 g pro.*

? Did you know?

Most vanilla comes from Madagascar and Reunion Island—formerly known as the Bourbon Islands—off the southeast coast of Africa. Bourbon vanilla is celebrated for its strong, clear vanilla flavor and creamy finish.

Apple Oatmeal Cookies F S C M

I brought these yummy cookies to work and they were gone in seconds. They're a great snack that's low in calories!

—**NICKI WOODS** SPRINGFIELD, MO

PREP: 10 MIN. • **BAKE:** 15 MIN./BATCH • **MAKES:** ABOUT 5 DOZEN

- 1 **package yellow cake mix (regular size)**
- 1½ **cups quick-cooking oats**
- ½ **cup packed brown sugar**
- 2 **teaspoons ground cinnamon**
- 1 **egg**
- ¾ **cup unsweetened applesauce**
- 1 **cup finely chopped peeled apple**
- ½ **cup raisins**

1. In a large bowl, combine the cake mix, oats, brown sugar and cinnamon. In a small bowl, combine the egg, applesauce, apple and raisins. Stir into oats mixture and mix well.

2. Drop by heaping teaspoonfuls 2 in. apart onto baking sheets coated with cooking spray. Bake at 350° for 12-14 minutes or until golden brown. Let stand for 2 minutes before removing to wire racks to cool.

PER SERVING *1 cookie equals 57 cal., 1 g fat (trace sat. fat), 0 chol., 55 mg sodium, 12 g carb., 1 g fiber, 1 g pro.* **Diabetic Exchange:** *1 starch.*

Toffee Meringue Drops F S C M

The original recipe called for mini chocolate chips and crushed peppermint candy. I didn't have those ingredients, so I substituted toffee bits and pecans. And I never looked back!

—**BETTE RICHARDS** CALEDONIA, ON

PREP: 25 MIN. • **BAKE:** 25 MIN. + STANDING • **MAKES:** 3 DOZEN

- 2 **egg whites**
- ⅛ **teaspoon cream of tartar**
- ½ **cup sugar**
- ½ **cup milk chocolate English toffee bits**
- ½ **cup finely chopped pecans**

1. Preheat oven to 250°. In a large bowl, beat egg whites and cream of tartar on medium speed until soft peaks form. Gradually add sugar, 1 tablespoon at a time, beating on high until stiff glossy peaks form and sugar is dissolved, about 6 minutes. Fold in toffee bits and pecans.

2. Drop by tablespoonfuls 2 in. apart onto parchment paper-lined baking sheets. Bake 25-30 minutes or until set and dry. Turn oven off; leave cookies in oven 1 hour.

3. Cool completely on pans on wire racks. Store in an airtight container.

PER SERVING *1 cookie equals 39 cal., 2 g fat (1 g sat. fat), 2 mg chol., 16 mg sodium, 5 g carb., trace fiber, trace pro.* **Diabetic Exchange:** *½ starch.*

Fresh Fruit Parfaits F S M

I fix this simple recipe when I want to prepare something impressive for company. It makes a low-calorie dessert that looks and feels indulgent.

—KARIN CHRISTIAN PLANO, TX

START TO FINISH: 30 MIN. • **MAKES:** 4 SERVINGS

- ½ cup mixed berry yogurt
- ¾ cup reduced-fat whipped topping
- 1 cup sliced ripe banana
- 1 cup sliced fresh strawberries
- 1 cup cubed fresh pineapple
- 1 cup fresh blueberries
- 4 whole strawberries

1. In a small bowl, combine yogurt and whipped topping; set aside 4 teaspoons for topping. Spoon half of the remaining yogurt mixture into four parfait glasses; layer with half of the banana, sliced strawberries, pineapple and blueberries. Repeat layers.

2. Top each parfait with reserved yogurt mixture and a whole strawberry. Chill until serving.

PER SERVING *149 cal., 2 g fat (2 g sat. fat), 2 mg chol., 22 mg sodium, 31 g carb., 4 g fiber, 2 g pro.* **Diabetic Exchanges:** *1½ fruit, ½ starch.*

Light & Creamy Chocolate Pudding F S M

This pudding is exactly what its name promises—light and creamy. Since it uses soy milk, it's a great choice if you're lactose-intolerant or are having a guest over who doesn't drink milk.

—DEBORAH WILLIAMS PEORIA, AZ

PREP: 10 MIN. • **COOK:** 15 MIN. + CHILLING • **MAKES:** 4 SERVINGS

- 3 tablespoons cornstarch
- 2 tablespoons sugar
- 2 tablespoons baking cocoa
- ⅛ teaspoon salt
- 2 cups chocolate soy milk
- 1 teaspoon vanilla extract

1. In a small heavy saucepan, mix cornstarch, sugar, cocoa and salt. Whisk in milk. Cook and stir over medium heat until thickened and bubbly. Reduce heat to low; cook and stir 2 minutes longer.

2. Remove from heat. Stir in vanilla. Cool 15 minutes, stirring occasionally.

3. Transfer to dessert dishes. Refrigerate, covered, 30 minutes or until cold.

PER SERVING *127 cal., 2 g fat (0 sat. fat), 0 chol., 112 mg sodium, 25 g carb., 1 g fiber, 3 g pro.* **Diabetic Exchange:** *1½ starch.*

Low-Fat Chocolate Cookies F S C M

These soft cake-like cookies have a mild cocoa flavor and cute chocolate chip topping. Better still, they're ready fast and have just 2 grams of fat!

—MARY HOUCHIN LEBANON, IL

PREP: 15 MIN. + CHILLING • **BAKE:** 10 MIN./BATCH
MAKES: ABOUT 3½ DOZEN

- ½ cup unsweetened applesauce
- ⅓ cup canola oil
- 3 egg whites
- ¾ cup sugar
- ¾ cup packed brown sugar
- 2 teaspoons vanilla extract
- 2⅔ cups all-purpose flour
- ½ cup baking cocoa
- 1 teaspoon baking soda
- ½ teaspoon salt
- ¼ cup miniature semisweet chocolate chips

1. In a large bowl, combine the applesauce, oil and egg whites. Beat in sugars and vanilla. Combine the flour, cocoa, baking soda and salt; gradually add to applesauce mixture and mix well. Cover and refrigerate for 2 hours or until slightly firm.

2. Drop dough by rounded teaspoonfuls 2 in. apart onto baking sheets coated with cooking spray. Sprinkle with chocolate chips. Bake at 350° for 8-10 minutes or until set. Remove to wire racks.

PER SERVING *1 cookie equals 78 cal., 2 g fat (trace sat. fat), trace chol., 63 mg sodium, 14 g carb., 1 g fiber, 1 g pro.* *Diabetic Exchange: 1 starch.*

PEACH 'N' PEAR CRISPS

Peach 'n' Pear Crisps S M

I have such a sweet tooth that even when I'm cutting calories, I don't like to skip dessert. So I adapted a favorite peach pie recipe to create this fiber-rich delight that makes just two servings.

—SUSAN WILSON MILWAUKEE, WI

PREP: 20 MIN. • **BAKE:** 20 MIN. • **MAKES:** 2 SERVINGS

- 1 medium peach, peeled and chopped
- 1 medium ripe pear, chopped
- 1 tablespoon honey
- 2 teaspoons all-purpose flour
- 1½ teaspoons lemon juice
- ¼ teaspoon ground cinnamon
- ⅛ teaspoon ground allspice

TOPPING

- 1 tablespoon all-purpose flour
- 1 tablespoon reduced-fat butter, melted
- 1 tablespoon honey
- ⅛ teaspoon ground allspice
  Dash ground cinnamon
- ⅓ cup old-fashioned oats
- 2 tablespoons coarsely chopped almonds

1. In a small bowl, combine the first seven ingredients. Divide mixture between two 8-oz. ramekins coated with cooking spray.

2. For topping, in a small bowl, combine the flour, butter, honey, allspice and cinnamon; stir in oats and almonds. Sprinkle over fruit mixture.

3. Bake at 375° for 18-20 minutes or until bubbly and golden brown. Serve warm.

PER SERVING *282 cal., 9 g fat (3 g sat. fat), 10 mg chol., 37 mg sodium, 52 g carb., 6 g fiber, 6 g pro.*

LOW-FAT CHOCOLATE COOKIES

Citrus Compote with Grapefruit Granita F S M

PREP: 25 MIN. + FREEZING • **MAKES:** 6 SERVINGS

- ½ cup sugar
- ½ cup water
- 1½ cups ruby red grapefruit juice
- 2 small navel oranges
- 2 small grapefruit
- 2 clementines
- ⅓ cup pomegranate seeds

1. In a small saucepan, bring sugar and water to a boil; cook and stir until sugar is dissolved. Remove from heat; cool slightly.

2. Stir in grapefruit juice. Transfer to an 8-in.-square dish. Freeze 1 hour. Stir with a fork. Freeze 2-3 hours longer or until completely frozen, stirring every 30 minutes.

3. Cut a thin slice from the top and bottom of each orange. Stand oranges upright on a cutting board. With a knife, cut off peel and outer membrane from oranges. Working over a bowl to catch juices, cut along the membrane of each segment to remove fruit. Place fruit in bowl. Repeat with grapefruit, removing any seeds.

Make granita no more than a day ahead of time for the best texture. If it freezes solid, it can be revived with pulsing in a food processor. This recipe was inspired by a trip I took with my husband to Italy. —JENNIFER BECKMAN FALLS CHURCH, VA

CITRUS COMPOTE WITH GRAPEFRUIT GRANITA

LITTLE ITALY PIGNOLI COOKIES

4. Peel and separate clementines into segments; add to oranges and grapefruit. Gently stir in pomegranate seeds.

5. To serve, stir granita with a fork. Alternately layer granita and fruit mixture into six dessert dishes. Serve immediately.

PER SERVING *149 cal., trace fat (trace sat. fat), 0 chol., 1 mg sodium, 38 g carb., 2 g fiber, 1 g pro.*

Little Italy Pignoli Cookies F S C M

Both my grandmas came from Italy. Of all the wonderful desserts they made, these were always the family favorite. Now I make them for every get-together. Lucky for me, they're easy and use just five ingredients!

—**FRAN GREEN** LINDEN, NJ

PREP: 25 MIN. • **BAKE:** 15 MIN./BATCH • **MAKES:** 5 DOZEN

- 1 cup almond paste
- 1 egg white
- 1 tablespoon honey
- ¾ cup confectioners' sugar
- ¾ cup pine nuts

1. Preheat oven to 325°. In a small bowl, beat almond paste, egg white and honey until crumbly. Gradually add confectioners' sugar; mix well.

2. Place pine nuts in a small bowl. Shape teaspoonfuls of dough into balls. Roll in pine nuts. Place 1 in. apart on parchment paper-lined baking sheets. Flatten slightly.

3. Bake 15-18 minutes or until lightly browned. Cool 1 minute before removing from pans to wire racks. Store in an airtight container.

PER SERVING *1 cookie equals 34 cal., 2 g fat (trace sat. fat), 0 chol., 1 mg sodium, 4 g carb., trace fiber, 1 g pro.*

ALMOND CHERRY COBBLER

Almond Cherry Cobbler M

This bubbling cherry cobbler is one of my favorite dishes. Serve warm with vanilla ice cream or whipped cream.

—**MELISSA WAGNER** EDEN PRAIRIE, MN

PREP: 20 MIN. • **BAKE:** 45 MIN.
MAKES: 6 SERVINGS

  3½ cups fresh dark sweet cherries, pitted
  1 cup all-purpose flour
  ¼ cup plus ½ cup sugar, divided
  1 teaspoon baking powder
  ¼ teaspoon salt
  ½ cup fat-free milk
  3 tablespoons butter, melted
  1 tablespoon cornstarch
  ¼ teaspoon ground cinnamon
  ¾ cup boiling water
  1 teaspoon almond extract

1. Preheat oven to 350°. Place cherries in an 8-in.-square baking dish coated with cooking spray.
2. In a small bowl, mix flour, ¼ cup sugar, baking powder and salt. Add milk and melted butter; stir in just until moistened. Spread over cherries.
3. In another bowl, mix cornstarch, cinnamon and remaining sugar; sprinkle over batter. Mix boiling water and almond extract; pour slowly over top. Bake, uncovered, 45-50 minutes or until bubbly and top is golden brown. Serve warm.
PER SERVING *297 cal., 6 g fat (4 g sat. fat), 16 mg chol., 225 mg sodium, 59 g carb., 1 g fiber, 3 g pro.*

Cherry Smarts

Dark sweet cherries are larger and firmer than sour cherries. While sweet cherries are popular and delicious for eating out of hand, they're often too sweet for making desserts. Sour cherries are generally considered better for baking. However, sweet cherries in a dessert recipe can allow you to get by with using less sugar.

MINI NEAPOLITAN BAKED ALASKAS

Mini Neapolitan Baked Alaskas F S M

Surprise—there's ice cream inside these tiny showstoppers! Dinner guests will be thrilled with the pretty presentation.

—*TASTE OF HOME* TEST KITCHEN

PREP: 30 MIN. • **BROIL:** 5 MIN.
MAKES: 4 SERVINGS

  4 foil muffin liners
  4 chocolate wafers
  1 cup reduced-fat strawberry ice cream
  3 egg whites
  6 tablespoons sugar
  ⅛ teaspoon cream of tartar
  ½ teaspoon vanilla extract

1. Flatten muffin liners; place on a baking sheet. Place a wafer on each. Scoop ¼ cup of ice cream onto each wafer; freeze.
2. Meanwhile, in a small heavy saucepan, combine the egg whites, sugar and cream of tartar; beat on low speed with a portable mixer for 1 minute. Continue beating over low heat until mixture reaches 160°, about 12 minutes. Remove from the heat; add vanilla. Beat until stiff peaks form and sugar is dissolved, about 4 minutes.
3. Remove baking sheet from freezer; immediately spread meringue over ice cream, sealing to edges of wafers. Broil 4-6 in. from the heat for 1-2 minutes or until meringues are lightly browned. Serve immediately.
PER SERVING *163 cal., 2 g fat (1 g sat. fat), 8 mg chol., 99 mg sodium, 32 g carb., trace fiber, 5 g pro.* **Diabetic Exchange:** *2 starch.*

Triple-Ginger Gingersnaps **F S C M**

Ginger cookies are always a hit during the holidays. Tuck them into clean upcycled coffee cans wrapped in decorative paper. With a glue gun, add decorative ribbon or trim.

—JESSICA FOLLEN WAUNAKEE, WI

PREP: 35 MIN. + CHILLING
BAKE: 10 MIN./BATCH • **MAKES:** 4 DOZEN

- ⅔ **cup butter, softened**
- 1 **cup packed brown sugar**
- ¼ **cup molasses**
- 1 **egg**
- 2 **teaspoons minced fresh gingerroot**
- 1 **cup all-purpose flour**
- ¾ **cup whole wheat flour**
- 3 **teaspoons ground ginger**
- 1½ **teaspoons baking soda**
- ½ **teaspoon fine sea salt or kosher salt**
- ½ **teaspoon ground nutmeg**
- ¼ **teaspoon ground cloves**
- 3 **tablespoons finely chopped crystallized ginger**
- ¼ **cup sugar**
- 1½ **teaspoons ground cinnamon**

1. In a large bowl, cream butter and brown sugar until light and fluffy. Beat in molasses, egg and fresh ginger.
2. Combine flours, ground ginger, baking soda, salt, nutmeg and cloves; gradually add to creamed mixture and mix well. Stir in crystallized ginger. Cover and refrigerate 1 hour or until easy to handle.
3. Preheat oven to 350°. In a small bowl, combine sugar and cinnamon. Shape dough into 1-in. balls; roll in sugar mixture. Place 3 in. apart on parchment paper-lined baking sheets.
4. Bake 10-12 minutes or until set. Cool 2 minutes before removing from pans to wire racks. Store in an airtight container.
PER SERVING *1 cookie equals 70 cal., 3 g fat (2 g sat. fat), 11 mg chol., 86 mg sodium, 11 g carb., trace fiber, 1 g pro.*
Diabetic Exchanges: *½ starch, ½ fat.*

Sonoran Sunset Watermelon Ice **F S M**

PREP: 15 MIN. + COOLING
PROCESS: 10 MIN. + FREEZING
MAKES: 6 SERVINGS

- ½ **cup sugar**
- ¼ **cup water**
- 4 **cups cubed seedless watermelon**
- 3 **tablespoons lime juice**
- 2 **tablespoons pomegranate juice**
- 1 **tablespoon minced fresh cilantro Dash salt**

1. In a small saucepan, bring sugar and water to a boil; cook and stir until the sugar is dissolved. Cool sugar mixture completely.
2. Place watermelon in a blender; cover and process until pureed. Transfer to a large bowl; stir in sugar mixture and remaining ingredients. Refrigerate until cold.
3. Pour watermelon mixture into cylinder of ice cream freezer; freeze according to manufacturer's directions. Transfer to freezer containers, allowing headspace for expansion. Freeze for 4 hours or until firm.
PER SERVING *102 cal., trace fat (trace sat. fat), 0 chol., 27 mg sodium, 25 g carb., 1 g fiber, 1 g pro.*

If you didn't think watermelon and cilantro could go together in dessert, this recipe will give you a pleasant surprise!
—JEANNE HOLT MENDOTA HEIGHTS, MN

SONORAN SUNSET WATERMELON ICE

LEMONY CREAM CHEESE BARS

Lemony Cream Cheese Bars M

Anytime I can take a recipe that has been handed down two generations and lighten it up while keeping the delicious flavor memories intact, I'm a happy girl.
—PATTI LAVELL ISLAMORADA, FL

PREP: 15 MIN. • **BAKE:** 25 MIN. + COOLING
MAKES: 2 DOZEN

- 1 **package lemon cake mix (regular size)**
- ½ **cup egg substitute, divided**
- ⅓ **cup canola oil**
- 1 **package (8 ounces) reduced-fat cream cheese**
- ⅓ **cup sugar**
- 1 **teaspoon lemon juice**

1. Preheat oven to 350°. In a large bowl, combine cake mix, ¼ cup egg substitute and oil; mix until blended. Reserve ½ cup mixture for topping. Press remaining mixture onto bottom of a 13x9-in. baking pan coated with cooking spray. Bake 11-13 minutes or until edges are light brown.

2. In a small bowl, beat cream cheese, sugar and lemon juice until smooth. Add remaining egg substitute; beat on low speed just until blended. Spread over crust.

3. Crumble reserved topping over filling. Bake 11-13 minutes longer or until filling is set. Cool on a wire rack for 1 hour. Cut into bars. Refrigerate the leftovers.

PER SERVING *1 bar equals 149 cal., 7 g fat (2 g sat. fat), 7 mg chol., 190 mg sodium, 20 g carb., 0 fiber, 3 g pro.* ***Diabetic Exchanges:*** *1½ fat, 1 starch.*

Easy Potluck

When setting up a potluck, mark the tables with sticky notes labeled for main dishes, sides, salads, drinks and desserts. Attendees will know where to place items and not have to ask. This will also help you plan a smooth flow of guests and reduce traffic jams.

CHOCOLATE-HAZELNUT
BANANA CREPES

Chocolate-Hazelnut
Banana Crepes M

Here's a wonderfully rich and delicious
treat: warm bananas and Nutella stuffed
into light and luscious homemade crepes.
—**CATHY HALL** LYNDHURST, VA

PREP: 15 MIN. + CHILLING • **COOK:** 15 MIN.
MAKES: 10 SERVINGS

- 2 **eggs**
- 2 **egg whites**
- ¾ **cup water**
- ½ **cup 2% milk**
- 1 **tablespoon canola oil**
- 1 **cup all-purpose flour**
- 1 **tablespoon sugar**
- ½ **teaspoon salt**
- 2 **tablespoons butter**
- 2 **tablespoons brown sugar**
- 4 **medium bananas, peeled and
  sliced**
- ⅓ **cup Nutella**

1. In a large bowl, whisk the eggs, egg
whites, water, milk and oil. Combine

the flour, sugar and salt; add to egg
mixture and mix well. Refrigerate for
1 hour.
2. Heat a lightly greased 8-in. nonstick
skillet over medium heat; pour ¼ cup
batter into center of skillet. Lift and tilt
pan to coat bottom evenly. Cook until
top appears dry; turn and cook 15-20
seconds longer. Remove to a wire rack.
Repeat with remaining batter,
greasing skillet as needed. When cool,
stack crepes with waxed paper or
paper towels in between.
3. In a large skillet, melt butter over
medium-low heat. Stir in brown sugar
until blended. Add bananas; cook for
2-3 minutes or until bananas are
glazed and slightly softened, stirring
gently. Remove from the heat.
4. Spread Nutella over each crepe;
top with bananas. Roll up and serve.
PER SERVING *208 cal., 8 g fat (2 g sat.
fat), 49 mg chol., 171 mg sodium, 31 g
carb., 2 g fiber, 5 g pro.* **Diabetic
Exchanges:** *2 starch, 1½ fat.*

Gingerbread
Meringue Bars S M

For the best of both worlds, I combined
my grandmother's gingerbread with my
aunt's special brown sugar meringue. The
result? These lovable holiday-perfect bars.
—**EDEN DRANGER** LOS ANGELES, CA

PREP: 20 MIN. • **BAKE:** 30 MIN. + COOLING
MAKES: 2 DOZEN

- ¼ **cup butter, softened**
- 1 **cup molasses**
- 2 **egg yolks**
- 1 **egg**
- ¼ **cup canned pumpkin**
- 1 **teaspoon vanilla extract**
- 1½ **cups whole wheat flour**
- 2½ **teaspoons ground cinnamon**
- 2 **teaspoons ground ginger**
- 1 **teaspoon baking powder**
- 1 **teaspoon baking soda**
- ¾ **teaspoon ground allspice**
- ¼ **teaspoon salt**
- 1 **cup miniature marshmallows**
- ½ **cup chopped pecans**
- ½ **cup semisweet chocolate chips**

MERINGUE
- 4 **egg whites**
- ½ **cup packed brown sugar**

1. In a large bowl, beat butter and
molasses until blended. Add egg yolks
and egg, one at a time, beating well
after each addition. Beat in pumpkin
and vanilla.
2. In a small bowl, combine the flour,
cinnamon, ginger, baking powder,
baking soda, allspice and salt.
Gradually add to the molasses
mixture. Pour into a greased 13x9-in.
baking pan. Sprinkle with
marshmallows, pecans and chocolate
chips. Bake at 350° for 20 minutes.
3. Meanwhile, in a small bowl, beat
egg whites on medium speed until soft
peaks form. Gradually beat in brown
sugar, 1 tablespoon at a time, on high
until stiff glossy peaks form and sugar
is dissolved.
4. Remove gingerbread from oven;
spread with meringue. Bake 9-11
minutes longer or until meringue is
lightly browned. Cool completely.
PER SERVING *1 bar equals 135 cal., 4 g
fat (2 g sat. fat), 31 mg chol., 129 mg
sodium, 24 g carb., 1 g fiber, 2 g pro.*
Diabetic Exchanges: *1½ starch, 1 fat.*

Chocolate-Pumpkin Cheesecake Bars M

I created these bars by taking my favorite cheesecake brownie recipe and adding pumpkin and spices. They disappear fast, so consider making two pans.

—JUDY CASTRANOVA NEW BERN, NC

PREP: 30 MIN. • **BAKE:** 20 MIN.
MAKES: 2 DOZEN

- ⅓ cup butter, cubed
- 1½ ounces unsweetened chocolate, coarsely chopped
- 1 tablespoon instant coffee granules
- ½ cup boiling water
- 1 cup canned pumpkin
- 2 eggs, lightly beaten
- 2 cups all-purpose flour
- 1½ cups sugar
- ¾ teaspoon baking soda
- ½ teaspoon salt

CHEESECAKE BATTER

- 1 package (8 ounces) reduced-fat cream cheese
- ½ cup canned pumpkin
- ¼ cup sugar
- 1 teaspoon vanilla extract
- ¾ teaspoon ground cinnamon
- ¾ teaspoon ground ginger
- ⅛ teaspoon ground cloves
- 1 egg, lightly beaten
- 1 cup (6 ounces) semisweet chocolate chips

1. In a microwave, melt butter and chocolate; stir until smooth. Cool mixture slightly.

2. In a large bowl, dissolve coffee in water. Stir in the pumpkin, eggs and chocolate mixture. Combine the flour, sugar, baking soda and salt; gradually add to chocolate mixture. Transfer to a 15-in. x 10-in. x 1-in. baking pan coated with cooking spray.

3. For cheesecake batter, in a small bowl, beat cream cheese and pumpkin until smooth. Beat in the sugar, vanilla and spices. Add egg; beat on low speed just until combined. Spoon over chocolate batter. Cut through batter with a knife to swirl the cheesecake portion. Sprinkle with chocolate chips.

4. Bake at 350° for 20-25 minutes or until a toothpick inserted near the center comes out with moist crumbs (do not overbake). Cool on a wire rack. Cut into bars. Refrigerate leftovers.

PER SERVING *1 bar equals 197 cal., 8 g fat (5 g sat. fat), 40 mg chol., 157 mg sodium, 29 g carb., 2 g fiber, 4 g pro. Diabetic Exchanges: 2 starch, 1 fat.*

Chili-Lime Grilled Pineapple F S M

START TO FINISH: 15 MIN.
MAKES: 6 SERVINGS

- 1 fresh pineapple
- 3 tablespoons brown sugar
- 1 tablespoon lime juice
- 1 tablespoon olive oil
- 1 tablespoon honey or agave nectar
- 1½ teaspoons chili powder
  Dash salt

1. Peel pineapple, removing any eyes from fruit. Cut lengthwise into six wedges; remove core. In a small bowl, mix remaining ingredients until blended. Brush pineapple with half of the glaze; reserve remaining mixture for basting.

2. Grill pineapple, covered, over medium heat or broil 4 in. from heat 2-4 minutes on each side or until lightly browned, basting occasionally with reserved glaze.

PER SERVING *97 cal., 2 g fat (trace sat. fat), 0 chol., 35 mg sodium, 20 g carb., 1 g fiber, 1 g pro. Diabetic Exchanges: ½ starch, ½ fruit.*

I love grilled pineapple. This recipe combines the fruit's natural sweetness with the tart and spicy flavors of lime and chili powder. It's great for dessert and even as a side dish to ham or pork chops.

—GERALDINE SAUCIER ALBUQUERQUE, NM

CHILI-LIME GRILLED PINEAPPLE

General Recipe Index

This index lists every recipe by food category, major ingredient and/or cooking method, so you can easily locate recipes that suit your needs.

•Table-ready in 30 minutes or less.

APPETIZERS & SNACKS

Cold Appetizers
•Roast Beef Aioli Bundles, 15
•Rosemary Beet Phyllo Bites, 10
•Shrimp Salad Appetizers, 16
Tangy Pickled Mushrooms, 12
•Yogurt & Honey Fruit Cups, 16
Zesty Marinated Shrimp, 10

Dips
•Chunky Mango Guacamole, 8
•Chipotle Avocado Dip, 9
Mediterranean Eggplant Dip, 15
Pomegranate Orange Salsa, 19
•Strawberry Salsa, 13
Thai Veggie Dip, 8
•Watermelon Salsa, 11
Zesty Spinach Dip, 213

Hot Appetizers
Asian Chicken Dumplings, 17
Cajun Crawfish Sliders, 13
•Grilled Nectarine & Cheese Crostini, 12
Grilled Shrimp Appetizer Kabobs, 19
Moo Shu Chicken Cones, 17
•Tomato & Artichoke Bruschetta, 18
Tri-Color Miniature Peppers, 9
Zucchini Crab Cakes, 11

APPLES

Apple-Cinnamon Pork Loin, 154
Apple Oatmeal Cookies, 236
Apple-Stuffed Pork Tenderloins, 150
Apple Sundaes, 213
Chunky Apple Snack Cake, 219
Cider Turkey Soup, 42
Curry-Apple Turkey Loaf, 138

ARTICHOKES

Grilled Artichoke-Mushroom Pizza, 187
Italian Chicken Chardonnay, 131
•Tomato & Artichoke Bruschetta, 18

ASPARAGUS

•Asparagus Omelet Tortilla Wrap, 69
•Garden Quinoa Salad, 186
Gingered Beef and Asparagus Stir-Fry, 111
•Roast Beef Aioli Bundles, 15
Tuscan-Style Roasted Asparagus, 55

AVOCADOS

•Avocado & Tomato Sandwiches, 183
•Chipotle Avocado Dip, 9
•Chunky Mango Guacamole, 8
•Shrimp Salad with Cilantro Vinaigrette, 30
•Tropical Fusion Salad with Spicy Tortilla Ribbons, 182

BACON

•Bacon-Swiss Pork Chops, 152
Black-Eyed Peas & Ham, 63

BANANAS

Banana-Pecan Sheet Cake, 222
•Chocolate Banana Bran Muffins, 200
Chocolate-Hazelnut Banana Crepes, 244
•Fresh Fruit Parfaits, 237
Monkey Bars, 233

BARS

Chocolate-Pumpkin Cheesecake Bars, 245
Gingerbread Meringue Bars, 244
Lemony Cream Cheese Bars, 243
Monkey Bars, 233

BEANS

Bean Soup with Sausage, 38
•Black Bean & Corn Quinoa, 82
Black Bean 'n' Pumpkin Chili, 48
Black Bean & White Cheddar Frittata, 74
Chipotle Turkey Chilaquiles, 141
•Coconut-Ginger Chickpeas & Tomatoes, 184
•Confetti Kielbasa Skillet, 140
•Corn, Rice & Bean Burritos, 181
Fiesta Beef Bowls, 105
Kale & Bean Soup, 43
•Mediterranean Turkey Skillet, 136
•Penne with Veggies 'n' Black Beans, 205
•Rosemary Chicken with Spinach & Beans, 121
Salsa Bean Burgers, 187
•Salsa Skillet Pork Chops, 150
•Skillet Cassoulet, 139
•Sweet Potato & Bean Quesadillas, 185
•Tilapia Tacos, 164
•Tropical Fusion Salad with Spicy Tortilla Ribbons, 182
White Bean Soup with Escarole, 51

BEEF (ALSO SEE GROUND BEEF)

Appetizers
•Roast Beef Aioli Bundles, 15
Main Dishes
•Beef & Spinach Lo Mein, 113
Beef Brisket Marinara, 117
Blue Cheese Flank Steak, 116
Braised Hanukkah Brisket, 110
•Chili Steak & Peppers, 86
Chipotle-Rubbed Beef Tenderloin, 115
•Cocoa-Crusted Beef Tenderloin, 112
Fiesta Beef Bowls, 105
Gingered Beef and Asparagus Stir-Fry, 111
Grilled Flank Steak, 108
Grilled Sirloin with Chili-Beer Barbecue Sauce, 111
•Italian Steaks for 2, 214
Moroccan Beef Kabobs, 116
Old-Fashioned Swiss Steak, 113
Peppered Filets with Tomato-Mushroom Salsa, 109
Round Steak Italiano, 100
•Sirloin in Wine Sauce, 108
Sirloin on the Grill, 211
Sizzling Beef Kabobs, 112
Slow Cooker Beef Bourguignonne, 96
•Southwest Steak & Potatoes, 117
•Sweet-and-Sour Beef with Broccoli, 84
•Wasabi Beef Fajitas, 82
Zesty Orange Beef, 115
Soups
Beef Barley Soup, 206
Chunky Beef & Vegetable Soup, 50

BEER

Grilled Sirloin with Chili-Beer Barbecue Sauce, 111
Sirloin on the Grill, 211

BEVERAGES

•Fruity Frappe, 77
•Ginger Cardamom Tea, 76
•Cherry Cobbler Smoothies, 79

BLUEBERRIES

Angel Food Cake with Berry Sauce, 225
Blueberry-Stuffed French Toast, 71
•Fresh Fruit Parfaits, 237
•Fruit-Filled Puff Pancake, 68
Granola Blueberry Muffins, 191

BREADS (SEE CORN BREAD & CORNMEAL; MUFFINS; QUICK BREADS & BISCUITS; YEAST BREADS & ROLLS)

BREAKFAST & BRUNCH RECIPES (ALSO SEE BEVERAGES)

Cereals
Autumn Power Porridge, 71
Carrot Cake Oatmeal, 76
•Cranberry-Walnut Oatmeal, 72
Michigan Fruit Baked Oatmeal, 77
Overnight Maple Oatmeal, 74
Slow Cooker Honey Granola, 68
Egg Dishes
•Asparagus Omelet Tortilla Wrap, 69
Black Bean & White Cheddar Frittata, 74
•Feta Scrambled Egg Wraps, 73
•Microwave Egg Sandwich, 70
Southwest Hash with Adobo-Lime Crema, 79
•Southwest Tortilla Scramble, 208
•Vegetable Omelet, 215
Veggie Egg Casserole, 69
Fruit
•Mixed Berry Sundaes for 2, 205
Rhubarb Compote with Yogurt & Almonds, 73
Meat
•Turkey Sausage Patties, 78
Pancakes, Waffles & French Toast
Berry Granola Pancakes, 78
Blueberry-Stuffed French Toast, 71
•Flaxseed Oatmeal Pancakes, 207

INDEX

•Fruit-Filled Puff Pancake, 68
•Whole-Grain Waffle Mix, 72

BROCCOLI
•Broccoli Slaw with Lemon Dressing, 32
•Chinese Takeout-on-a-Stick, 86
Ginger-Sesame Steamed Vegetable
   Salad, 22
•Peanut Chicken Stir-Fry, 129
•Sweet-and-Sour Beef with Broccoli, 84

BURGERS
•Grilled Turkey Burgers, 93
•Juicy & Delicious Mixed Spice Burgers, 115
•Portobello Pizza Burgers, 179
Salsa Bean Burgers, 187
Stuffed Pizza Burgers, 140

CABBAGE & COLESLAW MIX
Asian Veggie Glass Noodles, 178
Moo Shu Chicken Cones, 17
•Simple Sesame Chicken with Couscous, 87
•Tilapia Tacos, 164

CAKES & CUPCAKES
Almond Fudge Cake, 222
Angel Food Cake with Berry Sauce, 225
Banana-Pecan Sheet Cake, 222
Cappuccino Cupcakes, 218
Chocolate Peppermint Log, 227
Chunky Apple Snack Cake, 219
Cranberry-Pumpkin Spice Cake, 224
Mocha Frosted Snack Cake, 229
Mocha-Hazelnut Glazed Angel Food
   Cake, 221
Moist Lemon Chiffon Cake, 223
Orange Buttermilk Cupcakes, 225
Orange-Coconut Angel Food Cake, 228
Pear Bundt Cake, 218
Zucchini Carrot Spice Cake, 228

CARROTS
Carrot Cake Oatmeal, 76
•Roasted Carrot Fries, 56
Savory Braised Chicken with Vegetables, 128
Zucchini Carrot Spice Cake, 228

CHEESE (ALSO SEE CREAM CHEESE)
Appetizers
•Grilled Nectarine & Cheese Crostini, 12
•Rosemary Beet Phyllo Bites, 10
Breakfast & Brunch
Black Bean & White Cheddar Frittata, 74
•Feta Scrambled Egg Wraps, 73
Main Dishes
•Bacon-Swiss Pork Chops, 152
•Baked Fish with Cheese Sauce for 2, 207
Blue Cheese Flank Steak, 116
Chicken in Tomato-Caper Sauce, 130
Chipotle Turkey Chilaquiles, 141
Crispy Buffalo Chicken Roll-Ups for 2, 213
Grilled Artichoke-Mushroom Pizza, 187
Makeover Creamy Mac & Cheese, 184
Mama Rachel's Tomato & Kalamata
   Pizzas, 181
•Margherita Pita Pizzas, 91
•Parmesan Chicken Couscous, 132
Sausage & Peppers with Cheese Polenta, 130
•Shrimp with Tomatoes & Feta, 88

Salads
•Balsamic Cucumber Salad, 32
Grilled Vegetable Orzo Salad, 26
Side Dishes
Baked Parmesan Breaded Squash, 64
•Lemon Parmesan Orzo, 57
Tuscan-Style Roasted Asparagus, 55

CHERRIES
Almond Cherry Cobbler, 241
•Cherry-Chicken Lettuce Wraps, 124
•Cherry Cobbler Smoothies, 79

CHICKEN & CHICKEN SAUSAGE
Appetizers
Asian Chicken Dumplings, 17
Moo Shu Chicken Cones , 17
Main Dishes
•Apricot-Lemon Chicken, 83
•Bruschetta-Topped Chicken &
   Spaghetti, 120
Carolina-Style Vinegar BBQ Chicken, 105
•Cherry-Chicken Lettuce Wraps, 124
•Chicken & Vegetable Kabobs, 122
Chicken Cacciatore, 104
Chicken in Tomato-Caper Sauce, 130
•Chicken Sausages with Polenta, 133
Chicken Thighs with Ginger-Peach
   Sauce, 98
Chicken with Beans and Potatoes, 99
•Chinese Takeout-on-a-Stick, 86
Citrus-Marinated Chicken, 123
Coconut-Lime Chicken, 128
•Creole Blackened Chicken, 91
Crispy Buffalo Chicken Roll-Ups for 2, 213
•Greek-Style Chicken Skewers, 131
•Grilled Brown Sugar-Mustard
   Chicken , 132
•Herbed Chicken and Rice, 133
Honey Balsamic Chicken, 211
Indian Baked Chicken, 122
Italian Chicken Chardonnay, 131
•Lime-Ginger Chicken Tenders, 92
Mango-Pineapple Chicken Tacos, 127
Meaty Slow-Cooked Jambalaya, 97
Moroccan Chicken, 100
Orange-Spiced Chicken, 126
•Parmesan Chicken Couscous, 132
•Peanut Chicken Stir-Fry, 129
•Pecan-Crusted Chicken Nuggets, 127
Popcorn & Pretzel Chicken Tenders, 129
•Rosemary Chicken with Spinach &
   Beans, 121
Saucy BBQ Chicken Thighs, 120
•Saucy Peach-Balsamic Chicken, 121
Sausage & Peppers with Cheese Polenta, 130
Savory Braised Chicken with
   Vegetables, 128
•Simple Sesame Chicken with Couscous, 87
Slow-Cooked Coconut Chicken, 96
Southwest Grilled Chicken, 209
•Spicy Apricot-Glazed Chicken, 133
Spicy Shredded Chicken, 101 Spinach
   Chicken Manicotti, 124
•Tangy Chicken & Peppers, 123
•Thai Chicken Peanut Noodles, 126
Salads
•Cashew-Curry Chicken Salad, 35
•Chicken Salad with Dijon Vinaigrette, 33

Soup & Chili
Guilt-Free Chicken Chili, 46
Lemon Chicken & Rice Soup, 44

CHILI
Black Bean 'n' Pumpkin Chili, 48
Cincinnati-Style Chili, 42
Guilt-Free Chicken Chili, 46

CHOCOLATE (ALSO SEE COCOA)
Chocolate-Pumpkin Cheesecake Bars, 245
Fudge Sundae Pie, 227

COCOA
Almond Fudge Cake, 222
Cappuccino Cupcakes, 218
•Chocolate Banana Bran Muffins, 200
Chocolate Peppermint Log, 227
•Cocoa-Crusted Beef Tenderloin, 112
Light & Creamy Chocolate Pudding, 237
Low-Fat Chocolate Cookies, 238
Mocha Frosted Snack Cake, 229

COCONUT
Coconut-Lime Chicken, 128
Lime Muffins with Coconut Streusel, 191
Orange-Coconut Angel Food Cake, 228
•Pineapple Shrimp Stir-Fry, 169
Slow-Cooked Coconut Chicken, 96

COFFEE
Cappuccino Cupcakes, 218
Chocolate-Pumpkin Cheesecake Bars, 245
•Cocoa-Crusted Beef Tenderloin, 112
Mocha Frosted Snack Cake, 229
Mocha-Hazelnut Glazed Angel Food
   Cake, 221

COOKIES
Apple Oatmeal Cookies, 236
Cranberry Pistachio Biscotti, 234
Lemon Meringue Pie Cookies, 233
Little Italy Pignoli Cookies, 239
Low-Fat Chocolate Cookies, 238
Peanut Butter Cookies, 234
Snow-Puffed Meringues, 235
Triple-Ginger Gingersnaps, 242
Toffee Meringue Drops, 236

CORN
Basil Corn & Tomato Bake, 61
•Corn, Rice & Bean Burritos, 181
•Fresh Corn & Tomato Fettuccine, 178
Fresh Corn and Tomato Soup, 49
•Grilled Tomato with Fresh Corn, 64

CORN BREAD & CORNMEAL
Basil Polenta with Ratatouille, 182
Cajun Crawfish Sliders, 13
Jalapeno Buttermilk Corn Bread, 192
Sausage & Peppers with Cheese Polenta, 130

CRANBERRIES
Autumn Power Porridge, 71
Cranberry Orange Muffins, 193
Cranberry Pear Tart, 229
Cranberry Pistachio Biscotti, 234
Cranberry-Pumpkin Spice Cake, 224
•Cranberry-Walnut Oatmeal, 72

CRANBERRIES (CONTINUED)
Cranberry Whole Wheat Bagels, 196
Michigan Fruit Baked Oatmeal, 77
•Pork Medallions with Cranberry Sauce, 93
Roasted Brussels Sprouts with
    Cranberries, 65
Roasted Butternut Tossed Salad, 24

CREAM CHEESE
Arctic Orange Pie, 220
Chocolate Peppermint Log, 227
Chocolate-Pumpkin Cheesecake Bars, 245
Lemony Cream Cheese Bars, 243
Light Cheesecake, 220
Strawberry Cream Cheese Pie, 224
Zucchini Carrot Spice Cake, 228

CUCUMBERS
•Balsamic Cucumber Salad, 32
Brown-Sugar Salmon with
    Strawberries, 175
•Cajun Shrimp & Cucumber Wraps, 170
Cool as a Cucumber Soup, 40

DESSERTS (ALSO SEE BARS; CAKES & CUPCAKES; COOKIES; PIES & TARTS)
Almond Cherry Cobbler, 241
Apple Sundaes, 213
•Chili-Lime Grilled Pineapple, 245
Chocolate-Hazelnut Banana Crepes, 244
Citrus Compote with Grapefruit
    Granita, 239
•Fresh Fruit Parfaits, 237
Fresh Pear Ginger Crisp, 235
Light & Creamy Chocolate Pudding, 237
Light Cheesecake, 220
Mango Rice Pudding, 232
Mini Neapolitan Baked Alaskas, 241
•Mixed Berry Sundaes for 2, 205
Peach 'n' Pear Crisps, 238
Peach Ice, 209
Peach Melba Trifle, 232
Sonoran Sunset Watermelon Ice, 242

EGGPLANT
Basil Polenta with Ratatouille, 182
Mediterranean Eggplant Dip, 15
Pasta with Eggplant Sauce, 186

EGGS
Asian Veggie Glass Noodles, 178
•Asparagus Omelet Tortilla Wrap, 69
Black Bean & White Cheddar Frittata, 74
•Feta Scrambled Egg Wraps, 73
•Garden-Fresh Chef Salad, 34
•Microwave Egg Sandwich, 70
Southwest Hash with Adobo-Lime
    Crema, 79
•Southwest Tortilla Scramble, 208
•Stir-Fry Rice Bowl, 183
•Vegetable Omelet, 215
Veggie Egg Casserole, 69

FISH (ALSO SEE SEAFOOD)
Main Dishes
•Baked Fish with Cheese Sauce for 2, 207
•Blackened Halibut, 173
•Broiled Fish with Tarragon Sauce, 174
Brown-Sugar Salmon with Strawberries, 175

•Citrus Fish for 2, 208
Fish & Chips with Dipping Sauce, 162
•Fish & Vegetable Packets, 171
•Halibut Soft Tacos, 174
•Herb-Roasted Salmon Fillets, 172
•Hoisin & Honey Glazed Salmon, 166
•Lemony Parsley Baked Cod, 85
•Oven-Barbecued Salmon, 163
•Peppered Tuna Kabobs, 169
•Salmon with Tangy Raspberry Sauce, 165
•Savory Tomato-Braised Tilapia, 167
Simple Poached Salmon, 101
•Strawberry-Teriyaki Glazed Salmon, 89
•Sweet-Chili Salmon with Blackberries, 92
•Tilapia Tacos, 164
•Tuna with Citrus Ponzu Sauce, 167
Salads
•Crunchy Tuna Salad with Tomatoes, 172
•Salmon Salad with Glazed Walnuts, 24
Soup
•Veggie Salmon Chowder, 204

FLAXSEED
Cinnamon-Pecan Swirl Bread, 200
•Flaxseed Oatmeal Pancakes, 207
Multigrain Bread, 198

FRUIT (ALSO SEE SPECIFIC KINDS)
Berry Granola Pancakes, 78
Citrus Compote with Grapefruit
    Granita, 239
•Curried Apricot Pork Chops, 210
•Fresh Apple & Pear Salad, 29
•Fruity Frappe, 77
•Grilled Nectarine & Cheese Crostini, 12
•Honey-Lime Berry Salad, 31
Mango-Pineapple Chicken Tacos, 127
•Mixed Berry Sundaes for 2, 205
Pomegranate Orange Salsa, 19
Pork Medallions with Pomegranate
    Sauce, 148
Rhubarb Compote with Yogurt &
    Almonds, 73
Roasted Pork Loin with Fig Sauce, 159
•Ruby Red Spinach Salads, 29
Slow Cooker Honey Granola, 68
•Sweet-Chili Salmon with Blackberries, 92
•Tropical Fusion Salad with Spicy Tortilla
    Ribbons, 182
•Yogurt & Honey Fruit Cups, 16

GRAINS (ALSO SEE OATS; QUINOA)
•Beef Barley Soup, 206
•Shrimp & Chicken Sausage with Grits, 165
Texas Tabbouleh, 30
•Whole-Grain Waffle Mix, 72

GREEN BEANS
•Day-After-Thanksgiving Turkey
    Stir-Fry, 84
•Fresh Green Beans & Garlic, 54
Roasted Garlic Green Beans with
    Cashews, 62

GRILLED RECIPES
Appetizers
•Grilled Nectarine & Cheese Crostini, 12
Grilled Shrimp Appetizer Kabobs, 19

Burgers
•Grilled Turkey Burgers, 93
Stuffed Pizza Burgers, 140
Main Dishes
Blue Cheese Flank Steak, 116
Brown-Sugar Salmon with
    Strawberries, 175
•Chicken & Vegetable Kabobs, 122
•Chinese Takeout-on-a-Stick, 86
•Chipotle-Orange Pork Chops, 153
•Citrus-Marinated Chicken, 123
•Greek-Style Chicken Skewers, 131
Grilled Artichoke-Mushroom Pizza, 187
•Grilled Brown Sugar-Mustard
    Chicken, 132
Grilled Chipotle Tenderloin, 204
Grilled Pistachio-Lemon Pesto Shrimp, 163
Grilled Sirloin with Chili-Beer Barbecue
    Sauce, 111
Grilled Turkey Tenderloin, 139
•Halibut Soft Tacos, 174
•Juicy & Delicious Mixed Spice Burgers, 115
Lemony Shrimp & Tomatoes, 175
Moroccan Beef Kabobs, 116
Orange-Spiced Chicken, 126
•Peppered Tuna Kabobs, 169
•Salmon with Tangy Raspberry Sauce, 165
Shredded Pork Barbecue, 149
Sirloin on the Grill, 211
Sizzling Beef Kabobs, 112
Southwest Grilled Chicken, 209
•Southwest Steak & Potatoes, 117
•Spicy Shrimp 'n' Scallop Skewers, 85
•Sweet-Chili Salmon with Blackberries, 92
Walsh Family Grilled Pork Tenderloins, 156
Salads
Grilled Vegetable Orzo Salad, 26
•Salmon Salad with Glazed Walnuts, 24
Side Dishes
Grilled Potatoes & Peppers, 59
•Grilled Tomato with Fresh Corn, 64

GROUND BEEF
•Chili Beef Pasta, 109
•Juicy & Delicious Mixed Spice Burgers, 115
Meat Loaf with Chili Sauce, 99
Mexican Stuffed Peppers, 110
Skillet Pasta, 210
•Sweet-and-Sour Beef with Broccoli, 84

HAM & CANADIAN BACON
Black-Eyed Peas & Ham, 63
•Microwave Egg Sandwich, 70

HERBS
Appetizers
•Grilled Nectarine & Cheese Crostini, 12
•Roast Beef Aioli Bundles, 15
•Rosemary Beet Phyllo Bites, 10
•Strawberry Salsa, 13
•Watermelon Salsa, 11
Main Dishes
Basil Polenta with Ratatouille, 182
•Black Bean & Corn Quinoa, 82
•Broiled Fish with Tarragon Sauce, 174
•Cajun Shrimp & Cucumber Wraps, 170
•Citrus Fish for 2, 208
Grilled Pistachio-Lemon Pesto Shrimp, 163
•Herb-Roasted Salmon Fillets, 172

•Juicy & Delicious Mixed Spice Burgers, 115
Just-Like-Thanksgiving Turkey Meat
    Loaf, 144
Lemon-Basil Turkey Breast, 144
•Lemony Parsley Baked Cod, 85
Moroccan Beef Kabobs, 116
Portobello Turkey Bolognese, 138
Simple Poached Salmon, 101
•Zippy Zucchini Pasta, 91
Zucchini Pesto with Shrimp and
    Farfalle, 166

Salads
Fiesta Rice and Bean Salad, 31
•Mandarin Watermelon Salad , 29
•Minted Sugar Snap Pea Salad, 31
Texas Tabbouleh, 30
•Tomatoes with Buttermilk Vinaigrette, 23

Side Dishes
Basil Corn & Tomato Bake, 61
•Dilled New Potatoes, 57
•Grilled Tomato with Fresh Corn, 64
•Herb-Roasted Mushrooms, 65
•Thymed Zucchini Saute, 56

Soup
Roasted Tomato Soup with Fresh Basil, 48

HONEY
•Broiled Fish with Tarragon Sauce, 174
•Cherry Cobbler Smoothies, 79
Cranberry Whole Wheat Bagels, 196
•Fruity Frappe, 77
•Hoisin & Honey Glazed Salmon, 166
Honey Balsamic Chicken, 211
Honey-Glazed Pork Tenderloins, 158
•Honey-Lime Berry Salad, 31
Honey-Oat Pan Rolls, 199
Honey Wheat Loaves, 194
Oats & Honey Yeast Bread, 195

HOT PEPPERS
Cajun Crawfish Sliders, 13
•Chipotle-Orange Pork Chops, 153
•Watermelon Salsa, 11
Zesty Orange Beef, 115

JAMS, JELLIES & PRESERVES
•Apple-Balsamic Pork Chops, 88
•Apricot-Lemon Chicken, 83
•Chili-Apricot Pork Chops, 157
•Curried Apricot Pork Chops, 210
•Fig-Glazed Pork Tenderloin, 87
•Pork Medallions with Raspberry-Balsamic
    Sauce, 154
•Saucy Peach-Balsamic Chicken, 121
•Spicy Apricot-Glazed Chicken, 133
•Strawberry-Teriyaki Glazed Salmon, 89

KALE
Kale & Bean Soup, 43
•Kale Salad, 33

LEMON
•Apricot-Lemon Chicken, 83
•Broccoli Slaw with Lemon Dressing, 32
•Broiled Fish with Tarragon Sauce, 174
•Citrus Fish for 2, 208
Citrus-Marinated Chicken, 123
•Greek-Style Chicken Skewers, 131
Lemon-Basil Turkey Breast, 144

Grilled Pistachio-Lemon Pesto Shrimp, 163
Lemon Chicken & Rice Soup, 44
Lemon Meringue Pie Cookies, 233
•Lemon Parmesan Orzo, 57
Lemony Cream Cheese Bars, 243
•Lemony Parsley Baked Cod, 85
Lemony Shrimp & Tomatoes, 175
Moist Lemon Chiffon Cake, 223
•Turkey Cutlets in Lemon Wine Sauce, 141

LETTUCE
•Cherry-Chicken Lettuce Wraps, 124
•Chicken Salad with Dijon Vinaigrette, 33
•Garden-Fresh Chef Salad, 34
•Mandarin Orange & Romaine Salad, 23
•Red & Green Salad with Toasted
    Almonds, 22
•Salmon Salad with Glazed Walnuts, 24
•Shrimp Salad with Cilantro
    Vinaigrette, 30
•Turkey Taco Salad, 27

LIME
Coconut-Lime Chicken, 128
•Lime-Ginger Chicken Tenders, 92
Lime Muffins with Coconut Streusel, 191
Southwest Grilled Chicken, 209
Southwest Pork Tenderloin, 149

LOW-CARB MAIN DISHES
Apple-Stuffed Pork Tenderloins, 150
•Apricot-Lemon Chicken, 83
•Bacon-Swiss Pork Chops, 152
•Baked Fish with Cheese Sauce for 2, 207
Beef Brisket Marinara, 117
•Blackened Halibut, 173
Blue Cheese Flank Steak, 116
Braised Hanukkah Brisket, 110
•Caramelized Pork Tenderloin, 153
Carolina-Style Vinegar BBQ Chicken, 105
•Chicken & Vegetable Kabobs, 122
Chicken Cacciatore, 104
•Chicken Salad with Dijon Vinaigrette, 33
Chicken with Beans and Potatoes, 99
•Citrus Fish for 2, 208
Citrus-Marinated Chicken, 123
•Chili Steak & Peppers, 86
•Chinese Takeout-on-a-Stick, 86
Chipotle-Rubbed Beef Tenderloin, 115
Citrus-Herb Pork Roast, 156
•Cocoa-Crusted Beef Tenderloin, 112
•Creole Blackened Chicken, 91
Crispy Buffalo Chicken Roll-Ups for 2, 213
•Crunchy Tuna Salad with Tomatoes, 172
•Fish & Vegetable Packets, 171
•Garden-Fresh Chef Salad, 34
Grandma Edna's Cajun Pork, 98
•Greek-Style Chicken Skewers, 131
•Grilled Brown Sugar-Mustard
    Chicken , 132
Grilled Chipotle Tenderloin, 204
Grilled Flank Steak, 108
Grilled Pistachio-Lemon Pesto Shrimp, 163
Grilled Sirloin with Chili-Beer Barbecue
    Sauce, 111
Grilled Turkey Tenderloin, 139
•Herb-Roasted Salmon Fillets, 172
Honey Balsamic Chicken, 211
•Italian Steaks for 2, 214

•Juicy & Delicious Mixed Spice Burgers, 115
Lemon-Basil Turkey Breast, 144
•Lemony Parsley Baked Cod, 85
Lemony Shrimp & Tomatoes, 175
Light Turkey Cutlets Stroganoff, 145
Lime-Chipotle Carnitas Tostadas, 102
•Lime-Ginger Chicken Tenders, 92
Mango Chutney Pork Roast, 158
Mediterranean Shrimp Linguine, 162
Moroccan Beef Kabobs, 116
•Oven-Barbecued Salmon, 163
•Pecan-Crusted Chicken Nuggets, 127
Peppered Filets with Tomato-Mushroom
    Salsa, 109
•Pork Chops with Mushroom-Tarragon
    Sauce, 155
•Pork Medallions with Cranberry Sauce, 93
Pork Tenderloin with Marsala Mushroom
    Sauce, 155
•Salmon Salad with Glazed Walnuts, 24
•Salmon with Tangy Raspberry Sauce, 165
Saucy BBQ Chicken Thighs, 120
•Savory Tomato-Braised Tilapia, 167
•Shrimp with Tomatoes & Feta, 88
Simple Poached Salmon, 101
•Sirloin in Wine Sauce, 108
Sirloin on the Grill, 211
Sizzling Beef Kabobs, 112
•Skillet Sea Scallops, 170
Slow-Cooked Coconut Chicken, 96
Slow Cooker Beef Bourguignonne, 96
Southern Pulled Pork, 97
Southwest Grilled Chicken, 209
Southwest Pork Tenderloin, 149
•Southwestern Scallops, 164
Spicy Shredded Chicken, 101
•Spicy Shrimp 'n' Scallop Skewers, 85
•Strawberry-Teriyaki Glazed Salmon, 89
•Sweet-Chili Salmon with Blackberries, 92
•Tuna with Citrus Ponzu Sauce, 167
•Turkey Cutlets in Lemon Wine Sauce, 141
Walsh Family Grilled Pork Tenderloins, 156

LOW-FAT MAIN DISHES
Asian Veggie Glass Noodles, 178
•Broiled Fish with Tarragon Sauce, 174
•Buffalo Sloppy Joes, 136
Carolina-Style Vinegar BBQ Chicken, 105
•Greek-Style Chicken Skewers, 131
Lemon-Basil Turkey Breast, 144
Orange-Spiced Chicken, 126
•Peppered Tuna Kabobs, 169
Popcorn & Pretzel Chicken Tenders, 129
•Spicy Apricot-Glazed Chicken, 133

LOW-SODIUM MAIN DISHES
•Greek-Style Chicken Skewers, 131
•Herbed Chicken and Rice, 133
•Lemony Parsley Baked Cod, 85
Moroccan Beef Kabobs, 116
•Peppered Tuna Kabobs, 169
•Pork Medallions with Raspberry-Balsamic
    Sauce, 154
Simple Poached Salmon, 101
•Turkey Cutlets in Lemon Wine Sauce, 141

MANGOES
•Chunky Mango Guacamole, 8
•Halibut Soft Tacos, 174

MANGOES (CONTINUED)
Mango Chutney Pork Roast, 158
Mango Rice Pudding, 232
•Peppered Tuna Kabobs, 169

MAPLE
•Chipotle-Orange Pork Chops, 153
Overnight Maple Oatmeal, 74

MEAT LOAVES
Curry-Apple Turkey Loaf, 138
Meat Loaf with Chili Sauce, 99
Just-Like-Thanksgiving Turkey Meat
   Loaf, 144

MEATLESS RECIPES
Burgers
•Portobello Pizza Burgers, 179
Salsa Bean Burgers, 187
Main-Dish Salads
•Garden Quinoa Salad, 186
•Tropical Fusion Salad with Spicy Tortilla
   Ribbons, 182
Main Dishes
Asian Veggie Glass Noodles, 178
Basil Polenta with Ratatouille, 182
•Black Bean & Corn Quinoa, 82
Butternut Squash Enchiladas, 185
•Coconut-Ginger Chickpeas &
   Tomatoes, 184
•Corn, Rice & Bean Burritos, 181
•Fresh Corn & Tomato Fettuccine, 178
Grilled Artichoke-Mushroom Pizza, 187
•Linguine with Broccoli Rabe & Peppers, 83
Makeover Creamy Mac & Cheese, 184
Mama Rachel's Tomato & Kalamata
   Pizzas, 181
•Margherita Pita Pizzas, 91
Pasta with Eggplant Sauce, 186
•Penne with Veggies 'n' Black Beans, 205
Rosemary Butternut Squash Lasagna, 179
•Stir-Fry Rice Bowl, 183
•Sweet Potato & Bean Quesadillas, 185
Sandwiches
•Avocado & Tomato Sandwiches, 183
•Greek Salad Pitas, 206
Soups
Cool as a Cucumber Soup, 40
Creamless Creamy Squash Soup, 49
Healthy Gazpacho for 2, 214
Hearty Vegetable Split Pea Soup, 41
Kale & Bean Soup, 43
Roasted Tomato Soup with Fresh Basil, 48
Summer's Bounty Soup, 41

MOLASSES
A Bit Nutty Boston Brown Bread, 196
Gingerbread Meringue Bars, 244
Walsh Family Grilled Pork Tenderloins, 156

MUFFINS
•Chocolate Banana Bran Muffins, 200
Cranberry Orange Muffins, 193
Granola Blueberry Muffins, 191
Lime Muffins with Coconut Streusel, 191

MUSHROOMS
Braised Hanukkah Brisket, 110
Company Turkey Potpie, 143
Grilled Artichoke-Mushroom Pizza, 187
•Herb-Roasted Mushrooms, 65
Italian Chicken Chardonnay, 131
Light Turkey Cutlets Stroganoff, 145
Peppered Filets with Tomato-Mushroom
   Salsa, 109
•Pork Chops with Mushroom-Tarragon
   Sauce, 155
Pork Tenderloin with Marsala Mushroom
   Sauce, 155
•Portobello Pizza Burgers, 179
Savory Braised Chicken with
   Vegetables, 128
Skillet Pasta, 210
Slow Cooker Beef Bourguignonne, 96
Slow Cooker Mushroom Rice Pilaf, 59
•Sweet-and-Sour Beef with Broccoli, 84
Tangy Pickled Mushrooms, 12
Zesty Orange Beef, 115

NOODLES
Asian Veggie Glass Noodles, 178
Citrus-Herb Pork Roast, 156
•Peanut Chicken Stir-Fry, 129
Pork Satay with Rice Noodles, 157

NUTELLA
Chocolate-Hazelnut Banana Crepes, 244
Mocha-Hazelnut Glazed Angel Food
   Cake, 221
Snow-Puffed Meringues, 235

NUTS (ALSO SEE NUTELLA; PEANUTS
  & PEANUT BUTTER)
Breads
A Bit Nutty Boston Brown Bread, 196
Cinnamon-Pecan Swirl Bread, 200
Pecan Bread, 190
Breakfast & Brunch
Autumn Power Porridge, 71
Overnight Maple Oatmeal, 74
Desserts
Almond Pear Tart, 221
Banana-Pecan Sheet Cake, 222
Chunky Apple Snack Cake, 219
Cranberry Pistachio Biscotti, 234
Cranberry-Pumpkin Spice Cake, 224
Little Italy Pignoli Cookies, 239
Mocha-Hazelnut Glazed Angel Food
   Cake, 221
Toffee Meringue Drops, 236
Main Dishes
•Cherry-Chicken Lettuce Wraps, 124
•Herbed Chicken and Rice, 133
•Parmesan Chicken Couscous, 132
•Pecan-Crusted Chicken Nuggets, 127
Grilled Pistachio-Lemon Pesto Shrimp, 163
Salads
•Cashew-Curry Chicken Salad, 35
•Red & Green Salad with Toasted
   Almonds, 22
•Salmon Salad with Glazed Walnuts, 24
Sweet Potato Salad with Orange
   Dressing, 25

Side Dishes
Roasted Garlic Green Beans with
   Cashews, 62
•Walnut Zucchini Saute, 59

OATS
Apple Oatmeal Cookies, 236
Autumn Power Porridge, 71
Carrot Cake Oatmeal, 76
•Cranberry-Walnut Oatmeal, 72
•Flaxseed Oatmeal Pancakes, 207
Honey-Oat Pan Rolls, 199
Michigan Fruit Baked Oatmeal, 77
Oats & Honey Yeast Bread, 195
Overnight Maple Oatmeal, 74
Peach 'n' Pear Crisps, 238
Slow Cooker Honey Granola, 68
Swirled Pumpkin Yeast Bread, 194

OLIVES
Mama Rachel's Tomato & Kalamata
   Pizzas, 181
Mediterranean Shrimp Linguine, 162

ONIONS
Grilled Shrimp Appetizer Kabobs, 19
Old-Fashioned Swiss Steak, 113
Thyme-Roasted Vegetables, 63

ORANGE
Arctic Orange Pie, 220
Blueberry-Stuffed French Toast, 71
•Chipotle-Orange Pork Chops, 153
•Citrus Fish for 2, 208
Citrus-Herb Pork Roast, 156
Citrus-Marinated Chicken, 123
Cranberry Orange Muffins, 193
•Fruity Frappe, 77
Grilled Chipotle Tenderloin, 204
•Mandarin Orange & Romaine Salad, 23
•Mandarin Watermelon Salad , 29
Orange Buttermilk Cupcakes, 225
Orange-Coconut Angel Food Cake, 228
Orange-Spiced Chicken, 126
Pomegranate Orange Salsa, 19
Sweet Potato Salad with Orange
   Dressing, 25
•Tangy Chicken & Peppers, 123
Zesty Orange Beef, 115

PASTA (ALSO SEE NOODLES)
Main Dishes
•Beef & Spinach Lo Mein, 113
•Bruschetta-Topped Chicken &
   Spaghetti, 120
Chicken Cacciatore, 104
•Chili Beef Pasta, 109
•Fresh Corn & Tomato Fettuccine, 178
Italian Chicken Chardonnay, 131
•Linguine with Broccoli Rabe & Peppers, 83
Makeover Creamy Mac & Cheese, 184
Mediterranean Shrimp Linguine, 162
Moroccan Chicken, 10
•Parmesan Chicken Couscous, 132
Pasta with Eggplant Sauce, 186
•Penne with Veggies 'n' Black Beans, 205
Portobello Turkey Bolognese, 138

Rosemary Butternut Squash Lasagna, 179
•Sausage Pizza Pasta, 145
•Sesame Noodles with Shrimp & Snap
   Peas, 173
•Simple Sesame Chicken with Couscous, 87
•Sirloin in Wine Sauce, 108
Skillet Pasta, 210
Spinach Chicken Manicotti, 124
•Thai Chicken Peanut Noodles, 126
•Zippy Zucchini Pasta, 91
Zucchini Pesto with Shrimp and
   Farfalle, 166
Salads
Bow Tie Pasta Salad, 34
Grilled Vegetable Orzo Salad, 26
Side Dish
•Lemon Parmesan Orzo, 57
Soup & Chili
Cincinnati-Style Chili, 42
White Bean Soup with Escarole, 51

PEACHES
Chicken Thighs with Ginger-Peach
   Sauce, 98
Peach 'n' Pear Crisps, 238
Peach Ice, 209
Peach Melba Trifle, 232

PEANUTS & PEANUT BUTTER
Fudge Sundae Pie, 227
Ginger-Sesame Steamed Vegetable
   Salad, 22
Monkey Bars, 233
Peanut Butter Cookies, 234
•Peanut Chicken Stir-Fry, 129
Pork Satay with Rice Noodles, 157
•Thai Chicken Peanut Noodles, 126

PEARS
Almond Pear Tart, 221
Cranberry Pear Tart, 229
Fresh Pear Ginger Crisp, 235
Peach 'n' Pear Crisps, 238
•Pear & Turkey Sausage Rigatoni, 137
Pear Bundt Cake, 218

PEAS
Black-Eyed Peas & Ham, 63
Hearty Vegetable Split Pea Soup, 41
•Minted Sugar Snap Pea Salad, 31
•Sesame Noodles with Shrimp & Snap
   Peas, 173

PEPPERS (SEE HOT PEPPERS;
   SWEET PEPPERS)

PESTO
Grilled Pistachio-Lemon Pesto Shrimp, 163
Zucchini Pesto with Shrimp and
   Farfalle, 166

PIES & TARTS
Almond Pear Tart, 221
Arctic Orange Pie, 220
Cranberry Pear Tart, 229
Fudge Sundae Pie, 227

Marshmallow Pumpkin Pie, 219
Strawberry Cream Cheese Pie, 224

PINEAPPLE
Carrot Cake Oatmeal, 76
•Chili-Lime Grilled Pineapple, 245
•Fresh Fruit Parfaits, 237
Grilled Shrimp Appetizer Kabobs, 19
•Pineapple Shrimp Stir-Fry, 169
•Sweet-and-Sour Beef with Broccoli, 84
Tropical Pulled Pork Sliders, 102

PIZZAS
Grilled Artichoke-Mushroom Pizza, 187
Mama Rachel's Tomato & Kalamata
   Pizzas, 181
•Margherita Pita Pizzas, 91
Thin Crust Pizza Dough, 192

PORK (ALSO SEE BACON; HAM
   & CANADIAN BACON)
Main Dishes
•Apple-Balsamic Pork Chops, 88
Apple-Cinnamon Pork Loin, 154
Apple-Stuffed Pork Tenderloins, 150
•Bacon-Swiss Pork Chops, 152
•Caramelized Pork Tenderloin, 153
•Chili-Apricot Pork Chops, 157
•Chipotle-Orange Pork Chops, 153
Citrus-Herb Pork Roast, 156
•Curried Apricot Pork Chops, 210
•Fig-Glazed Pork Tenderloin, 87
Grandma Edna's Cajun Pork, 98
Grilled Chipotle Tenderloin, 204
Honey-Glazed Pork Tenderloins, 158
Lime-Chipotle Carnitas Tostadas, 102
Mango Chutney Pork Roast, 158
Pork & Potato Supper, 148
•Pork & Vegetable Stir-Fry, 152
•Pork Chops with Mushroom-Tarragon
   Sauce, 155
•Pork Medallions with Cranberry Sauce, 93
Pork Medallions with Pomegranate
   Sauce, 148
•Pork Medallions with Raspberry-Balsamic
   Sauce, 154
Pork Satay with Rice Noodles, 157
Pork Tenderloin with Marsala Mushroom
   Sauce, 155
Roasted Pork Loin with Fig Sauce, 159
•Salsa Skillet Pork Chops, 150
Southern Pulled Pork, 97
Southwest Pork Tenderloin, 149
Walsh Family Grilled Pork Tenderloins, 156
Sandwiches
Shredded Pork Barbecue, 149
Tropical Pulled Pork Sliders, 102

POTATOES
Butternut Squash & Potato Mash, 55
Chunky Beef & Vegetable Soup, 50
•Dilled New Potatoes, 57
Fish & Chips with Dipping Sauce, 162
Golden Clam Chowder, 47
Grilled Potatoes & Peppers, 59
Mediterranean Mashed Potatoes, 62
Pork & Potato Supper, 148

Red Potato Salad Dijon, 27
Round Steak Italiano, 100
•Southwest Steak & Potatoes, 117
Thyme-Roasted Vegetables, 63
Veggie Egg Casserole, 69

PUMPKIN
Autumn Power Porridge, 71
Black Bean 'n' Pumpkin Chili, 48
Chocolate-Pumpkin Cheesecake Bars, 245
Cranberry-Pumpkin Spice Cake, 224
Marshmallow Pumpkin Pie, 219
Pumpkin Dinner Rolls, 198
Swirled Pumpkin Yeast Bread, 194
•Tuscan Turkey Soup, 39

QUICK BREADS & BISCUITS
A Bit Nutty Boston Brown Bread, 196
Favorite Irish Soda Bread, 199
•Flaky Whole Wheat Biscuits, 190

QUINOA
Autumn Power Porridge, 71
•Black Bean & Corn Quinoa, 82
•Garden Quinoa Salad, 186

RAISINS
A Bit Nutty Boston Brown Bread, 196
Apple Oatmeal Cookies, 236
Carrot Cake Oatmeal, 76
•Cashew-Curry Chicken Salad, 35
Chicken Thighs with Ginger-Peach
   Sauce, 98
Favorite Irish Soda Bread, 199
Swirled Pumpkin Yeast Bread, 194
•Tropical Fusion Salad with Spicy Tortilla
   Ribbons, 182

RASPBERRIES
Almond Fudge Cake, 222
Angel Food Cake with Berry Sauce, 225
Peach Melba Trifle, 232

RICE
Dessert
Mango Rice Pudding, 232
Main Dishes
•Coconut-Ginger Chickpeas &
   Tomatoes, 184
Coconut-Lime Chicken, 128
•Confetti Kielbasa Skillet, 140
•Corn, Rice & Bean Burritos, 181
Fiesta Beef Bowls, 105
Gingered Beef and Asparagus Stir-Fry , 111
•Herbed Chicken and Rice, 133
Meaty Slow-Cooked Jambalaya, 97
•Pineapple Shrimp Stir-Fry, 169
Pork Medallions with Pomegranate
   Sauce, 148
•Sesame Turkey Stir-Fry, 137
•Stir-Fry Rice Bowl, 183
•Sweet-and-Sour Beef with Broccoli, 84
•Tangy Chicken & Peppers, 123
Zesty Orange Beef, 115
Salad
Fiesta Rice and Bean Salad, 31

RICE (CONTINUED)

Side Dishes
Slow Cooker Mushroom Rice Pilaf, 59
Spring Green Risotto, 54
Soups & Chili
Cider Turkey Soup, 42
Guilt-Free Chicken Chili, 46
Lemon Chicken & Rice Soup, 44

SALADS

Fruit Salads
•Fresh Apple & Pear Salad, 29
•Honey-Lime Berry Salad, 31
•Mandarin Watermelon Salad , 29
Green Salads
•Mandarin Orange & Romaine Salad, 23
•Red & Green Salad with Toasted
    Almonds, 22
Roasted Butternut Tossed Salad, 24
•Ruby Red Spinach Salads, 29
Main-Dish Salads
•Cashew-Curry Chicken Salad, 35
•Chicken Salad with Dijon Vinaigrette, 33
•Crunchy Tuna Salad with Tomatoes, 172
•Garden-Fresh Chef Salad, 34
•Garden Quinoa Salad, 186
•Salmon Salad with Glazed Walnuts, 24
•Shrimp Salad with Cilantro
    Vinaigrette, 30
•Tropical Fusion Salad with Spicy Tortilla
    Ribbons, 182
•Turkey Taco Salad, 27
Pasta & Grain Salads
Bow Tie Pasta Salad, 34
Fiesta Rice and Bean Salad, 31
Grilled Vegetable Orzo Salad, 26
Texas Tabbouleh, 30
Potato Salads
Red Potato Salad Dijon, 27
Sweet Potato Salad with Orange
    Dressing, 25
Vegetable Salads
•Balsamic Cucumber Salad, 32
•Broccoli Slaw with Lemon Dressing, 32
Ginger-Sesame Steamed Vegetable
    Salad, 22
•Italian Fresh Vegetable Salad, 26
•Kale Salad, 33 •Minted Sugar Snap Pea
    Salad, 31
My Underground Vegetable Salad, 35
•Tomatoes with Buttermilk Vinaigrette, 23

SALSA

Peppered Filets with Tomato-Mushroom
    Salsa, 109
Pomegranate Orange Salsa, 19
Salsa Bean Burgers, 187
•Southwest Tortilla Scramble, 208
•Strawberry Salsa, 13
•Sweet Potato & Bean Quesadillas, 185
•Tangy Chicken & Peppers, 123
•Turkey Taco Salad, 27
•Watermelon Salsa, 11

SANDWICHES & WRAPS
(ALSO SEE BURGERS)
•Asparagus Omelet Tortilla Wrap, 69
•Avocado & Tomato Sandwiches, 183

Buffalo Sloppy Joes, 136
•Cajun Shrimp & Cucumber Wraps, 170
•Feta Scrambled Egg Wraps, 73
•Greek Salad Pitas, 206
•Microwave Egg Sandwich, 70
Shredded Pork Barbecue, 149
Tropical Pulled Pork Sliders, 102

SAUSAGE

•Chicken Sausages with Polenta, 133
•Confetti Kielbasa Skillet, 140
Italian Sausage and Vegetables, 104
•Pear & Turkey Sausage Rigatoni, 137
Sausage & Peppers with Cheese Polenta, 130
•Shrimp & Chicken Sausage with Grits, 165
•Skillet Cassoulet, 139
Stuffed Pizza Burgers, 140

SEAFOOD (ALSO SEE FISH)

Appetizers
Cajun Crawfish Sliders, 13
Grilled Shrimp Appetizer Kabobs, 19
•Shrimp Salad Appetizers, 16
Zesty Marinated Shrimp, 10
Zucchini Crab Cakes, 11
Main Dishes
Grilled Pistachio-Lemon Pesto Shrimp, 163
Lemony Shrimp & Tomatoes, 175
Meaty Slow-Cooked Jambalaya, 97
Mediterranean Shrimp Linguine, 162
•Pineapple Shrimp Stir-Fry, 169
•Sesame Noodles with Shrimp & Snap
    Peas, 173
•Shrimp & Chicken Sausage with Grits, 165
•Shrimp with Tomatoes & Feta, 88
•Skillet Sea Scallops, 170
•Southwestern Scallops, 164
•Spicy Shrimp 'n' Scallop Skewers, 85
Zucchini Pesto with Shrimp and
    Farfalle, 166
Salads
•Shrimp Salad with Cilantro
    Vinaigrette, 30
Sandwiches
•Cajun Shrimp & Cucumber Wraps, 170
Soup
Golden Clam Chowder, 47

SIDE DISHES

Miscellaneous
Black-Eyed Peas & Ham, 63
Pasta
•Lemon Parmesan Orzo, 57
Potatoes
•Dilled New Potatoes, 57
Grilled Potatoes & Peppers, 59
Mediterranean Mashed Potatoes, 62
Rice
Slow Cooker Mushroom Rice Pilaf, 59
Spring Green Risotto, 54
Vegetables
Baked Parmesan Breaded Squash, 64
Basil Corn & Tomato Bake, 61
Butternut Squash & Potato Mash, 55
•Fresh Green Beans & Garlic, 54
•Grilled Tomato with Fresh Corn, 64
•Herb-Roasted Mushrooms, 65
•Rainbow Vegetable Skillet, 60
Roasted Brussels Sprouts with Cranberries, 65

•Roasted Carrot Fries, 56
Roasted Fall Vegetables, 60
Roasted Garlic Green Beans with
    Cashews, 62
•Sweet Onion & Carrot Medley, 61
Thyme-Roasted Vegetables, 63
•Thymed Zucchini Saute, 56
Tuscan-Style Roasted Asparagus, 55
•Walnut Zucchini Saute, 59

SLOW COOKER RECIPES

Breakfast & Brunch
Carrot Cake Oatmeal, 76
Slow Cooker Honey Granola, 68
Main Dishes
Apple-Cinnamon Pork Loin, 154
Carolina-Style Vinegar BBQ Chicken, 105
Chicken Cacciatore, 104
Chicken Thighs with Ginger-Peach
    Sauce, 98
Chicken with Beans and Potatoes, 99
Citrus-Herb Pork Roast, 156
Fiesta Beef Bowls, 105
Grandma Edna's Cajun Pork, 98
Italian Chicken Chardonnay, 131
Italian Sausage and Vegetables, 104
Lime-Chipotle Carnitas Tostadas, 102
Mango-Pineapple Chicken Tacos, 127
Meat Loaf with Chili Sauce, 99
Meaty Slow-Cooked Jambalaya, 97
Moroccan Chicken, 100
Pork Satay with Rice Noodles, 157
Round Steak Italiano, 100
Saucy BBQ Chicken Thighs, 120
Simple Poached Salmon, 101
Slow-Cooked Coconut Chicken, 96
Slow Cooker Beef Bourguignonne, 96
Southern Pulled Pork, 97
Spicy Shredded Chicken, 101
Zesty Orange Beef, 115
Sandwiches
Tropical Pulled Pork Sliders, 102
Side Dishes
Black-Eyed Peas & Ham, 63
Slow Cooker Mushroom Rice Pilaf, 59
Soups
Black Bean 'n' Pumpkin Chili, 48
Cincinnati-Style Chili, 42
Hearty Vegetable Split Pea Soup, 41
Lemon Chicken & Rice Soup, 44
Turkey Sausage Soup with Fresh
    Vegetables, 44
Summer's Bounty Soup, 41

SOUPS (ALSO SEE CHILI)

Bean Soup with Sausage, 38
•Beef Barley Soup, 206
Chunky Beef & Vegetable Soup, 50
Cider Turkey Soup, 42
Cool as a Cucumber Soup, 40
Creamless Creamy Squash Soup, 49
Fresh Corn and Tomato Soup, 49
Golden Clam Chowder, 47
Healthy Gazpacho for 2, 214
Hearty Vegetable Split Pea Soup, 41
Kale & Bean Soup, 43
Lemon Chicken & Rice Soup, 44
Roasted Sweet Potato Soup, 39
Roasted Tomato Soup with Fresh Basil, 48

Summer's Bounty Soup, 41
Turkey Gnocchi Soup, 43
Turkey Sausage Soup with Fresh
    Vegetables, 44
•Tuscan Turkey Soup, 39
•Veggie Chowder, 40
•Veggie Salmon Chowder, 204
White Bean Soup with Escarole, 51

SPINACH
•Beef & Spinach Lo Mein, 113
Cajun Crawfish Sliders, 13
Chicken in Tomato-Caper Sauce, 130
Ginger-Sesame Steamed Vegetable
    Salad, 22
•Rosemary Chicken with Spinach &
    Beans, 121
Spinach Chicken Manicotti, 124

SQUASH (SEE WINTER SQUASH; ZUCCHINI & SUMMER SQUASH)

STRAWBERRIES
Angel Food Cake with Berry Sauce, 225
Brown-Sugar Salmon with
    Strawberries, 175
•Fresh Fruit Parfaits, 237
Light Cheesecake, 220
Strawberry Cream Cheese Pie, 224
•Strawberry Salsa, 13

SWEET PEPPERS
Greek Stuffed Banana Peppers, 143
Grilled Potatoes & Peppers, 59
Mexican Stuffed Peppers, 110
•Peppered Tuna Kabobs, 169
•Roast Beef Aioli Bundles, 15
Tri-Color Miniature Peppers, 9

SWEET POTATOES
Roasted Sweet Potato Soup, 39
Southwest Hash with Adobo-Lime
    Crema, 79
•Sweet Potato & Bean Quesadillas, 185
Sweet Potato Salad with Orange
    Dressing, 25
•Veggie Salmon Chowder, 204

TOMATOES
Appetizers
•Strawberry Salsa, 13
•Tomato & Artichoke Bruschetta, 18
Bread
Tomato-Herb Focaccia, 201
Main Dishes
•Avocado & Tomato Sandwiches, 183
Basil Polenta with Ratatouille, 182
Chicken Cacciatore, 104
Chicken in Tomato-Caper Sauce, 130
•Crunchy Tuna Salad with Tomatoes, 172
•Fresh Corn & Tomato Fettuccine, 178
Grilled Artichoke-Mushroom Pizza, 187
Italian Sausage and Vegetables, 104
Lemony Shrimp & Tomatoes, 175
Mama Rachel's Tomato & Kalamata
    Pizzas, 181
•Margherita Pita Pizzas, 91
Old-Fashioned Swiss Steak, 113
Pasta with Eggplant Sauce, 186

Peppered Filets with Tomato-Mushroom
    Salsa, 109
•Rosemary Chicken with Spinach &
    Beans, 121
Saucy BBQ Chicken Thighs, 120
•Savory Tomato-Braised Tilapia, 167
•Shrimp with Tomatoes & Feta, 88
•Skillet Cassoulet, 139
•Tilapia Tacos, 164
•Zippy Zucchini Pasta, 91
Salad
•Tomatoes with Buttermilk Vinaigrette, 23
Side Dish
•Grilled Tomato with Fresh Corn, 64
Soups
Fresh Corn and Tomato Soup, 49
Healthy Gazpacho for 2, 214
Roasted Tomato Soup with Fresh Basil, 48

TORTILLAS
•Asparagus Omelet Tortilla Wrap, 69
Butternut Squash Enchiladas, 185
Chipotle Turkey Chilaquiles, 141
•Corn, Rice & Bean Burritos, 181
•Feta Scrambled Egg Wraps, 73
•Halibut Soft Tacos, 174
•Southwest Tortilla Scramble, 208
•Sweet Potato & Bean Quesadillas, 185
•Tilapia Tacos, 164
•Wasabi Beef Fajitas, 82

TURKEY & TURKEY SAUSAGE
Appetizers
Tri-Color Miniature Peppers, 9
Breakfast & Brunch
•Turkey Sausage Patties, 78
Burgers
•Grilled Turkey Burgers, 93
Stuffed Pizza Burgers, 140
Main Dishes
Chipotle Turkey Chilaquiles, 141
Company Turkey Potpie, 143
•Confetti Kielbasa Skillet, 140
Curry-Apple Turkey Loaf, 138
•Day-After-Thanksgiving Turkey
    Stir-Fry, 84
Greek Stuffed Banana Peppers, 143
Grilled Turkey Tenderloin, 139
Italian Sausage and Vegetables, 104
Just-Like-Thanksgiving Turkey Meat
    Loaf, 144
Lemon-Basil Turkey Breast, 144
Light Turkey Cutlets Stroganoff, 145
•Mediterranean Turkey Skillet, 136
•Pear & Turkey Sausage Rigatoni, 137
Portobello Turkey Bolognese, 138
•Sausage Pizza Pasta, 145
•Sesame Turkey Stir-Fry, 137
•Skillet Cassoulet, 139
•Turkey Cutlets in Lemon Wine Sauce, 141
Salad
•Turkey Taco Salad, 27
Sandwiches
•Buffalo Sloppy Joes, 136
Soups & Chili
Bean Soup with Sausage, 38
Black Bean 'n' Pumpkin Chili, 48
Cider Turkey Soup, 42
Cincinnati-Style Chili, 42

Turkey Gnocchi Soup, 43
Turkey Sausage Soup with Fresh
    Vegetables, 44
•Tuscan Turkey Soup, 39

VEGETABLES (ALSO SEE SPECIFIC KINDS)
Appetizers
•Rosemary Beet Phyllo Bites, 10
•Shrimp Salad Appetizers, 16
Thai Veggie Dip, 8
Zesty Spinach Dip, 213
Breakfast & Brunch
•Vegetable Omelet, 215
Main Dishes
Asian Veggie Glass Noodles, 178
•Avocado & Tomato Sandwiches, 183
•Black Bean & Corn Quinoa, 82
Braised Hanukkah Brisket, 110
•Chicken & Vegetable Kabobs, 122
•Chili Steak & Peppers, 86
Chicken with Beans and Potatoes, 99
Company Turkey Potpie, 143
•Confetti Kielbasa Skillet, 140
•Fish & Vegetable Packets, 171
•Garden Quinoa Salad, 186
Indian Baked Chicken, 122
Italian Sausage and Vegetables, 104
Lemon-Basil Turkey Breast, 144
•Linguine with Broccoli Rabe & Peppers, 83
•Mediterranean Turkey Skillet, 136
Moroccan Chicken, 100
•Penne with Veggies 'n' Black Beans, 205
•Pineapple Shrimp Stir-Fry, 169
•Pork & Vegetable Stir-Fry, 152
Portobello Turkey Bolognese, 138
Sausage & Peppers with Cheese Polenta, 130
•Sausage Pizza Pasta, 145
Sizzling Beef Kabobs, 112
•Skillet Cassoulet, 139
•Stir-Fry Rice Bowl, 183
•Tangy Chicken & Peppers, 123
•Thai Chicken Peanut Noodles, 126
Zesty Orange Beef, 115
Salads
Bow Tie Pasta Salad, 34
•Garden-Fresh Chef Salad, 34
Grilled Vegetable Orzo Salad, 26
•Italian Fresh Vegetable Salad, 26
My Underground Vegetable Salad, 35
Roasted Butternut Tossed Salad, 24
•Ruby Red Spinach Salads, 29
•Shrimp Salad with Cilantro
    Vinaigrette, 30
Texas Tabbouleh, 30
Sandwich
•Greek Salad Pitas, 206
Side Dishes
Basil Corn & Tomato Bake, 61
•Rainbow Vegetable Skillet, 60
Roasted Brussels Sprouts with
    Cranberries, 65
Roasted Fall Vegetables, 60
Spring Green Risotto, 54
•Sweet Onion & Carrot Medley, 61
Thyme-Roasted Vegetables, 63
Soups
•Beef Barley Soup, 206
Chunky Beef & Vegetable Soup, 50

Alphabetical Index

This index lists every recipe alphabetically, so you can easily find the dishes you enjoy most.

•Table-ready in 30 minutes or less.

VEGETABLES
Soups (*continued*)
Healthy Gazpacho for 2, 214
Hearty Vegetable Split Pea Soup, 41
Kale & Bean Soup, 43
Summer's Bounty Soup, 41
Turkey Sausage Soup with Fresh
   Vegetables, 44
•Veggie Chowder, 40

WATERMELON
•Mandarin Watermelon Salad , 29
Sonoran Sunset Watermelon Ice, 242
•Watermelon Salsa, 11

WINTER SQUASH
Butternut Squash & Potato Mash, 55
Butternut Squash Enchiladas, 185
•Rainbow Vegetable Skillet, 60
Roasted Butternut Tossed Salad, 24
Roasted Fall Vegetables, 60
Rosemary Butternut Squash Lasagna, 179

YEAST BREADS & ROLLS
Cinnamon-Pecan Swirl Bread, 200
Cranberry Whole Wheat Bagels, 196
Honey-Oat Pan Rolls, 199
Honey Wheat Loaves, 194
Multigrain Bread, 198
Oats & Honey Yeast Bread, 195
Pecan Bread, 190
Pumpkin Dinner Rolls, 198
Seeded Whole Grain Loaf, 201
Sunflower Seed Wheat Bread, 193
Swirled Pumpkin Yeast Bread, 194
Tomato-Herb Focaccia, 201

WINTER SQUASH
Creamless Creamy Squash Soup, 49
Butternut Squash & Potato Mash, 55
Butternut Squash Enchiladas, 185
•Rainbow Vegetable Skillet, 60
Roasted Butternut Tossed Salad, 24
Roasted Fall Vegetables, 60
Rosemary Butternut Squash Lasagna, 179

ZUCCHINI & SUMMER SQUASH
Baked Parmesan Breaded Squash, 64
•Thymed Zucchini Saute, 56
•Walnut Zucchini Saute, 59
•Zippy Zucchini Pasta, 91
Zucchini Carrot Spice Cake, 228
Zucchini Crab Cakes, 11
Zucchini Pesto with Shrimp and
   Farfalle, 166

A
A Bit Nutty Boston Brown Bread, 196
Almond Cherry Cobbler, 241
Almond Fudge Cake, 222
Almond Pear Tart, 221
Angel Food Cake with Berry Sauce, 225
•Apple-Balsamic Pork Chops, 88
Apple-Cinnamon Pork Loin, 154
Apple Oatmeal Cookies, 236
Apple-Stuffed Pork Tenderloins, 150
Apple Sundaes, 213
•Apricot-Lemon Chicken, 83
Arctic Orange Pie, 220
Asian Chicken Dumplings, 17
Asian Veggie Glass Noodles, 178
•Asparagus Omelet Tortilla Wrap, 69
Autumn Power Porridge, 71
•Avocado & Tomato Sandwiches, 183

B
•Bacon-Swiss Pork Chops, 152
•Baked Fish with Cheese Sauce for 2, 207
Baked Parmesan Breaded Squash, 64
•Balsamic Cucumber Salad, 32
Banana-Pecan Sheet Cake, 222
Basil Corn & Tomato Bake, 61
Basil Polenta with Ratatouille, 182
Bean Soup with Sausage, 38
•Beef & Spinach Lo Mein, 113
•Beef Barley Soup, 206
Beef Brisket Marinara, 117
Berry Granola Pancakes, 78
•Black Bean & Corn Quinoa, 82
Black Bean 'n' Pumpkin Chili, 48
Black Bean & White Cheddar Frittata, 74
Black-Eyed Peas & Ham, 63
•Blackened Halibut, 173
Blue Cheese Flank Steak, 116
Blueberry-Stuffed French Toast, 71
Bow Tie Pasta Salad, 34
Braised Hanukkah Brisket, 110
•Broccoli Slaw with Lemon Dressing, 32
•Broiled Fish with Tarragon Sauce, 174
Brown-Sugar Salmon with
   Strawberries, 175
•Bruschetta-Topped Chicken &
   Spaghetti, 120
•Buffalo Sloppy Joes, 136
Butternut Squash & Potato Mash, 55
Butternut Squash Enchiladas, 185

C
Cajun Crawfish Sliders, 13
•Cajun Shrimp & Cucumber Wraps, 170
Cappuccino Cupcakes, 218
•Caramelized Pork Tenderloin, 153
Carolina-Style Vinegar BBQ Chicken, 105
Carrot Cake Oatmeal, 76
•Cashew-Curry Chicken Salad, 35

•Cherry-Chicken Lettuce Wraps, 124
•Cherry Cobbler Smoothies, 79
•Chicken & Vegetable Kabobs, 122
Chicken Cacciatore, 104
Chicken in Tomato-Caper Sauce, 130
•Chicken Salad with Dijon Vinaigrette, 33
•Chicken Sausages with Polenta, 133
Chicken Thighs with Ginger-Peach
   Sauce, 98
Chicken with Beans and Potatoes, 99
•Chili-Apricot Pork Chops, 157
•Chili Beef Pasta, 109
•Chili-Lime Grilled Pineapple, 245
•Chili Steak & Peppers, 86
•Chinese Takeout-on-a-Stick, 86
•Chipotle Avocado Dip, 9
•Chipotle-Orange Pork Chops, 153
Chipotle-Rubbed Beef Tenderloin, 115
Chipotle Turkey Chilaquiles, 141
•Chocolate Banana Bran Muffins, 200
Chocolate-Hazelnut Banana Crepes, 244
Chocolate Peppermint Log, 227
Chocolate-Pumpkin Cheesecake Bars, 245
Chunky Apple Snack Cake, 219
Chunky Beef & Vegetable Soup, 50
•Chunky Mango Guacamole, 8
Cider Turkey Soup, 42
Cincinnati-Style Chili, 42
Cinnamon-Pecan Swirl Bread, 200
Citrus Compote with Grapefruit
   Granita, 239
•Citrus Fish for 2, 208
Citrus-Herb Pork Roast, 156
Citrus-Marinated Chicken, 123
•Cocoa-Crusted Beef Tenderloin, 112
•Coconut-Ginger Chickpeas &
   Tomatoes, 184
Coconut-Lime Chicken, 128
Company Turkey Potpie, 143
•Confetti Kielbasa Skillet, 140
Cool as a Cucumber Soup, 40
•Corn, Rice & Bean Burritos, 181
Cranberry Orange Muffins, 193
Cranberry Pear Tart, 229
Cranberry Pistachio Biscotti, 234
Cranberry-Pumpkin Spice Cake, 224
•Cranberry-Walnut Oatmeal, 72
Cranberry Whole Wheat Bagels, 196
Creamless Creamy Squash Soup, 49
•Creole Blackened Chicken, 91
Crispy Buffalo Chicken Roll-Ups for 2, 213
•Crunchy Tuna Salad with Tomatoes, 172
•Curried Apricot Pork Chops, 210
Curry-Apple Turkey Loaf, 138

D
•Day-After-Thanksgiving Turkey
   Stir-Fry, 84
•Dilled New Potatoes, 57

F

Favorite Irish Soda Bread, 199
•Feta Scrambled Egg Wraps, 73
Fiesta Beef Bowls, 105
Fiesta Rice and Bean Salad, 31
•Fig-Glazed Pork Tenderloin, 87
Fish & Chips with Dipping Sauce, 162
•Fish & Vegetable Packets, 171
•Flaky Whole Wheat Biscuits, 190
•Flaxseed Oatmeal Pancakes, 207
•Fresh Apple & Pear Salad, 29
•Fresh Corn & Tomato Fettuccine, 178
Fresh Corn and Tomato Soup, 49
•Fresh Fruit Parfaits, 237
•Fresh Green Beans & Garlic, 54
Fresh Pear Ginger Crisp, 235
•Fruit-Filled Puff Pancake, 68
•Fruity Frappe, 77
Fudge Sundae Pie, 227

G

•Garden-Fresh Chef Salad, 34
•Garden Quinoa Salad, 186
•Ginger Cardamom Tea, 76
Ginger-Sesame Steamed Vegetable
  Salad, 22
Gingerbread Meringue Bars, 244
Gingered Beef and Asparagus Stir-Fry , 111
Golden Clam Chowder, 47
Grandma Edna's Cajun Pork, 98
Granola Blueberry Muffins, 191
•Greek Salad Pitas, 206
Greek Stuffed Banana Peppers, 143
•Greek-Style Chicken Skewers, 131
Grilled Artichoke-Mushroom Pizza, 187
•Grilled Brown Sugar-Mustard
  Chicken , 132
Grilled Chipotle Tenderloin, 204
Grilled Flank Steak, 108
•Grilled Nectarine & Cheese Crostini, 12
Grilled Pistachio-Lemon Pesto Shrimp, 163
Grilled Potatoes & Peppers, 59
Grilled Shrimp Appetizer Kabobs, 19
Grilled Sirloin with Chili-Beer Barbecue
  Sauce, 111
•Grilled Tomato with Fresh Corn, 64
•Grilled Turkey Burgers, 93
Grilled Turkey Tenderloin, 139
Grilled Vegetable Orzo Salad, 26
Guilt-Free Chicken Chili, 46

H

•Halibut Soft Tacos, 174
Healthy Gazpacho for 2, 214
Hearty Vegetable Split Pea Soup, 41
•Herb-Roasted Mushrooms, 65
•Herb-Roasted Salmon Fillets, 172
•Herbed Chicken and Rice, 133
•Hoisin & Honey Glazed Salmon, 166
Honey Balsamic Chicken, 211
Honey-Glazed Pork Tenderloins, 158
•Honey-Lime Berry Salad, 31
Honey-Oat Pan Rolls, 199
Honey Wheat Loaves, 194

I

Indian Baked Chicken, 122
Italian Chicken Chardonnay, 131
•Italian Fresh Vegetable Salad, 26
Italian Sausage and Vegetables, 104
•Italian Steaks for 2, 214

J

Jalapeno Buttermilk Corn Bread, 192
•Juicy & Delicious Mixed Spice Burgers, 115
Just-Like-Thanksgiving Turkey Meat
  Loaf, 144

K

Kale & Bean Soup, 43
•Kale Salad, 33

L

Lemon-Basil Turkey Breast, 144
Lemon Chicken & Rice Soup, 44
Lemon Meringue Pie Cookies, 233
•Lemon Parmesan Orzo, 57
Lemony Cream Cheese Bars, 243
•Lemony Parsley Baked Cod, 85
Lemony Shrimp & Tomatoes, 175
Light & Creamy Chocolate Pudding, 237
Light Cheesecake, 220
Light Turkey Cutlets Stroganoff, 145
Lime-Chipotle Carnitas Tostadas, 102
•Lime-Ginger Chicken Tenders, 92
Lime Muffins with Coconut Streusel, 191
•Linguine with Broccoli Rabe & Peppers, 83
Little Italy Pignoli Cookies, 239
Low-Fat Chocolate Cookies, 238

M

Makeover Creamy Mac & Cheese, 184
Mama Rachel's Tomato & Kalamata
  Pizzas, 181
•Mandarin Orange & Romaine Salad, 23
•Mandarin Watermelon Salad , 29
Mango Chutney Pork Roast, 158
Mango-Pineapple Chicken Tacos, 127
Mango Rice Pudding, 232
•Margherita Pita Pizzas, 91
Marshmallow Pumpkin Pie, 219
Meat Loaf with Chili Sauce, 99
Meaty Slow-Cooked Jambalaya, 97
Mediterranean Eggplant Dip, 15
Mediterranean Mashed Potatoes, 62
Mediterranean Shrimp Linguine, 162
•Mediterranean Turkey Skillet, 136
Mexican Stuffed Peppers, 110
Michigan Fruit Baked Oatmeal, 77
•Microwave Egg Sandwich, 70
Mini Neapolitan Baked Alaskas, 241
•Minted Sugar Snap Pea Salad, 31
•Mixed Berry Sundaes for 2, 205
Mocha Frosted Snack Cake, 229
Mocha-Hazelnut Glazed Angel Food
  Cake, 221
Moist Lemon Chiffon Cake, 223
Monkey Bars, 233
Moo Shu Chicken Cones, 17
Moroccan Beef Kabobs, 116
Moroccan Chicken, 100

Multigrain Bread, 198
My Underground Vegetable Salad, 35

O

Oats & Honey Yeast Bread, 195
Old-Fashioned Swiss Steak, 113
Orange Buttermilk Cupcakes, 225
Orange-Coconut Angel Food Cake, 228
Orange-Spiced Chicken, 126
•Oven-Barbecued Salmon, 163
Overnight Maple Oatmeal, 74

P

•Parmesan Chicken Couscous, 132
Pasta with Eggplant Sauce, 186
Peach 'n' Pear Crisps, 238
Peach Ice, 209
Peach Melba Trifle, 232
Peanut Butter Cookies, 234
•Peanut Chicken Stir-Fry, 129
•Pear & Turkey Sausage Rigatoni, 137
Pear Bundt Cake, 218
Pecan Bread, 190
•Pecan-Crusted Chicken Nuggets, 127
•Penne with Veggies 'n' Black Beans, 205
Peppered Filets with Tomato-Mushroom
  Salsa, 109
•Peppered Tuna Kabobs, 169
•Pineapple Shrimp Stir-Fry, 169
Pomegranate Orange Salsa, 19
Popcorn & Pretzel Chicken Tenders, 129
Pork & Potato Supper, 148
•Pork & Vegetable Stir-Fry, 152
•Pork Chops with Mushroom-Tarragon
  Sauce, 155
•Pork Medallions with Cranberry Sauce, 93
Pork Medallions with Pomegranate
  Sauce, 148
•Pork Medallions with Raspberry-Balsamic
  Sauce, 154
Pork Satay with Rice Noodles, 157
Pork Tenderloin with Marsala Mushroom
  Sauce, 155
•Portobello Pizza Burgers, 179
Portobello Turkey Bolognese, 138
Pumpkin Dinner Rolls, 198

R

•Rainbow Vegetable Skillet, 60
•Red & Green Salad with Toasted
  Almonds, 22
Red Potato Salad Dijon, 27
Rhubarb Compote with Yogurt &
  Almonds, 73
•Roast Beef Aioli Bundles, 15
Roasted Brussels Sprouts with
  Cranberries, 65
Roasted Butternut Tossed Salad, 24
•Roasted Carrot Fries, 56
Roasted Fall Vegetables, 60
Roasted Garlic Green Beans with
  Cashews, 62
Roasted Pork Loin with Fig Sauce, 159
Roasted Sweet Potato Soup, 39
Roasted Tomato Soup with Fresh Basil, 48
•Rosemary Beet Phyllo Bites, 10

Rosemary Butternut Squash Lasagna, 179
•Rosemary Chicken with Spinach & Beans, 121
Round Steak Italiano, 100
•Ruby Red Spinach Salads, 29

S
•Salmon Salad with Glazed Walnuts, 24
•Salmon with Tangy Raspberry Sauce, 165
Salsa Bean Burgers, 187
•Salsa Skillet Pork Chops, 150
Saucy BBQ Chicken Thighs, 120
•Saucy Peach-Balsamic Chicken, 121
Sausage & Peppers with Cheese Polenta, 130
•Sausage Pizza Pasta, 145
Savory Braised Chicken with Vegetables, 128
•Savory Tomato-Braised Tilapia, 167
Seeded Whole Grain Loaf, 201
•Sesame Noodles with Shrimp & Snap Peas, 173
•Sesame Turkey Stir-Fry, 137
Shredded Pork Barbecue, 149
•Shrimp & Chicken Sausage with Grits, 165
•Shrimp Salad Appetizers, 16
•Shrimp Salad with Cilantro Vinaigrette, 30
•Shrimp with Tomatoes & Feta, 88
Simple Poached Salmon, 101
•Simple Sesame Chicken with Couscous, 87
•Sirloin in Wine Sauce, 108
Sirloin on the Grill, 211
Sizzling Beef Kabobs, 112
•Skillet Cassoulet, 139
Skillet Pasta, 210
•Skillet Sea Scallops, 170
Slow-Cooked Coconut Chicken, 96
Slow Cooker Beef Bourguignonne, 96
Slow Cooker Honey Granola, 68
Slow Cooker Mushroom Rice Pilaf, 59
Snow-Puffed Meringues, 235
Sonoran Sunset Watermelon Ice, 242

Southern Pulled Pork, 97
Southwest Grilled Chicken, 209
Southwest Hash with Adobo-Lime Crema, 79
Southwest Pork Tenderloin, 149
•Southwest Steak & Potatoes, 117
•Southwest Tortilla Scramble, 208
•Southwestern Scallops, 164
•Spicy Apricot-Glazed Chicken, 133
Spicy Shredded Chicken, 101
•Spicy Shrimp 'n' Scallop Skewers, 85
Spinach Chicken Manicotti, 124
Spring Green Risotto, 54
•Stir-Fry Rice Bowl, 183
Strawberry Cream Cheese Pie, 224
•Strawberry Salsa, 13
•Strawberry-Teriyaki Glazed Salmon, 89
Stuffed Pizza Burgers, 140
Summer's Bounty Soup, 41
Sunflower Seed Wheat Bread, 193
•Sweet-and-Sour Beef with Broccoli, 84
•Sweet-Chili Salmon with Blackberries, 92
•Sweet Onion & Carrot Medley, 61
•Sweet Potato & Bean Quesadillas, 185
Sweet Potato Salad with Orange Dressing, 25
Swirled Pumpkin Yeast Bread, 194

T
•Tangy Chicken & Peppers, 123
Tangy Pickled Mushrooms, 12
Texas Tabbouleh, 30
•Thai Chicken Peanut Noodles, 126
Thai Veggie Dip, 8
Thin Crust Pizza Dough, 192
Thyme-Roasted Vegetables, 63
•Thymed Zucchini Saute, 56
•Tilapia Tacos, 164
Toffee Meringue Drops, 236
•Tomato & Artichoke Bruschetta, 18
Tomato-Herb Focaccia, 201
•Tomatoes with Buttermilk Vinaigrette, 23

Tri-Color Miniature Peppers, 9
Triple-Ginger Gingersnaps, 242
•Tropical Fusion Salad with Spicy Tortilla Ribbons, 182
Tropical Pulled Pork Sliders, 102
•Tuna with Citrus Ponzu Sauce, 167
•Turkey Cutlets in Lemon Wine Sauce, 141
Turkey Gnocchi Soup, 43
•Turkey Sausage Patties, 78
Turkey Sausage Soup with Fresh Vegetables, 44
•Turkey Taco Salad, 27
Tuscan-Style Roasted Asparagus, 55
•Tuscan Turkey Soup, 39

V
•Vegetable Omelet, 215
•Veggie Chowder, 40
Veggie Egg Casserole, 69
•Veggie Salmon Chowder, 204

W
•Walnut Zucchini Saute, 59
Walsh Family Grilled Pork Tenderloins, 156
•Wasabi Beef Fajitas, 82
•Watermelon Salsa, 11
White Bean Soup with Escarole, 51
•Whole-Grain Waffle Mix, 72

Y
•Yogurt & Honey Fruit Cups, 16

Z
Zesty Marinated Shrimp, 10
Zesty Orange Beef, 115
Zesty Spinach Dip, 213
•Zippy Zucchini Pasta, 91
Zucchini Carrot Spice Cake, 228
Zucchini Crab Cakes, 11
Zucchini Pesto with Shrimp and Farfalle, 166